MANAGING IP NETWORKS

MANAGING IP NETWORKS

Challenges and Opportunities

Edited by

SALAH AIDAROUS
THOMAS PLEVYAK

With Contributions by

JAVIER ARACIL
ANDREA FUMAGALLI
PAUL LEVINE
JOBERTO SÉRGIO BARBOSA MARTINS
MOSTAFA HASHEM SHERIF
BURKHARD STILLER
LUCA VALCARENGHI

IEEE Press Series on Network Management
Salah Aidarous and Thomans Plevyak, *Series Editors*

IEEE Communications Society, *Sponsor*

IEEE PRESS

A JOHN WILEY & SONS, INC., PUBLICATION

Library of Congress Cataloging-in-Publication Data:

Managing IP networks : challenges and opportunities / edited by Salah Aidarous, Thomas Plevyak.
    p. cm. — (IEEE Press series on network management)
   Includes bibliographical references and index.
   ISBN 978-0-471-39299-6
   1. Computer networks—Management.   2. TCP/IP (Computer network protocol)   I.
Aidarous, Salah. II. Plevyak, Thomas. III. IEEE series on network management

TK5105.5.M3577 2003
004.6'2—dc21   2003053465

In memory of
Salah Aidarous
co-editor of this book
and an outstanding technical professional
in the field of communications

CONTENTS

3   Quality of Service in IP Networks   57

Joberto Sérgio Barbosa Martins

4 A Survey of Charging Internet Services   143

Burkhard Stiller

**6   The Future Optical Internet: Integration of Optical and   287
IP Technologies**

Andrea Fumagalli, Javier Aracil, and Luca Valcarenghi

CONTRIBUTORS

The late **Salah Aidarous** worked in the Network Management Division, NEC America, on the planning and development of integrated network management systems. Before his employment at NEC, he was with Nortel Technology (formerly BNR) working on a broad range of assignments in telecommunications networks and services planning and development. Dr. Aidarous received a B.S. and an M.S. in Electrical Engineering from Ain Shams University, Cairo, and a Ph.D. in Electrical Engineering from Louvain University, Belgium.

Thomas Plevyak is a past president of the IEEE Communications Society (ComSoc). He served as ComSoc President in 1998 and 1999. Mr. Plevyak is a past director of publications of ComSoc and a former editor-in-chief of *IEEE Communications Magazine*. He retired after 28 years with Bell Laboratories and AT&T Network Systems (now Lucent Technologies) and is now a Distinguished Member of Technical Staff with Verizon in Arlington, Virginia, responsible for operations and network management standards. He is also an IEEE Fellow. Mr. Plevyak is the former vice chairman of the Inter-American Telecommunications Commission (CITEL), Permanent Consultative Committee 1 (PCC.1), a unit of the Organization of American States (OAS). He is a member of the United States ITU Association (USITUA) Board of Directors. He is co-editor and an author of *Telecommunications Network Management Into the 21st Century: Techniques, Standards, Technologies, and Applications* and is co-editor of the series on network management, which includes this book.

Javier Aracil received the MSc. and Ph.D. degrees (Honors) from Technical University of Madrid in 1993 and 1995, both in Telecommunications Engineering. In 1995, he was awarded a Fulbright scholarship and appointed a postdoctoral researcher of the Department of Electrical Engineering and Computer Sciences, University of California, Berkeley. In 1998, he was a research scholar at the Center for Advanced Telecommunications,

Systems and Services of The University of Texas at Dallas. He is currently a tenured associate professor at Public University of Navarra, Spain. Dr. Aracil's research interests are in IP over WDM networks, Internet services analysis, and performance evaluation of communication networks. Dr. Aracil is a member of the editorial board of SPIE/Kluwer *Optical Networks Magazine*.

Andrea Fumagalli holds a Ph.D. in Electrical Engineering (1992) and a Laurea Degree in Electronics Engineering (1987) from the Politecnico di Torino, Italy. Since 1997, he has been an associate professor of Electrical Engineering at the University of Texas as Dallas and became the head of the Optical Networking Advanced Research (OpNeAR) Lab in 1000. His research interests include high speed and optical networking, survivable networks, and sensor networks. He servers on the editorial boards of ACM/IEEE Transactions on Networking and the Elsevier *Journal of Computer Networks*.

Paul Levine has held leadership roles in many standards bodies and information/communications industry forums with the objective of converging standardization initiatives to common approaches for B2B interoperability. Mr. Levine has enjoyed a 34-year career with Bell Laboratories, Bellcore, and Telcordia Technologies, in various positions dealing with design and administration of shared information. Most recently he held the position of Standards Development Director, COMMON LANGUAGE® Products,* the Telcordia business unit which provides a data administration service essential for operability within and interoperability among telecommunications service providers. He holds BME and MSME degrees from Rensselaer Polytechnic Institute, Troy, NY.

Joberto Sérgio Barbosa Martens received his Ph.D. in Computer Science, Université Paris VI, France, 1986; M.Sc. in Electronic Engineering, PII, Eindhoven, Netherlands, 1979 and B.S. in Electronic Engineering, UFPb, Brazil, 1977. Dr. Martens has also worked as visiting scientist at ICSI, Berkeley University at Berkeley, California in 1995 and worked as full professor at UFPb from 1977 to 2000. Currently, he develops activities as full professor and director of Research Activities of the Computer Networks Group (NUPERC) at University Salvador (UNIFACS), Brazil. Dr. Martens' main areas of research and activities include Quality of Service, Multimedia over IP, Telecommunications Systems, High-Speed Networks and Mobile Agents. He is a project manager, expert consultant, and course instructor in these areas for various institutions, international congresses, and enterprises. Additional information about his professional activities can be found in *www.jsmnet.com*.

Mostafa Hashem Sherif is a principal member of the Technical Staff at AT&T. He received a B.Sc. in Electronics and Communications and an M.Sc. in Electrical Engineering from Cairo University, Egypt in 1972 and 1975, respectively, and a Ph.D. in Engineering from the University of California, Los Angeles in 1980. In 1996, he obtained a Masters of Science in the Management of Technology from Stevens Institute of Technology, Hoboken, NJ. He is a senior member of the IEEE, a standards editor for the *IEEE Communication Magazine* and the author of *Secure Protocols for Electronic Commerce* published by CRC Press, 2002. The French version, co-authored with Professor A. Sehrouchni from the ENST of Paris, is published by Eyrolles under the title *La monnaie électronique*. Dr.

*COMMON LANGUAGE® is a registered trademark of Telcordia Technologies, Inc.

Sherif is a certified project manager from the Project Management Institute. He has participated in standardization activities in the International Telecommunication Union (ITU), T1A1, and the ATM Forum. He is a founding member of the series of conferences on management of technology sponsored y the International Association for the Management of Technology (IAMOT) and of the IEEE International Symposium on Computers and Communications (ISCC). He is a core member of the Awards and Recognition working committee of the AT&T Project Management Council and a member of the evaluation committee for the Commission on Science and Technology, State of New Jersey.

Professor Dr. Burkhard Stiller received his diploma degree in computer science and his doctoral degree from the University of Karlsruhe, Germany in October 1990 and February 1994, respectively while being a Research Assistant at the Institute of Telematics, University of Karlsruhe. After working as a research fellow at the University of California, Irvine and the University of Cambridge, Computer Laboratory, England, he joined the Computer Engineering and Networks Laboratory TIK, Swiss Federal Institute of Technology ETH Zurich, Switzerland. Currently, Dr. Stiller is a full professor at the University of Federal Armed Forces Munich, German, in charge of the Information Systems Laboratory IIS, and an assistant professor at ETH Zurich, TIK. His primary research interests include Internet communications, Quality-of-Service models, charging and accounting for packet-based services, pricing schemes, mobility and AAA architectures, and peer-to-peer systems. He published more than 50 papers and headed a number of national and international projects in areas such as CATI, Mac/MicPay, M3I, MMAPPS, or MobyDick. Professor Stiller is member of the editorial board of the Kluwer's Netmonics journal on economic research and electronic networking, the ACM, and the German Society for Computer Science GI.

Luca Valcarenghi earned a Laurea degree in Electronics Engineering in 1997 from the Politecnico di Torino, Italy, a M.S. degree in Electrical Engineering in 1999 and a Ph.D. in Electrical Engineering-Telecommunications in 2001, from the University of Texas at Dallas. In January 2002, he was appointed as research associate of the Optical Networking Advanced Research (OpNeAR) Lab of the University of Texas at Dallas Erik Jonsson School of EE/CS. He is currently assistant professor at the Scuola Superiore Sant'Anna of University Studies and Doctoral Research of Pisa, Italy. Dr. Valcarenghi co-authored more than a dozen papers published in international journals and presented in leading international conferences. He is a member of the IEEE, feature editor of the SPIE/Kluwer *Optical Networks Magazine,* and has been part of the Organizing Committee and Technical Program Committee of international conferences, such as OptiComm2000 and Optical Networking and Systems Symposium at IEEE Globecom 2003. His main research interests are optical networks design, analysis, and optimization; artificial intelligence optimization techniques; communication networks reliability and IP over WDM Networking.

MANAGING IP NETWORKS

INTRODUCTION

VINT CERF AND BOB KAHN

I.1 INTRODUCTION

There can be little doubt in 2002 that Internet protocol (IP) networks, among which the public portion of the Internet is but one, have become essential elements in this century's communications repertoire. A broad definition of current-day network management might include order entry, provisioning, billing, fault detection, isolation and repair, traffic engineering, performance monitoring, and assurance. One might even include network security under the general rubric of network management. As these IP networks assume greater importance with their proliferation and increased use, a number of challenges in their management and operation emerge along with new areas of concern that have little relationship to current network-management problems.

I.2 SCALING

Chief among the existing challenges for the larger networks is the problem of scaling. As networks get larger, they incorporate increasing numbers of components. The information records describing the current configuration of the network also increase in size and the cascading effects of specific failures produce larger quantities of alarm indications. New techniques may be required to evaluate such alarms in real-time, as well as to filter and classify them as to severity, priority, and origin. Rule-based systems that apply artificial intelligence techniques to the assessment of alarms have proven to be useful tools, but this area is likely to remain people intensive for the indefinite future. Another side effect of

Managing IP Networks. Edited by Saleh Aidarous and Thomas Plevyak
ISBN 0-471-39299-5 © 2003 Institute of Electrical and Electronics Engineers

scale is the difficulty of assuring that the actual configuration of the network is matched in detail by the service provider's information records that are supposed to represent the same information. New tools and new companies are being formed to address this verification and validation challenge. Key to this will be the use of unique identifiers and other network metadata, as the number of entities increase and the use of more convenient terminology takes hold. A good example of this is in the use of familiar names to denote the burgeoning set of IPv6 addresses within a given organization.

A related complexity arises from the increasingly common practice of implementing IP networks atop virtual communications substrates. The dedicated, hard-wired, point-to-point circuits of yesterday are being replaced with virtual circuits derived from asynchronous transfer mode (ATM), frame-relay, synchronous optical (SONET), sychronous digital hierarchy (SDH), and multiprotocol label switching (MPLS) networks. These virtual resources have their own provisioning and configuration complexities, not the least of which is that virtual misconfiguration of a network resource is sometimes harder to detect than physical misconfiguration. From the network-management point of view, even when physical circuits are working properly, virtual circuits derived from them may be inoperable, making fault detection, isolation, and repair that much more complex. A related equipment problem may occur when embedded computing hardware is working, but certain software functions are rendered inoperable. Increasing scale exacerbates all of these problems.

Another measure of scale comes from the increasing numbers of networks that are interlinked in the Internet. Some of the network-management problems may be the result of faulty interactions between the networks (or due to equipment at the boundary of the networks). As the component networks increase in number, the number of potential interactions among the networks can increase more than linearly. Virtually all of the fault isolation, detection, and repair challenges of one network are multiplied as we attempt to resolve operational problems in the global Internet.

I.3   TRAFFIC ENGINEERING

Traffic engineering in IP networks is usually accomplished in several "layers." The primary management of traffic flow is a consequence of traffic routing at the IP layer and is animated by a variety of routing protocols including border gateway protocol (BGP), intelligent scheduling and information system (IS-IS) and open shortest path first (OSPF) to name three. These protocols are generally destination-based in the sense that for each possible IP destination, each router picks a particular "next-hop" router to which to send that traffic. In the future, the notion of layer may not accurately describe the situation accurately enough, particularly where dynamic interactions take place among various data structures to produce a given result. For example, agent-based systems will likely operate on this principle, and various operations may actually be composite and require cooperation at various "layers."

Network operators have found it useful to introduce an additional layer of traffic management mechanism in the form of virtual circuits below the IP layer. Traffic is typically categorized by destination and then distributed across alternative paths so as to make efficient use of the underlying transmission capacity. Virtual circuits (e.g., ATM or frame relay permanent virtual circuits, MPLS label switched paths) are used to created *adjacencies* between routers at layer 2, and the standard routing procedures are used to determine the next-hop router at layer 3. In effect, the topology of the links between routers and their capacity can be altered at layer 2 in accordance with the apparent traffic flow requirements between pairs of routers. At layer 3, it is possible that all routers might appear to be one hop from each other in a fully connected virtual network.

To achieve the benefits of this form of traffic engineering, it is useful to gather information about the flow of traffic across the network. Some vendors offer systems for gathering such data directly from routers; but under heavy traffic loads, such data gathering may potentially interfere with forwarding of traffic. An alternative is to gather the data directly from the physical circuits that connect routers (or the lower-level switches) together by copying the traffic to an analyzer that can filter source and destination Internet addresses and packet sizes from the traffic and produce a database of source/destination traffic requirements for the network. Such noninvasive measurement methods are attractive when the backbone circuit bandwidths and traffic loads are sufficiently high that self-monitoring by a router has a negative impact on its ability to forward traffic. Finally, it may be useful to send typed data through the network such that the network operators are aware of the nature of the digital information being routed in the network and can organize the network-management system to handle it accordingly.

I.4 SERVICE QUALITY

Among the key performance metrics in IP networks are delay, throughput, and any related measures of packet loss. Even in the absence of any service quality guarantees, it is vital for network operators to have concrete measures of network performance. Packet loss has powerful and negative effects on performance, especially for transmission control protocol (TCP) that interprets loss as congestion and responds by reducing its rate of transmission and retransmission of packets. While the discard of a small percentage of packets in transit by routers may be useful in avoiding localized congestion, packet loss, in general, will adversely affect throughput and delay, and can have a deleterious effect on real-time packet communications. Consequently, it is important for operators of IP networks to know whether and when a network is approaching limits to capacity. Once again, measurements are key and network-management engineering must take this into account.

There is increasing interest in the user population to find ways to assure the quality of service on IP networks. Requirements range from constraining end-to-end packet delay and loss to prescribed parameters or even to assure that the variance in packet interarrival times ("jitter") can be constrained. The latter may prove very important for real-time applications, where information communicated in digital form to the user is converted at the user's site into what is usually known as voice or video or some combination thereof. In addition to these performance characteristics, there is increasing interest by the network providers in being able to assure capacity for preferred customers or applications.

In times of crisis, the ability of the network to guarantee performance for a subset of critical applications can be a high priority. Finding ways to achieve this effect while circumscribing its abuse (e.g., by users who have *not* been subscribed to such preferred service) is an important design challenge. For example, the ability to mark packets as having priority needs to be balanced by the ability to confirm that the originator of the packets has the authority to make such markings. Alternatively the markings might be applied by an edge router only after verifying that packets originating on a given access circuit should be given priority (or a subset of them based on the class of traffic/packet type).

Even this becomes a challenge if traffic is flowing *between* networks operated by different service providers. In this case, either the providers must trust one another to properly mark the traffic or all such markings might have to be ignored. Even if there is trust, there may be a question about a commercial agreement between the service providers to give priority to such traffic, perhaps at a premium charge associated with a net settlement commercial arrangement. Few if any service providers are prepared to offer such internetwork services, but it seems likely that this will become an important requirement in the not-to-distant future. Of course, this determination may be further governed by terms and conditions in associated metadata that can be communicated with the data themselves.

I.5   ORDER ENTRY, PROVISIONING, BILLING

Network management depends in large measure on the use of repositories of information that describe existing network topology, the connectivity among various monitored devices, and the way in which customers at the edge are connected and serviced. Without reliable and accurate information, billing may be difficult to impossible; fault detection, isolation, and repair an impossible challenge; and traffic engineering a distant hope. In designing network-management systems, then, it is vital that the design include considerations for obtaining customer orders, correctly calculating the provisioning required to service the order, and properly capturing all of these data to enable effective fault detection, billing, and traffic engineering. Actual data capture to meet these requirements can also be subject to considerable engineering debate. The use of alarms versus polling for status is one such area for debate. The larger the network, the longer it may take to capture critical information through polling. But, if information is sent automatically, under some circumstances the data gathering can be overwhelmed by an excess of alarm data. The design of the network-management system must balance these competing alternative methods, using hierarchies of polling, alarm, and filtering to cope with the scaling problems.

As discussed earlier, interactions between networks can produce unanticipated problems. For example, lack of sufficient buffering in the hand-off of traffic from one network to another can result in loss of packets during specific high traffic intervals. It is conceivable that neither network may be aware of the problem, or know how to fix the anomaly without collaborating. Indeed, two such providers may not even know they have a problem without the specific input of others. More subtle problems, such as changes in the variance of key performance parameters, may only be determined on a "black-box" type of network characterization at the boundary of the network, or at the boundaries of a collection of networks.

Finally, in a multinetwork environment, the costs for various services may be the result of costs incurred by several parties (both network operators and applications providers). While end users may not need to know the detailed breakdown of costs, the parties involved in providing the services may eventually need to know the detailed breakdown of charges, in order to keep end-user costs under control.

I.6   NETWORK SECURITY

Because network management includes the provisioning of network resources, it is vital that this capability be enabled only for authorized personnel and systems. In the wrong hands, a network-management system can simply disable the entire network. Consequently, the design of the network-management system must incorporate highly reliable authentication of individuals empowered to operate the system and also authentication of various network control subsystems, so that the controlled components can confirm the authenticity and authority of these subsystems to issue commands that affect the configuration of all managed network components. In the wake of an increasing incidence of various forms of network attacks and potential for *inside* abuse by disgruntled or compromised employees, it is no longer sufficient to rely on systems such as firewalls to defend the network from various forms of attack. Security methods including the incorporation of strong authentication technology are called for. Plainly these techniques are only as effective as the observation of procedures for their use. Installing locks does no good if people fail to lock doors or if they leave the keys lying about.

Key management may be an increasingly important part of network management. Already the number of services that require passwords and other forms of authentication is beyond the ability of many to treat them separately. Keeping large "key rings" is one possibility, but more likely is the use of a few services that provide identity-management services. These will also be useful for managing internal network operations, and could also be offered to users of the network. Authenticity of users may require a combination of network-management techniques combined with identity management.

I.7   FUTURE CONSIDERATIONS

As we peer into a somewhat uncertain future, it is possible to discern some interesting possibilities. In addition to finding billions of people and Internet-enabled devices on the network, information itself may become a kind of first class citizen requiring its own management infrastructure. The idea that *digital objects* have an identity and a configuration analogous to the physical devices of the Internet leads one to imagine management requirements for constellations of active digital objects. The elevation of information to a place in the network once reserved only for physical devices suggests that network management will be a lively and challenging area in which to work in the coming decade.

One can imagine accessing digital objects whose location (whether inside the net or provided as an external service) is transparent to a given user. If such objects cannot be accessed, should this be treated as an applications failure and not the responsibility of the network? What if the network makes the selection of where on the network to access the digital object? How can the operator determine the overall health of the system in this context, independent of whether a given user has lodged a complaint or not?

A major concern within today's intellectual property community is the unauthorized access to literary and/or musical works structured in various digital forms. The provision of moving pictures experts group (MPEG) audio layer-3 (MP3) song files over the Internet being easily achieved technically has brought this issue to the forefront. Higher-speed network access may soon make access to audiovisual works in digital form (e.g., "movies") economical over IP networks as well, further compounding the matter, if acceptable solutions are not found.

Today's network infrastructure does not provide required service levels based on a determination of content (i.e., based on the nature of a digital form of expression), but rather attempts to do so based on stated "quality of service" (QOS). If agreement can be reached with the owners of intellectual property on how to determine if a given object is allowed to be accessed, as a prerequisite for performing expressly stated operations on it, then the use of QOS may suffice, even if the underlying information is unknown or even encrypted. This issue is also likely to be controversial, as network operators have historically had no obligation to consider such matters. In the wake of recent terrorist actions, this issue may have ramifications for other types of communication as well. Issues of successful binding of content (in whatever form) to authorizations for communication will have network-management implications as well as free-speech overtones. This will be especially true when the need to track unauthorized access and other communication services is raised for national security purposes.

I.8 SUMMARY

Network management has become more complex as networks have evolved in capacity, scale, and capability. The Internet is no exception. Its implementation has made increasing use of virtual resources that must themselves be managed in addition to managing the system as seen from an IP perspective. As the Internet becomes increasingly ubiquitous, and as traditional applications such as telephony, radio, and video are converted to various digital forms for purposes of access and other communication services, the network-management challenges for Internet operators will continue to evolve and make new engineering demands. These challenges will also appear with regard to other applications, such as interactive games, peer-to-peer services, mobile services, and Internet-enabled appliance management. They will have high priority as service quality *between* Internet service providers (ISPs) becomes as important as service quality *within* an ISP. As with many infrastructure problems, the perceived value of the new communications services is evolving along with the importance of discovering solutions to the associated network-management challenges associated with them.

CHAPTER 1

CURRENT PRACTICE AND EVOLUTION

SALAH AIDAROUS

The development of Internet protocol (IP) and its applications during the last decade make it one of the technological breakthroughs that will shape the new century. Its wide application possibilities make it attractive for service providers and their customers. However, its deployment faces challenges that need more attention from the academic community as well as industry. This chapter and the ones that follow address potential opportunities that IP-based networks and applications offer, and the challenges facing their deployment.

1.1 INTRODUCTION

IP-based technology trends and their impact on the evolution of networking (e.g., traffic value, expenditures) have changed the perception of the industry. Service providers are looking for new opportunities by moving their current environment to databased networking. At the same time, they are faced with the challenge of interworking with the current legacy environment. Manufacturers are responding to these requirements by introducing new technologies at the core and access networks.

Traditionally, a basic network consists of an access telephone switch connected to each subscriber by a dedicated wire pair (metallic loop). These switches, within a geographic area, in the incumbent local exchange carrier (ILEC) or the competitive local exchange carrier (CLEC), are interconnected to provide local calling. They are connected through points of presence (POP) to various interexchange carriers (IECs). The long-distance network can be a flat or hierarchal-based mesh. In a flat network, every switch is connected to every other switch directly, with calls arriving into the network at an originating switch and leaving

Managing IP Networks. Edited by Saleh Aidarous and Thomas Plevyak
ISBN 0-471-39299-5 © 2003 Institute of Electrical and Electronics Engineers

the network at a terminating switch based on the dialed number. In this arrangement there are only two long-distance switches involved in the call. In the hierarchal-based mesh, a hierarchy switches exist where a call enters the network and traverse over four to five intermediate switches, depending on the originating and terminating locations.

This chapter provides the requirements of IP-based service management (what needs to be managed, management objectives, management applications). It discusses present opportunities and challenges in managing the resultant infrastructure. An overview of the book is given.

1.2 EVOLUTION OF NETWORK ARCHITECTURES

No one can ignore the current important role of IP-based networks and services in the business community, and the expectations the industry has build on the opportunities that will be available in the future. With the current growth of the electronic business (eBusiness) coupled with the phenomenal growth of wireless access, the move toward the electronic society (eSociety) is happening at a fast rate.

Public networks (voice) and data networks have been following different philosophies in their architecture and operations. Public networks have been conceived according to a connection (circuit switching) model, with guaranteed quality of service (QoS) and availability (7/24). This requires an operational model that satisfies the real-time and related requirements for voice. Voice is an important application that drives the business of a service provider. In general, subscribers are expected and ready to pay for using the network for either local or long-distance calls. On the other hand, transmitting data over public networks does not attract the same revenue as voice.

Since deregulation of the local network, this can be either ILEC or CLEC. Both serve a determined geographical area, and are connected to each other to provide local calling. They are also connected through POP sites to various IECs. Networks, as shown in Figure 1.1, consist of switches and transmission facilities that process and connect the calls.

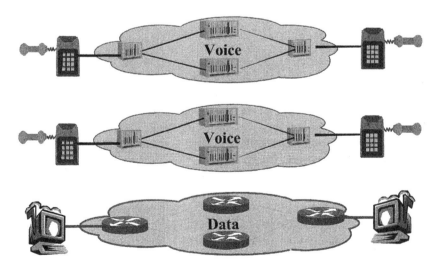

Figure 1.1 Public versus data networks.

IP-based networks followed a connectionless model (packet networks) with best-effort philosophy, which does not maintain the real-time requirements, and mainly satisfies data requirements (accuracy). The main focus was on voice over IP (VoIP) telephony, which was perceived as one of the main drivers for IP.

IPs best-effort philosophy is not optimally designed for voice conversation. Thus, the QoS, reliability and performance can't be guaranteed. There are a lot of basic telephony functions that need to be supported by IP-based networks. For example, dial tone, tone or pulse dial signals, ringing, busy signals, timeout signals, manual flash signals, automatic number identification, answering and disconnect supervision.

1.3 TECHNOLOGY BREAKTHROUGH

One of the major reasons for the time-division multiplexing (TDM) technology is the efficient utilization of costly transmission resources. With fiber and dense-wavelength division multiplexing (DWDM) technology, this constraint is no longer valid. Service providers have gone through massive deployment of fiber in their networks, even to the extent that they have highly underutilized backbone networks. In other words, the cost of bandwidth was not an issue.

Figure 1.2 shows how the future network is based on the technology advancement of IP-based equipment. There are number of factors that cause packet delay in such a network:

1. Transmission link
2. Multiplexing buffer
3. Processing
4. Switching
5. Routing
6. Coding

Subjective voice quality is very sensitive to the total round-trip delay and should be held to a minimum (not to exceed 200 ms). Total delay also impacts the use of echo cancellers and their specifications. On the other hand, as shown in Figure 1.3, the advancements in data networking technology from superrouters to photonic routers and ultimately

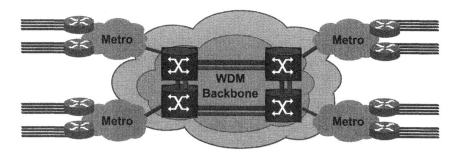

Figure 1.2   Next generation non-TDM world.

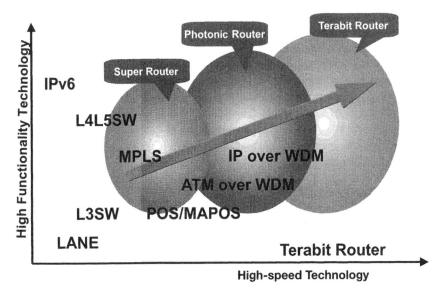

Figure 1.3   Evolution of data networks technology.

to terabit routers will handle many of these issues. This has been driven by the evolution of DWDM and switching technology.

1.4   IP MANAGEMENT CHALLENGES

The traditional business model has been influenced by the scarcity of resources and use by service providers. When bandwidth became available, the business model shifted to customer QoS and relationship management. It is clear that generating revenue was the main business objective of Internet service providers (ISPs). With the current downturn in the telecom industry, that has changed to survivability of the ISP.

Network management has been evolving in the public network over the last two decades. With the declining cost of technology and the rising cost of software, it became clear to service providers that capital is no longer a major decision in operating the network. Expense to operate and maintain, this capital is the key factor for successful business. This has not been the case for IP-based networks (e.g., Internet), where less attention was given to end-to-end network management.

Examining the current status of IP-based networks, there are many major challenges facing service providers in their operations and management. Figure 1.4 is a simplified representation of the major operations and management function needed to provide and maintain services to the service providers' customers.

It is clear that business objectives and marketing activities associated with IP are well developed. There is a good buy-in by the market and industry to the importance of IP-based networks and services.

In the network design area, there are many activities that address the issues of congestion, performance, reliability, QoS, charging, provisioning, security, and maintenance. One critical issue is the lack of a model of the user base and load factors. For example,

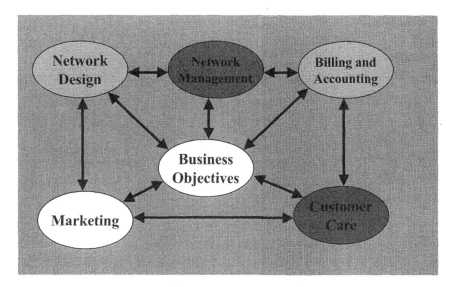

Figure 1.4   Operations and management processes.

traffic control is static in IP but dynamic in the public switched telephone network (PSTN). Measurement criteria, monitoring, and maintenance tools are needed to support QoS and reaction to traffic flow. Classes of QoS and guaranteed minimum performance of network delivery provided traffic parameters need to be offered. Security of information over IP networks is critical from an eBusiness perspective. Security of access jeopardizes the ability of the ISP to provide service.

Billing for packet-based services is an area that started to get more attention in the last years. Both ISPs and SPs are looking for a mechanism for billing for IP-based services. There is no agreement on time, bandwidth, throughput, or flat-rate billing, among others. However, there are several tools for collecting an IP data record (IPDR).

Customer care does not exist in the overall picture of IP networks. It took the public network over 10 years since divestiture to realize the importance of customer care as a survivability issue for their business. It should be expected that IP-based networks should not follow the same strategy. Customer care should be considered at an early stage!

Network-management functions have been receiving less attention and the industry started to realize their importance in sustaining a successful business model for the IP-based network and services. Availability, performance, QoS, and reliability are hard to measure and to guarantee.

1.5   IP/PSTN INTEGRATION

IP interconnection to the PSTN requires that computer hardware and software emulate the PSTN signaling and transmission functions in such a way that the customer can make a call without noticing any difference in that function or in the quality. This will require that signaling conversion, echo cancellation, and other service features are supported by the IP-based part of the network. One big challenge that is facing the industry is the evolution of the current infrastructure to the required IP-based one.

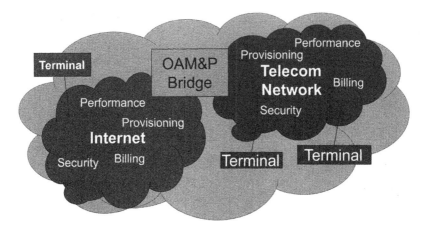

Figure 1.5 Internet and PSTN convergence.

Figure 1.5 shows an interworking approach rather than the replacement approach, which was dominant for many years. The main reason to the interworking approach is the desire of service providers to preserve their current network investment and avoid any major expansion to their capital.

Interconnection to the PSTN requires that the IP network emulate the transmission and signaling characteristics in such a way that a user can make a call to the PSTN, and neither end can notice any difference in the quality of function and transmission. This will require that the operation, administration, maintenance, and provisioning (OAM&P) bridge provides the proper data protocol conversions (for voice, signaling, and echo cancellation) to achieve a satisfactory service.

Interconnected IP to PSTN has to support both residential and business customers. Each uses a wide range of services. There is a need to support the interworking of ISDN, SS7, H.323, for example. Customers may have significant investments in customer-provided equipment (CPE) to interconnect to the various services with standard serial and parallel interfaces which will need to be connected or rerouted to IP transport equipment. This may require reengineering and/or replacement in order to work with IP transport equipment.

1.6 SUMMARY

This chapter and the book itself describe how IP-based networks and applications can be used to create opportunities to enable services of value to the user. After summarizing these opportunities, it is clear that more work needs to be done in QoS for IP services that include end-to-end real-time requirements (e.g., VoIP), eBusiness, security of access and applications, performance of applications, and network reliability. Billing is another area that needs to be considered. The evolution of IP-based networks is also considered, along with current developments in optical technology.

CHAPTER 2

eCOMMERCE

PAUL LEVINE

2.1 INTRODUCTION

Concepts such as electronic data interchange (EDI) and now electronic commerce (eCommerce) have a high profile among users and suppliers alike, not to mention standards bodies. These concepts/terms have many different meanings in various contexts and perspectives [1].[1] In addition, marketing people and those seeking to raise investment funds use these terms in a variety of ways. However, the underlying principles and characteristics of eCommerce include:

1. Being business transaction-based (of both a financial and nonfinancial nature).
2. Using information technology (IT) (computers and telecommunications).
3. Interchanging electronic data involving establishment of commitments among Persons, where "Person" is a committing entity or party in a business transaction.

"From a commercial, legal and standardization perspective, one can view electronic commerce as:

Electronic commerce: a category of business transactions, involving two or more Persons, enacted through electronic data interchange, based on a monetary and for profit basis. Persons can be individuals, organizations, and/or public administrations" [2].

---

[1]The International Organization for Standardization/International Electrotechnical Commission Joint Technical Committee (ISO/IEC JTC 1) Business Team on Electronic Commerce (BT-EC) in its report to JTC 1 stated "BT-EC recognizes that Electronic Commerce (EC) can be defined in many different ways. But rather than attempting to provide a satisfactory definition, the Team has chosen to take a more heuristic approach to EC and to do so from a global perspective, that is, world-wide, cross-sectorial, multi-lingual, various categories of participants (including consumers)."

Managing IP Networks. Edited by Saleh Aidarous and Thomas Plevyak

13

ISBN 0-471-39299-5 © 2003 Institute of Electrical and Electronics Engineers

Electronic Commerce can be broadly categorized into the following scenarios, with the understanding that each scenario holds in both directions.

- Business to business
- Business to public administration
- Individual to business
- Individual to public administration
- Public administration to public administration

eCommerce requirements in Section 2.2 are taken from the BT-EC report, which focused on individual-to-business and individual-to-administration scenarios, in order to bring human needs for eCommerce into play.

This chapter focuses on satisfying the overarching requirement that information to be exchanged is publicly defined and available so that it can be shared. Standards bodies and industry forums have been addressing this need over the past decade in two respects: (1) semantic definition of data entities as building blocks for information exchange, and (2) organization and registration of the data-element descriptions so that the information can be shared. Standards activity has more recently evolved business-process and information modeling, where information exchange occurs within a business collaboration framework using business-collaboration protocol patterns. This chapter highlights standardization activity related to the information exchange requirements from the business perspective, i.e., the "why," "what," "when," and "with whom," with respect to information to be shared as driven by business needs. Not to minimize the importance of "how" this is done, that aspect of information exchange is left to other chapters in this volume.

The remaining sections of this chapter provide a broad overview of activity being conducted in standards bodies and industry forums in connection with standardized definition and exchange of information. Section 2.2 gives a picture of the global view of the requirements driving eCommerce. The foundation underlying standards activity related to the next generation of electronic exchange of business information is covered in Sections 2.3 and 2.4. Section 2.5 discusses standardized semantic components as a requisite for eCommerce. Section 2.6 provides an overview of standards activities related to interchanging standardized semantic components among organizations according to well-defined business collaboration protocols.

2.2 eCOMMERCE REQUIREMENTS

2.2.1 Consumer Interest in eCommerce Standardization

According to the ISO/IEC JTC 1 Business Team on Electronic Commerce (BT-EC), there are several reasons for consumer interest in eCommerce and its standardization [1, Sec. 5.2]:

- eCommerce will first touch most facets of society and daily living, including fundamental services such as banking, shopping, etc. If the individual cannot cope with this, she or he will become socially disadvantaged and a two-tier society will be created.
- A second, closely related point, is that eCommerce may be the only way certain products or services will be offered for sale in the future. Not being conversant with

eCommerce will reduce an individual's choice (choice being a fundamental consumer right).

- Third, eCommerce can, through economies of scale, provide better offers to the consumer than traditional city-center stores. Those conversant with eCommerce may be able to enjoy lower prices; those not conversant, may pay higher prices.

- Fourth, eCommerce may be the most suitable way for people living in remote areas, single parent families, people at work, or for disabled consumers to shop. Consumers who are not able to use eCommerce systems or do not trust them will be disadvantaged when this becomes a means of purchase.

- eCommerce currently presupposes that the user has access to a computer and a modem. The costs associated with this (equipment, software, installation, and, not least of all, training costs) will be a barrier to some. The use of other delivery techniques where the user already has invested in existing equipment (e.g., TV sets, screen phones) needs to be considered according to market requirements.

- Following on from the preceding point is the issue of eCommerce delivery systems being compatible with other emerging technologies (e.g., smart house control technologies). Through compatible systems, the user would be able to avoid purchasing, installing, and learning several different pieces of incompatible equipment and systems.

A concern that underpins several of the previous points is the ease of use of eCommerce systems. This concern has derived from the problem many users have when using existing low functionality self-service, or smart card systems.

One way of achieving ease of use is consistency at the user interface. Today's user interface solutions can hardly be described as consistent. If the systems are not easy to use, large numbers of users will not be able to use them, or will use them inefficiently. This will in turn impact market acceptance.

On a positive note, users can achieve advantages using eCommerce, provided that the systems are easy and consistent to use, and physically and psychologically accessible. eCommerce should also be available via technologies other than the PC, e.g., through TVs, screenphones, and mobile phones.

2.2.2 Consumer Requirements for eCommerce

The following consumer requirements are not necessarily specific to eCommerce, but generic for information and communication technologies (ICT). Some of them are already met, partially or in full, by computerized information systems currently in use.

It should be noted that it is important to see all the requirements in relation to each other, as they are interlinked. Resolving just one or two of the issues will not ensure that consumer interests are satisfactorily taken into account.

Requirements are not presented in any hierarchical order of importance. This is because the relevance and thereby importance of each and every requirement is situation-dependent. In some situations, some of the requirements may not be applicable.

1. **Ease of Use** (a) eCommerce must be easy to use for all intended user groups. Following ergonomics software principles for user interface design[2] should help

---

[2]For example, ISO/IEC 9241—10 Dialogue Principles, and ISO/CD 13407—2 Human Centered Design Processes for Interactive Systems.

achieve ease of use. Information presentation should follow a natural flow. A system should be designed taking into account the mental models of the users. The model of a systems designer should be behind the scenes, but should not intrude on the users' perception of the system. (b) eCommerce standards should address ergonomical aspects of hardware, software, services, and support. Existing standards should be applied.[3] (c) Metaphors and supporting icons should be standardized to help facilitate ease of use. (d) A usability metrics tool is needed. [*Note:* Ease of use can be measured in terms of performance (e.g., the time taken by users to complete a predetermined task, and/or number of errors, and/or satisfaction with a service: see ISO/IEC 9241—11 Guidance of Usability). Goals for ease of use (known as usability statements) should be developed.]

2. **Consistent User Interface Elements**   A system must have consistent user interface elements. It is especially important that the methods of processing, storing, and accessing the systems are consistent for the user. [*Note:* A consistent user interface can be achieved by different means, e.g.:

   (a) All components of the user interface are uniform; this requires standardization.

   (b) The user interface adapts to the user, so that the user always meets a personalized uniform interface. This principle is the subject of the prEN 1332-4 "Identification Card Systems; Man Machine Interface:—Coding of User Requirements on Smart Cards."]

3. **Adaptability**   A system should be adaptable to meet a user's specific requirements and abilities. For example, a system should provide output in a format and at a pace that meets the individual's needs.

4. **Provision of System Status Information**   The status of a system (e.g., waiting for input, checking, fetching) should always be available for the user (i.e., feedback). Different mechanisms should be employed to give complete feedback to the user. Messages should be positive and not place blame on the user. Equally, mechanisms for feedforward (especially of consequences of actions) should be available ("if you start downloading the file you have selected it will take 76 minutes. Press «Cancel download» or «Download»"). Feedforward is an attribute that helps build trust in the system.

5. **Error Tolerance and System Stability**   The system should anticipate errors of operation and be forgiving. Informative error messages should lead the user forward. The system should be robust and should remain stable if users try services that cannot be delivered or make choices that are redundant.

6. **Minimize the User's Need to Remember System Operation**   A system should display dialog elements to the user and allow them to choose from items generated by the system or to edit them. Menus are a typical technology to achieve this goal.

7. **Explorability**   The system should encourage users to discover its functions, without the system crashing.

8. **Design for All**   eCommerce standards should support the principle of "design for all." This is a process of creating products, systems, and services that are accessible and usable by people with the widest possible range of abilities operating

---

[3]For example, ISO 9241.

within the widest possible range of situations. This could be facilitated by standards on the interchange of different input/output devices needed to match the individual's requirements (e.g., a blind person wants voice output). Equally, an individual's requirements could be encoded in a standardized way (see below) so that the user interface of the system is adapted to the individual's requirements (language preference, input mode preference, etc.).

9. **Functionality of Solution**   A standard supporting eCommerce should take into account the requirements of different user groups and the user tasks that a system conforming to the standard is able to support. In the scope of an eCommerce standard, it should be stated by which groups and for which tasks the system should be used, and in which operating environments. This statement should be open for review. There may be occasions where a system is not intended for all users, e.g., it is intended to be childproof. In these instances, the scope of the underlying standard should state which users and tasks the system is not designed for and why these groups' requirements are not taken into account.

10. **Multicultural Aspects**   Multicultural aspects (these are regarded by some as geographical localization issues) need to be considered when developing eCommerce standards. These aspects might be affected by religion (e.g., no shopping on Sunday, national legislation, the shape and size of clothing/footwear). (See Section 2.2.3.3 for more discussion on cultural adaptability.)

11. **Multilinguistic Aspects**   Multilinguistic aspects need to be considered. Existing standards should be applied and where necessary new ones developed. (See Section 2.2.3.2 for more discussion on multilinguistic aspects.)

12. **Terminology**   As part of a user-centered design, the terminology used in user interfaces, (including brochures, user instructions, and information presented by the system) should meet basic generic user requirements.[4]

13. **Comprehensible Standards**   Standards on consumer input should be unambiguous and easy to understand, i.e., written in plain language so that nontechnical people can comprehend them and contribute. ISO Guidelines on standards writing must be met.

14. **Interoperability**   Different services should be interoperable so that, in theory, any service can be accessed on any appropriate network on any relevant device, thus avoiding the acquisition of access to several different networks and terminals for similar services.

15. **Compatibility**   Compatibility within a system should be ensured; for example, new versions of systems should be compatible with previous versions of the same system. Components for systems originating from different manufacturers should also be compatible. Different systems should be compatible so as to allow their joint operation.

16. **Privacy**   The system should ensure the privacy of the individual.

17. **Security of Information**   It should not be possible for unauthorized people to follow a user's activities on an electronic network. Electronic footprints are to be avoided. Standards should help provide methods for checking this, especially in open and decentralized networks. Necessary system-generated footprint data

---

[4]Or meet ISO Guide 37 requirements.

should be deleted after an appropriate time. The system should not allow disclosure of information about the user to unauthorized people and should indicate clearly to whom information is given. Security of information sent, stored, received or deleted must be ensured. The level of security should be clearly stated to the user. Electronic signatures and encryption devices are clear candidates for standardization.

18. **Cost Transparency**   The system must be transparent regarding all costs involved. Cost information should be presented in a standardized way. This includes both initial costs incurred by the user and subsequent costs for subscribing to and operating the system, especially when interworking on networks, or when using on-line help or other fundamental services (e.g., directory enquiries or short-message service on a mobile phone). Disconnecting from a service must be free of charge or the charge must be stated in a standardized way at the point of purchase.

19. **Reliability of Information**   The system should indicate reliability of information (possibly by quoting sources) provided on the system (e.g., "Balance of account is xxx ECU at 1000 hours on yyyy-mm-dd. Note: Bank clearing system has been out of action last two days").

20. **Quality of Service and System Reliability**   There should be a way to determine and present quality-of-service and system reliability. This should include the development of performance indicators. This information should be displayed at the point of sale.

21. **Rating and Grading Systems**   eCommerce standards should allow for the application of rating and grading systems. Standards for evaluating and presenting ICT systems in terms of ease of use, cost, durability, system reliability, and information reliability (source and content) will need to be developed.

22. **Consumer Participation Throughout the System Development Process**   Active consumer participation should be ensured throughout all phases of the standardization process in order to ensure user-friendly systems. This includes the programming of standardization work, priority setting, and participating in the technical work.

23. **Ecological Aspects**   Developments should be sustainable in an ecological sense. Scientific and objective methods are needed to assess the environmental friendliness of products over their entire lifetime. This information should be indicated in a standardized way.

24. **Ethical Aspects**   Scientific and objective methods are needed to assess ethically sound products (e.g., no child labor, no support of ideologies based on discrimination or violence). This information should be indicated in a standardized way.

2.2.3 Horizontal Aspects

The BT-EC [1, Sec. 6.1] identified four horizontal issues as being of general relevance for all scenarios involving eCommerce and gave these horizontal issues prominent attention in its work. These issues are:

- IT enablement
- Localization, including multilingualism

- Cross-sectorial aspects
- Cultural adaptability

From a user perspective, these four horizontal issues need to be addressed in a harmonious manner.

2.2.3.1 IT Enablement

2.2.3.1 IT Enablement A key characteristic of commerce worldwide, in particular in the business-to-business and business-to-administration domains, is that it consists of business transactions that:

1. Are rule-based, i.e., mutually understood and accepted sets of business conventions, practices, procedures, etc.; and
2. make extensive use of "codes," often table-based, representing predefined possible choices for common aspects of business transactions. Examples include countries, currencies, languages, and manufacturers and their products.

Many of these sets of agreed-upon rules used in business worldwide and their associated lists of tables/codes are de jure and de facto standards. The BT-EC noted that numerous international standards are already in use in support of commerce worldwide. The problem is that most are paper-based and lack a computer-processable version. Even if distributed in electronic form, these standards cannot be "plugged-in" for use in eCommerce. Much of the intelligence in these international standards is humanly understandable explicitly or implicitly. They have not been described formally using formal description techniques, i.e., in their present form they do not support "computational integrity." Consequently, each enterprise using these code sets has to spend considerable time and effort to (1) determine their meaning and interpret them; (2) build applications; and, (3) hope that they interoperate with other networks or enterprises.

2.2.3.2 Localization/Multilingualism Human beings like to name objects. But the approach of using names is not very IT friendly, cost-efficient, or time-efficient. Depending on the interplay of multilingual and localization requirements, in eCommerce, a singular product or service being offered for sale will have multiple names and differing names even in the same language. Thus, if we wish to ensure rapid and widespread use of eCommerce globally, we must on the one hand identify objects, i.e., products or services being offered for sale, in an unambiguous, linguistically neutral, and IT-processable and eCommerce-facilitated manner, and, on the other hand, present the same via a range of linguistic names (and associated character sets) from a point-of-sale perspective, i.e., human-readable user interface, as required by the local marketplace.

In order to provide a focus for its work on horizontal issues, the BT-EC utilized four real-world examples, namely:

- Currency Codes
- Country Codes
- Language Codes
- Commodity Codes

These examples represent standards used for commerce worldwide and are currently implemented by enterprises and their information systems in a wide variety of ways. There are also no standard ways for the interworking among these and similar standards. This impedes global interoperability. The widespread use of the Internet is exacerbating existing ambiguities.

From a BT-EC perspective, these four examples underline the fact that with respect to eCommerce there may be less of a need for new standards. Rather, the immediate challenge may well be the development of a category of information technology standards that will facilitate the development of information-technology-enabled versions of existing standards used in commerce, and do so in a manner that also supports the interplay of localization and multilingual requirements, i.e., "bridging standards."

The BT-EC recommended the following objectives for such standardization work in support of eCommerce:

1. Standards must focus on the interface (as opposed to implementation) as the best means of arriving at globally harmonized solutions for interoperability from both a business and information technology perspective.
2. Standard interfaces among information systems must be technology neutral, accommodating advances in technology to the extent possible. Further, such standard interfaces must be linguistically neutral to the furthest extent possible.
3. In order to empower users and consumers, standards should be adaptable to local and multilingual requirements at national and regional levels, while ensuring full transparency of available market solutions to the consumer. Multilingualism must be considered. The expansion of open, multilingual standards could significantly increase the volume and value of worldwide eCommerce.

2.2.3.3 *Cross-Sectorial/Cultural Adaptability*   Cross-sectorial issues pertain to differing, at times conflicting, understandings of business practices, object identification, etc., among economic sectors [1, Sec. 6.4]. The challenge here is that of resolving two sets of issues:

1. Industry sectors, scientific fields, and professional disciplines assign their own uses or meanings to the terms of a natural language. Quite often natural languages are used in a manner called "technical languages": the same word/term frequently has very different meanings in other industry sectors. This reflects the trend in various sectors toward using existing nontechnical "common language" words as terms with new technical meanings.
2. "Scientific language" terminology arising from efforts to create multilingual equivalency in addition to cross-sectorial interoperability in support of eCommerce adds to the complexity. A case study on the cross-sectorial issues [3], with respect to scientific languages, led to the conclusion that a scientific language can be considered a culturally neutral exchange language, which, in turn, has multiple natural language and culturally dependent linguistic equivalent terms.

Technical languages and their use in particular industry sectors present particular challenges to cultural adaptability and cross-sectorial interoperability, because they do not have the attributes of scientific languages. Technical languages as linguistic subsystems are difficult enough to handle even within their industry sector, in one natural language. To this are added the challenges of localization, multiculturalism, and cross-sectorial interactions in eCommerce. Associating technical languages with a controlled vocabulary of terms is one means of providing cross-sectorial interoperability. Cultural adaptability is accomplished by making multilingual equivalents to the controlled vocabulary terms.

In conclusion, it should be noted that within industry sectors established standards and conventions exist for unambiguous identification and referencing of unique objects, and for naming them (often multilingually), along with associated rules. Although not originally designed to interoperate across and among industry sectors, many of these sectorial standards have common core constructs that could be utilized to support cross-sectorial eCommerce and in a manner that accommodates localization and multilingual needs.

2.3 OPEN-EDI

eCommerce standardization activity, addressing the requirements of Section 2.2, has taken place in the past 12 years under a banner referred to as "Open-edi." Not to be confused with electronic data interchange (EDI), Open-edi, which is a term for "the automated exchange of any predefined and structured data for business purposes among information systems of two or more organizations," provides a reference model framework for the standards that are needed for the next generation of information exchange [3].

Open-edi is defined as "electronic data interchange among multiple autonomous organizations to accomplish an explicit shared business goal according to Open-edi standards" [4]. Defining a totally new paradigm from traditional EDI, the Open-edi Reference Model provides the foundation for current developments in eCommerce, eBusiness in particular, where eBusiness is defined as "a generic term covering information definition and exchange requirements within and between enterprises, including customers." [5] The scope of Open-edi is to provide standardization in the field of generic information technology standards for open electronic data interchange needed to attain global interoperability among the systems used by organizations. Such interoperability is viewed from both a business and information technology perspective. The Open-edi vision is that there will be:

- Cross-sectorial information exchange, with
- Information to be exchanged, structured, and predefined, requiring
- No prior agreements among trading partners, nor
- Human intervention in interfacing with computer applications,
- Specified in a manner that is independent from underlying IT systems.

2.3.1 Open-edi Conceptual Model

A conceptual model for electronic data interchange standards and services was created by the Special Working Group on Electronic Data Interchange (SWG-EDI) as a framework for positioning and harmonizing all edi-related standards and activities into a cohesive whole [6]. Particular attention was given to a top-down approach for modeling multilateral information flows. Figure 2.1 is a schematic representation of an Open-edi transaction. The transaction consists of information exchanges among autonomous parties shown by the various shaped objects.

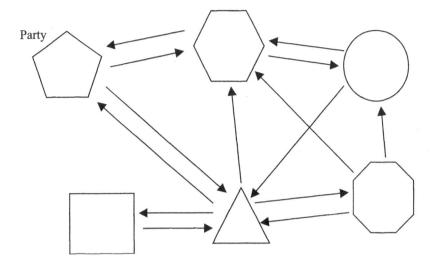

Party

Figure 2.1 Schematic representation of an Open-edi transaction.

The SWG-EDI found three aspects of information flow to be important considerations in Open-edi:

1. The independent decision-making capabilities of the autonomous parties must be preserved in the associated information flow. Each party must be allowed the freedom to make decisions based on the semantic content of the information interchanges and on factors known only to itself.

2. Rule-based techniques can be applied to the business and semantic behavior of the parties within an information flow. By requiring that each participant engage in specific interchange scenarios according to predefined rules, it is possible to reduce or eliminate operational ambiguities and misinterpretations.

3. Infrastructure support services are required to realize the exchange of information. They must operate according to mutually accepted standards in all aspects of the exchange, such as data usage and representation, security, auditing, and communications.

These three aspects are also reflected in the organizational capabilities of parties. Figure 2.2 illustrates this concept as three concentric ovals representing an abstraction of a party (shown as a pentagon in Figure 2.1) referred to as an information management domain (IMD). It provides more detail about the parties shown in Figure 2.1. The innermost oval (the edi Principal) represents the logical part of an IMD that is responsible for the decision-making, goal-oriented business activities of a real organization. The second ring (the Business Agreement Service) represents the activities related to the business rules and semantics involved in information exchange. The outer ring (the edi Support Service) represents the IT infrastructure required to realize the goals of an information exchange.

Only the interorganizational aspects of information flows should be standardized. Therefore the model is not concerned with the internal decision-making aspect, because

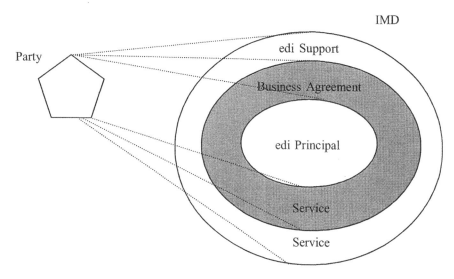

Figure 2.2   Breakdown of an information management domain (IMD).

this deals with proprietary, nonstandard activities. The other two aspects represent the areas important to Open-edi.

The Open-edi Conceptual Model provides a framework and specification of those aspects of Open-edi transactions that require standardization. Business and organizational requirements provide input to the model, but are not within the model itself. Further, the model is ultimately realized by Open-edi implementations, which are also outside the scope of the model. Figure 2.3 illustrates the components of the Open-edi Conceptual Model.

2.3.2   Open-edi Reference Model

In Figure 2.3 the Open-edi Conceptual Model contains a part called the Open-edi Reference Model, which contains descriptions, or the requirements and constraints on the functional components. It is concerned with the business rules and activities that must take place and not with the standards required to specify them. The reference model is subdivided into two views, or perspectives:

1. The business operational view focuses on high-level operations and their associated requirements and constraints, as regarded from the business user's perspective.
2. The functional service view focuses on the infrastructure requirements for realizing the operations described in the business operational view.

In summary, by viewing a multilateral Open-edi transaction as a schematic of parties and information flows, as in Figure 2.1, we can better see the overall scope of a business transaction. However, by looking more closely at the parties involved, we find that each organization can be abstractly modeled as a three-tiered entity, i.e., an IMD, as shown in Figure 2.2. Further, the two outer portions of the IMD abstraction can be related directly to the two views represented within the Open-edi Reference Model. These relationships are illustrated in Figure 2.4.

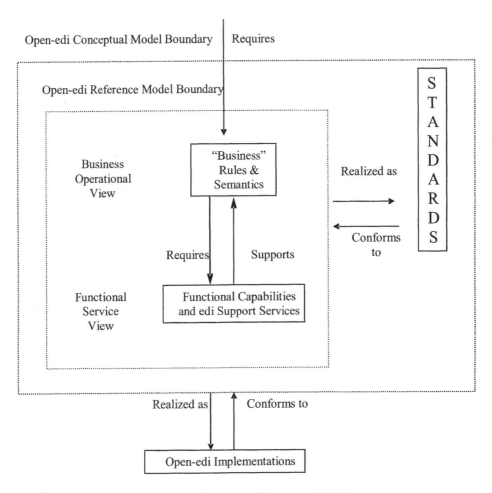

Figure 2.3   The Open-edi Conceptual Model.

2.3.2.1 *Problems with EDI*   Interoperation among application programs requires that there be "common ground" in their exchange of information, so that there can be common understanding and agreement on the information being jointly processed. Common ground in this exchange of information is accomplished in current EDI methodology through a neutral, application independent syntax, i.e., typically for business data, a translated X12 or UN/EDIFACT interchange file. All consideration of application programs, how to facilitate their interoperation, functionality variations, and the business practices behind them are deliberately ignored. Instead, the current EDI standardization process in X12 and UN/EDIFACT concentrates solely on the structure and content of the translated interchange file.

Problems associated with X12 and UN/EDIFACT standards and the standards-development process, are well documented and begin with the lack of an agreed upon semantic

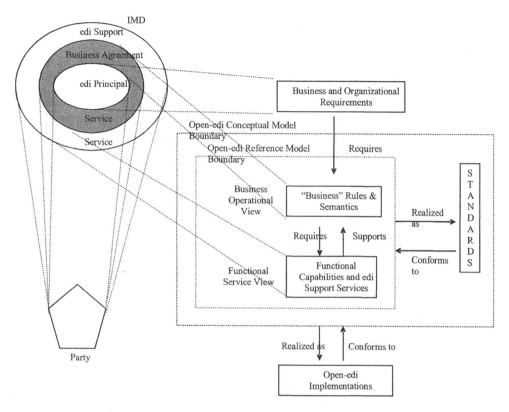

Figure 2.4 Relationship between the Open-edi Reference Model and IMDs.

definition of the information to be exchanged. Data-centric EDI standards that are organized into service segments that control the data interchange information content, and messages that provide the generic interchange structure attempt to include the solution for every industry. For example, the UN/EDIFACT Purchase Order (PO) transaction set contains over 1200 data elements. However, a paper PO contains about 40 different data fields (assuming a single item is ordered). Why does the EDI equivalent have 30 times as many data possibilities? The reason is that the PO transaction set includes more than just the data related to a specific order being placed. As the PO standard was created and maintained over time, it was predominantly IT experts who participated in the work. Their knowledge was mostly based on "what" was in their corporate databases. Because of that, they expected that their data requirements would be fulfilled in the PO standard. There was no analysis as to whether the corporate purchasing application (or any other one) actually "used" or "required" those data. As more companies used the PO (as well as other EDI transaction sets), more data elements were added. Because many of the EDI transaction sets were used across many industries, this addition of data requirements proliferated.

To help bring true data requirements back to a manageable level, industry groups created implementation conventions (ICs) (not standards) that would limit the use of data elements to what the companies in a given industry agreed to. This generally resulted in an 80% reduction, i.e., 240 data elements in the case of the PO, still six times as many as a paper PO. Additional problems with this approach were that changes in EDI standards were not coordinated with changes in ICs, and international coordination of ICs was especially rare.

Individual companies further limited their implementation to a subset of an industry IC, eliminating another 80%, thus resulting in 45–50 data elements, which is almost the same number as a paper-based PO. However, if one compares the POs of any two companies in the same industry, their data requirements are not identical. Further, even if a particular company is big enough to dominate another company with its requirements, not every partner it trades with can deliver all the data it requires, thus resulting in different implementations. Trading partner agreements must be made on which EDI transactions they intend to use, which IC will be used for each transaction, individual data elements to be used in each IC, etc.

Before one can engage in EDI with a particular partner, resources are required not only to identify the requirements for data to be exchanged, but also to integrate the IC into the business process, particularly at the receiving end. Finally, the information exchange must be tested before going live. Time and expertise needed to navigate new transactions and changes through the standards process took anywhere from 18 months to several years.

This process is required for each new trading partner, and for each EDI message with that partner—a very costly effort that only the Fortune 1000 companies in each country could afford. The resultant EDI standards are not really standards at all, only a tool to be used as a starting point in the analysis of information to be exchanged in a business process. The initial X12 and UN/EDIFACT goal of developing standard semantics was not realized. As summarized in the Open-edi Reference Model [4],

> The economic advantages of Electronic Data Interchange (EDI) are widely recognized. However, the cost of setting up an EDI relationship is still very high due to the need for a detailed bilateral business and technical agreement between the involved business partners. The initial high cost of establishing such an agreement does not justify short-term partnerships. It has also been found that implementations involving the management of a large number of partners and their associated agreements are not productive. Consequently, most EDI implementations have been successful only:
>
> In long term partnerships
> Between a limited number of partners

An example of this situation is taken from the Healthcare EDI Coalition (HEDIC) where "the cost and complexity of EDI have prevented many small-to-medium enterprises from participating in electronic commerce." Even where "the explosive growth of the Internet and the rapid development of web-based applications are the primary drivers for creating a new *Virtual e-marketplace* in healthcare, the effects of the web on healthcare eCommerce have been minimal. The market drivers in healthcare eCommerce have traditionally been manufacturers, distributors and GPOs. The eCommerce sites developed by these companies are simply IP-based versions of existing relationships using the Internet to provide access to additional product information, server-based electronic order status and purchasing options for their customers" [7].

2.3.2.2 The Open-edi Solution It is essential to understand that for Open-edi to overcome the current impediments to implementing EDI, a new paradigm must be envisioned that shifts the focus on EDI standards from the interchange file to the information contained in the business processes.

In the words of the Open-edi Reference Framework

Open-edi lowers these barriers by introducing standard business scenarios and the necessary services to support them. Once a business scenario is agreed upon, and the implementations conform to the Open-edi standards, there is no need for prior agreement among trading partners, other than the decision to engage in the Open-edi transaction in compliance with the business scenario. Since Open-edi takes a generic approach, it enables organizations to establish short-term relationships quickly and cost effectively. Business scenarios and the necessary supporting services would be available to all that wish to use them, thus providing the necessary means for implementing Open-edi.

The field of application of Open-edi is the electronic processing of business transactions among autonomous multiple organizations within and across sectors (e.g., public/private, industrial, geographic). It includes business transactions that involve multiple data types such as numbers, characters, images and sound.

The Open-edi Reference Model has been developed primarily to provide standards required for inter-working of organizations, through interconnected information technology systems. This model is independent of specific:

- Information technology implementations
- Business content or conventions
- Business activities
- Organizations

The Open-edi Reference Model identifies required standards for Open-edi and provides a reference for those standards by defining the basic concepts used to develop them. It serves as the basis for coordination of work between the different agencies involved in EDI standardization. It provides the framework for this co-ordination and for the integration of existing and emerging standards and the development of future standards. [4, Clause 0, Introduction]

2.3.3 MoU Management Group Concerning Standardization in the Field of eBusiness

In order to follow through with on-going activities according to the Open-edi framework, a Memorandum of Understanding (MoU) has been established among international standardization organizations, namely:

- The International Electrotechnical Commission (IEC)
- The International Organization for Standardization (ISO)
- The International Telecommunication Union (ITU)
- The United Nations Economic Commission for Europe (UN/ECE)

Along with the participation of International User Groups, these organizations coordinate relevant work programs at the highest level to optimize the use of scarce resources. Figure 2.5 shows a MoU matrix of standards activity [2].[5]

---

[5]Annex J update to Memorandum of Understanding between the International Electrotechnical Commission, the International Organization for Standardization, the International Telecommunication Union and the United Nations Economic Commission for Europe concerning Standardization in the Field of Electronic Business, Annex A: Division of Responsibilities.

	Meta-standards	Standards	Guidance	Produce Product	Conformance and Certification	Used by
Environment	Cultural Adaptability	International National Bilateral	Lawyers		Courts	Commerce and government
Formal recognition	ISO/IEC JTC 1/SC 32	ISO, ISO/IEC, ITU National and regional standards bodies UN/ECE CEN IETF ASTM OASIS	ISO/IEC JTC1 SC 32 UN/ECE ASTM		ISO/IEC	Standards bodies Suppliers Users
BOV activity models	ISO/IEC JTC 1/SC 7 and SC 32 ISO TC 184	ISO, IEC and ITU sectorial bodies CEN National standards bodies WfMC	WfMC	Non-standard products		Users
BOV data models	ISO/IEC JTC 1 SC 21/WG 3 and SC 32 ISO TC211	Trade bodies User groups WTO WCO ICAO IMO SWIFT ebXML UN/ECE	as previous column plus sectorial groups	Suppliers	UN/CEFACT	Suppliers Users
FSV technology	ISO/IEC JTC 1 ISO TC211 IETF	ISO/IEC various TCs and JTC1/SCs CEN IETF W3C	ISO/IEC JTC 1/SC 32 JTC1/SC27 TC 215 CEN TC 251 IETF W3C	Manufacturers Suppliers	Many NIST Open Group	Suppliers Users

Figure 2.5   MoU Matrix: A road map for electronic business.

2.4 BUSINESS OPERATIONAL VIEW

The remainder of this chapter on eCommerce focuses on aspects of the business operational view (BOV) as defined in the Open-edi Reference Model. The BOV is defined as "a perspective of business transactions limited to those aspects regarding the making of business decisions and commitments among organizations, which are needed for the description of a business transaction" [4, Clause 4, The Open-edi Reference Model].

2.4.1 Emphasis on Semantics

Key to the BOV perspective is the semantic definition of information being exchanged in business transactions. This point has been evident in the recent work of eBusiness eXtensible Markup Language (ebXML), an 18-month international initiative, the purpose of which is "to research and identify the technical basis upon which the global implementation of XML can be standardized" [8]. As noted in ebXML, XML is really not a language, but a framework for developing an unlimited number of languages. XML by itself provides a syntax (schema for describing data or message structures), not semantics (meaning, behavior, or presentation). XML is flexible and extensible, easy to implement, and small enough for processing by Web browsers. XML standardizes the syntax of information exchange in a text-based notation designed to be obvious to both people and processes.

However, ebXML was established with the understanding that semantic definition of information is the real issue in information exchange. XML is catching on quickly because of the obvious appeal of being able to quickly develop a new document or message type, which contrasts greatly with the lengthy organizational debates by which new UN/EDIFACT message standards are developed. Anyone using XML can invent new tags for particular subject areas and define the document schema. However, this can lead to the proliferation of multiple schemas for the same application or business process, with the same content being described using different element or attribute names, or different content using the same names. XML contains a namespace mechanism that avoids naming collisions by associating an element with the authority for that element, but this is a syntactic remedy for avoiding collisions that does not address the issue of semantic incompatibility. The lack of standard content models and semantics clearly impedes interoperability.

In contrast,

Open-edi describes flows of information using Information Bundles (IBs) which cause predefined changes in the states of the parties to the exchange. Parties using Open-edi make the commitment that they will adhere to the predefined rules associated with the registered scenario attributes, roles and IBs (including registered Semantic Components (SCs)) necessary to support the exchanges of commitments applicable to the parties involved in the business transaction.

The characteristics by which Open-edi is recognized and defined are:

- Actions based upon following predefined rules
- Commitment of the parties involved
- Communications among parties are automated
- Parties control and maintain their states
- Parties act autonomously
- Multiple simultaneous transactions can be supported [2, Clause 5]

Business process and information models, described in Section 2.6, facilitate business process and business information integration among trading partners that is needed to accomplish these Open-edi objectives.

2.4.2 BOV Requirements

The evolution of information and communications technologies has created a need and opportunity for different user groups to engage in business relationships, using these technologies. This requires automated methods to carry out information exchange among organizations.

Standards required for Open-edi cover a wide spectrum of areas and include commercial aspects, support for national and international laws and regulations, information technology perspectives, and telecommunications and interconnections security, etc. To these are added public policy requirements of a generic and horizontal nature such as consumer protection and privacy. [4]. Figure 2.5 describes how the Open-edi Reference Model serves as the basis for coordination of work of different standardization areas and types of standardization for Open-edi.

In addition, the widespread adoption and use of Internet and World Wide Web (WWW)-based technologies, by organizations as well as individuals, has added urgency to the need to identify and specify the key components of a business transaction. For such specifications to be carried out as electronic business transactions supported by automated methods of the functional support services requires a standard-based approach for business semantic descriptive techniques in support of the BOV of Open-edi.

The sources of requirements on the BOV aspects that need to be integrated and/or taken into account in the development of business descriptive techniques for Open-edi-based business transactions include.[6]

- Commercial frameworks and associated requirements.
- Legal frameworks and associated requirements.
- Public policy requirements, particularly those of a generic nature such as consumer protection and privacy.
- Sectorial and cross-sectorial requirements.
- Requirements arising from the need to support cultural adaptability requirements. This includes meeting localization and multilingualism requirements, i.e., as may be required to meet requirements of a particular jurisdiction or desired for providing a good, service, and/or right in a particular market [9]. Here distinguishing between IT interfaces and their multiple human interface equivalents is the recommended approach [9].

Figure 2.6 provides an integrated view of the business operational requirements" [2, Sec. 0.2].

2.4.3 BOV Methodology

Taking Unified Modeling Language (UML) as the FDT of choice, many standards bodies and industry consortiums have adopted a UML-based methodology for modeling business processes involving information exchange, e.g., SWIFT, RosettaNet and Uniform Code Council/(UCC/EAN), Accredited Standards Committee (ASC) T1, ITU—Sector Telecommunication (ITU-T), and the United Nations Centre for Trace Facilitation and Electronic Business (UN/CEFACT). This is in keeping with Objective 2 of Section 2.2.3.2, where UML artifacts capture and represent the business process and information exchange semantics independent of any data protocol, e.g., XML.

Looking at the telecommunications industry as an example, many years have been spent in efforts to adopt business process and information modeling in a way that any technology can be utilized to exchange the data. This came about as a result of enormous efforts in migrating the data protocol of interface specifications from OSI/CMIP to Com-

---

[6]This list of sources of requirements is basically a summary of two Annexes of [4]: Annex A (Informative) Standardization Areas and Types of Standardization Activities [ISO/IEC 14662 (E), pages 25–29]; Annex B (Informative) Requirements for Open-edi Standards [ISO/IEC 14662 (E), pages 30–33].

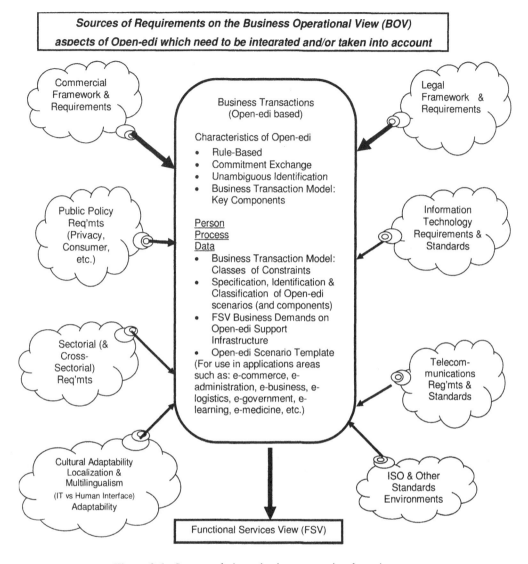

Figure 2.6 Integrated view—business operational requirements.

mon Object Request Broker Architecture (CORBA) to Extensible Markup Language (XML). Business process and information modeling is now seen as the means to "future-proof" the interface standardization work. The Unified TMN Requirements, Analysis, and Design (UTRAD) methodology of ITU-T Study Group 4 "specifies an iterative three-phase process with features that allow traceability across the three phases. The three phases (i.e., requirements, analysis, and design) apply industry-accepted techniques using object oriented analysis and design principles. The techniques should allow the use or development of commercially available support tools" [10]

In the case of UN/CEFACT, the organization set up under UN/ECE that oversees international trade facilitation, including administration of UN/EDIFACT standards, XML is considered to be a protocol-specific derivative of a protocol-neutral UML business process and information model. CMIP and CORBA would be related to XML through the common protocol-neutral UML artifacts. Going straight to XML implementations falls short as a data-centric view that is not capable of capturing the business process context and behavior of a UML specification. XML-based standards, if such could ever be developed and administered, would not be sufficient. Pair-wise trading partner agreements would continue, not addressing the problems that exist today with UN/EDIFACT or X12 EDI.

An example of UML-based requirements, analysis, and design methodology, facilitating knowledge transfer from business experts to IT developers, uses workflows starting with business modeling, as follows:

- The UN/CEFACT Modeling Methodology (UMM) Business Modeling Workflow elicits and organizes business processes and information in the business-to-business domain. This includes the creation of packages to categorize key concepts and business models. The type of questions that are asked by the modeler of the business domain expert and the business process analyst in this workflow are:

  —What are the business(es) and domain(s) to accomplish the business goal?

  —What are the Business Goals and Level 1 Business processes?

  —What are the Business Area(s)?

  —What are the Process Area(s)?

  —Are there existing Business Processes in libraries that meet our needs (key component of the reusability of UMM model components)?

  —What disciplines or expertise areas does this process cross?

  —What is the scope of the process and who are the stakeholders?

  —What are the process constraints?

- The UMM Requirements Workflow uses Business Modelling Workflow artifacts (deliverables) as input to understand the requirements of the resulting business-to-business solution. This includes the creation of detailed requirements, the discovery of business entities and UMM use case diagrams. The type of questions that are asked by the modeller of the business domain expert and business process analyst in this work flow are:

  —What is the purpose of this process?

  —What business roles such as manager signature authority, clerk, etc., participate in the process?

  —What business entities are engaged?

  —What are the collaborations between business roles?

  —How does the process start, what are the conditions, inputs and how does it stop, what are the outputs?

  —How do we know the process is done?

  —What should the availability of the process be: 24/7 or 8/5?

- The UMM Analysis Workflow further elaborates the Requirements Workflow use cases by detailing the activities that occur, collaborations between roles, and initial UMM class diagrams. These IBs can be expressed as conceptual UML class diagrams. The artifacts produced in the Analysis Workflow draw upon information in UMM Library(ies), or may populate the UMM Library(ies) where relevant information is not available. The type of questions that are asked by the modeller of the business process analyst in this workflow are:

—What are the business transaction patterns?

—What are the IBs (business documents) that flow between roles?

—What level of security do I need on this process?

• The UMM Design Workflow precisely defines the dynamics of the collaboration, along with the structure of data (IBs) exchanged between business partners. The type of questions that the modeler asks herself/himself for this workflow are:

—What business information entities should be used for structuring the business documents ?

—What network technology should we implement this process in?

—How does the business document relate (map) to the database structure? [11]

2.5 SEMANTICS (DATA DEFINITION STANDARDS)

This section focuses on defining the semantic content of information, whereas Section 2.6 provides an overview of standards activities related to interchanging commonly defined information among organizations.

2.5.1 IT-Enablement

"IT-enablement" is the term used to identify the need to transform currently accepted standards used in commerce worldwide from a manual to a computational perspective. eCommerce, in particular the business-to-business or business-to-administration categories, introduces a requirement for standards that are prepared, structured, and made available for unambiguous usage within and among information systems. This requirement can be expressed as "computational integrity," in particular

the expression of standards in a form that ensures precise description of behaviour and semantics in a manner that allows for automated processing to occur, and the managed evolution of such standards in a way that enables dynamic introduction by the next generation of information systems. [1, Sec. 6.2]

The objective of IT-enablement is to capture in a computer-processable manner, and one that maximizes interoperability, the implicit rules and relations (i.e., those known to "experts") of the code sets found in standards used in commerce worldwide. That is, specify the standard code sets within an entity relationship and/or object technology perspective, using formal description techniques. Also, address issues arising from change management in "code tables," i.e., synchronization, backward compatibility, migration. IT-enablement is based on the premise that a detailed and exhaustive identification of standards and "conventions," etc., used in support of existing commerce, will eliminate many barriers to eCommerce.

IT-enablement recognizes that within ISO, IEC, and ITU, there are committees that have the domain responsibility and expertise in areas of work, the primary purpose of which is to manage and control the content. IT-enablement also recognizes that outside of ISO/IEC/ITU, there are many other organizations that have domain responsibility and expertise in subject areas relevant to global eCommerce. Their "content" and industry sector domain-oriented standards require an IT-enabled version for use in eCommerce.

2.5.2 Data Definition Standards Examples

2.5.2.1 T1 Standards A number of T1 standards describe information that must be exchanged across the Telecommunications Management Network (TMN) X-Interface, i.e., interenterprise, to support the preordering and ordering of services between a service customer and a service provider. Such services are exchange-access services, administrative services, local exchange services, and customer account record exchange (CARE) services to support the requirements of the open telecommunications environment. These T1 standards describe shared information that was developed to support the regulatory and business requirements resulting from interconnection of network operators/service providers, initially within the United States, and more recently within the global telecommunications industry.

The T1 standards, listed in Figure 2.7 and partially described in the following subsections are examples of IT-enabled codes. These codes are critical codes used in the exchange of information. These codes are IT-enabled in that they are "prepared, structured and made available for unambiguous usage within and among information systems" by virtue of having:

- Semantic definition as agreed to in due process development of standardized codes
- Unambiguous format and structure
- Coordinated assignment of codes on demand from a centralized reference database
- Availability through on-line access via the Internet

T1 Standard Name	T1 Standards Reference
Telecommunications Service Priority Code	ANSI T1.211
Equipment Entity Identification Code	ANSI T1.213
Manufacturers Identification Code	ANSI T1.220
Network Channel Code	ANSI T1.223
Network Channel Interface Code	ANSI T1.223
Facility Identification Code	ANSI T1.238
Exchange Carrier Code	ANSI T1.251
IAC Code	ANSI T1.251
Company Code	ANSI T1.251
Location Entity Identification Code	ANSI T1.253
Circuit Identification Code	ANSI T1.266

Figure 2.7 T1 standards utilized in the TMN-X interface.

The key success factor in this use of common standards for designating operator's network interconnections has been the delegation of maintenance responsibility for the codes by the standards organization. While the design of information format structures is evolutionary and relatively stable, the assignment of code values is extremely volatile. This is especially true of the identification of network operators/service providers, and network locations, where new industry entrants demand new codes, sometimes with one-day turnaround. Only through the use of a dedicated resource with technical knowledge and tools to administer coding would this be possible.

Questions are often raised on funding the cost of a maintenance agent. Standards are assumed to be publicly available from the Standards Development Organization (SDO) as part of the benefit of paying an annual membership fee to the SDO. What justification is there for additional charges for maintenance agent services such as:

- Coordinated assignment of codes on demand from a centralized reference database
- Availability of IT-enabled codes through on-line access via the Internet
- Technical advisory groups that provide opportunity for user input to coding requirements and administration rules/conventions
- User documentation and training
- On-site consultation for code conversion and implementation
- On-call resource for subject matter expert consultation

From a maintenance agent perspective, such services are mandatory in order to facilitate implementation of standardized codes needed to accomplish interoperability and flowthrough. Users of maintenance agent services in connection with T1 standards have expressed sentiments that these are services that they "can't live without." Yet, the value of maintenance agent services is extremely difficult to quantify. It is the author's opinion that the telecommunications industry needs to be educated on the necessity of maintenance agents and brought to a realization that the cost of maintenance services must be factored in as part of the cost of doing business. In providing an essential service to the industry, maintenance agents should be permitted to recover their costs by charging reasonable and nondiscriminatory prices.

2.5.2.1.1 Location Entity Identification Code A detailed description of the Location Entity Identification Code format and structure of T1.253 is provided in this subsection as an illustration of an IT-enabled code. The Location Entity Identification Code has four formats [12].

1. **Location Entity Identification Code/Network Site Format** The Network Site Format of the Location Entity Identification Code is a standardized code that uniquely identifies a physical location, e.g., a telecommunications service company structure housing equipment or personnel. This format consists of a sequence of Geographical Code, Geopolitical Code, and Network Site Code data elements, resulting in a code that totals eight characters, as shown in Figure 2.8.

   Character positions that require alphabetic (A–Z), numeric (0–9), or either alphabetic or numeric characters are represented by A, N, and A/N, respectively. Allowing both AA and NN for the Network Site Code data structure provides for the maximum number of Network Site Codes, for use in the Network Site Format and

Elements/Positions	1	2	3	4	5	6	7	8
Geographical Code	A	A	A	A				
Geopolitical Code					A	A		
Network Site Code							A	A

or

Elements/Positions	1	2	3	4	5	6	7	8
Geographical Code	A	A	A	A				
Geopolitical Code					A	A		
Network Site Code							N	N

Figure 2.8   Location Entity Identification Code/Network Site Format.

Network Entity Format (see following), without conflicting with the Network Support Site Format (see following) or the Customer Site Format (see following).

2. **Location Entity Identification Code/Network Entity Format**   The Network Entity Format of the Location Entity Identification Code is a standardized code that uniquely identifies the function of equipment or personnel housed in a telecommunications service company structure. This format consists of a sequence of Geographical Code, Geopolitical Code, Network Site Code, and Network Entity Code data elements, resulting in a code that totals eleven characters, as shown in Figure 2.9.

3. **Location Entity Identification Code/Network Support Site Format**   The Network Support Site Format of the Location Entity Identification Code is a standardized code that uniquely identifies the geographical location and function of telecommunications service company equipment normally outside of a telecommunications service company structure. This format consists of a sequence of Geographical Code and Geopolitical Code data elements plus a Network Support Site Code data element, resulting in a code that totals eleven characters, as shown in Figure 2.10.

4. **Location Entity Identification Code/Customer Site Format**   The Customer Site Format of the Location Entity Identification Code is a standardized code that uniquely identifies a customer's presence at a location at which network elements or network systems equipment exists. This format consists of a sequence of Geographical Code and Geopolitical Code data elements plus a Customer Site Code data element, resulting in a code that totals eleven characters, as shown in Figure 2.11.

2.5.2.1.2 Company Code   A second illustration of an IT-enabled code is the Company Code (CC) Format of T1.251. Company Code is a unique four-character alphanumeric code (N A/N A/N A/N) assigned, as appropriate, to all telecommunications service providers. Based on company operations, more than one code may be required for each entity [13].

Elements/Positions	1	2	3	4	5	6	7	8	9	10	11
Geographical Code	A	A	A	A							
Geopolitical Code					A	A					
Network Site Code							A	A			
Network Entity Code									A/N	A/N	A/N

or

Elements/Positions	1	2	3	4	5	6	7	8	9	10	11
Geographical Code	A	A	A	A							
Geopolitical Code					A	A					
Network Site Code							N	N			
Network Entity Code									A/N	A/N	A/N

Figure 2.9 Location Entity Identification Code/Network Entity Format.

Elements/Positions	1	2	3	4	5	6	7	8	9	10	11
Geographical Code	A	A	A	A							
Geopolitical Code					A	A					
Network Support Site Code							A	N	A/N	A/N	A/N

Figure 2.10 Location Entity Identification Code/Network Entity Format.

Elements/Positions	1	2	3	4	5	6	7	8	9	10	11
Geographical Code	A	A	A	A							
Geopolitical Code					A	A					
Customer Site Code							N	A	A/N	A/N	A/N

Figure 2.11 Location Entity Identification Code/Network Entity Format.

Company Codes are assigned to telecommunications service providers for unique identification. The code set is used in mechanized systems throughout the industry to facilitate the exchange of information. Applications of the Company Code include, but are not limited to:

- NECA FCC Tariff No. 4.
- Routing and rating practices.
- Industry-recognized guidelines, including Access Service Requests (ASR), Multiple Exchange Carrier Access Billing (MECAB), Small Exchange Carrier Access

Billing (SECAB), Carrier Access Billing Systems (CABS), and Exchange Message Record (EMR).

- Interexchange Carrier systems used to audit Exchange Access bills.
- Telecommunications companies operating in the international arena.

2.5.2.2 ITU-T Recommendation M.1400

Similar discussions related to the TMN X-Interface information requirements are taking place internationally in the ITU-T. ITU-T Recommendation M.1400, *Designations for Interconnections among Operators' Networks*, defines designations and additional information primarily for human-to-human communication between various telecommunications operators. It defines both identification and additional information to be exchanged between two operators. Recommendation M.1400 defines the presentation format of data at human–computer interfaces, but does not define the data communication format for interaction between computer systems.

The definition of information is independent of which function or stakeholder in the virtual enterprise it supports. Provisioning, maintenance management, performance management, testing, and trouble administration are within the currently understood scope of Recommendation M.1400. Also, this Recommendation is intended to support communication between network operators, but may also support communication between a network operator and service operators, brokers, retailers, customers, and installation providers.

Because Recommendation M.1400 is presented in informal natural language, tables, and figures, it has been agreed that a new draft Recommendation be added to the ITU-T Question 2/4 work plan for the purpose of developing a formalized Recommendation, while at the same time keeping Recommendation M.1400 stable and maintainable for functional enhancements. The new draft Recommendation is ITU-T Recommendation M.fides (Formalization of Interconnection Designations). Figure 2.12 shows an application schema graph of the "kernel" of Recommendation M.fides, i.e., an external terminology schema for grammar used in codification and screen presentation [14].

Since the TMN-X Interface requires a computer-to-computer exchange of information over the entire life cycle of the interactions between a service provider and a service customer, the scope of operations to be supported by M.fides may be greater than that currently covered by Recommendation M.1400. Since the definition of information is independent of which function it supports, it should not only be consistent whenever it is used, but it should be organized in interface specifications according to the requirements of each function, referred to in eCommerce as business collaborations. Initially a service provider may indicate a catalog of network services/products available at specific locations. A service customer would select from the catalog what it wants to order and provide minimal information necessary for ordering. The service provider would confirm the order and initiate design activity, adding to the information. Eventually maintenance and billing records would be completed, etc.

Recommendation M.fides could be developed assuming the UML-based UTRAD methodology, starting with business process requirements (including mechanization), and continuing with formalized analysis and design. Information requirements should be modeled and standardized as business information objects, cross industry to the extent possible. In support of this, TSC T1M1 has proposed that the telecom industry build a TMN-X interface registry, referred to as a Global Telecommunications Data Dictionary (GTDD), that could be used as a protocol-neutral reference database for interface imple-

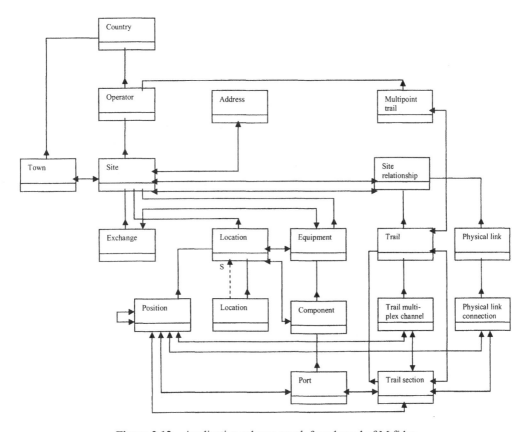

Figure 2.12 Application schema graph for a kernel of M.fides.

mentations, XML being one. For example, a repository of XML schemas would reference the standard information items in the GTDD (see Section 2.6.4).

An ITU-T project that covers the entire scope of the TMN X-Interface would require a registration authority for all of the X-Interface. Each ITU-T experts group would continue its stewardship responsibilities, but would channel its information to the registration authority. Further, the registration authority would require the support of maintenance agents to carry out the day-to-day activity of coordinating the updates to the reference databases.

2.5.2.3 *ITU Carrier Code*

A prime GTDD candidate that requires the support of a maintenance agent is the ITU Carrier Code (ICC). The ITU-T currently maintains a list of ICCs for the purpose of identifing network operators or service providers ("Operators") that are recognized by the national regulatory administrations. Specification of ICCs for interconnecting operators is a mandatory requirement of ITU-T Recommendation M.1400.

The ICC equivalent in North America is the four-character CC based on the T1.251 standard (see Section 2.5.2.1). Company Codes are used to uniquely identify telecommunications carriers or operators in North America and internationally.

Currently, there is no complete and accurate list of international and domestic operators. The creation of a single, integrated code set based on ICCs and CCs would facilitate the exchange of information between operators regarding call routing, maintenance, and billing issues across international and North American networks. In addition, a single, accurate, up-to-date list of operator identifiers would facilitate the increase of mechanization and the growth of electronic business and commerce by providing an industry standard that uniquely identifies an operator. Such a list of operator identifiers would fully support the requirements of Recommendation M.fides (see Section 2.5.2.2).

In recognition of this situation ITU-T Study Group 4 proposed a new approach to administering ICCs, opening the door for maintenance agents in the ITU-T. In the proposal, the ITU Telecommunications Service Bureau (TSB) would establish a central Web page for the ICC list. In order to simplify updating the data on the ICC list for national administrations that have a large number of ICCs and to keep the list up-to-date, it was proposed that national administrations can maintain a list of their ICCs on their own Web page, or authorize an organization to establish a Web page on their behalf. It was proposed that through a Web link on the ITU ICC Web page, one could access the national administration's Web page. Together, the central ITU ICC Web page and the linked national administrations' Web pages would be referred to as the ITU distributed ICC Web.

A trial of the ITU distributed ICC Web was implemented in January 2002. The National Exchange Carrier Association (NECA), maintenance agent for T1.251 Company Codes, revised its Web site and created a new Web page to provide information on ICCs along with a list of approximately 3000 ICCs for North American operators. The list of North American ICCs was developed from the publicly available Company Codes that comprise a subset of the complete list of greater than 9600 Company Codes. The list of North American ICCs is updated monthly. This compares with approximately 670 ICCs in the TSB ICC database as of April 2002.

The TSB revised the ITU Web site to provide a separate page for the ICCs for each national administration, in its corresponding role with respect to the ITU distributed ICC Web. In addition, the TSB and NECA coordinated the removal of ICCs for North American operators on the ITU ICC list and the addition of those ICCs to the list on NECA's Web site.

The ITU-distributed ICC Web trial was demonstrated to ITU-T Study Group 4 in April 2002. The TSB ICC link to the NECA Company Code Web site seamlessly showed over 3000 ICCs/publicly available Company Codes and corresponding contact information for North American operators within the context of the TSB ICC Web page for the United States. The successful trial of the ITU Distributed ICC Web capability was characterized by one expert as "providing a quick look for recent information." It is expected that such maintenance agent capability will be extended to other enumerated lists in the development of the GTDD.

2.5.3 Harvest Existing Business Information

Efforts are underway to identify existing code sets that are already rule-based (explicitly or implicitly) and where the rule base has a "source authority," such as relevant ISO or ISO/IEC committees for code sets originating in those SDOs. One such effort is a New Work Item recommended by the ISO/IEC JTC 1 BT-EC titled, "IT-enablement of Widely Used Coded Domains" [15], which focuses on "coded" rather than "encoding" and provides a tool for the preparation of new standardized codes as well as for IT-enablement of existing standards.

In proposing the creation of the ebXML Initiative, the Techniques and Methodologies Working Group (TMWG) of UN/CEFAFCT recommended that UN/EDIFACT standard semantics be used in XML applications to provide a firm foundation for interoperability

[16]. The proposal went on to say "it is essential that XML Document Type Descriptions (DTDs) (or Schemas, when standards for them exist) encode information about the mapping between element and attribute definitions and their foundation semantics." Efforts to create IT-enabled codes such as in ebXML will benefit from the vast repository of data semantics that has been assembled in UN/EDIFACT and X12 directories. In addition, encoding UN/EDIFACT and X12 data semantics in XML applications will provide a clear migration path for traditional EDI applications that choose to take advantage of the Internet and provide reassurance that existing EDI implementations will interoperate with XML implementations in the meantime.

This motivation leads one to seek the best method for mapping UN/EDIFACT data items directly to XML. Several organizations and industry initiatives are investigating the translation of EDI data items to XML, but there is as yet little consensus on the best way to achieve it. Some are developing algorithms to autogenerate XML elements and DTDs directly from EDI directories. However, the TMWG has advised against this approach. Autogeneration can lead to semantically meaningless names that are hard to use and that do not facilitate reuse. Furthermore, because of redundancy in the data dictionaries, autogeneration would result in semantically equivalent elements with different names.

The TMWG believed that industry consensus could be achieved on a methodology for mapping EDI to XML, such as the appropriate use of elements and attributes, naming rules, and the granularity of the XML constructs. Further, the TMWG recommended that best practices be identified through cooperation with other organizations working on XML specifications for eCommerce, anticipating that the recommended practices will include human input to cleanse the generated output.

The TMWG recommendations have been partially realized in efforts of the ebXML Initiative. Subject matter experts have focused on data requirements for a variety of application domains. Walking through real-world business scenarios, data entities involved in information exchange have been identified, both in generic definition and subtype definitions based on the context of the business process and imposed constraints. Such data entities are then specified as attributes in business entity types that will become prime candidates for standardization.

A recommended procedure for developing the business information content, i.e., "payload," of an ebXML message according to this approach follows:

1. Describe eBusiness requirements, drawing from common business processes and business entity types in the ebXML Registry/Repository that have been developed independently of any existing or developing business processes.
2. Use the business process context characteristics to extend/adjust the business entity types in completing the attributes of the eBusiness requirements class diagram, showing business-entity-type classes, attributes, and relationships together with class definitions.
3. In the analysis workflow, transform the eBusiness requirements class diagram into a precise object-oriented class diagram, built on registered, normalized business information entities.
4. The business documents to be exchanged will contain instantiations of the attributes of the business information entities and formed into XML constructs. (It should be noted that in addition to XML constructs, the transformation from UML artifacts to any other protocol-specific data syntax is the intended objective, as discussed in Section 2.4.3.)

2.6.   SHARED SEMANTICS FOR INTEROPERABILITY (DATA EXCHANGE STANDARDS)

Once the semantic content of shareable information is defined and standardized, it needs to be organized and related to eCommerce applications, i.e., interoperable business processes, such that the benefits of common semantics can be realized among trading partners.

Sections 2.3 and 2.4 discussed the Open-edi concept of exchanging electronic data among organizations without prior agreement. In an effort to accelerate an implementation approach to the Open-edi Reference Model, the predecessor to the UN/CEFACT TMWG, an ad hoc committee (AC.1) of the UN/ECE WP.4 was created to investigate the available technologies for creating the next generation for electronic information exchange among business trading partners.

AC.1 reported that the most promising technology to address the shortcomings of EDI was that of business process and information modeling (BPIM). Through BPIM, information standards would not have the problem of ambiguity. Instead, as per the Open-edi Reference Model, scenarios, i.e., complete processes and their information requirements, including constraints, execution options, exceptions, etc., would be specified. Further, AC.1 recommended that object technology should be used in BPIM, since it offered many, if not all, aspects required to describe the real world, which consists of objects.

AC.1 recognized that even with BPIM, business policies would dictate doing things differently, even in regard to external processes. AC.1 proposed that the next generation standards would be BPIMs, standardized for a particular business goal, such as "catalog ordering." The standardized BPIM would contain "all" the possible activities that could be part of that goal. In other words, the standardized BPIM would be a supermodel for a given business process. Since such models would have many execution alternatives (paths through the model) each path would be identified as a scenario. Depending on their internal processes, one trading partner may be able to execute all the scenarios of a model, whereas another may only execute a certain number of them. For two trading partners to engage in the same business process, they must both be able to execute at least one scenario in common. In regard to small- and medium-size enterprises (SMEs), it is envisioned that the software providers would create applications that implement BPIMs for the most popular scenarios.

As WP.4 transitioned itself to the new organization, now known as UN/CEFACT, AC.1's BPIM recommendation became the foundation for the new work. UN/CEFACT created the TMWG in order to continue the work of AC.1. Based on the original recommendation, UN/CEFACT also created the Business Process Analysis Working Group (BPAWG) and encouraged UN/EDIFACT and other working groups to move toward adopting BPIM as a requisite for maintaining UN/EDIFACT.

As the TMWG identified the necessity to decompose business processes to their more generic components, it also concluded that a consistent modeling methodology and technique for conducting the analysis and design must be utilized. Thus, it became important to explore the benefits of using modeling techniques and methodologies to identify the data requirements and data flows of a particular business process. Resulting models would provide an interface specification that enables nonstandard data, internal to a business process, to be mapped and translated to a representation of standardized data in a standardized business process collaboration.

Models that provide the interface specification would constitute the new eBusiness standards, once they are certified as satisfying the business requirements. These new standards would be independent of the interchange data syntax, transport infrastructure, and server software.

2.6.1 Business Process Modeling in ebXML

The first application of BPIM is the ebXML Initiative. ebXML is an international initiative established by UN/CEFACT and the Organization for the Advancement of Structured Information Standards (OASIS). Phase one of this initiative extended for 18 months and completed in May 2001. Technical work on ebXML now moves forward as a coordinated activity between members of UN/CEFACT and OASIS. Figure 2.13 shows the foundational role of BPIM in the ebXML technical architecture [17].

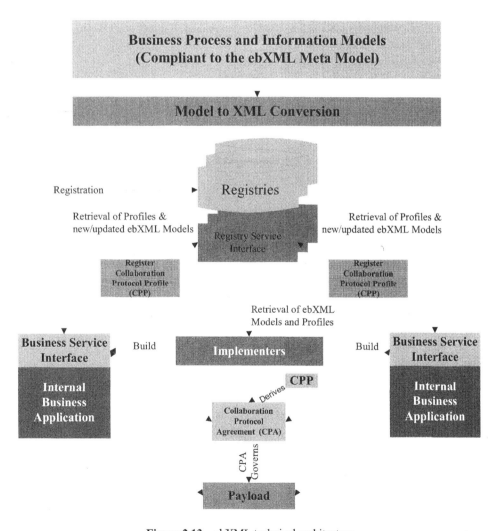

Figure 2.13   ebXML technical architecture.

2.6.1.1 Business Process Modeling Requirements According to the ebXML Requirements Specification,

The *Business Process Project Team* detailed requirements and deliverables will:

- Provide a technical specification for business process definition (BPDS), enabling an organization to express its business processes so that they are understandable by other organizations, thereby enabling integration of business processes (see, for example, eCo strategic framework-services and interactions)
- Provide an explicitly specified process metamodel that is not merely implied by instantiations or derivations
- Provide a BPDS that is usable—
  —globally
  —cross-industry
  —by small, medium, and large organizations
  —by for-profit and government and/or non-profit organizations
- Provide a BPDS that enables an organization to express its business processes to such an extent that other organizations can discover—
  —the kind of organization the process belongs to
  —the business processes belonging to an organization
  —the interaction points in the organization's business process in order to determine whether and how to engage in business
  —the kinds of information exchanges required to conduct a particular interaction in the business process
  —company interactions and services and categorize them
- Provide for BPDS compatibility by—
  —allowing for forward migration from existing frameworks to the degree possible
  —carrying forward accumulated best of breed experience such as—OAG, RosettaNet, HL7—into the ebXML "superset"
  —enabling mapability between content provider defined processes
  —enabling organizations or industry verticals to be able to compare business processes
- Provide for BPDS re-usability/extensibility by—
  —allowing a company to 're-use' and extend standard, template, or actual business processes as starting points for definition of specific business processes
  —encouraging industry verticals to base their model on the high level framework
  —supporting re-usable data components
  —supporting re-usable process components
- Enable business processes to be accessible and readable by—
  —making BPDS-based processes machine readable
  —expressing processes defined under BPDS in parsable, navigable XML
  —making processes defined under BPDS visually (diagrammatically) viewable
  —identifying at least one industry standard based tool or technique, through which BPDS compliant processes can be defined through diagrammatic drawing
- Provide a process to create and maintain a—
  —glossary of terms related to business process methodology vocabulary such as—functional, non-functional, vertical, message, segment, data type—using TMWG Unified Modeling Methodology document Annex 1 as a starting point

—glossary of terms specific to each business process to be modeled

—glossary of XML tags

—library of documents based on identified services and interactions

—web site for ready access to glossaries

- Be developed in conjunction with the *Registry and Repository Project Team* to incorporate technical specifications, models, and required glossaries into the ebXML repository" [18]

2.6.1.2 Business Process Modeling Methodology

Many of the requirements just listed were fulfilled through the use of the UN/CEFACT modeling methodology (UMM) metamodel, contributed as part of the *Business Collaboration Framework* of Edifecs Commerce. To provide a flavor of this metamodel, the Executive Summary of the Edifecs Commerce submission follows:

Business partners must collaborate if they are to remain competitive. A high level of collaboration is possible when business partners link their businesses processes through an interface of network computer e-business services that enforce commercial trading agreements modeled as collaborative exchanges of business information, in agreed sequences and within agreed timeframes. A commercial trading agreement is modeled as a business process model expressed with the Unified Modeling Language (UML) and the Object Constraint Language (OCL). The UML is a language expressive enough to specify the structure and behavior of objects that interact in any conceptual domain of discourse. A process model, however, is a specification of the structure and behavior of objects interacting at business partner interfaces, a specialized domain of discourse. This document describes an extension to UML to include business process domain specific syntax and semantics. This extension is termed the e-Business Process Metamodel. The metamodel is organized into the following views so that each process model can be viewed from a number of perspectives. [19]

These perspectives, as incorporated into the UMM, are:

- The Business Domain View (BDV)—the partitioning of business domain into business areas and process areas and business processes. This view establishes the business context of the process which is a precursor to evaluating the likelihood of finding reusable previously defined process descriptions or terminology in the UMM libraries.

- The Business Requirements View (BRV)—the view of a business process model that captures the use case scenarios, inputs, outputs, constraints and system boundaries for business processes and their interrelationships within business process collaborations. This view is how the business domain expert sees and describes the process to be modeled. This is in the language and concepts of the business domain expert.

- The Business Transaction View (BTV)—the view of a business process model that captures the semantics of business information entities and their flow of exchange between roles as they perform business activities. This view is an elaboration on the business requirements view by the business process analyst and is how the business process analyst sees the process to be modeled. This is in the language and concepts of the business process analyst, who may have to help convey ideas to the software designer and the business domain expert.

- The Business Service View (BSV)—the view of a business process model that specifies the component services and agents and their message (information) exchange as interactions necessary to execute and validate a business process. This is in the language and technical concepts of the software developer. [11]

These perspectives support an incremental model construction methodology and provide levels of specification granularity that are suitable for communicating the model to business practitioners, business application integrators, and network application solution providers.

2.6.1.3 REA, Economic Ontology for Business Requirements View   The business semantics of the UMM BRV perspective are based on an accounting ontology called resource–event–agent (REA). REA is a framework for specifying the accounting concepts and relationships involved in business collaborations. REA is an elementary set of concepts derived from basic definitions in accounting and economics. A business transaction or exchange joins two parties together in a pair of commitments, noting that the two parties to a simple market transfer expect to receive something of value in return when they trade. For example, a seller, who delivers a product to a buyer, expects a cash payment in return. REA provides a foundational business collaboration pattern that consists of a pair of commitments between agents (Persons in Open-edi terms) that are fulfilled by events that signal the transfer of resources.

An ontology, according to the most generally accepted eCommerce definition of that word, is a "specification of a conceptualization" [20]. The REA ontology is a specification of the declarative semantics involved in a business collaboration (or more generally, in a business process). The theory behind REA comes from the field of microeconomics with specific ties in many instances of the use of economic definitions in the practice of building enterprisewide information systems. The UMM BRV applies the REA ontology definitions to the collaborative space between enterprises where market exchanges occur in closely synchronized fashion among two or more trading partners.

2.6.1.3.1 The Basic REA Ontology   The basic REA model was first published in the July 1982 issue of *The Accounting Review* [21]. Figure 2.14 illustrates the basic class structure of REA ontology. The left-to-right configuration of economic *R*esources, economic *E*vents, and economic *A*gents in a typical business collaboration pattern is the source of the model's REA name.

A successful business collaboration involves first and foremost two types of *Economic Events,* each of which details the *Economic Resources* involved in an exchange between two Trading *Partners.* For example, a supplier (trading partner) transfers ownership of an automobile (economic resource) to a customer (trading partner), in return for which (*duality* association) the Customer will provide money (economic resource) to the supplier. There are two mirror-image instantiations of the object pattern shown in Figure 2.14, where one transfer represents the legal or economic consideration given for the other.

The declarative semantics shown here are central to all trading relationships. Economic resources are objects that have value and are under the control of one of the two collaborative agents. Trading partners always expect requited transfers of resources when they engage in commerce. Hence, Figure 2.14 is a pattern for all economic exchanges [22].

2.6.1.3.2 Adding Commitments to the Basic Exchange Ontology   In electronic commerce, the actual trading phase of an exchange is well accommodated by the object

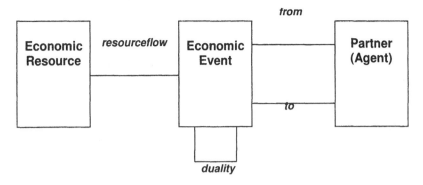

Figure 2.14   Basic REA ontology.

structure shown in Figure 2.14. However, trading partners in long-term relationships need more trusted and predictable structures where both parties contract for their exchange behavior in advance. The REA ontology accommodates this expansion with the addition of the classes shown as *Economic Commitments, Economic Contract,* and *Agreement* in Figure 2.15.

A *Commitment* is a promise by a trading partner to initiate an economic event in the future. Performing the economic events *fulfills* that commitment. A commitment should always be *reciprocated* by the other trading partner, who commits to initiate another type of economic event in return. An *Economic Contract* is a bundle of reciprocating commitments between trading partners, who bind themselves to one or more economic exchanges

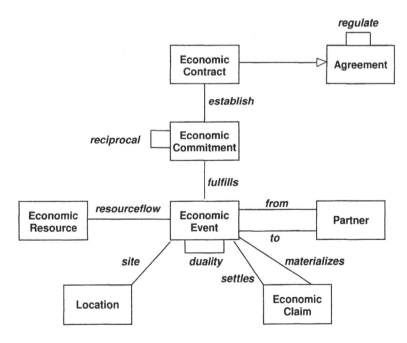

Figure 2.15   REA ontology with commitments.

in the future. A contract is a subtype of the more general object class called *Agreement,* and agreements can regulate other agreements.

In the case of the automobile-for-money exchanges discussed in the prior section, commitments would involve the customer agreeing to accept delivery of an automobile on a certain date, in return for which he or she would be contractually obligated to making a series of cash payments to the supplier for that purchase.

In the bottom part of Figure 2.15, two additional objects of the REA ontology are illustrated: *Economic Claim* and *Location.*

- Materialization of a *Claim* is sometimes needed when trading partners insist on documentation of partially completed exchanges (for example, when a customer takes possession of an automobile before paying for it in full). If needed, claims can be instantiated by documents like invoices or by accounting artifacts like accounts receivable. Their inclusion here is more a matter of business custom than ontological completeness.

- A *Location* is another object that is sometimes needed to fill out the specification for a full economic transfer. A location simply identifies the place where an Economic Event takes place.

The economic and ontological foundations of commitments are explained more completely by Geerts and McCarthy [23].

2.6.1.3.3 Adding Types to the Basic REA Exchange Ontology

The object pattern portrayed in Figure 2.15 is primarily *descriptive* in the sense that it illustrates what actually occurred in an economic exchange or what has been committed to. In the UMM and the business entity type (BET) [24] specification, these *descriptive* components have been augmented by *prescriptive* components that allow the specification of control policies or collaboration patterns. These prescriptive components are enabled by the inclusion of type images of the basic descriptive objects [25]. The class diagram of Figure 2.16 shows these additions.

The addition of Types to Figure 2.16 proceeds in two stages:

- Four of the base descriptive classes—Economic Resource, Economic Event, Partner, and Location—have classes added for their types. These new classes are connected to the descriptive objects by *typifies* associations. An example of a Resource Type could be different models of automobiles. An example of an Economic Event Type could be the classes of retail transaction and wholesale transactions, each with different pricing structures. An example of Partner Type could be different classes of employees, each type with separate training requirements. And finally, an example of Location Type might be different types of loading docks with different sizes and stress capability levels.

- The full design of the Economic Commitment would necessitate associations between the commitment and each of the new Type-level objects. These are illustrated in the figure with *specifies* associations.

In addition to these two groups of additions, there are other REA associations in the UMM that are not illustrated here in an effort to minimize diagram complexity. These include:

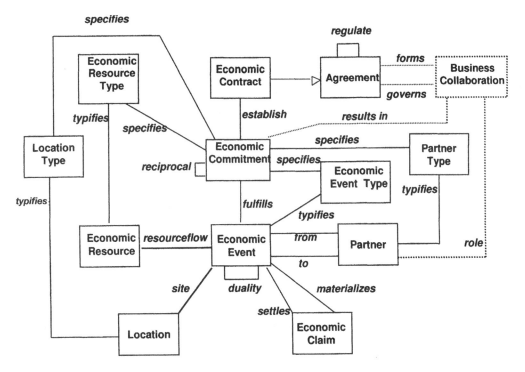

Figure 2.16   REA ontology with Types.

- Partner—*participates*—Economic Commitment
- Economic Commitment—*destination*—Location
- Partner—*participates*—Agreement
- Partner—*participates*—Economic Commitment
- Economic Commitment—*reserves*—Economic Resource

And finally with regard to Figure 2.16, the partial integration of the elements of the REA ontology with the components of the UMM business collaboration framework is illustrated by showing the class for Business Collaboration (with dotted lines) and some of its associations with REA classes (also illustrated with dotted lines). Outside of its use with the UMM, the REA ontology has a three-level architecture that is explained by Geerts and McCarthy [26]. In the UMM, this three-level architecture is effected by the integration of REA components within the business collaboration framework and by the connection of the BRV to the BDV above it and the BTV below it.

REA concepts are more fully specified in working drafts of the UN/CEFACT eBusiness Transition Working Group [27], base documents for *UMM User Guide* to be released in 2003.

2.6.2 tML Framework

A telecommunications industry application of XML, *tML Framework,* was approved as ITU-T Recommendation M.3030 in August 2002 under the ITU-T alternate approval process (AAP). (This can also be thought of as a specific industry extension of ebXML.) The tML Framework is a framework for the development of standards for the management of telecommunications networks based on a markup language derived from XML for telecommunications network management. The markup language derived from XML is referred to as the telecommunications Markup Language (tML).

The current version of the tML Framework focuses on the TMN X-Interface. Subsequent versions may add scope to include other TMN interfaces. Figure 2.17 shows the scope of the tML Framework.

The scope of Recommendation M.3030 includes Rules, Objectives, and Guidelines for:

- Specifying business document structure (i.e., tML Schemas) for X interface applications of tML
- Use of common vocabulary structure

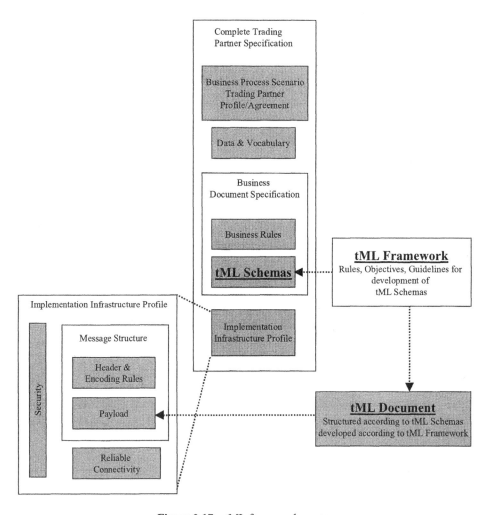

Figure 2.17   tML framework scope.

- Use of namespaces
- Mapping from existing standards to tML
- Specification of metadata used

The scope of this Recommendation does not specify the following items because trading partners specify these items through negotiation:

- Business Process Scenario
- Implementation Infrastructure Profile—Specification of any particular communications protocol profile (including provisions for reliability, availability, and survivability, or RAS), and provisions for security, privacy, and non-repudiation.
- Data and Vocabulary content [28]

2.6.3   Business Application Contracts in TM Forum's New-Generation OSS

A third BPIM application is current work in the TeleManagement Forum (TM Forum) on new-generation operation support systems (NGOSS). In this BPIM application, shared semantics for interoperability are shown to apply within an enterprise as an extension to the business-to-business discussion. It is apparent that distinctions in information exchange between enterprises versus within an enterprise are diminishing with ever-increasing interoperation among competitive service providers and outsourcing of operations. Information is exchanged between computer application components via business application contracts, defined as "the central concept of interoperability in the NGOSS™ Architecture. Through contracts, public shared services are described and defined in a technology-neutral fashion" [29]. Upon invocation of a contract, a logical business component can carry out one or more operations to produce the agreed upon set of outputs.

2.6.3.1 Business View   A business application contract specification can be thought of as a UML use case at the level of a business transaction within a collaborative business process. A collaborative business process is identified in the UMM in the recursive decomposition of the business domain to a business area to a process area to a business process [11]. Such a business process is at the granularity level of a "business collaboration," where individual business transactions can each be identified that conform to one of six business transaction design patterns. Business transaction design patterns currently defined in the UN/CEFACT business collaboration metamodel, and which may apply to contract specifications, are:

- Commercial Transaction—Used to model the "offer and acceptance" business transaction process that results in a residual obligation between both parties to fulfill the terms of the contract.
- Query/Response—Used to query for information that a responding partner already has, e.g., against a fixed data set that resides in a database.
- Request/Response—Used for business contracts when an initiating partner requests information that a responding partner already has and when the request for business information requires a complex interdependent set of results.
- Request/Confirm—Used for business contracts where an initiating partner requests confirmation about their status with respect to previously established contracts or with respect to a responding partner's business rules.

- Information Distribution—Used to model an *informal* information exchange business transaction that therefore has no nonrepudiation requirements.

- Notification—Used to model a *formal* information exchange business transaction that therefore has nonrepudiation requirements.

All six patterns can have an outcome of "success" or "control fail," i.e., for any control parameter violation such as timeout, processing exceptions, nonrepudiation, and authorization exceptions.

Contract specifications are under development in Phase 2 of the NGOSS project as a result of TM Forum plug-and-play catalyst activity, and otherwise as identified through the TM Forum enhanced Telecom Operations Map (e-TOM) [30] activity. As in the development of a TM Forum Business Agreement (BA) specification, a contract specification should be accompanied by detailed, categorized requirement statements, including information exchange requirements, for business application contracts at a conceptual level.

2.6.3.2 *Systems View*   Contract specification artifacts may include:

1. An activity diagram for the "Business Process," referred to as a System Process Plan, that identifies each contract specification, characterized as a business transaction design pattern.

2. An activity graph for each contract specification according to its respective business transaction design pattern.

3. A conceptual class diagram, initially without attributes, for the information to be exchanged.

4. Sequence diagram for the interactive protocol for the contract specification, as available in UN/CEFACT business service interaction design patterns.

5. For information provider contracts, identification of attributes of business entities to be exchanged via the contract, by reference to a registry of shareable data (see Section 2.6.4). Shareable data entities would be represented in shared information models as attributes of business entities. Data types of the data elements would be specified utilizing the TMF Common Information Structure [31]. Since business application contracts may require data entities not yet in the shared information models, rules must be developed for reference to and change management for the business entity library as the shared information models are incrementally constructed as required by the contract activity.

Taking the business application contract attributes from the NGOSS Architecture Technology Neutral Specification [32] into account, as well as the characteristics of the business application contract definition just listed, these artifacts could be the basis for a business application contract template. Once validated, the template could be released for widespread contract specification, utilizing distributed resources that agree to work in close cooperation with the centralized registry/repository of shared information models.

It has been recommended that the shared information modeling activity lay some groundwork using "something that already exists," e.g., the Distributed Management Task Force (DMTF) methodology and framework model [33]. In particular, any business entities that already may have been modeled, such as product, service, or order would be useful, at least as a reference. In addition, it has also been recommended to refer to the TM

Forum Systems Integration Map (SIM) as a means to organize the knowledge base of NGOSS system artifacts such as system process plans, business application contracts, and shared information models [29].

The NGOSS Shared Information/Data Model (SID) is a fundamental component for achieving interoperability in the NGOSS Technology Neutral Architecture. SID represents a synthesized view of information derived from various industry models. As stated by the SID team, the SID model represents a federation of model fragments. This converged model should be very attractive to service providers, independent software vendors, equipment vendors, and others who have the objective of creating a common model and a language that expresses shared information/data terminology. The SID work should be related to the ITU-T SG4 and T1M1 GTDD (see Section 2.6.4) for information to be exchanged on the TMN X-Interface.

2.6.4 Global Telecommunications Data Dictionary
The GTDD is a structure that stores telecommunications terminology and its semantic description. It is a catalog of terminology that can be used by administrators, designers, applications developers, and standards developers for information resource management. As such, the GTDD is a resource to be used in developing standards for interoperable information interchange in telecommunications OAM&P applications. Such standards would permit consistency in data interchange and understanding. Also, the GTDD is a resource for applications developers that may have a need to discover terminology used in information interchange. ITU-T Recommendation M.1400 is a primary source for describing information that is shared among network operators, i.e., designations for interconnection, and is thus likely to provide a substantial contribution to the GTDD.

The most substantive work to date on GTDD requirements has been in the context and support of the tML Framework project. With the ITU-T Recommendation M.3030, tML Framework, having been approved in August 2002 , there is more urgency in completing the requirements for a GTDD that is capable of gathering the telecommunications terminology and semantic description required for tML implementations.

One of the goals of the GTDD is to reuse applicable terms that are available in commercial libraries. Initial studies have shown this to be a promising approach. Preliminary work in Eurescom has utilized CommerceOne's Common Business Library (CBL) as a reference. Also, analysis of CBL applicability to the tML initiative in T1M1 has been documented, showing a significant percentage of direct application of CBL data elements [34].

2.7 SUMMARY

This chapter provides a snapshot view in time of some eCommerce standardization activities from the business perspective of information exchange. In particular, standardization activities with which the author has been directly engaged in an effort to influence the convergence of telecommunications and cross-sectorial information exchange standards, are highlighted. In terms of the Open-edi conceptual model, emphasis has been placed on the business operational view, which "focuses on high-level operations and their associated requirements and constraints, as regarded from the 'business' user's perspective." The functional services view of Open-edi is left to the IT infrastructure, i.e., IP networks in the context of this volume.

The key concept to be noted is that information exchange standards are ideally developed within the context of a business collaboration framework and are represented by a formal description technique that is independent of data protocol syntax. A business process and information modeling methodology is the key to making interface standards future-proof in the onset of evolving data exchange protocols. The challenge of managing eCommerce, as defined in the Introduction to this chapter, is fundamentally met through the development and implementation of standards that provide for process and information interoperability. Formulation of business user's requirements on the IT infrastructure would then be a natural outcome of such information exchange standards, which would in turn drive IP network solutions.

REFERENCES

1. The ISO/IEC JTC 1 Business Team on Electronic Commerce (BT-EC) report to JTC 1.
2. ISO/IEC 15944-1: 2002, "Business Agreement Semantic Descriptive Techniques -Part 1: Operational Aspects of Open-edi for Implementation."
3. JTC 1/BT-EC N 045.
4. ISO/IEC 14662: 2003, "Information Technologies—Open-edi Reference Model."
5. Memorandum of Understanding between the International Electrotechnical Commission, the International Organization for Standardization, the International Telecommunication Union, and the United Nations Economic Commission for Europe Concerning Standardization in the Field of Electronic Business.
6. ISO/IEC JTC 1 Information Technology SWG-EDI Report on the Open-edi Conceptual Model.
7. G. E. Hegemeier, *The E-Marketplace Case for Industry-wide Electronic Product Data Synchronization,* Heathcare EDI Coalition.
8. ebXML Terms of Reference.
9. ISO/IEC JTC 1 N5296, "Report of the ISO/IEC JTC 1 Business Team on Electronic Commerce," Chapter 6, Horizontal Aspects, pp. 22–28.
10. ITU-T Recommendation M.3020, *TMN Interface Specification Methodology* (Revised July 1999), Section 2.2.
11. UN/CEFACT Modeling Methodology, UN/CEFACT TMG N090 Rev. 12, Chapter 1.
12. T1.253-2000 American National Standard for Telecommunications Information Interchange—Code Description and Codes for the Identification of Location Entities for the North American Telecommunications System.
13. T1.251-2001 American National Standard for Telecommunications Information Interchange—Identification of Telecommunications Service Provider Codes for the North American Telecommunications System.
14. ITU-T COM 4-C30, Report of Question 2/4 (Designations for Interconnections among Operators' Networks) Rapporteurs Group interim meeting in Oslo Norway, September 2002.
15. New Standard ISO/IEC 18022 "IT-enablement of Widely Used Coded Domains."
16. UN/CEFACT TMWG N089 (Revision 5) *TMWG Recommendations on XML.*
17. ebXML Technical Architecture Specification Version 1.0.4.
18. ebXML Requirements Specification Version 1.06, Section 7.3.
19. Business Process Project Team Technical Specification Document Draft Version 3.0: Collaboration Modeling Metamodel & UML Profile, Executive Summary.
20. T. Gruber, *A Translation Approach to Portable* Ontologies in Knowledge Acquisition, pp. 199–220, 1993.

21. W. E. McCarthy, "The REA Accounting Model: A Generalized Framework for Accounting Systems in A Shared Data Environment," *Accounting Review,* pp. 554–578, July 1982.

22. G. Geerts and W. E. McCarthy, "An Accounting Object Infrastructure for Knowledge-based Enterprise Models," *IEEE Intelligent Systems and Their Applications,* pp. 89–94, July/August 1999.

23. G. Geerts and W. E. McCarthy, "The Ontological Foundation of REA Enterprise Information Systems," paper presented at the Annual Meeting of The American Accounting Association, August 2000.

24. eBTWG—*Business Entity Types Technical Specification,* Revision 0.12, July 2002.

25. G. Geerts and W. E. McCarthy, "An Ontological Analysis of the Primitives of the Extended-REA Enterprise Information Architecture" *International Journal of Accounting Information Systems,* 2002, vol. 3, pp. 1–16.

26. G. Geerts and W. E. McCarthy: *Using Object Templates from the REA Accounting Model to Engineer Business Processes and Tasks* in The Review of Business Information Systems, Vol. 5, no. 4, 2001, pp. 89-108.

27. eBTWG—*Business Collaboration Patterns/Business Commitment Patterns Technical Specification (BCP²)*—"Monitored Commitments," evision 0.13, June 2002.

28. ITU-T Recommendation M.3030, telecommuications Markup Language (tML) Framework, August 2002.

29. TeleManagement Forum GB 914 System Integration Map, Draft/Version 1.5, May 2002, NGOSS is a trademark of the TeleManagement Forum.

30. TeleManagement Forum GB 921, TM Forum Approved Version 3.0, *Enhanced Telecom Operations Map (eTOM), the Business Process Framework for the Information and Communication Services Industry,* June 2002.

31. TeleManagement Forum TMF 045, *Common Information Structure,* Member Evaluation Release 1.1, March 2000.

32. TeleManagement Forum TMF 053, *NGOSS Architecture Technology Neutral Specification,* Version 2.1, May 2002.

33. Distributed Management Task Force, *Common Information Model (CIM) Core Model,* Version 2.4, August 2000.

34. B. Kabatepe, T1M1/2000-080, *Contribution to tML Framework Document—Common XML Data Elements Across eCommerce Applications,* November 2000.

CHAPTER 3

QUALITY OF SERVICE IN IP NETWORKS

JOBERTO SÉRGIO BARBOSA MARTINS

INTRODUCTION

Transmission control protocol/IP (TCP/IP) has become a de facto platform for most of the computer systems in the world. Besides that, it is a common well-known fact that IP has to be somehow "adjusted" to work adequately with multimedia and other general applications, becoming very popular in networks, including the Internet and other TCP/IP networks. QoS provisioning to application and end users in IP networks then becomes the challenging task for network designers, managers, researchers and, generically, technical staff.

The objective of this chapter is to elaborate on this subject by presenting an introductory overview of the main technical solutions available for QoS in IP networks. We will first elaborate on the importance of this field and then review the most important solutions and propositions for QoS provisioning in IP networks.

The plan of the chapter is as follows:

Section 3.1, "IP Context and Quality of Service," introduces the importance of the field, identifies the overall perspectives and makes an attempt to foresee IP evolution.

Section 3.2, "Quality of Service," examines some common basic principles for QoS, presents a taxonomy for applications, and introduces the most important basic parameters frequently used to characterize, analyze, and manage QoS requirements.

Section 3.3, "Quality of Service: Approaches and Initiatives for IP Networks," summarizes the main approaches used to control and manage QoS and presents some additional basic concepts.

Managing IP Networks. Edited by Saleh Aidarous and Thomas Plevyak
ISBN 0-471-39299-5 © 2003 Institute of Electrical and Electronics Engineers

Section 3.4, "Packet Conditioning, Queue Scheduling and Congestion Control in Routers," explores the techniques used by routers for QoS provisioning.

Sections 3.5 and 3.6 sequentially present the Integrated Service Architecture and the Differentiated Services Architecture, examining their goals and implementation issues.

Section 3.7, "Multiprotocol Label Switching," idescribes multiprotocol label switching (MPLS) technology in the context of the IP network.

Selected references are listed at the end of the chapter in order to provide guidance for additional reading.

3.1 IP CONTEXT AND QUALITY OF SERVICE

Quality of service (QoS) is a very important issue for computer networks in general and for IP networks in particular.

Over the past few years, data networks have been growing at enormous rates while, simultaneously, a totally new set of applications has emerged. Generically, these new applications can be broadly grouped as multimedia applications, since they manipulate many different media types, e.g., real-time applications, mission-critical applications, or another specific denomination (Fig. 3.1). This new set of applications needs to be supported by the "conventional" data networks in use, which, in turn, are mainly TCP/IP networks. Therefore, an understanding of the QoS concept and solutions is essential to design, implement, operate, maintain and manage TCP/IP networks adequately in this new context.

The discussion about quality of service at first requires an answer to this very simple question: How can the term "quality of service" be defined considering the application

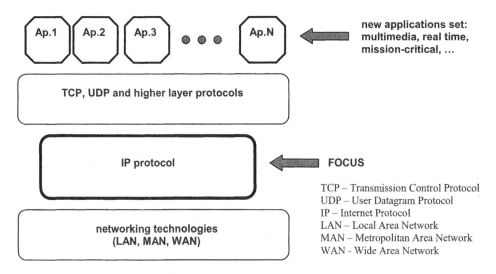

Figure 3.1 QoS and TCP/IP.

scenario just mentioned? In the following introductory sections we elaborate on the basic concepts about QoS before discussing the strategies used in IP networks to achieve a "QoS-ready network."

3.1.1 IP Network Context and Perspectives

To understand how the QoS issue is important requires a general overview of the wide-spread use of computer networks and their importance in our lives and society. This discussion is beyond the scope of this text, but the general context and the perspectives involved are easily identifiable. In effect, there is a plethora of networked users, and certainly none would possibly appreciate the chaotic effect of turning off all these very practical and troublesome "appliances." Industry, banks, retail stores, universities, schools, in short, all segments of our "civilized and efficient" society, will simply not work as expected without the "networks."

The estimated installed number of IP users is impressive and, beyond that, is continuously growing in all numbers available. The very strong growth of IP-installed base and widespread use are measurable effects of well-known facts:

- The explosive growth of the Internet global network and its continuous dissemination among end users all over the world;
- The de facto standardization of IP as a network platform for supporting distributed applications by companies and institutions in almost all areas of business.

Certainly, the use of IP as a network platform (Figure 3.1) for distributed applications could be understood as a consequence of Internet success. For developers, IP is an extremely natural "business option," as the number of users is large and, fueled by the World Wide Web (WWW), will continue growing over the long term.

At this point, a fundamental question may be asked: Is IP *the platform* for supporting distributed applications in local, metropolitan, and wide-area networks (WANs)?

There are various approaches to answering this question, and ours will focus on QoS issues. In this context there are other important technological options to consider that are discussed in the following section.

As far as the IP perspective is concerned, all indicators point to the widespread use of this solution in all application areas.

3.1.2 Switched Networks, IP Networks, and Applications

There is general agreement among computer scientists and specialists that cell, frame, or packet switching is a better option when compared to circuit switching or message switching.

As a matter of fact, there is a global trend to employ switching technologies in all networking areas, such as:

- Backbones for local, metropolitan and WANs
- Optical communications
- Supporting multimedia, voice, fax, video-conferencing, mobile, and industrial applications, among others

When analyzing available switching technology alternatives, designers frequently consider certain options:

- Ethernet is an important switching technology option for local areas
- Asynchronous transfer mode (ATM)
- Frame relay
- IP

In the context of our discussion, an important point to understand is how user applications are supported, considering the switching technologies just mentioned.

There are two basic approaches to discuss:

1. The application support is based on level 2 switching.
2. The application support is based on level 3 switching.

In the first approach, ATM, frame relay, or another level 2 switching technology, is used in the backbone. User applications communicate and are effectively distributed across the backbone, directly using the services and features available for the chosen technology. When the chosen technology is ATM, the application would control and use an ATM virtual circuit mesh on top of the backbone. Voice over ATM (VoATM) and voice over frame relay (VoFR) are examples of frequently used applications following the level 2 switching approach.

The favorable point in using this approach is the set of technical advantages of the chosen technology. For instance, ATM will provide a great deal of control to user applications for the characteristics of the communication channels. The application quality of service needs would be mapped to specific services on the ATM backbone. For frame relay, another set of favorable characteristics would be available to applications, such as, controlled bandwidth utilization by committing to the information rate and flow control mechanisms to avoid congestion. These advantages are extensively discussed in many books treating metropolitan and WAN technologies.

The level 3 switching applications support is basically an IP-based approach. Applications are on top of the IP network, and use its services and features through a dual choice of transport services (TCP or user datagram protocol (UDP)) discussed later in this chapter. In this context, the application is fully dependent upon packet switching datagram services and characteristics. This means, in principle, no guarantees for bandwidth, delay, jitter, and others communication channel characteristics. As a matter of fact, there are more technical drawbacks than straight advantages in using native level 3 IP switching support for applications.

The favorable points in using IP-based switching to support end-user applications are the following:

- Massive Internet and corporate IP use results in having IP in almost all computers, or in other words, high availability.
- High availability implies reduced costs as a consequence of good market share.
- Level 2 switching advantages could always be preserved in terms of backbones used by IP switching as a "transport mechanism" for packets.

Level 3 switching is technically far less satisfactory for supporting multimedia, real-time, and other applications that require a better control of network parameters. But the fact is, level 3 switching will prevail as *the alternative* for all applications.

In effect, the indicated advantages are apparently pushing IP switching in such a way that it will have to support all types of applications.

Level 2 switching apparently will not prevail as a general solution for supporting applications in all networking areas (local, metropolitan, and wide area). To understand this trend, we should consider the following:

- Level 2 switching is an excellent solution for backbones, but it does not get to the end user with enough capillarity.
- Level 2 switching is often much more expensive.

So, pragmatically, we will consider level 2 switching technologies like ATM and frame relay as mainly representative for backbone implementations and specific applications support. We will concentrate on IP as the "global end-user platform" in the near future. This being so, a big technical challenge is presented: How to obtain QoS guarantees on top of IP networks? That is the subject discussed next and the technical focus of this chapter.

3.1.3 IP and Quality of Service: Basic Issues

IP was conceived two decades ago to improve a networking scenario of links with very low performance communication and few hosts. This being the case, IP was designed to target simplicity and use a best-effort model, which has properties such as:

- Connectionless
- Routing forwarding decisions taken on a hop-by-hop basis (simplicity)
- No recovery mechanism for errors (let to TCP)
- Support for diverse layer 2 technologies
- Very little control and management over protocol behavior at network nodes

Nowadays, the scenario is quite different, with very high performance communication links being used for router interconnection and many thousands of hosts to interconnect. Their number is not precisely known, but is certainly increasing continuously. In this scenario, new applications with explicit QoS requirements have to run over IP and, as a consequence, QoS has to be addressed somehow by the protocol.

QoS issues are directly addressed in IP version 4 (IPv4) basically by defining the "Type of Service" (ToS) byte in its header (Fig. 3.2).

The ToS byte is defined as follows (Fig. 3.3). Precedence bits (3 bits) specify the priority associated with that particular packet while the remaining bits (bit 3 to 6) specify requirements that could be used for route definition during routing processing. The encoded QoS information is as follows:

IP Precedence (bits 0 to 2):
    000 to 111 → priorities

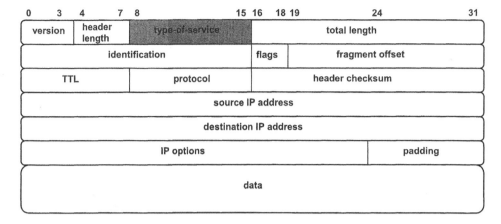

Figure 3.2 IP version 4 packet header.

Type of Service (bits 3 to 6):

All zero—normal service

Bit 3—minimize delay

Bit 4—maximize throughput

Bit 5—maximize reliability

Bit 6—minimize monetary cost

The ToS byte was not effectively used in practice by routers until the recent Internet explosion. In this new scenario, IP Precedence bits have been extensively used to provide a simple priority mechanism for differentiating among packet flows through the network.

IPv4 basic routing processing presents some problems for high-performance routers, which have an impact on the overall network QoS provided. In effect, the IPv4 header was not optimized for gigabit or terabit packet processing and, as such, presents overhead problems. These include:

- Address matches for packet forwarding are processed by using mainly matches to network address prefixes of variable length using a table look-up search method.
- Fragmentation, when necessary, is an important overhead component for routers through the packets path.

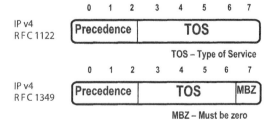

Figure 3.3 ToS in IP header.

- Checksum computation was necessary at every hop due to TTL (time-to-life) manipulation.
- IP options processing implies a variable header length and represents an additional overhead for router packet processing, specially when options are present in the header.

IP version 6 (IPv6), sometimes denoted IP new generation (IPng), is the new IP. IPv6 design addresses the indicated problems of IPv4 and, as such, IPv6 better supports the requirements for high-performance IP forwarding in routers and switches. It is important to mention that IPv6 design addresses many other technical aspects, which are beyond the scope of this chapter. These include:

- A solution to the IP address exhaustion problem, which resulted from explosive Internet growth all around the world
- A security framework at layer 3, targeted at supporting applications
- An overall IP processing optimization (fewer parameters in the header, optional headers, and no fragmentation, among other improvements)
- Other more specific improvements, like autoconfiguration, well-structured address hierarchy, and easy migration path form IPv4, just to mention a few.

The format of the IPv6 header is illustrated in Figure 3.4. IPv6 addresses directly QoS issues by defining specific fields in its header. These include:

- A "flow label"
- A "traffic class"

The flow-label byte may have a general-purpose use, but the basic principle it supports is the concept of flow manipulation. In IPv6, flow identification (flow label) may be used to efficiently manipulate the packet. For instance, a labeled IPv6 packet can be forwarded by

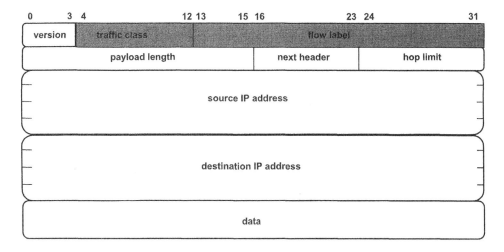

Figure 3.4   IPv6 header format.

using the label, disregarding any other field in the IPv6 header. As we discuss in the following sections, "label identification" may be used by solutions like integrated services architecture (IntServ) and MPLS to implement QoS-aware solutions.

The "traffic class" byte is also oriented to support QoS. It allows applications to specify priorities for the packets they generate. In this sense, IPv6 introduces the principle of "class" which, in practice, corresponds to considering packets from different flows belonging to the same aggregate or grouping. This is another important concept used by QoS solutions like, for instance, the Differentiated Service Architecture (DiffServ).

3.2 QUALITY OF SERVICE

QoS is a fundamental issue for many applications. Once we examine some common definitions about QoS, we will develop a more precise analysis on how to control and manage IP networks in order to obtain the expected operating characteristics or, in other words, the expected QoS.

3.2.1 Quality of Service: Trying a Definition

The definition of QoS depends on the perspective adopted. It is possible to define QoS based on either the user point-of-view, the application point-of-view, or the network and equipment point-of-view, among some of the mostly used perspectives. The following statement is an attempt to provide a more monolithic understanding of QoS, considering the scope of our discussion:

> Quality of service is an application requirement expressed by a set of characterization parameters (typically, a *service-level agreement (SLA)*), which should be provided by the network on an *end-to-end basis,* in order to preserve an adequate application operational behavior and end-user "satisfaction."

SLA is not a unique way to express QoS requirements, but it is certainly the one mostly used. Later in this chapter we will identify other alternatives for expressing QoS requirements.

End-to-end QoS is a challenging requirement for designers. Like a long chain, QoS guarantees are achieved by a set of equipment and services through the network. In the event that one of these equipments or services fail, the entire chain is compromised. Unique and monolithic approaches to provide end-to-end QoS are indeed one of the most promising research and development areas for this subject.

3.2.2 Quality of Service: How to Proceed?

Once we have defined an end-to-end meaning for quality of service, we need to refine the concept by pointing out what technical issues, control procedures, and management actions are necessary to handle it.

Typically, implementing a QoS-ready network requires a rather broad set of techniques, control procedures, and management actions. These include:

- Identifying applications requirements.
- Understanding how network components (routers, switches, hosts, and other devices) behave as far as QoS is concerned.

- Requesting specific QoS in networks and equipment using an appropriate method and formulation.
- Making use of signaling protocols.
- Controlling the router operation for QoS-dependable applications.
- Integrating alternative QoS enforcement control options in complex and heterogeneous networks, such as the Internet, for instance.

Applications should be clearly understood as far as their needs are concerned. The overall network and equipment behavior is fundamental in distributing the need for QoS through the network being used. We must have a clear method of expressing QoS needs in terms of applications requirements and, beyond that, we need to map it on the networks and equipment involved. Signaling protocols are the way in which user requirements are translated in specific network requirements to the equipments adopted. Finally, the router is a very important element for QoS enforcement strategies, since it handles IP packets. Thus, router control and queue management techniques are essential for a successful QoS-ready network. In the following section these issues are briefly discussed.

3.2.3 Application's Taxonomy: Quality of Service

As far as QoS is concerned, applications behave differently and, as such, may be grouped in classes. In this section we identify how they differ and what possible classification could be adopted.

In global terms, applications are classified in two main groups (Fig. 3.5):

1. Adaptable applications
2. Real-time applications

Adaptable applications are also frequently denoted as elastic, satisfactory, and flexible applications. They have the basic characteristic of being able to tolerate fluctuations in network performance and continue to work satisfactorily.

Real-time applications do not tolerate variations in network performance. The basic characteristic of real-time applications is their stringent requirements for QoS parameters, such as packet loss and delay. Variations on the required QoS parameters result in serious degradation of application behavior, and consequently reduce user satisfaction. A good example of real-time application is medical imaging. A system supporting a real-time surgical operation should maintain network performance parameters as required to maintain

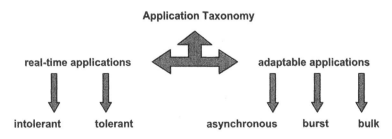

Figure 3.5. Application taxonomy.

perfect images, thus preserving the health and tranquility of the patient. In these applications, QoS enforcement and network performance relying on agreed values is a must.

The adaptable applications mentioned so far can be further refined in another classification as follows:

- Asynchronous application
- Bulk transfer applications
- Burst applications

Asynchronous applications, as their name implies, have a rather asynchronous behavior between their peers. Application peers have to communicate, but there are no strict requirements established. In other words, the requirements are "soft" and easily accomplished as long as the network is operational. The cited requirements concern delay, loss, and jitter in any combination. Thus, the term "asynchronous" can be understood in a broader perspective, meaning flexible applications that are capable of adapting to various network conditions.

A good example of asynchronous applications is email. It is desirable to have email transfers processed as soon as possible, but it is not necessary to enforce bounds to the communication exchange between mail servers. This means that other more demanding applications may borrow network resources from email applications, as long as they can wait for available resources without significant loss. Also, if the network drops packets with email, the application will recover from this situation and preserve the application service.

An interesting aspect of asynchronous applications is how asynchronous they really are. The required response time (which is one possible parameter to identify how asynchronously peers communicate) can vary significantly for different asynchronous applications. As an example, email data transfers, which are TCP-based, can wait for minutes before reacting to any impediment to sending messages. In another situation, hypertext transfer protocol (HTTP) transfers may have their response time dictated by external factors like the maximum waiting time to display a Web page to a customer. Generally, it is assumed that asynchronous applications support network performance variations and that their time limits are typically beyond the minimum the network is able to guarantee.

Burst and bulk applications behave differently in the way they generate data (packets). Burst applications, as the name suggests, produce bursts or peaks of data. The instantaneous data rate may substantially vary from the average data rate for this type of application.

Bulk-transfer applications are more reliable with respect to data generation. In bulk transfers, there is a huge volume of data, and also the instantaneous data rate does not significantly vary from the average data rate for long periods of time. File transfer is one example of bulk application.

The burst or bulk characteristic of the application is important for buffer dimensioning and management. Buffers in routers and switches are a valuable resource that has to be used efficiently. To know beforehand that some supported applications generate data in peaks is fundamental to determining buffer size or, alternatively, to managing and smooth peaks in order to regulate the flow of data in network nodes.

Real-time applications can also be further refined and grouped as follows:

- Real-time tolerant applications
- Real-time intolerant applications

Tolerant applications do have real-time requirements, but can wisely support "fluctuations" of specified QoS parameters without compromising the user's "satisfaction." For instance, Moving Picture Experts Group (MPEG) video applications have the possibility of guaranteeing "graceful degradation" in case network performance suffers fluctuations.

Intolerant real-time applications (also called hard real-time applications) do not accept QoS parameter variability. This means that the requirements are absolutely stringent and violations on parameter agreement (SLA violation) might compromise the "satisfaction" (QoS) of the user.

3.2.4 Quality of Service Parameters

QoS has to be expressed in precise terms. This is an important issue, especially for planners and designers, in order to have a common understanding of the requirements involved.

The QoS requirements for applications are frequently expressed in terms of:

- Bandwidth
- Latency
- Jitter
- Packet loss
- Reliability

The following discussion will consider the definition of these parameters, the factors in a network that affect them, and the possibilities for managing and controlling them.

Figure 3.6 depicts a very simple network comprising two logical LANs interconnected by a router based WAN. There are two applications communicating with QoS requirements on an end-to-end basis. This simple setup will be used to exemplify the QoS parameters just listed, their dependency, and their relationship with network equipment and services.

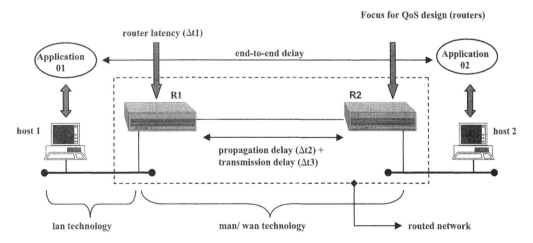

Figure 3.6 QoS parameters in IP networks: an example.

3.2.4.1 Bandwidth Bandwidth is a straightforward parameter representing the amount of *capacity* the network has to guarantee for the application on an end-to-end basis. In simple terms, the bandwidth parameter expresses the *data rate* that the network is supposed to guarantee for the application.

Bandwidth requirements have been identified for the most commonly used applications. Table 3.1 shows typical bandwidths for network applications. Typically, bandwidth requirements are expressed in units of packets per second (PPS) or bits per second. This metric reflects once again the global trend to adopt layer 3 (IP) switching for supporting end-user applications. There are also other parameters that are used to express bandwidth requirements. These include:

- Minimum data rate
- Maximum data rate
- Committed average data rate
- Burst size (expressed in amount of data and/or burst time duration)

In effect, overall bandwidth requirements have to be identified by network managers. Methodologies to identify these requirements for a set of user applications distributed over the network (physical topology dependency) are available in the literature [1]. Subsequently, the network has to be provisioned, as far as bandwidth is concerned. There are various alternative ways to provision a network. These include:

- Contracting services
- Acquiring adequate equipment
- Choosing network technology which matches requirement needs

Bandwidth requirements are not a critical problem for LAN design. This fact is due to technology evolution from shared to switched and their low cost. As an example, single-user ethernet interfaces at 10 Mbps, 100 Mbps, 1 Gbps and, soon, 10 Gbps, are large pipes that give designers enough flexibility and accommodate user needs.

Bandwidth requirements could be a point of concern for WAN and metropolitan area network (MAN) design. The reasons are the following:

Table 3.1 Typical Bandwidth for Some Networking Applications

Application	Bandwidth (Typical)
Voice	6 kbps to 64 kbps
Whiteboard	10 kbps to 100 kbps
Web applications	10 kbps to 500 kbps
File transfer	10 kbps to 1 Mbps
Video (Streaming)	100 kbps to 1 Mbps
Video-conferencing	128 kbps to 1 Mbps
Video MPEG	1 Mbps to 10 Mbps
Medical images	10 Mbps to 100 Mbps
Virtual reality	> 80 Mbps

- Overall communications cost
- Bandwidth limitations on router interconnections
- Availability

Bandwidth is usually an expensive and limited resource for router interconnection. High-speed technologies like synchronous optical networks (SONET), DWDM, and ATM, capable of delivering hundreds of megabits per second, are certainly available, but their use is still precisely adjusted to application needs. In other words, this means that a precise or even an underdimensioned design is mostly a common practice. Also, there is sometimes a rigid budget to maintain, which finally results in using much less bandwidth than necessary. These approaches result in a more affordable global overall cost for network operation, but may compromise QoS requirements. Besides that, availability of high-speed data communication services may be a problem for remote sites.

The concerns about bandwidth limitation for network design just discussed have a direct impact on router operation. In effect, the router might become a bottleneck, since the available bandwidth for their interconnections is not necessarily dimensioned to guarantee the flow of packets from all applications simultaneously at all times. IP processing in routers has to handle packets efficiently to guarantee overall QoS requirements. The issues on router IP processing and router control are discussed further in Section 3.4.

In the near future, it might be possible to have enough bandwidth on all router interconnections for all types of networks (private networks, Internet, etc.). In this desirable and optimum scenario, the point of concern for QoS would be the IP processing capacity of the equipment involved (router, multilayer switch, routing switch, layer 3 switch, or any other type of equipment for switching IP packets).

3.2.4.2 *Latency and Delay*   Latency is a general denomination for the various types of delays experienced by packets when traveling through the network.

Although "latency" and "delay" can be used indistinctly to express slowness in the packet's journey through the network, "latency" is often used in relation to equipment and network services (e.g., switch latency, router latency), while "delay" is often used in data communications (e.g., transmission delay, propagation delay).

Latency and delays can be expressed using different terminology. Figure 3.7 illustrates the terms considered for the scope of the discussion in this text.

Network Latency   In general terms, network latency (NL) can be considered as the result of summing up all end-to-end delays produced by network and end-user equipment (hosts). This includes, as an example, delays introduced by network equipment (hubs, LAN switches, and routers), delays introduced by network service

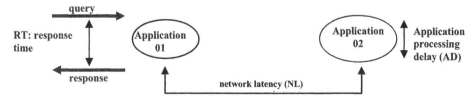

Figure 3.7   Latency and delays.

providers (carriers), delays introduced by signals propagating in a communications medium (fiber, wireless, twisted-pair, and coaxial), and the network stack processing delay at the hosts (Fig. 3.8). The network stack processing delay at the hosts is frequently ignored by designers, but may become an important component when low-performance hosts are using high-performance networks.

Application Processing Delays   As the name suggests, the application processing delay (AD) indicates the amount of delay introduced by data processing in the application program. As illustrated in Figure 3.8, the AD may include a protocol component. In effect, it is assumed that the AD incorporates delays introduced by the application code, which, typically, has components such as:

- The application program itself
- The protocol layers reaching up to the application programming interface (API) used

For most TCP/IP networks, this interface is located at layer 4 (TCP/UDP API). The AD is totally dependent on the end-user application program, its computer performance, and local operating system.

End-to-End Delay   For the scope of this discussion, end-to-end delay (EE) is equivalent to the previously defined NL, since it incorporates all delays introduced by the network itself and the host's network stack. The EE delay approximately represents the overall time a packet takes from leaving its source to arrival at its destination, except for the processing time in higher layers in the host. This parameter is frequently used to specify QoS requirements for user-to-user applications like, for instance, VoIP.

Response Time   Response time (RT) is a typical way of expressing QoS requirements for client/server applications. RT has end-user significance and depends on both round-trip NL and ADs at both communicating parties' ends, as follows:

$$RT = \Sigma\ (NL_{\text{round-trip}}, AD_{\text{source}}, AD_{\text{destination}})$$

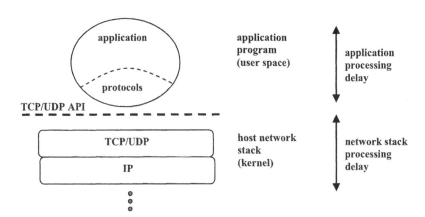

Figure 3.8   Host network stack and application program.

From the application point-of-view, network latency is frequently the main component of the response time. Therefore, let us consider in detail the delay components influencing it. They are the following:

- Propagation delays
- Transmission speed
- Equipment latency
- Communication service latency

3.2.4.2.1 Network Latency Components Here is a brief discussion presenting the main NL components.

Propagation Delay Propagations delays are immutable physical parameters. They represent the time the signals (electrical, optical, or electromagnetic) take to propagate in the media being used in the physical network. For long runs and satellite networks, these delays reach hundreds of milliseconds, and may become critical for certain applications and have to be considered as a NL component. For LANs these values are normally ignored, since they are very small when compared with other delay components.

Transmission Speed The second factor contributing to NL is the transmission speed used by routers and communications equipment. The transmission delay resulting from packet transmission will contribute to the NL.

The transmission speed used in the various network links are defined by project and provisioned for the network by means of any public data communications services carrier or, alternatively, private network. In any event, this is a manageable parameter for QoS provisioning. The points to consider in defining data communication services for IP networks are:

- Router links in local area design are high speed and do not contribute significantly to the overall network latency.
- Router links in long-distance design may become a major source of delay for the overall network latency.

Cost issues and limited availability of services are the main causes of delays in long-distance router links. As an example, 1000-byte packets routed through 1.5-Mbps links, would experience 5.3-ms transmission delay per router link, assuming all links use the same transmission speed. The cumulative effect of transmission delay in multihop router paths can result in long delays. In brief, propagation delay and transmission speed are important design issues for long-distance and metropolitan networks.

Equipment Latency The third network latency component is due to processing in network equipment. Examples of network equipment contributing to increased network delay include:

- Routers
- Hubs and LAN switches

- Firewalls
- Remote-access servers

All network equipment traversed by the packet introduces a delay component typically denoted as *equipment latency* (router latency, LAN switch latency, and so on). This delay is basically due to packet, frame, or higher layer processing within the equipment. In general terms, equipment latency may be considered as the time period between when the packet enters and exits the equipment.

The impact of this delay component on overall delay depends on equipment type and its internal design characteristics. As an example, let us consider a brief discussion of the most important equipment:

- LAN switches normally introduce delays of a few microseconds and, as such, they have very low impact on overall delay. As technology is always in evolution, it is expected that this equipment will not represent a point of concern for QoS.
- Routers, depending on their internal implementation, introduce processing delays that could vary from microseconds to milliseconds. Low-performance routers therefore introduce important delay components, and high-performance routers are equivalent to LAN switch when considering delay components.

Since routers are fundamental equipment for packet processing, their implementation has been the subject of much attention from manufactures. In effect, since QoS emerged as a must for network design, routers have evolved and many techniques have been applied to their implementation. These include:

- Switching techniques (router switch model).
- Integrated multilayer implementation (integrates switching of layer 2 and 3 in a single piece of equipment).
- Hardware integration, especially by using application-specific integrated circuits (ASIC) techniques.
- Multiprocessing implementation.

In general, all equipment should be considered potential delay component elements. QoS design demands careful identification of the equipment's latency in order to guarantee overall delay requirements.

Communication Services Latency Another delay component for applications is communication service latency. Normally, this component plays an important part in overall delay. Communication services are requested by an SLA, and latency is one of the specified QoS parameters. Other parameters typically include bandwidth, packet loss, and availability. As an example, using a frame relay point-to-point communication link between routers R1 and R2 (Figure 3.6) may introduce delays of hundreds of milliseconds for packets. Network design with QoS guarantees should consider public communication services as a potential delay component.

3.2.4.3 Jitter Jitter is another important QoS parameter. In the context of IP, jitter can be defined as the delay variation experienced by packets (packet-delay variation).

Jitter control is important for applications whose correct processing depends on packets being delivered in guaranteed time intervals by the network. As an example, VoIP and fax-over-IP (FoIP) applications do not behave adequately if packets do not arrive at a given rate at the destination for decoding.

As discussed in earlier sections, equipment introduces delay for packets that are variable. Factors influencing the variability of equipment latency are:

- Variable processing time at intermediate equipment (routers, switches, and others)
- Variable public communication services latency
- Congestion
- Other factors related to network operation

Considering the processing and latency variability, it is evident that time processing is different for each incoming packet due to the unpredictable behavior of the distribution of resources in the equipment. Also, it is important to mention that congestion is a critical issue for jitter. Once the network or its equipment reaches a congested state, processing delays increase, contributing to increased jitter.

The Figure 3.9 illustrates the jitter effect for applications. In this simple example, it is important to notice that jitter not only causes variability in packet delivery but also may cause packets to be received out of order.

For TCP-based applications, this last problem is promptly corrected by the TCP protocol. For UDP-based applications (which correspond to a large number of real-time and multimedia applications), there must exist another high-level protocol or procedure to eventually recover from this situation. As an example, real-time protocol (RTP) is used in VoIP applications to help the application in fixing this problem.

Once the jitter can be controlled and kept within defined bounds, there must be an additional mechanism to guarantee that packets will be received in precise time windows for applications. The most common mechanism to eliminate jitter or delay fluctuations is *jitter buffer*. The basic idea is to create a buffer that will keep incoming packets for processing in such a way that the receiver will always have an incoming packet ready for processing. The controlled jitter bounds is the basic parameter used to dimension the required buffer in this approach.

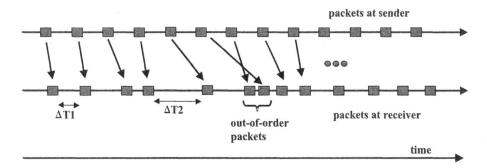

Figure 3.9 Jitter effect for applications.

3.2.4.4 Packet Loss Packet loss occurs in networks mainly due to factors such as:

- Dropping packets at routers
- Transmission errors
- Routing processing decisions

Packets dropped during congestion or due to resource limitation in routers is the main contributing factor for this specific QoS parameter.

Transmission error is a much less important factor contributing to packet loss, since error rates have been considerably reduced by the use of fiber optics and other communication techniques for interfaces and systems. In effect, transmission error rates fall below 10^{-9} for many communication systems.

Packet loss due to routing processing decisions corresponds to the situation in which a packet is routed incorrectly and, because of this, is dropped somewhere in the network. These misrouted-packet possibilities are a less important factor contributing to packet loss.

Packet loss is a very important parameter for certain applications. As an example, VoIP applications will tolerate packet loss up to a certain limit (typically 5%). Beyond that, the recovered voice quality becomes inadequate for user perception.

3.2.4.5 Availability and Reliability Availability and reliability are related parameters considered for QoS. In practice, availability and reliability are parameters typically considered during the network design phase. When considering network operation, these parameters specify directly or indirectly the time constraints for equipment and systems to execute without disruption or failure. For end-user applications, the execution without disruption or failure is dependent on such factors as:

- Network equipment reliability (private networks)
- Public service availability and reliability (when used)

When using public services, SLA should specify availability and/or reliability of parameters required for network operation.

Computer networks are frequently the mission-critical infrastructure for companies and institutions in areas such as electronic commerce, banking, industrial, and retail. In this scenario, availability and reliability are critical issues. As an example, availability requirements above 99.9% are common for Web applications, client/server applications, VoIP applications, and other applications that strongly interact with users.

3.3 QUALITY OF SERVICE: APPROACHES AND INITIATIVES FOR IP NETWORKS

In this section we discuss some basic definitions concerning QoS and we indicate the main existing and proposed alternatives to enforcing QoS requirements in IP networks. The Internet Engineering Task Force (IETF) proposed most of these initiatives, all of which have a very important role in IP network evolution. Besides IETF, other forums, such as the ATM Forum, Frame Relay Forum, WWW, and private companies have contributed, but less intensively, to promoting solutions to QoS enforcement in IP networks.

3.3.1 Quality of Service: Some Basic Definitions

For the purpose of discussing QoS, some basic definitions, which are commonly used with standardized strategies, will be briefly introduced. Also, alternative QoS approaches, like overdimensioning, will be briefly revisited in order to provide a contextual overview of the set of technical alternatives involved.

3.3.1.1 Flow-Based and Class-Based IP Processing   In general, quality of service packet processing in routers and switches can use two different approaches:

- Flow-based packet processing
- Class-based packet processing

Before detailing these approaches, we must first give the meaning of the terms "flow" and "class." For the purposes of this chapter, a flow is identified as follows:

- A flow corresponds to a unidirectional (source-to-destination) data stream between applications.
- A flow is typically identified by parameters such as IP addresses (source and/or destination) and port numbers (source and/or destination). Alternatively, a flow can be identified by a label like the flow label used by IPv6 and resource reservation protocol (RSVP) (Fig. 3.10).

Using the concept and identification just described, a flow may correspond, for instance, to packets exchanged by end-user applications. A flow is a fine-grain concept with high capillarity for applications and its associated QoS.

The important concept to retain for now is that the term flow is associated with high capillarity. This means that, eventually, additional parameters may be applied for flow identification. As an example, the ToS parameter in an IP header can be used together with an address and port number to further refine flow's identification.

In our discussion, the term "packets flow" represents the packets being delivered to the network, and that are delivered for one (unicast) or multiple destinations (multicast and broadcast). In this chapter we will use the terms "flow" and "packets flow" interchangeably.

Flows and packets can be identified and grouped together in different ways; for instance, packets originating from a specific machine, a subnetwork, or any other combina-

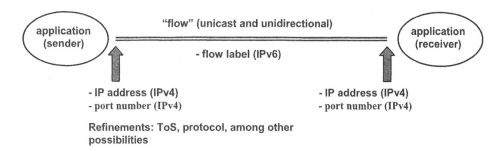

Figure 3.10   A flow between applications.

tions of machines and subnetworks. Also, IP header parameters like addresses, port numbers, and protocols can be used to identify a specific group of packets belonging to an "aggregate" or assigned to a "class." The term "class" or "aggregate" represents a group of packets with some common identification (IP prefix, from the same machine, etc.), which, in effect, corresponds to two or more flows.

For the purposes of this chapter, aggregate and class are terms representing the same basic idea. The term class is often used to indicate a group to which the packet belongs, and the term aggregate typically represents a group of packets flowing through the network that belong to the given class.

For now, let us discuss the main characteristics when flow-based and class-based packet processing is used in strategies to enforce QoS.

In flow-based packet processing, the processing is done at the flow level. In other words, packets belonging to a specific pair of applications (sender/receiver) are processed to enforce the expected QoS.

The main advantages of flow-based packet processing are:

- High capillarity, since processing can be tuned to end-users individually.
- Good resource distribution, since applications can be tuned individually.

The main drawbacks of flow-based packet processing are:

- Flow identification with high capillarity typically requires additional processing.
- Does not scale well, since flow-based packet processing is subject to "state explosion" in big networks with many users.
- The amount of per-flow information to be maintained by the network nodes may also become a scaling problem.

In class-based packet processing, the processing is done for an aggregate or class of packets. Flows are not considered individually anymore.

The main processing advantages of a class-based packet are:

- Class-based processing scales well with many users since, for instance, state information is kept to a minimum.
- Flow aggregates reduce the analysis of packet header parameters by routers, and consequently reduces overhead.
- Processing by class eases operation management and price policy implementation.

The main processing drawback of a class-based packet is related to the fact that individual users cannot be tuned adequately as far as their specific requirements are concerned.

3.3.1.2 *Token Bucket* IP quality of service control approaches like the IntServ and the differentiated service architecture (DiffServ) use, typically, a token-bucket scheme. We will therefore introduce the basic concepts related to this scheme.

QoS strategies need to keep track (monitoring, controlling, etc.) of the characteristics of different packet streams, such as average data rate, peak data rate, and bursts. Identification of these characteristics is necessary for the network, because the traffic from most applications is quite variable and, besides that, the traffic does not necessarily follow predefined service contracts due to the behavior of intrinsic applications. Networks thus need to have a scheme to limit traffic at network borders, to shape bursts, and to identify out-of-profile traffic, among other needs.

The token-bucket scheme can be used to address some of the listed network needs. In its most basic operation, the token-bucket principle is as follows (Fig. 3.11):

- Tokens representing "credit" are generated at contracted rate "r."
- Tokens/credits accumulate in the bucket till the limit "b" (the bucket size).
- Packets require credit to enter the network.
- Packets arriving at average rate "p" get access to the network with credit that is available at the bucket.
- Packets experience a predefined action, in case the accumulated credit is insufficient.

This very simple scheme can be used to create some necessary functionality in networks like policy modules, packet markers, and shapers.

As illustrated in Figure 3.12, a token-bucket filter implements a "policy module" that limits out-of-bound traffic by dropping packets that do not obtain enough credit when arriving at network entry point. The operation is as follows:

- Tokens representing credits are generated at contracted rate "r," which is supposed to be the average contracted rate for the incoming packet stream.
- Tokens/credits accumulate in the bucket until the limit "b" (the bucket size), which allows the instantaneous packet input rate to vary (input data rate fluctuation).
- Arriving packets require credit proportional to their size to get access to the network.
- Any arriving packet is dropped, in case the accumulated credit in the bucket is insufficient at arrival time.

The token-bucket scheme has advantages. For example, it can be used by the network to enforce a traffic contract, by identifying conforming and nonconforming packets. Also,

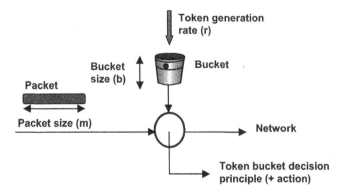

Figure 3.11 Token-bucket principle.

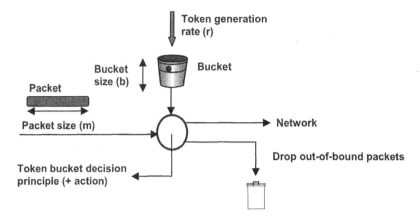

Figure 3.12 Token-bucket as a policy module.

the token-bucket scheme provides a boundary on the average rate and limits the maximum amount of traffic during any period of time. The last mentioned advantage is important because it adequately limits the buffer size used in devices like routers and switches.

Slight variations of the preceding operation and the concatenation of parameterized token-buckets produce shapers, markers, limiters, and other modules, which are essential to QoS control and management.

3.3.2 IP Quality of Service: How to Handle It?   Having examined some common definitions relating to IP QoS, we will now develop a more precise view of how to enforce QoS requirements in IP networks. The most common alternatives for enforcing QoS parameters in IP networks are the following:

- Overdimensioning
- Queue and congestion management in routers and switches
- Integrated services architecture
- Differentiated services architecture
- Multiprotocol label switching
- Proprietary and hybrid solutions

Each one of these solutions has its own set of characteristics that we will describe and discuss in the remainder of this chapter.

3.3.3 Do We Need Quality of Service Control?

Networking technologies have evolved significantly in the last few years. This evolution becomes apparent when we consider, for instance, the data rates supported by the actual and under-development technologies. Following is a brief review of frequently used technologies:

- Ethernet has evolved from a 10-Mbps shared-hub solution to a switched solution (eventually dedicated) ranging from 100 Mbps, 1 Gbps, and beyond to 10 Gpbs.

- ATM supports data rates that typically range from 1.5 Mbps to 622 Mbps.
- SONET and synchronous digital hierarchy (SDH) can, typically, deliver data rates ranging from 52 Mbps to 622 Mbps and beyond to 2.4 Gbps.
- DWDM is another high-speed technology with data rates that can achieve hundreds of Gbps and beyond to Tbps (terabits per second, or 10^{12}).

Besides the increase in supported data rates, another important aspect of networking technology's evolution is that the cost per bit has been considerably reduced over the last few years. In principle, this aspect stimulates the widespread use of the technologies.

This being so, a fundamental question can be asked: Do we really need do deploy any form of *QoS control* in networks?

The point is: with high-speed technologies available, we could just provide as much bandwidth as necessary for applications. This approach, called overprovisioning or overdimensioning, is discussed next.

3.3.3.1 *Overdimensioning Approach.*

Strictly speaking, overdimensioning is not a technique for QoS control. In effect, the basic idea is to provide as much bandwidth as necessary for any application. Since technologies have evolved and are capable of delivering hundreds and even thousands of megabits per second, overdimensioning might be applicable in some circumstances.

The context for overdimensioning utilization is mainly the private and local-area networking. In this context, it is a possible alternative, considering that:

- Users are, in principle, well known (number, traffic characteristics).
- The global cost for installing the network is, apart from network operations and management maintenance costs, mainly the measurable initial investment.

For wide and metropolitan area networking, the use of such big pipes typically implies higher monthly costs for public services, which prevents the use of this approach for network provision.

The possibility of using overdimensioning may also be discussed using another perspective. The question is: In order to guarantee overdimensioned output links, is it enough for applications to behave as expected?

Intuitively, the straightforward answer is yes, since we assume that large output pipes will guarantee that routed or switched packets and cells will be delivered very quickly. In routers and switches, this behavior guarantees that output queues will be nearly empty and, thus, delays are reduced and the jitter is minimized in the network.

The preceding supposition raises two additional basic questions:

- Do the networking devices (routers and switches) have enough processing capacity so that we can assume minimal latency and processing time?
- Can we be sure that users and applications will not evolve in parallel to consume the "pretended" overdimensioned resources?

For the first question it is necessary to understand the existing limitations for network devices. Focusing on routers, the fact is that processing capacity and network design features have, for the moment, eliminated eventual internal-capacity bottlenecks in these devices. High throughput routers and level 3 switches, for instance, can deliver thousand of packets with minimal latency (on the order of microseconds) and, as such, do not yet represent a serious concern for QoS. Also, virtual networking and careful design can overcome excessive traffic concentration at some network points, which would create a potential bottleneck. As such, the actual router limitation is the output interface capacity, often limited in metropolitan and wide-area design by cost or availability. Beside this, there is no clear evidence that "free bandwidth" will emerge as a network design scenario in the near future.

Analysis of the second point may be better tackled by looking back at the network evolution. The fact is that historically user-application demands have always risen to meet network technology's evolution. In other words, network evolution has been followed by new applications with tougher requirements concerning data rate, delays, and jitter. In this evolving scenario, it may happen that the overdimensioning approach does not work at all and the network designer will have to adopt QoS strategies to adjust the network to attain user demands.

In conclusion, the fundamental resource is the output link rate. Therefore, network designers and managers will need algorithms, techniques, and end-to-end strategies to help them in controlling requirements and delivering QoS for end-user applications.

3.4 PACKET CONDITIONING, QUEUE SCHEDULING, AND CONGESTION CONTROL IN ROUTERS

As stated earlier, routers are a point of concern for QoS since they could become potential bottlenecks for packet flow. In effect, for high packet volumes flowing through routers, low-speed links used in interconnections and low processing capacity, among other factors, may cause packets to slow down or even to be dropped at routers.

As illustrated in Figure 3.13, basic router operation can be described in very simple terms:

- Packets are picked up at input queues, where they arrive asynchronously or, eventually, synchronously.
- Packets are processed according to basic IP routing operation (TTL control, address handling, and so on).
- Packets are switched to output queues for transmission.

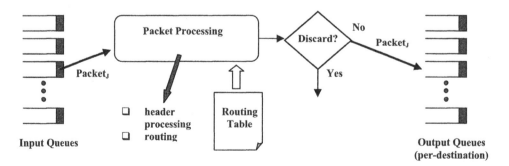

Figure 3.13 Basic router operation.

This very simple view of the router operation has a set of potential problems for QoS. Here is a short summary of some of the problems encountered in routers:

- Packet latency in routers is dependent, for instance, on router processing capacity and transmission speed at output interfaces. Low-capacity routers will lead to greater router latency since packets will take longer to be internally processed. Also, low-speed interfaces will lead to bigger router latency because packets wait longer to be transmitted on output queues.
- Packet loss has a great deal of dependency on router capacity, queue memory size, and transmission speed at output interfaces. Packets may be lost by combining situations, for instance, like queue overflow due to low transmissions speed or queue overflow due to peaks of input traffic.
- Jitter is another QoS parameter influenced by router operation. Since there is no prior guarantee that packets from the same sources will be handled "homogeneously" (given the same amount of router capacity, processed at same time, and so on), internal packet delays in routers tend to be quite variable, thus increasing the jitter.

Overall router operation can be managed by applying a set of basic control methods to packets and queues such as:

- Packet conditioning
- Queue scheduling
- Congestion control

In the remainder of this section we will elaborate on each of these control methods in more detail and review their application to routers.

3.4.1 Packet Conditioning

In general terms, packet conditioning corresponds to the set of actions carried out on packets in an attempt to establish and preserve their relative importance or priority in relation to any other packet in the network.

Packet conditioning can be accomplished by the following techniques:

- Packet prioritization
- Packet classification and markup
- Traffic shaping
- Policing

It is important to observe that these functions are, in practice, typically used in conjunction. Depending on the QoS strategy used, these functionalities may be combined to achieve the expected result. So, classification may precede traffic shaping or prioritization may result from traffic shaping results. This being so, the following discussion will focus on the description of basic functionalities, and their interoperation will be elaborated later when we discuss the scheduling algorithms and QoS strategies.

In an attempt to give some insight on how these functionalities might interoperate, Figure 3.14 shows a typical router implementation. Packet prioritization is one of the most

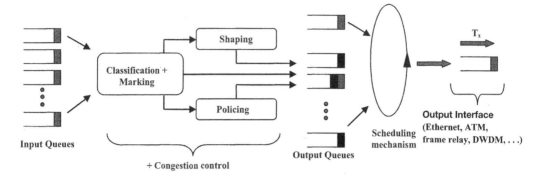

Figure 3.14 Packet conditioning, scheduling, and congestion control in typical interoperation.

frequently used and straightforward packet conditioning techniques. Packets are "marked" as having a specific priority and, as an example, will receive network resources like memory and bandwidth depending on its priority.

In IP routers, the scheduling algorithms used to decide which packet would be serviced next typically employ packet prioritization. Alternatively, packet prioritization also may be used to decide which packet will be dropped during congestion. Figure 3.15 illustrates QoS and routing functionalities using priority-based decisions.

Packet classification and markup is another fundamental and very frequently used conditioning technique. The idea is to investigate packet content (IP header, TCP/UDP header, and so on) in order to identify the flow or application to which that packet belongs, and therefore infer the packet's characteristics. As a very simple example, this technique allows a router to know that for the two packets waiting for service, one carries synchronous time-sensitive traffic and the other carries asynchronous traffic. This information is valuable to various aspects of router operation.

Figure 3.16 illustrates the basic principles for classification and markup functions. In routers, packet classifications typically occur when moving packets from input queues to output queues. The markup technique, normally associated with packet classification, allows some sort of relative identification of packets within the router, or within a network of routers and switches. There are various approaches to marking packets (labeling pack-

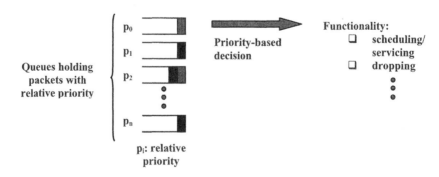

Figure 3.15 Typical functionalities using priority-based decisions.

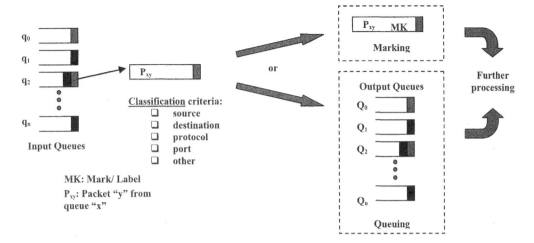

Figure 3.16 Classification and markup functions.

ets) and distributing labeling information (RSVP, MPLS, etc.) that will be further discussed later in this chapter.

Packet classification and packet markup are separate functions, but intrinsically associated. It means that for markup, some classification has to be executed, but classification does not necessarily apply in marking or labeling packets. The way these functions interoperate depends on the QoS strategy used.

Traffic shaping is a very important technique necessary in many scheduling algorithms in routers. When applied to a classified stream or flow of packets, traffic shaping allows, among other possibilities, the control of packet bursts. The incoming traffic is "shaped" by defining upper bounds, for instance, on the packet's average rate and burst. The token-bucket filter is a typical example of shaper functionality implementation.

In routers, traffic shaping is typically used to limit incoming traffic to predetermined profiles. Alternatively, traffic shaping also can be used at network borders to deliver packets according to predetermined flow characteristics. In effect, predetermined short- and long-term traffic behavior is an essential condition for many algorithms used in routers.

Traffic-shaping techniques also can be used, for instance, in conjunction with a monitoring function to make decisions about dropping packets. In this particular situation, the bursts of traffic are detected. Depending on the accumulated volume of traffic generated, new out-of-bound packets might be elected to be discarded or not.

Before discussing policing functionality in the router context, it is important to understand the general meaning of the term "policy." Generally speaking, policy is a set of rules associated with services (Fig. 3.17). The principle is such that these rules define the criteria for obtaining related services. In other words, policy describes the set of conditions that must be satisfied before actions related to the service can be taken. Policy is applied to many aspects of computers, such as security, management, and administrative issues.

In the specific context of router operation, typical examples of possible policy rules are:

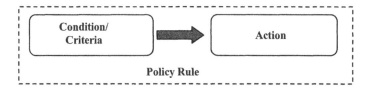

Figure 3.17 Policy rule.

- Mark packets out-of-bounds with respect to negotiated SLA for dropping.
- Drop packets over the agreed medium rate.
- Lower the priority of packets over the agreed burst size.

In the first example of a policy rule the condition is: "packets are out-of-bounds with respect to negotiated SLA"; while the action is: "mark packets for dropping".

Policy management is a broad technical issue, and for further reading a visit to the IETF Policy Framework Working Group Web site (www.ietf.org) is recommended.

3.4.2 Queue Scheduling

Queue scheduling corresponds to the set of algorithms or mechanisms used to control the way packets are sent from an input to output queue in routers. The scheduler analyzes packets from queues for eligibility. The best eligible packet per queue and per algorithm is scheduled and serviced.

In IP routers, the queue scheduling algorithms are targeted to optimize IP operation and improve QoS parameters.

The main goals for queue scheduling mechanisms used in IP routers are the following:

- To share bandwidth fairly.
- To guarantee QoS parameters like bandwidth and delay for certain types of applications, for instance, time-sensitive ones.
- To reduce jitter.
- To prevent bandwidth starvation among IP users.

There are many alternatives for scheduling IP packets on router queues, most of which have proprietary implementations. Some of the most frequently used algorithms found in IP routers are:

- First-in first-out (FIFO)
- Round-robin (RR) and weighted round-robin queuing (WRR)
- Priority queuing (PQ)
- Weighted-fair queuing (WFQ).

3.4.2.1 First-In First-Out First-in first-out (FIFO), also called first-come first-served algorithm (FCFS), is the simplest and most typical default solution found in routers. As the name suggests, packets are switched from input to output queues in order of arrival independently of their size, type, contents, or any other packet characteristics (Fig. 3.18).

Considering IP routing, the FIFO algorithm's main advantage is simplicity and that it behaves well in the absence of network congestion. It consumes far less processing than any subsequently discussed algorithms, and thus can be used with very high-speed interfaces.

With heavy traffic or during congestion, the FIFO algorithm creates a potential problem for QoS enforcement in routers.

First, since it does not distinguish packet lengths, small packets may experience long delays while long packets are transmitted. Assuming the short packets are generated by a real-time or QoS-demanding application, this characteristic contributes to increased router blindness to critical applications.

Second, packet dropping is executed at random, as far as the type of packet or type of packet content is concerned. Usually, routers using FIFO execute tail drop (arbitrarily). This characteristic is very undesirable or even unacceptable for most critical applications since it increases packet loss without criteria. Besides that, in this operation, packets with low priority may pass through while critical packets are being dropped out.

In brief, the disadvantages of FIFO include unfairness and the impossibility of guaranteeing bandwidth or delay parameters for QoS enforcement over routers.

3.4.2.2 *Priority Queuing*
Priority queuing (PQ) is a very common solution in routers. In PQ, packets are typically sent to n queues, which are assigned relative priorities (0 to $n - 1$). These priorities set a relative ordering (high to low) for servicing the queues for a given interface. In PQ, packets in higher priority queues are serviced first. Besides that, packets in queue k are serviced only if queues 0 to $K - 1$ are empty. Figure 3.19 illustrates PQ operation.

Considering IP routing, the main advantages of PQ are high throughput, lower delay, and higher bandwidth to packets in higher priority queues.

Queues in PQ may experience resource starvation, which is one of its most serious problems. Since there is an order for servicing queues, it may happen that low-priority

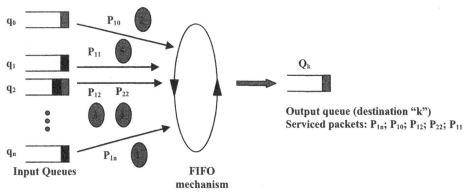

P_{xy}: Packet "x" at queue "y"

Order of arrival: P_{1n}; P_{10}; P_{12}; P_{22}; P_{11}. (packets to destination "k")
FIFO queuing: P_{1n}; P_{10}; P_{12}; P_{22}; P_{11}

Figure 3.18 Basic FIFO operation.

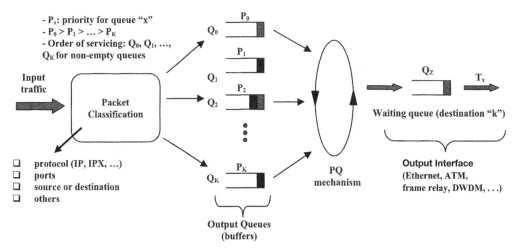

Figure 3.19   Priority queuing operation.

queues starve for resources, which happens when any highest-priority queue remains occupied. There is, therefore, a compromise between the traffic receiving the lowest possible delay and the low-priority traffic, which should receive minimum resources. Often, the use of PQ assumes that admission policies and control are used to limit the amount of high-priority traffic in high-priority queues, somehow regulating the starvation problem.

In PQ, several levels of granularity for traffic classification are possible. For instance, traffic may be prioritized by the type of packet (IP, IPX, or other), or by the type of application (VoIP, HTTP, FTP, etc.). In the first case, IP packets may be delivered before IPX packets and, in the second case, packets carrying VoIP application data identified by the RTP protocol may go ahead of packets carrying HTTP application data. Higher levels of granularity have the disadvantage of increasing the packet processing overhead for classification and queuing, and, as such, have often to be limited in practical PQ applications. One of the resulting considerations of the previous discussion is that PQ does not scale well for higher levels of granularity.

In general terms, PQ can be considered to be the most "primitive" method to differentiate traffic for scheduling. For this reason, more "refined" algorithms exist and are the focus of the following discussion.

3.4.2.3 Round-Robin and Weighted Round-Robin Queuing   In round-robin (RR), packets are classified and sent to m queues. Classification, as seen previously, may be performed by type of packet, type of application or any other packet characteristic. The queues in the basic RR algorithm are serviced in order (0 to $m - 1$), one packet at a time (Fig. 3.20).

RR solves the starvation problem, since all queues are periodically served by the RR discipline, but introduces new problems.

First, RR does not consider packet size, and is consequently unfair. In some cases, small critical packets may wait for long periods in queues while large noncritical packets are serviced. Second, RR cannot provide guarantees for bandwidth or delays.

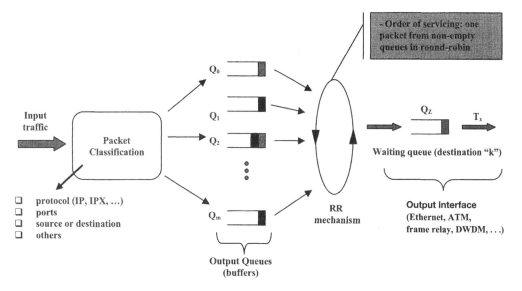

Figure 3.20   Round-robin operation.

Weighted round-robin (WRR) is one possible variation of the RR discipline. In WRR, more than one packet can be serviced in turn for a particular queue. As in the RR algorithm, if packet sizes are different, the algorithm deviates from a strict relative resource allocation strategy and is therefore unfair.

3.4.2.4 Weighted-Fair Queuing
Weighted-fair queuing (WFQ) is another algorithm used in routers in an attempt to provide fairness, to deliver predictable behavior to packet flow, and to avoid the resource starvation problem.

WFQ is an approximation of the generalized processor sharing (GPS) algorithm. GPS is an algorithm that provides fairness by visiting each active (nonempty) queue in turn and servicing it bit by bit (infinitesimal service). The basic problem with GPS is that it does not have a feasible implementation, since it can serve only whole packets.

In WFQ, packets are served in order of their "finish times." To compute finish times, the WFQ operation maintains two variables (assuming weights are 1 for all queues):

- The current round number
- The finish time (packet state information maintained per queue)

The round number, as the name suggests, corresponds to the number of rounds of service completed by the round-robin scheduler, supposing that the algorithm serves one bit from each active queue. The round number reflects the amount of traffic served for the active queues. The round number may be fractional, where fractions represent partially completed rounds.

To show the computation of the "finish time" (F_i) at queue, i, suppose a packet of length L, arrives to an empty queue when the round number is R. The finish time for this packet corresponds to the time of transmitting its last bit $(F_i = R + L)$. This packet will be served by WFQ discipline only when its finish time is the smallest among the queues.

When a packet arrives at an active queue (not empty), its finish time is equal to the previous packet finish time plus its size.

The following expression computes the finish time for a packet in a given queue, i:

$$F_i(x, t) = \max \{F_i(x - 1, t), R(t)\} + S_i(x, t)$$

where

$F_i(x, t)$ = finish time for packet "x" on queue "i" at arrival time "t";

$R(t)$ = round number at packet arrival time "t";

$S_i(x, t)$ = Size of packet x arriving on queue i at time t.

The round number is updated on the arrival or departure of each packet. Packet departure resulting in empty queues increases the round rate for servicing. On packet departure, the queue is considered inactive when the largest finish time in the queue is smaller than the round number. On packet arrival, the round number is recalculated and the finish time is computed.

When weights are allocated to queues, the computation of the finish time takes the weighted size packets into account as follows:

$$F_i(x, t) = \max \{F_i(x - 1, t), R(t)\} + S_i(x, t)/w(i)$$

where $w(i)$: weight on queue i. The larger the weight, the smaller the resulting finish time for a given packet size, which in practice means that more bandwidth is effectively allocated for that queue.

In brief, WFQ operation can be resumed as follows:

- On packet arrival, classification allocates the packet to a queue.
- The round number is recomputed.
- The packet finish time is computed (relative to either its previous packet on queue or the round number).
- Service the packet with the smaller finish time.

On packet departure, the WFQ algorithm services the packet with the lowest finish time. When queues are empty the algorithm goes idle.

Figure 3.21 illustrates the basic WFQ operation. In brief, the general characteristics of WFQ are fair in that:

- Traffic with small sized packets are not compromised and have an effective priority.
- Traffic of large packets does not hog bandwidth.
- The use of weights for queues allows an intrinsic allocation of more resources (bandwidth) for time sensitive traffic.

WFQ also provides performance guarantees:

- Bandwidth bound
- End-to-end delay bound

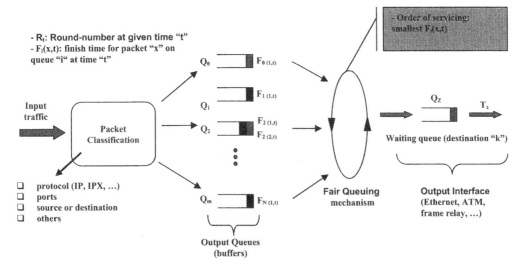

Figure 3.21 The WFQ operation.

Bandwidth bound is achieved by rating link capacity, thus allowing queues to receive minimum amounts of the available bandwidth. End-to-end delay bound is achieved if queues are regulated, for instance, by a token-bucket filter; otherwise, too many packets will arrive and will be stuck in queues.

3.4.2.5 Other Scheduling Approaches There are additional technical alternatives for queue scheduling, such as:

- Virtual clock
- Deficit round-robin (DRR)
- Distributed weighted-fair queuing (DWFQ)
- Class-based queuing (CBQ).

These alternatives are either variations of the basic queue scheduling algorithms previously discussed, proprietary implementations of generic solutions, or new ideas, which may be implemented in routers. For further details of these solutions, the references at the end of this chapter should be consulted.

3.4.3 Congestion Control

Congestion control is the general term for the set of mechanisms used to both prevent and eliminate congestion in networks.

Congestion occurs because packets can go "from any input queue, to any output queue," at any moment. In other words, for an unpredictable period, T, up to $(n-1)$ of n possible input queues could be directed to a single output queue. Since bandwidth is normally limited in packet-switched networks and IP routers, in particular, congestion can occur at any time.

Congestion control techniques are installed capabilities available on routers and switches that have the ability to control flow and deal with excessive traffic during congestion periods.

One of the first basic points concerning congestion is the perception of its effects on data flows. Congestion may influence basic QoS parameters:

- Congestion can increases packet loss
- Congestion can increases delay and jitter

During congestion periods, packets are dropped out, causing packet loss to increase for the corresponding data flows. Depending on the level of congestion, all flows may experience packet losses.

Transport protocols (TCP or UDP) are also influenced by congestion. In TCP, lost packets are interpreted as signaling congestion and cause resynchronization among TCP peers. In effect, lost packets trigger the TCP slow-start algorithm and other procedures to adapt TCP flow to the underlying network throughput capacity. TCP slow-start triggering results in delay increase and jitter variation.

In UDP, delay and jitter variation result mainly from either additional packet processing and overload at output queues or resynchronization procedures, whenever they are used at the application level. Longer output queues result in longer delay for packets waiting on these queues.

The congestion control techniques differ in the threshold the moment they start to deal with the congestion problem. It is worthwhile to distinguish between congestion management and congestion avoidance techniques. *Congestion management* deals with techniques and strategies used to eliminate congestion once it begins. Congestion management comprises reactive techniques, which typically try to manage congestion by reducing data flow intensities over the network. *Congestion avoidance* comprises techniques and strategies that try to prevent congestion from occurring. These strategies are proactive techniques that basically try to avoid the nasty effects of congestion on data flows.

Another important aspect of congestion is the identification or detection of a congestion situation or congestion period. The point is: How can congestion be identified, for instance, in a router?

Typically, an excessive queue length can signal a congestion situation. In other words, the queue length is normally the most usual parameter used to identify congestion. The actual optimal queue length depends on a number of factors, such as traffic type (bursty, adaptative, etc.).

The basic approaches used to control congestion are the following:

- Tail drop
- Random early detection (RED)
- Explicit congestion notification (ECN)

Tail drop is a straightforward mechanism in which incoming packets are dropped if the output queue for the packet is full. RED is a general technique in which packets are discarded with a certain probability in order to prevent congestion [2]. ECN is another technique proposed for routers to modify a congestion situation to ECN-capable end systems.

3.4.3.1 Tail Drop As previously indicated in this section, tail drop is a straightforward mechanism in which incoming packets are dropped if the output queue overflows. Tail drop is a very simple procedure, but it has disadvantages, among which are the unfair queue utilization with FIFO queue management, and TCP synchronization and recovery problems.

The main disadvantages with TCP are the global synchronization problem [3] and the recovery procedure for multiple packet losses in a single window. If many TCP hosts are sending packets simultaneously during a congestion period, tail drop will discard packets, and, consequently, TCP hosts will stop sending them in an attempt at synchronization using the slow-start algorithm. Also, multiple packet drops in the same TCP window will cause long delays on recovering. The unfair queue utilization problem occurs when a small set of flows "monopolize" the link by generating packets at a higher rate (lockout). In this condition, packets from "well behaved" flows will have a greater probability of being discarded.

3.4.3.2 Random Early Detection Random early detection (RED) is a recommended active queue management technique that attempts to prevent highly congested situations. The basic idea is to discard packets early and, in doing so, to avoid the output queues to become completely congested (queue overflow for long periods). RED discards packets proportionally from competing flows according to their average bandwidth usage once a precongestion situation is detected. As illustrated in Figure 3.22, this precongestion situation is identified by having the weighted average output queue size between a minimal (Q_{min}) and a maximum value (Q_{max}).

The RED algorithm uses a weighted average of the total queue length instead of current queue length to determine when to drop packets. This prevents RED from reacting from packet bursts, effectively allowing reaction to long-term flows.

Packets are sent to an output queue whenever the weighted-average queue length is smaller than Q_{min}. Early drop verification is performed on packets whenever the weighted-average queue length is greater than Q_{min} and smaller than Q_{max}. A forced drop will occur whenever the weighted average queue length is greater than Q_{max}.

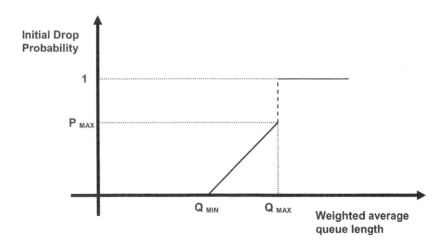

Figure 3.22 RED thresholds.

The main RED control parameters are illustrated in Table 3.2. In RED, the probability of early drop packet discarding depends on various parameters. The packet drop probability calculation follows [2]:

$$P_b = P_{max} \, (\text{avg} - Q_{min})/(Q_{max} - Q_{min}) \qquad (3.1)$$

$$P_a = P_b \, / \, (1 - \text{count} * P_b) \qquad (3.2)$$

Where:

P_b = initial drop probability

P_a = actual drop probability

avg = weighted-average queue length

P_{max} = maximum drop probability

count = number of enqueued packets since the last dropped packet

It follows that initial probability varies from 0 (zero) to P_{max}, and the actual drop probability increases with the number of enqueued packets since the last one was dropped. The general effect is that higher rate flows will have a higher number of dropped packets, since their packets arrive at a higher rate than slower rate flows.

RED operation assumes a higher-level protocol (transport); otherwise, the application eventually will somehow react to packet loss as an indication of congestion.

With TCP, the slow-start algorithm is activated and causes the reduction of packets flowing among TCP peers for the TCP connection that experienced a packet loss. Generally, it is expected that this effect will help reduce the precongestion condition and bring the total amount of enqueued packets to below the minimal threshold (Q_{min}). In the case where congestion persists, packets are systematically discarded after the maximum threshold (Q_{max}) is reached.

There are variations of RED in which the thresholds are chosen according to traffic priority, or the discard probability is adjusted to guarantee fairness, among other possibilities. Examples of these variations are weighted RED (WRED), distributed weighted RED (DWRED), fair RED (FRED), stabilized RED (SRED), and balanced RED, among other alternatives [4].

RED has no effect on UDP data flows. This is because, contrary to TCP, UDP does not back off during congestion. Also, some TCP flows may behave as a nonresponsive flow or, in other words, as an aggressive flow. That happens, for instance, with optimized TCP implementations that do not implement TCP congestion avoidance mechanisms, as proposed by IETF [5].

Table 3.2 RED Control Parameters

RED Parameter	Description
Q_{LEN}	Maximum queue length
Q_{min}	Queue length threshold for triggering probabilistic drops
Q_{max}	Queue length threshold for triggering forced drops
P_{max}	Maximum probability of early dropping

3.4.3.3 *Explicit Congestion Notification*   Explicit congestion notification (ECN) is another alternative for preventing congestion; it allows routers to set a congestion signaling bit (congestion experienced bit (CE)) in packets from ECN-capable transport protocols. The basic idea behind ECN is to signal congestion explicitly, instead of signaling congestion by dropping packets.

Using ECN instead of packet drop as a mechanism to signal congestion has the following advantages:

- Signaling congestion reduces packet loss.
- ECN allows different actions on end nodes.
- Coupled with active queue management, in which routers detect congestion and precongestion situations, ECN effectively separates the policies for queuing and dropping from the policies for indicating congestion.

To this end, ECN signaling must be carried in IP packets. The bits used are illustrated in Figure 3.23.

The ECN-capable transport bit is set by the data sender to report that ECN capability is available on the endpoints. The CE bit is set by the router to indicate congestion to the endpoints.

Basic ECN operation is very simple, as illustrated in Figure 3.24. Once a router receives a packet from an ECN-capable transport source and congestion is detected, the CE bit is set and the packet is forwarded to its destination (in RED, the packet would be even-

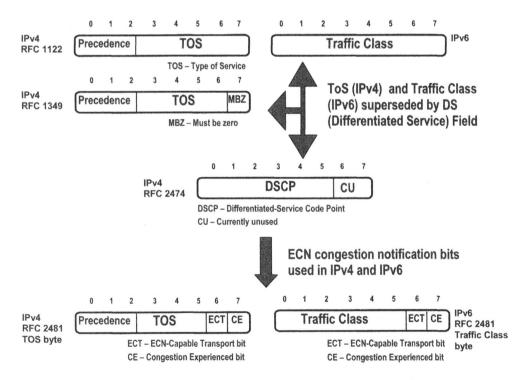

Figure 3.23   ECN bits in IPv4 and IPv6 packet headers.

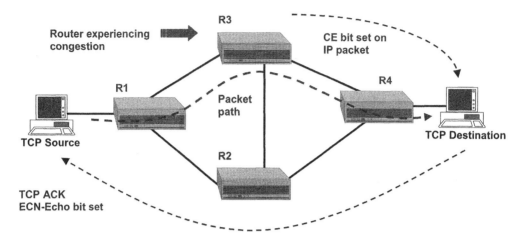

Figure 3.24 ECN notification between IP and TCP peers.

tually dropped). At the destination, ECN assumes that the transport protocol (for instance, TCP) will signal back to source the congestion indication. Upon receipt of that signal, the source will execute essentially an equivalent congestion-control algorithm as that used for packet dropping. This last condition is essential for the coexistence between ECN and non-ECN endpoints and nodes, allowing the gradual adoption of this solution.

As indicated earlier, the transport protocol must support ECN. In TCP, three mechanisms are required:

- Negotiation between endpoints to identify ECN capabilities.
- An ECN-echo flag is designated to signal back to the TCP source the congestion indication bit (CE).
- A congestion window reduced (CWR) flag is designated to indicate when the TCP destination should stop sending the congestion indication bit (CE).

The ECN-echo flag is set by the TCP destination in the next TCP ACK (ECN-echo ACK packet) whenever a CE bit is received. When a TCP ACK with ECN-echo set is received by the TCP source, it triggers the TCP congestion control algorithm:

- TCP halves the congestion window (cwnd)
- TCP reduces the slow start threshold (ssthresh)

0	1	2	3	4	5	6	7	8	9	10	11	12	13	14	15

IPv4 - RFC 2481 TCP header ECN bits

Header length	Reserved bits (4)	CWR	ECN*	TCP Flags

ECN* – ECN-Echo Flag bit
CWR – Congestion Window Reduced bit
TCP Flags – URG (10), ACK (11), PSH (12), RST (13), SYN (14), FIN (15)
(bit position)

Figure 3.25 ECN bits in TCP header.

After these steps cause the TCP data flow to back off, the TCP source will set the CWR bit in the next TCP data packet in order to signal to the TCP destination to stop sending TCP ACK with ECN-echo.

In the TCP header, the ECN bits are positioned as indicated in Figure 3.25.

3.5 INTEGRATED SERVICES ARCHITECTURE

In this section we will introduce the main initiatives being proposed by the IETF, and we will elaborate on the IntServ [6].

3.5.1 IETF Quality of Service Strategies and Initiatives

The IETF has been actively involved in the development of a standardized support for multimedia applications over IP networks and, in particular, for the Internet.

For the scope of this discussion, we will consider three major standardized alternatives, which can be used to provide QoS for multimedia applications:

- The IntServ
- The DiffServ
- The MPLS solution

This section presents and discusses IntServ, a proposed IETF strategy oriented to provide QoS to individual flows.

3.5.2 Goals and Basics

The main idea behind the IntServ architecture initiative is to expand the Internet basic service model.

The basic Internet model is based on best-effort services. Best-effort services do not guarantee QoS parameters like bandwidth and delay and, thus, are very limited for supporting many user applications.

The IntServ architecture proposes an "Integrated Service Model." In this model, individual flows are identified and specific QoS flow requirements may be enforced on an end-to-end basis. IntServ effectively allows an application to request QoS from the network with high capillarity and thus is of great importance to end users.

In IntServ, all types of digitally represented information (conventional data, voice, video, text, graphics, and so on) are transported in a single and unique network infrastructure, with their QoS requirements being either controlled or guaranteed.

Obviously, the benefits of this new set of capabilities have a great impact on IP networks:

- For corporate networks, merging different networks onto fewer or, eventually, just one network, may result in significant economic benefits.
- The Internet represents the possibility of supporting multimedia applications with high capillarity.

It is important to observe that this goal is not a new idea. The integrated services digital network (ISDN) in the 1970s and the broadband ISDN (B-ISDN) in the 1980s were earlier attempts to provide a common or integrated infrastructure for a wide range of applications. IntServ, the new architecture proposed, targets IP networks and, in particular, the Internet.

The point now is how to implement the "Integrated Services Architecture" or, in other words, how to put this new model into practice?

The proposed new capabilities of integrated services require the following basic functionalities:

- Network nodes, mainly routers, must be able to support and control QoS delivered for IP packets.
- Application of QoS requirements must be signaled to all network nodes involved in the end-to-end path from source to destination.

The first functionality mentioned earlier corresponds to the "service" supported by the IP network nodes (routers) and must be precisely defined. The following services have been defined for IntServ compliant networks:

- Guaranteed service
- Controlled-load service

The second functionality can be provided by a signaling protocol. RSVP [7] is the protocol frequently used in IntServ implementations (Fig. 3.26). Thus, RSVP can be considered as an essential component of the IntServ initiative, responsible for signaling QoS requirements for nodes in the network's infrastructure. RSVP characteristics are detailed in Section 3.5.5, and have great importance on the overall IntServ applicability.

Before discussing RSVP in more detail, we will explore the IntServ architecture, its characteristics, and basic services.

3.5.3 Integrated Service Architecture: Characteristics and Services

There is a basic conception principle adopted by the IntServ architecture: "The Quality of Service in IntServ compliant network infrastructures is supported by a *resource reservation mechanism* applied to packet flows."

This conception principle requires IntServ nodes and users to follow an operational model summarized as follows:

Figure 3.26   IntServ and RSVP.

- First, QoS parameters have to be identified by users in order to be properly request-ed from network nodes.

- Once users identify their QoS application requirements, they must request IntServ nodes to support them. This is done, for instance, by requesting services using the RSVP signaling protocol between end-user and network nodes.

- Since IntServ uses a reservation-based model, nodes must perform validation steps before granting access to the required QoS parameters. In other words, network nodes must perform admission control before accepting any new flow of packets between users.

- Once access is granted to the network, IntServ nodes must continuously identify flows, provide the required QoS for the flows, verify conformance to flow charac-teristics, and police traffic flows.

Other important characteristics of IntServ are:

- IntServ uses state information to keep track of IP packet flows through the network. State information is kept on IntServ routers and is necessary for service processing. This characteristic differs considerably from the classic IP assumption in which packets are processed independently at every node, and it has some scalability im-plications discussed later.

- IntServ does not attempt to alter basic packet routing. In effect, routing paths are processed and maintained using any routing protocol (unicast or multicast) like open shortest path first (OSPF) and border gateway protocol (BGP), among other alternatives.

- Best effort traffic is the default service for packets that are not part of defined flows. Also, best effort traffic has to be considered in the overall IntServ design. In effect, the allocated resources for IntServ services (bandwidth, memory) should not cause best effort flows to starve.

In the next section, flow definition and flow requirements that the IntServ will support are discussed.

3.5.3.1 *Flow Definition and Requirements*   Data flows have to be characterized as signaled source, destination, and network nodes. Figure 3.27 illustrates a typical flow specification signaling for a given packet flow between a source and a destination.

TSpec defines the source packet's flow specification, giving characteristics of the data traffic to be handled. TSpec indicates transmitter configuration parameters such as peak rate, average transmission rate, and packet size.

RSpec defines the receiver packet's flow specification. RSpec indicates the desired ser-vice or, alternatively, the receiver configuration. Parameters defined in RSpec are the ser-vice requested and its characterization, for instance, in terms of delay bounds.

3.5.4 Services

The services defined in IntServ architecture have the philosophical intention of eliminat-ing, as much as possible, the randomness characteristics of delay, jitter, and bandwidth

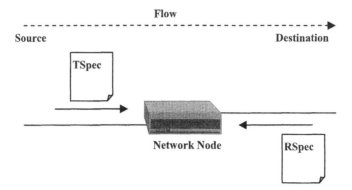

Figure 3.27   IntServ flow specification.

found in basic IP services. In other words, IntServ services will attempt to guarantee some QoS parameters on an end-to-end basis.

As stated earlier, there are two basic services defined in IntServ architecture, which are also called service elements:

- Guaranteed service
- Controlled-load service

3.5.4.1 Guaranteed Service   Guaranteed service guarantees limited delays for packets on a policed flow with no queuing loss. The resulting end-to-end behavior for this service is such that a maximum delay bound is guaranteed all along the application's flow path. Guaranteed service also guarantees bandwidth limits, since there is an agreement about the maximum flow bandwidth the user is supposed to deliver at any time. This property of the flow is actually policed at every network node.

Guaranteed service can also be understood as the equivalent of a conventional leased-line service where there is a precise definition for the available bandwidth and corresponding transmitting delay.

IntServ specifies requirements for achieving a guaranteed reservation, but does not specify how to set up these requirements. Various setup methods can be used to guarantee reservations in the IntServ model. Here are some alternatives:

- To use a signaling protocol, for instance, like RSVP.
- To use a management protocol, for instance, like SNMP to properly configure reservation parameters at every network node.
- To manually configure the nodes.

It is important to observe that only queuing delay limits are guaranteed by IntServ. As discussed in Section 3.2.4.2, end-to-end networking delay is a more general definition and has three basic components:

- Propagation delays
- Transmission delays
- Processing delays

Transmission delays refer mostly to the time required to send and receive packets over data communications links, and can be easily calculated once the link properties (speed, packet length, technology) being used are specified.

Processing delays comprise both frame processing delay, packet processing delay, and upper-level processing delay at hosts. In routers, it is a reasonable approximation to consider the processing delay component to be the summation of queuing delay processing and packet encapsulating delay processing since most of the processing involved is related to queuing mechanisms and packet encapsulation. Guaranteed service, therefore, could also be roughly understood as a solution that defines limits on processing delay for routing.

IntServ users must properly identify the queue limit when making a request of the network by analyzing the various delay components present in a network end-to-end path.

Guaranteed service is intended for hard real-time applications, which need to have guarantees, for instance, that packets will arrive at the destination within a maximal arrival time limit. Multimedia applications are potential users of IntServ guaranteed service. VoIP, for instance, is an example of an application that has well-defined parameters for packet arrival time and, as such, could benefit from this service.

3.5.4.2 *Controlled-Load Service*

The controlled-load service element is intended to guarantee QoS under overloaded traffic conditions. The basic idea of this service is that the QoS provided to the user's flow is quite close to the QoS this flow would receive under unloaded conditions, even if the network element were actually overloaded. Also, the applicability of this service is based on the observation that for the specific flow using controlled-load service the IP network works adequately if it is not heavily loaded. Therefore, the controlled-load services are adequate only for certain classes of application, in particular, those applications (like the Web-based ones) that are elastic or adaptable to modest fluctuations in network performance.

The principle behind controlled-load service is the service element's ability to keep QoS guarantees under heavily loaded conditions by controlling flow admissions and adopting queuing mechanisms with priorities to differentiate flows.

Controlled-load QoS guarantees in terms of parameters should be understood as follows:

- A high percentage of packets is successfully transmitted.
- The transit delay variation experienced by packets is kept small for a high percentage of transmitted packets.

In general terms, the behavior of a series of controlled-load service elements (routers, switch routers, or subnetworks) always resembles the best effort service provided by the same network element under unloaded conditions. If overload occurs, the QoS of controlled-load flows will behave better in relation to best effort serviced flows.

An Implementation of controlled-load services, for instance, may use a queuing mechanism with priorities to distinguish between controlled-load flows and best effort flows.

Applications should request controlled-load services to obtain, for instance, a more "stable" behavior under overloaded traffic conditions. Since the reservation-style used in IntServ is dynamic, any application capable of self-monitoring performance can benefit from IntServ controlled-load service. In this case, anytime the application monitors an unacceptable performance degradation when using a best effort service, it could dynamically switch to controlled-load service in order to improve its performance. Controlled-load service is also recommended for applications whose traffic characteristics are reasonably approximated by a TSpec. Applications characterized by more "precise" TSpecs generate less out-of-profile packets, and consequently have a more stable behavior guaranteed by network design.

In summary, IntServ architecture provides two basic solutions for QoS as follows:

- A leased-line style solution, oriented to hard real-time applications having strict delay requirements, called guaranteed service.

- A less strict solution, whose main objective is to keep the approved flows QoS parameters more invariant to instantaneous loading conditions on network nodes, known as controlled-load service.

3.5.5   Resource Reservation Protocol

The resource reservation protocol (RSVP) is a signaling protocol used by senders and receivers in a path to reserve the network resources that they need to guarantee proper application functioning. After proper setup, applications using RSVP perform with QoS.

What does the term "signaling" mean for RSVP and the integrated service model?

RSVP is not a transport protocol or, in other words, it does not transport data. In effect, RSVP carries a series of commands requesting and granting the resources (signaling) necessary for the proper execution of applications. IntServ supports requests for QoS parameters like minimal bandwidth and maximum delay. The reservation commands carried by RSVP are described in Section 3.5.5.3.

The RSVP protocol has various important characteristics. A brief discussion of each one follows.

Receiver-Oriented Protocol   RSVP is a receiver-oriented protocol, which means that receivers request reservation services. This is a flexible solution, since receivers know exactly what QoS they need, independently of transmitter capacity. It often happens that a receiver requires much fewer networking resources than the transmitter's full capacity. As an example, a video flow of 1.5 Mbps may be supported by a video server, but the personal computer receiving this data flow is only capable of handling 258 kbps of video flow due to processing limitations. In this case, RSVP receiver-oriented characteristics allows the flow to be adjusted to the receiver's capacity, thereby reducing utilization of network resources.

Soft State   RSVP uses soft state to keep track of flow reservations and their characteristics. Each network node maintains state control for all defined flows with reservations. Periodically, RSVP sends refresh messages (REFRESH) to maintain the state in all the nodes along the used path. The principle is that if no refresh message arrives in time, the actual state is destroyed and a new one has to be built upon. Soft state supports the dynamics of RSVP. In effect, users can change their reservations anytime either by application or end-user requirements. Also, new users can be added to flows dynamically. Reservations can also change due to routing reconfiguration or route failure. RSVP soft-state characteristics provide flexibility and dynamics to the network operation.

RSVP Data Flow RSVP data flows are called "sessions." The receiver side of RSVP sessions is identified by:

- Destination address (unicast or multicast);
- Protocol identification; and
- Destination port (optional).

Each data flow is considered independently of any other data flow in RSVP. The destination port should be thought of as a general identification used to separate flow information at the transport or application level. Frequently, TCP and UDP ports are used as destination port parameters.

Simplex operation RSVP is a simplex signaling protocol. Specifically, reservations are requested separately for each flow direction (source to destination and destination to source). This characteristic is relevant since, for many applications, the flow resulting from the user's communications is not balanced. As an example, in client/server applications the server-to-client flow normally carries much more application data than the flows in the opposite direction.

RSVP and Routing Protocols RSVP does not attempt to route IP packets or flows. RSVP uses routing tables created by current routing protocols (OSPF, BPG, RIP, MOSPF, etc.) to find paths between users through the network. Also, RSVP is designed to operate with any future unicast and multicast routing protocol. These considerations have two implications. First, reservations requested using RSVP do not necessarily cause any traffic engineering action on the network. In this context, reservations are only used to allocate available resources independently of any global network optimization. Second, in case of route failure or route modification, the reservation process has to be repeated, since the reservation is set up for a routing path between sender and receiver.

IPv4 and IPv6 Both IPv4 and IPv6 protocols support RSVP. As stated earlier, RSVP uses these routing protocols by reading their routing database for forwarding packets. IPv6 packets can be tagged with "flow labels" in their headers. As the name suggests, flow labels can be used to mark packets as belonging to a certain flow. As such, this label can be used by classifiers in RSVP to identify which service has to be delivered to the packet.

3.5.5.1 *RSVP Functionalities* RSVP operation requires the following functionalities on network nodes:

- Admission control
- Policy control
- Classifier
- Scheduling

The interoperation of these functions on hosts and routers is illustrated in Figure 3.28.

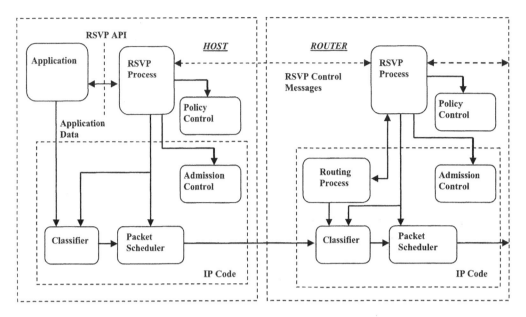

Figure 3.28   RSVP functionalities in hosts and routers.

The admission-control functionality is invoked for any new request for service. It is a decision module necessary for verifying the availability of resources at every node for new incoming requests during reservation setup.

The policy control module determines whether the user requesting a reservation has the necessary permissions. The policy control module is also invoked during reservation setup.

The classifier and packet scheduler are modules invoked during data exchange between senders and receivers. The classifier executes packet classification. Packets are associated with their specific flow and, as such, they will receive a particular QoS during forwarding processing at the packet scheduler module. Specifically, the packet scheduler identifies the packet flow and, eventually, the route information associated with the packet.

The packet scheduler module implements the scheduling mechanism for packet flows according to the service requested by the user.

In the hosts, the RSVP requests generated by applications are passed to RSVP processes through an API. This API is also responsible for passing any information or signaling generated by the RSVP process to the application programs.

Both the RSVP process and policy control modules are a user process in many RSVP implementations. The other modules composing the RSVP—the classifier, admission control, and packet scheduling—strongly interact with the IP code. As such, these modules are typically system modules within the operating system or kernel.

3.5.5.2   RSVP Operation   Now that we have examined the basic RSVP functionalities, let us develop a more precise understanding of its operation. The basic operation principle used by RSVP is that senders announce their flows to all possible receivers and receivers subsequently reserve resources for these flows according to their needs.

RSVP signaling protocol operates as illustrated in Figure 3.29, and its operation is summarized below.

First of all, senders (the origin of flows) must characterize the packet's flow that they will generate. The TSpec identifies the traffic generated by any sender in IntServ.

A sender must inform all possible unicast or multicast receivers about its packet flow. *PATH messages* containing a TSpec are then send from the sender to all receivers. PATH messages are thus used to "inform" routers and end users of possible flows.

When unicast routing is being used, there is a one-to-one relationship between sender and receiver. When multicast routing is being used, the PATH message will follow the multicast tree, ultimately reaching all active receivers for that tree. As we stated before, RSVP uses the "normal " routing protocols (unicast or multicast) supported by network nodes.

PATH messages will then follow the routing "path" provided by the normal IP routing process all the way downstream from the sender to the receivers. All RSVP-compliant routers downstream will establish a "path identification" that will keep information about the upstream sender of the PATH message. Specifically, they know the address of the upstream router from which they receive the PATH message. This information is necessary for establishing a "reservation path" along the network for the TSpec flow.

The receiver reserves resources at each network node (for instance, routers) by sending a *RESV (reservation request) message* along the upstream "path" to the sender. The RESV message will flow upstream, hop-by-hop, through the previous "marked PATH" defined by the PATH message.

The RESV message defines the service requested (guaranteed or controlled-load) and carries the *RSVP reservation* composed by the sender flow specification, called TSpec, the receiver specification, called RSpec, and a filter specification called "Filter Spec" (Fig. 3.30).

The TSpec identifies and characterizes the transmitter's flow to which the reservation and requested service should be applied. Receivers recover TSpec objects from PATH messages sent earlier by transmitters.

The RSpec specifies the requested QoS for the flow. RSpec includes information such as the service requested and parameters needed for that service.

The "Filter Spec" defines IPv4 or IPv6 filters to specify the flow (addresses, port numbers, and flow descriptor—IPv6) to which the reservation applies. The filter specification is used to set parameters in the packet classifier (Figure 3.28). The filter specification al-

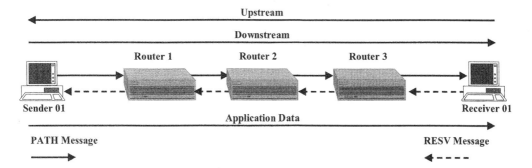

Figure 3.29   RSVP control messages.

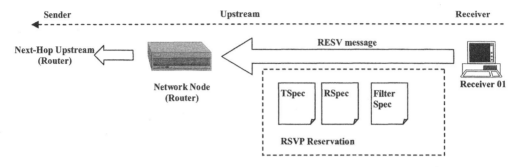

Figure 3.30 RSVP reservation with RESV message.

lows fine-coarse-grained filters. As an example, IPv6 packets with the same flow descriptor, but from different sources (different IPv6 addresses), might have different reservations and QoS guarantees in RSVP networks.

Upon reception of a RESV message, RSVP nodes must execute admission control. First, the user requesting a reservation is authenticated, and second, the node verifies if there are enough resources available to satisfy the reservation requested. In case of failure (authorization denied or unavailable resources), the node returns an error back to the receiver. Otherwise, the RESV message is sent upstream to the next network node in the path.

When the RESV message reaches the last network node and is accepted, a confirmation message is sent back to the receiver and the reservation setup process is completed. A confirmation message resulting from merging it with another already established reservation might also be sent by a node.

Receivers, senders, or intermediate nodes along the reserved path can initiate the teardown process. The teardown process removes reservations, thus releasing the corresponding allocated resources. Since the reservation is merged in the routers, the teardown process can result in selective pruning of state and resources. For instance, the teardown of one multicast receiver using less bandwidth than another multicast receiver causes the router to assign the allocated resources to the receiver remaining active.

There are two RSVP teardown messages, PATHTear and RESVTear. The first travels from receivers or routers, whichever one initiated the teardown process, in the direction of all senders. The second travels from senders or routers to all receivers in the reserved path.

3.5.5.3 RSVP Messages
The RSVP protocol uses the set of control messages indicated in Table 3.3 to allow users to make reservations.

PATH and RESV are the most important RSVP commands. A brief summary of their operation is in Table 3.4

3.5.5.3.1 PATH Message
To state their traffic specifications within an RSVP session, senders generate PATH messages. Since both unicast and multicast are supported, PATH messages can reach one or multiple receivers within an RSVP session.

PATH messages carry two basic objects (Fig. 3.31):

- TSpec (transmitter specification)
- ADSpec (advertising specification)

Table 3.3   RSVP Messages

Control Message	Action	Generation
PATH	Inform sender's traffic flows	Sender → Receiver
RESV	Reserve resources for sessions	Receiver → Sender
RESVConf	Confirm reservation request	Sender → Receiver
		Node → Receiver
PATHTear	Teardown process	Sender → Receiver
		Router → Receiver
RESVTear	Teardown process	Receiver → Sender
		Router → Sender
PATHErr	Error reporting in PATH message processing	Router → Sender
RESVErr	Error reporting in RESV message processing	Router → Receiver

As stated later, TSpec carries the senders data flow characteristics in terms of a token-bucket traffic model and identifies the sender, while ADSpec carries information generated by either senders or intermediate nodes all along the downstream path. The ADSpec objective is to support the identification of the QoS parameters, available services, and network characteristics that will be used by applications to properly request the network service. As an example, information carried by ADSpec include:

- The services (guaranteed, controlled-load) supported by nodes.
- If there are weak points for end-to-end QoS guarantees, such as a network node not supporting RSVP reservations.
- The minimal path maximum transfer unit (MTU), which is a necessary parameter to avoid packet fragmentation all along the reserved path.
- Identify the "C" and "D" delay bounds necessary for determining guaranteed service reservation parameters.

Table 3.4   RSVP Messages PATH and RESV

RSVP Message	RSVP Message Processing
PATH message	Send by sources of data flow
	Information provided to receivers:
	• source data flow characteristics
	• network resources
	Nodes processing:
	• identifies path upstream from receivers to source
	• finds route to receiver
RESV message	Send by data flow's receiver
	Information provided by receivers:
	• service requested
	• service parameters
	Nodes processing:
	• checks resources availability
	• establishes reservation

ADSpec information is altered and updated by routers all along the reserved path, but TSpec remains unaltered.

ADSpec provides an enhancement to the reservation setup process. In effect, receivers request reservations sending RESV messages that are either accepted or rejected at each node. Upon rejection, receivers have little recourse beyond guessing the next request, unless they have some previous knowledge of network parameters. ADSpec, also called "one pass with advertising" (OPWA), provides "knowledge" to receivers by collecting network characteristics and parameters.

Once PATH messages reach their destination(s), TSpec and ADSpec objects are passed to user application. The application then computes its RSpec reflecting its QoS needs based on the information gathered.

Figure 3.32 illustrates the exchange of PATH and RESV control messages during the reservation setup process.

3.5.5.4 *Reservation Models* Resource reservations in RSVP can have different styles or reservation models. The style or reservation model determines the treatment a RSVP node will apply to data flow sources within a RSVP session. Figure 3.33 illustrates possible alternatives. First, when multiple senders are in the same RSVP session, resources might or might not be shared among then. For instance, resources might be shared among data sources, or each source could use "separate" resources. Second, the sender's choice in RSVP reservations may be deterministic (for instance, including all source IP address) or, alternatively, reservations may use a wildcard representation to senders. The possible reservation styles actually defined are:

- Fixed-filter style
- Shared-filter style
- Wildcard-filter style

In the fixed-filter style (FF), "separate" reservations are created for "explicit" senders. In that case, different senders for the same session will have separate network resources reserved by the RSVP node. The RSVP representation for the FF style is:

$$FF(S\{Q\}) \tag{3.3}$$

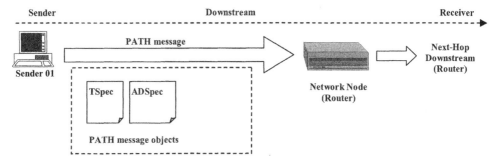

Figure 3.31 PATH message.

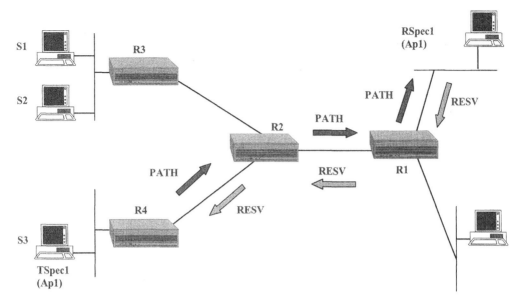

Figure 3.32 Control message exchange during setup process.

where

S = sender

Q = flow specification (flowspec)

In the shared filter style (SF), reservations (implicitly network resources) are "shared" among "explicit" senders. In this case, a group of senders "share" resources allocated for a session. The RSVP representation for the SF style is:

$$SF(S1\{Q\}, S2\{Q\}, \ldots) \qquad (3.4)$$

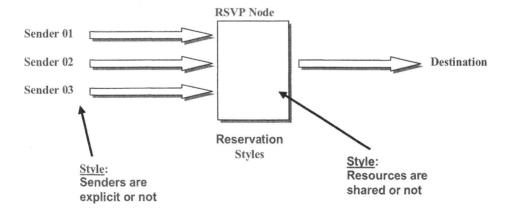

Figure 3.33 Alternative styles for RSVP reservations.

In the wildcard-filter style (WF), reservations are "shared" among wildcard-selected senders. WF reservations correspond to having a single reservation being used by flows from all upstream senders. With the WF style, new senders can join the session at any time and share the reserved resources. The RSVP representation for the wildcard-filter style is:

$$WF(*\{Q\}) \qquad (3.5)$$

3.5.5.4.1 Reservation Merging   The RSVP operation allows reservations to merge in an appropriate and efficient way. Reservation merging results in optimized network resource utilization. The point is that network resources (bandwidth, memory, etc.) are scarce and therefore they should not be wasted. As an example, Figure 3.34 illustrates reservation merges with different resources. At router R1 reservations are merged such that the same flows receive, when available, the highest level of requested resources. From R1 to R3, for instance, an upstream RESV message will carry an RSpec requesting QoS levels defined by Q1, which is assumed to be higher than Q2.

By definition, different reservation styles cannot be merged since erroneous situations may occur.

Figure 3.35 illustrates another example of reservation merge, where the WF style is used. Multicast applications could use this reservation style to reserve resources. In that case, the multicast receiver sends reservation request to any sender. The RESV message follows the multicast tree upstream to all possible active senders. From the RSVP point of view, active senders are those senders that previously sent PATH messages. Also, it is important to notice that RSVP allows many-to-many configurations, in which multiple senders are simultaneously sending flows to multiple receivers.

3.5.6   RSVP: Final Considerations

Now that we have examined the overall RSVP operation, let us discuss its application to networks in more detail. The following technical aspects are considered:

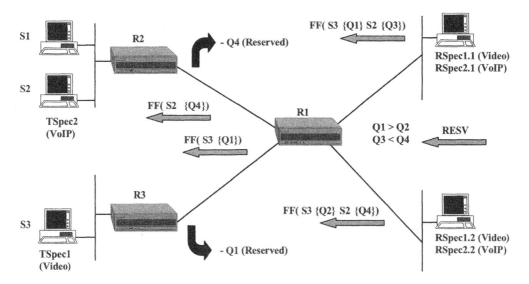

Figure 3.34   A RSVP reservation merge for the FF style.

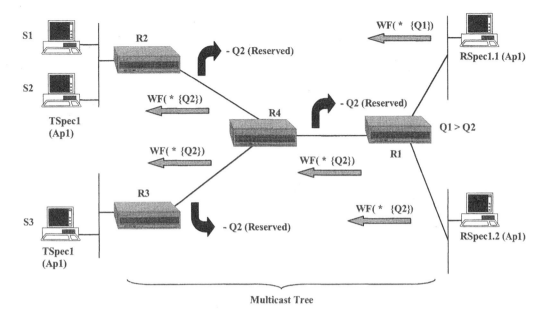

Figure 3.35   Reservation merge with the WF style.

- Signaling complexity
- State control
- Granularity
- Migration path

In brief, there is a scalability problem to handle when using RSVP as a generalized solution for supporting QoS guarantees over complex network infrastructures.

In effect, RSVP requires interior nodes to keep information on the state of each flow. In large networks, this leads to the so-called "state explosion problem," and effectively represents a potential problem for RSVP implementation. For reasonably sized networks, in which the number of total flows is somehow limited, the scalability problem does not represent a potential problem.

Another problem faced in large networks by RSVP is signaling complexity. Here, we have two basic considerations: the complexity involved in RSVP message processing and the number of messages necessary to set up and maintain a reservation. RSVP message processing requires a great deal of processing and may be a limitation for high-speed routers. The number of exchanged messages is another potential problem. As an example, reservations are kept in "soft" states and, as such, must be periodically refreshed. This characteristic limits RSVP applicability to networks in which the number of simultaneous flows is large.

A final concern about RSVP implementation is related to the migration path necessary for adopting the solution. In effect, RSVP requires a "system" to be installed. In other words, routers, hosts, and applications must be updated in order to guarantee an end-to-end support for this solution in the network. Since this requires time and investment, migration is not necessarily straightforward.

Granularity is an important characteristic of RSVP protocol and its corresponding integrated services model. In effect, real-time, mission-critical, and other new applications require QoS flows to be explicitly enforced. In this context, RSVP and the integrated service approach is certainly necessary.

In the context of complex networks, where applications require flow control, it may be possible that an IntServ solution will be integrated with other QoS initiatives in order to provide both flow control and high-performance processing at network nodes.

3.6   DIFFERENTIATED SERVICES ARCHITECTURE

There are three major standardized alternatives to support QoS enforcement for multimedia applications: the IntServ architecture, the differentiated services (DiffServ) architecture, and MPLS. This section presents DiffServ [8], a coarse-grained approach providing QoS to aggregated traffic. This initiative has been standardized in IETF.

3.6.1   Goals and Basics

The main idea of the DiffServ architecture initiative is to provide differentiated services to an "aggregate of flows" in an IP network.

In DiffServ, flows are not treated individually but are considered in groups. In effect, only a few services or behaviors are instantiated at network nodes and, as such, user's flows must be treated in aggregates if they are to to receive the available services. It is expected that DiffServ will support a large number of user flows, thus allowing this solution to adequately support QoS in very large networks, such as the Internet.

As in the previously discussed solution, the DiffServ initiative intends to expand the basic Internet best effort service model. In its basics, DiffServ allows all types of digitally represented information (conventional data, voice, video, text, graphics, and so on) to be transported in a single and unique IP network infrastructure, while their QoS requirements are being supported.

The question we can now ask is how to put this new proposition to work in practice.

DiffServ architecture proposes a "differentiated service model." This model requires the following basic functionalities to be implemented in IP networks:

- Network nodes must be able to support and control the QoS required for IP packet aggregates.
- IP packets must be "marked" with their QoS requirements.

The first function just mentioned corresponds to the "services" actually supported by IP network nodes in DiffServ. IETF defines the following services:

- The Expedited Forwarding (EF) service
- The Assured Forwarding (AF) service

The second function can be provided by simply "marking" packets according to their required QoS. This marking procedure in DiffServ is often realized at network borders, but it is also possible to mark or remark packets at nodes within the network.

As an illustration, the packet markings in DiffServ compliant networks are realized by the differentiated service byte (DS byte), which is equivalent to a packet tag (Figure 3.36). Once marked, a packet is said to belong to a specific "class" that will receive a specific service at network nodes. This simple yet powerful principle allows, for instance, service providers to classify user's flows in a limited number of classes and provide to these classes a set of basic common services.

In the next section, we will explore in more detail the model and the services supported by a DiffServ-compliant network and how these services are mapped to network node operation.

3.6.2 Differentiated Service Architecture

First, it is important to realize what the main focus for DiffServ architecture services is EF and AF and what the operational model defined by the DiffServ architecture is.

The DiffServ model has been proposed to mainly support the QoS services in complex networks with many network nodes, like routers, and many simultaneous user applications demanding QoS. This is a situation with potential scaling problems, which is why the DiffServ architecture is made to scale to a large number of users.

Roughly, the basic idea is to:

- Aggregate user's flow and application traffic streams in a small and manageable number of *traffic classes*.
- Process and forward packets according to their assigned classes.
- Avoid using signaling at every hop.

Traffic stream aggregation is an important aspect in DiffServ. Users of the DiffServ network-capable infrastructure benefit from the services they need by having their packets marked with DSCP. Marking can be done, for instance, at DiffServ network borders, although packets can be also marked elsewhere:

- In hosts
- At the first hop router after the host
- In a specific equipment such as a VoIP gateway

This simple approach has a number of advantageous features for large and complex networks:

- First of all, packet processing is considerably reduced in network core nodes with respect to the total number of end-user flows (also called microflows). This happens

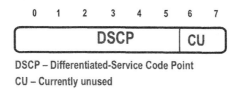

DSCP – Differentiated-Service Code Point
CU – Currently unused

Figure 3.36 Differentiated services field (DS byte).

because there is no per-flow state, with packets being processed according to their class.

* Network provisioning is defined by the characteristics of the services provided for each class.

The DiffServ model presents potential benefits, for instance, in ISP networks. In effect, ISPs normally negotiate a service profile with their clients (users and applications). This negotiation is formalized by typically defining an SLA in which QoS or other traffic and service characteristics are agreed upon.

Once a user's SLA is defined, packets from users and applications have to be processed according to the services negotiated. For scaling reasons, SLAs ("service profiles") are negotiated and policed in the DiffServ network for a set of *aggregate flows.*

From the technical point of view, this means that ISP networks using the DiffServ model benefit from the fact that services provided in network nodes may be the same for various end-user flows (microflows), as long as packets from these flows are assigned for the same DiffServ class. Marking packets appropriately in a small number of predefined and negotiated classes is a more scalable solution, since there is less router processing involved.

Finally, ISP network service provisioning can be adjusted to the number of users, network resources available, and type of services supported by the network.

From the previous discussion we can write the basic conception principle used by DiffServ architecture:

A reservationless model supports the QoS in DiffServ-compliant network infrastructures where *marked packets,* corresponding to a *group of end-user applications,* receive a predefined *service* or processing in network core nodes.

To understand this principle in more detail, let us consider more carefully the network nodes, the functionality, and the terminology adopted by DiffServ architecture. Figure 3.37 illustrates a typical DiffServ network or DiffServ domain.

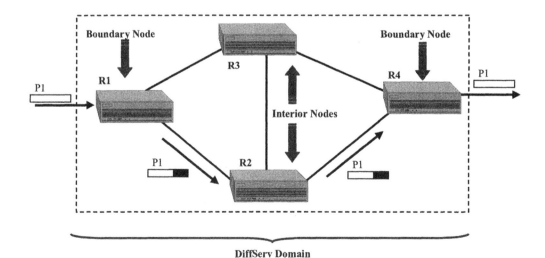

Figure 3.37 Basic DiffServ network elements.

First, let us consider the DiffServ *domain* concept. A DiffServ domain is a set of network nodes, typically routers, cooperating to provide predefined services (EF and AF) to packet streams classified into classes. There are two types of nodes in DiffServ domains: boundary nodes and interior nodes. Boundary nodes connect the DiffServ domain cloud to other domains. Interior nodes are connected to other interior nodes or boundary nodes and always belong to the same DiffServ domain. Boundary nodes can be either ingress nodes or egress nodes, depending on packet flow direction. As an example, the router located at the entry point is called an "ingress router" (Fig. 3.38). It typically implements a set of functions to allow "normal IP packets" to benefit from DiffServ services.

Core routers (internal routers) are mainly responsible for the optimized IP processing for marked packets. These marked packets are supposed to receive AF and EF services while traveling hop to hop through the DiffServ domain. In DiffServ terminology, the way the routers process the marked packets is termed "per-hop behavior" (PHB) (Fig. 3.38).

The router located at the outer edge of a DiffServ domain is called an "egress router." Egress routers process marked packets according to their required services and, may also unmark packets when they leave the DiffServ domain. Egress routers may also condition the outgoing traffic to make it compliant with interdomain traffic agreements.

3.6.3   Service-Level Specification and Traffic Conditioning Specification

As stated earlier, services are negotiated beforehand between customers and service providers and are typically defined in terms of service-level agreements (SLA) and traffic conditioning agreements (TCA) by the large majority of network service providers.

An SLA is a service contract between a customer and a service provider that typically defines all business and technical aspects of their interaction, such as:

- Services provided and their basic properties
- QoS parameters for each service

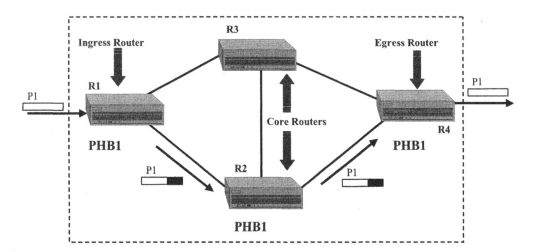

Figure 3.38   Per-hop behavior in DiffServ networks.

- Other technical aspects (availability, resilience, etc.)
- Rules for services (TCA)
- Contractual basis (pricing, discounts, etc.)
- Other technical or business aspects

TCAs can be understood as the definition of *requirements or rules for services*. In other words, it is necessary to precisely define the traffic stream (bandwidth, bursts, and other traffic characteristics) the service provider will handle for each customer and negotiated service. This is certainly essential for network resources provisioning and many other network operational characteristics, such as billing and fairness. An SLA may include the rules for services, which constitute the TCA.

SLA and TCA are general terms that encompass parameters and characteristics beyond the scope of DiffServ. This being so, new terms have been proposed for DiffServ-compliant networks.

Services provided by a DiffServ domain are defined in *service-level specifications* (SLS), and rules for this service are expressed in *traffic conditioning specifications* (TCS) (Figure 3.39).

SLS, like SLA, is a service contract that defines the service provided by the DiffServ domain, and typically specifies:

- The specific DiffServ service (AF, EF) the customer should receive
- Service parameter values
- The rules for that service (TCS)

TCS is an integral element of an SLS, and specifies traffic rules and requirements, such as:

- Traffic profiles
- Classifier rules
- Action on traffic streams (in-profile and out-of-profile traffic)

Traffic profiles specify the expected temporal properties of a traffic stream, the classifier rules specify how input traffic is classified, and actions are defined under various instantaneous and long-term traffic stream conditions.

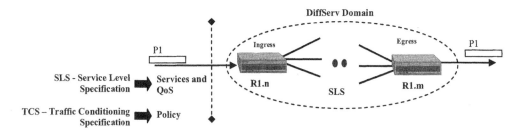

Figure 3.39 Service Level Specifications and Traffic Conditioning Specification in a DiffServ Domain.

In simple terms, DiffServ domains have an entry point and an exit point with respect to the stream of packets and negotiated services. In terms of the SLS, it defines the services that are implemented within the DiffServ domain.

In multi-domain DiffServ implementations, SLSs should be agreed at each network entry point and boundaries between DiffServ domains are not covered by SLSs (Figure 3.40).

3.6.4   DiffServ Functionalities

As mentioned earlier, ingress, core, and egress routers have to process marked packets within a DiffServ domain in order to implement predefined services (EF and AF) and to have PHBs.

In DiffServ architecture, the network nodes support the following functionalities:

- Packet classification
- Traffic monitoring
- Packet marking
- Traffic conditioning (shaping and dropping)
- Behavior classification
- Packet scheduling

Figure 3.41 illustrates a typical distribution of these functions among DiffServ network nodes. As illustrated in the figure, ingress routers are responsible for packet classification, stream monitoring, marking, and conditioning. Obviously, ingress routers also do forwarding processing for each packet according to its marked behavior. In most cases, core routers do only basic packet forwarding processing by identifying the correspondent packet behavior and scheduling it accordingly.

Egress routers, for instance, may optionally classify and condition packets at the DiffServ domain exit point for multidomain infrastructures. In this case, egress routers may be responsible for SLS/TCS conformance.

Let us now consider each one of these functions in more detail. Figures 3.42 and 3.43 illustrate how they interoperate in DiffServ routers.

Packet Classification   The first functionality required is to classify packets in a traffic stream. The classifier is the entity within the ingress router that checks incoming packets against *service profiles*. Service profiles indicate the following:

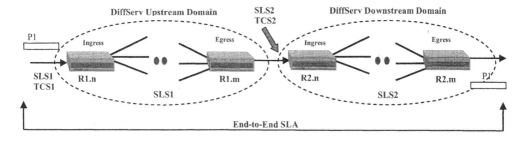

Figure 3.40   Multidomain DiffServ infrastructure.

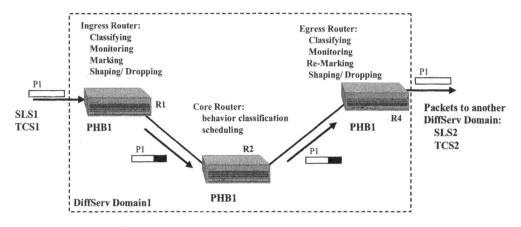

Figure 3.41 Typical functionalities in DiffServ routers.

- The flow of packets that will receive service
- The corresponding service.

Packets can be classified by IP address, protocol type, ToS, source port, destination port number, and other packet parameters or information. Multifield classification is allowed to obtain a fine-grain flow or microflow identification. There are two types of classifiers:

- Behavior aggregate (BA) classifier
- Multifield (MF) classifiers

The first classifies packets based on the DS code point only. The second classifies packets based on the value of a combination of packet header parameters, as indicated earlier. Packet classification is a time-consuming processing task realized once at the network border. Core routers do not normally execute this functionality.

Traffic Monitoring Traffic monitoring is a functionality intended to measure and keep track of the temporal properties (rate, bursts, etc.) of classified traffic streams.

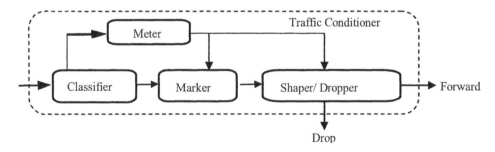

Figure 3.42 Typical ingress router functionalities.

Figure 3.43 Typical core nodes functionalities.

TCS defines the expected temporal properties of the monitored traffic streams. Essentially, traffic monitoring determines whether packets for a selected traffic streams are in-profile or out-of-profile. This classification state can be used by the marking and conditioning functions (shaping and dropping) in many other ways. Some possibilities are:

- In-profile packets are normally allowed to enter the DiffServ network, since they conform to the traffic requirements and rules.
- Out-of-profile packets can be shaped, discarded, and remarked or receive other specific actions defined in SLS.

Typically, out-of-profile packets, if allowed to enter the network, receive inferior services in relation to in-profile packets.

Packet Marking Packet marking is a functionality required to set the DSCP in classified packets. Once marked, a packet will experience a defined PHB within the DiffServ domain. In other words, once marked, a packet will belong to a specific DiffServ behavior aggregate. The DiffServ field (DS field) holds the DSCP and uses six bits of the so-called DS byte, as illustrated in Figure 3.44. The value encoded in the DS field is called DSCP. The DS byte is placed in a packet's header and corresponds to either the previous "Type of Service" octet in IPv4 or the "Traffic Class" octet in IPv6. DSCPs are used in the packet-forwarding path to differentiate the services they will receive. DSCPs are mapped to PHBs at each network node.

Traffic Conditioning Traffic conditioning is a function that verifies and eventually alters the temporal properties of a traffic stream to bring it into compliance with a specific traffic profile. In the DiffServ model, traffic conditioning is performed by combining the classifier, meter, marker, shaper, and dropper functions. In brief, traffic conditioning can mark or remark packets, shape temporal traffic properties, or drop packets in accordance with traffic conditioning rules defined in SLS/TCS.

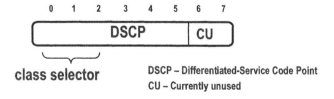

Figure 3.44 DSCP code point in DS byte.

Traffic Shaping   Traffic shaping, as the name suggests, is the process of adapting a packet stream to conform to some defined traffic profile. Traffic shaping can be achieved, for instance, by delaying out-of-profile packets within a packet stream. Traffic shaping is a necessary function in the DiffServ model because traffic sources are typically unpredictable, both in short-term and long-term perspectives. As an example, a customer may negotiate an SLS with the following traffic-stream profile:

- R = rate of packets arrival (bytes/s)
- B = allowed burst size (bytes)

Eventually, the source may alter its traffic-stream properties, either in terms of rate of packets or peak bursts. The traffic shaper would then guarantee that packets out of the shaper are always in accordance with the former temporal properties independent of any unpredictable behavior experienced by the traffic generator.

Packet Dropping   Packet dropping is another possible action for out-of-profile packets. In this case, packets are discarded as a result of *policing* the packet stream.

To summarize, classifiers and traffic conditioners are used in the DiffServ model to select which packets are to be added to a particular aggregate.

Behavior Classification   Marked packets are grouped according to their DS byte values. This functionality corresponds to aggregating traffic flows into classes to receive predefined behaviors (PHB).

Packet Scheduling   This last function schedules packets on a per-class basis.

Several scheduling mechanisms may be employed to deliver the defined PHBs. As an example, PHBs can be implemented by using PQ or WFQ, among other possibilities.

3.6.5 Differentiated Services and Per-Hop Behaviors

In the DiffServ architecture, the per-hop behavior (PHB), can be understood as the basic building block for "network services." At this point, it is important to observe that overall services are obtained as a result of multiple behaviors experienced by packets in network nodes. The term per-domain behavior (PDB), is used to express the overall behavior expected in a DiffServ domain.

Considering the packets themselves, PHBs define the specific forwarding treatment each one will receive at every node along its path within the network. In a more precise view, PHBs define how traffic belonging to a particular behavior aggregate or, simply, aggregate, is treated at individual nodes in a domain. In effect, packets from multiple sources may experience identical treatments at the same node or, in other words, may experience identical behaviors.

Another way to define PHB is presented by the IETF: PHB can be understood as the description of the externally observable forwarding behavior of a DiffServ node applied to an aggregate of packets flow.

Packets are allocated to behaviors (PHBs) in each DiffServ domain node according their marked DSCP encoding or code point.

3.6.5.1 *DSCP Encoding and PHB Mapping*

The DSCP encoding or code point is the value attributed to the DSCP part of the DS field (Figure 3.44) and maps to PHBs. The code-point mapping considers the following:

- Standardized PHBs (EF, AF) have specific code points defined.
- Code point DSCP = 0 maps to a default PHB, for instance, best effort PHB.
- Experimental PHBs and local defined PHB mapping are allowed.
- Mapping between code points and PHBs is locally defined (although there is a mapping recommendation for standardized PHBs).

There are 64 possible DSCP values and there is a recommended standardized PHB mapping, as illustrated later. Also, DiffServ implementations are allowed to choose alternative mappings.

The standardized code-point encoding is the following:

- Best effort service (default behavior) → 000 000
- EF service → 101 110

The code points for the assured forwarding services are illustrated in Table 3.5.

Mapping between code points and PHBs is flexible and may use various relations such as 1-to-1 or N-to-1. The later relation means that multiple code points could be mapped to a single PHB, for instance, when considering experimental DSCPs or locally defined DSCPs. Also, the "class selector" bits, as illustrated in Figure 3.44, are intended to preserve IP precedence compatibility.

DiffServ defines two standardized PHBs: EF and AF. A discussion on the characteristics of these services follows.

3.6.6 Expedited Forwarding

Expedited forwarding (EF) behavior, also known as premium service, determines that the departure rate of the aggregate's packet from the DiffServ node must be equal or greater than a predefined rate.

EF service delivers minimum guaranteed bandwidth. EF guarantees at any time that the packet stream will always be allowed to use its minimum guaranteed bandwidth. From the user's point of view, the EF service has assured bandwidth with low latency, low jitter, and low loss. In other words, this service model emulates a leased-line service for its user.

Table 3.5 DSCPs for Assured Services

Dropping Precedence	Class 1	Class 2	Class 3	Class 4
Low	001 010	010 010	011 010	100 010
Medium	001 100	010 100	011 100	100 100
High	001 110	010 110	011 110	100 110

Several queue-scheduling mechanisms for delivering EF PHB are possible. These include:

- Priority queuing (PQ), with EF queue having maximum priority.
- Weighted round-robin (WRR) with bandwidth allocated to the EF queue equal to Ag_DRT_{min}.

Figure 3.45 illustrates the EF service with the following definitions:

$\Sigma_n AG_n$ = packet-arrival rate for all aggregates
L_Q = queue length
AG_N_ARt = aggregate's arrival rate
AG_N_DRt = aggregate's departure rate

Fundamentally, the queue scheduling mechanism adopted to implement the EF PHB should guarantee a minimum departure rate ($AG_N\_DRt_{min}$) for a given aggregate (AG_N) mapped to EF behavior.

EF behavior implementation, for a given aggregate, has also to consider other aspects, such as:

- The aggregate's maximum arrival rate should be less than or equal to the aggregate's minimum departure rate in order to keep queue length empty as long as possible, leading to minimum latency, low jitter, and low losses.
- The queue scheduling mechanism used for EF PHB should behave invariantly with respect to traffic stream variation for any other aggregate.

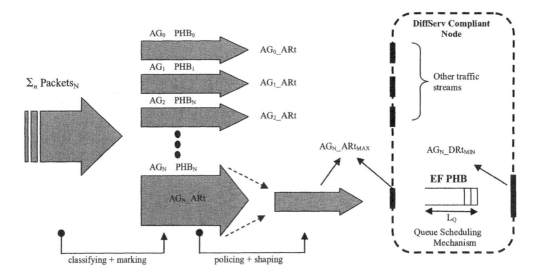

Figure 3.45   The expedited forwarding (EF) per-hop behavior (PHB).

Since various queue-scheduling alternatives (PQ, WRR, etc.) are possible to implement EF PHB, implementations should take the following into consideration:

- When an optimized use of network resources is intended, the maximum departure rate for a given aggregate should be kept as close as possible to the minimum guaranteed by the service:

$$AG_n\_DRt_{max} \cong AG_n\_DRt_{min}$$

- It is recommended that scheduling mechanisms that may cause "loss" to other aggregates be avoided.

The first consideration is related to the fairness of distribution for overprovisioned resources at each node. Network resources are scarce, and so the scheduling mechanism used should provide a way to distribute extra resources in a fair way. For instance, if bandwidth is available beyond the minimum required by all aggregates, this extra resource should be distributed in a fair and intelligent way.

3.6.7 Assured Forwarding

In general terms, assured forwarding (AF) services (AF PHB) offer a mechanism for service discrimination by creating "classes" for incoming traffic. In AF, each class corresponds to a certain level of service (greater or smaller probability of forwarding) that is scalable without the need for per-flow or signaling at every node.

In technical terms, AF PHB guarantees that packets belonging to a particular class have a defined probability of being forwarded. AF PHB services do not define any specific restriction on bandwidth or delay for packets. Instead, AF PHB distributes available resources in such a way that a relative probability exists for forwarding packets from different classes.

From the customers point of view, AF PHB services do not assure forwarding, but rather offer different levels of forwarding assurance for IP packets.

For ISPs or any service provider, offering service differentiation (services with different levels of forwarding assurance) is a flexible solution for billing and accounting. Customers can agree on the expected forwarded probability and be billed as such. Also, over-billing strategies for extra levels of guarantees are also possible to implement for customers.

AF PHB services are defined as follows:

- N = independent classes
- M = different levels of dropping precedence within each defined AF class

Each AF class is allocated a certain number of forwarding or networking resources at DiffServ nodes. All AF classes are independent, having their own forwarding resources. Within an AF class, drop precedence is mainly intended for deciding on packet priority during congestion. Once the network becomes congested, packet precedence will define which ones will be dropped first.

The standardized AF PHB is the following (IETF):

- 4 AF classes
- 3 drop precedences within each AF standardized class

DiffServ domains may define additional AF classes for local use.

The convention adopted for representing the classes and corresponding drop precedences is as follows:

$$AF_{IJ} \rightarrow AF \text{ PHB class "I" with drop precedence "J."}$$

At this point, the next basic question is: How can AF classes and drop precedences be defined and implemented in DiffServ domains?

As stated earlier, first packets have to be conditioned at DiffServ network borders. Figure 3.46 represents the incoming stream of packets being conditioned for an AF PHB class "N".

The AF behavior states for the AF-defined class N that:

$$P_{F\_IN} > P_{F\_OUT}$$

$$P_{F\_OUT} \geq 0$$

where:

P_{F_IN} = forwarding probability for in-profile traffic
P_{F_OUT} = forwarding probability for out-of-profile traffic

Dropping precedence is configured by management within each AF class using microflow traffic parameters. Figure 3.47 illustrates dropping precedence configured for microflows within an AF class N.

Convention packets with smaller drop precedence values within an AF class are forwarded before packets with higher drop precedence values.

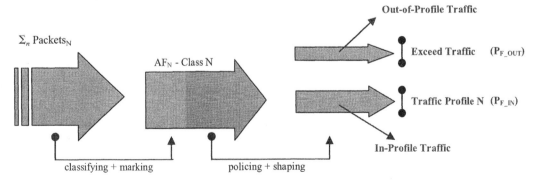

Figure 3.46 AF class conditioning.

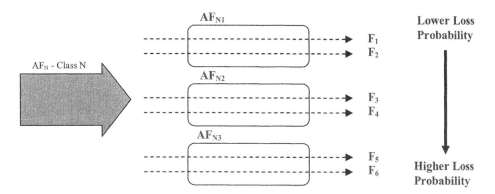

Figure 3.47   Dropping precedence configured for microflow traffic.

Figure 3.48 represents a generic view for an AF node in DiffServ domain having three classes implemented.

The number of forwarding resources allocated for each class is statically defined according to the scheduling mechanism chosen. As an example, percentage of available bandwidth or relative priority among AF classes are, among others, alternative ways for resource allocation.

Forwarding resources allocated for AF classes may not be in use and may be allocated to other AF classes. The utilization of these excess-forwarding resources results in higher efficiency for individual nodes, but has the drawback of being more complex.

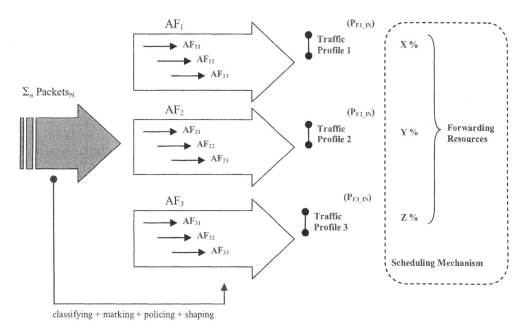

Figure 3.48   AF PHB with three classes.

3.6.8 Differentiated Service: Final Considerations

DiffServ architecture has important advantages. These include:

- Scalability
- Reduced packet-processing overhead

Scalability is one of the most important requirements for deploying any QoS strategy in complex networks like, for instance, the Internet. Scaling problems can be considered in two circumstances:

- Scaling to a large number of flows
- Scaling to high speed flows in routers and switches

Scaling to a large number of flows is a fundamental requirement of core routers in ISPs and complex networks. These routers frequently have to forward a large number of flows and, in this context, the differentiated service approach tries to minimize the amount of per-flow information required in routers by forwarding packet aggregates. The per-flow processing complexity is left to border routers, which normally handle a significantly smaller number of flows.

Scaling to high-speed flows is a requirement resulting from the evolution of technology. In effect, network interfaces are capable of very high sustained transmission rates (ATM, DWDM, SONET, etc.). In this scenario, applications will probably require high-speed flows with QoS to be maintained through the network, and simple DiffServ processing at core nodes may represent a considerable implementations advantage to guarantee these implementations.

As just mentioned, simplified processing is one major advantage for core routers in DiffServ. Since complexity is relegated to network borders, forwarding can be optimized, and this represents an implementation advantage with respect to other alternatives, in particular, with respect to IntServ.

DiffServ also has some potential problems. In particular, end-to-end behavior is not easily derived from the individual node's PHB. Also, specifying the distribution of network resources among nodes supporting various PHBs has potential difficulties. In particular, with both static and dynamic SLA requirements, there must be a global schema to allocate resources and to accept new flows or aggregates. This scheme presents challenging problems. One possible approach to deal with the allocation-of-resource problem and admission-control problem is to use bandwidth brokers.

As a final consideration, DiffServ is a network-oriented solution and is not the best solution for providing QoS requirements to microflows when they are needed for end users.

3.7 MULTIPROTOCOL LABEL SWITCHING

Multiprotocol label switching (MPLS) [9] is an initiative being proposed by IETF, which addresses many important requirements for today's network backbones.

In this section we elaborate on the importance of MPLS as a packet-switching technique for backbone networking. We will introduce its basic characteristics and operation, focusing on the use of IP as the network protocol, although this technique can be applied to any network layer protocol (IP, IPX, among others).

3.7.1 Identifying Routing and Switching Basics and Possible Variations

Before presenting MPLS's operational principles, let us first identify the new technical aspects it introduces.

Routers and switches perform two basic functions: *forwarding* and *control*. Forwarding functions are performed for operations at level 3 (routing) or level 2 (switching) and for both connection-oriented and connectionless operation.

As an example, in routers the control function corresponds to the set of protocols and algorithms used to maintain the routing table. Route calculation and updating are performed by well-known protocols, such as OSPF, intermediate system to intermediate system (IS-IS), and BPG, that calculate paths and determine reachability. These protocols use different approaches with algorithms based on link-state or distance-vector information to define paths (routes) to destinations. Typically in routers, a user process executing on the equipment's processor performs route calculation.

The forwarding in routers is independent from route calculation. It corresponds to switching (routing) packets from input to output interfaces based on routing information available from the routing table. The forwarding function uses the routing table maintained by control protocols. The forwarding function in high-performance routers is typically executed by a piece of dedicated hardware (integrated function) as an attempt to increase the equipment's forwarding capacity.

In ATM switches the control function is also present. The private network-to-network interface (PNNI) is an example of a control function performed in ATM switches. The basic principle is about the same when compared with router operation. In effect, PNNI controls and establishes virtual connections between ATM users. Since the operation is connection-oriented, establishing virtual circuits (VCs) can take into consideration a great number of parameters and functionalities when choosing the path between ATM users. VCs in ATM switches are typically established by a user process executing on the equipment's processor.

The forwarding function in ATM switches is independent from VC control and establishment. In this function, ATM cells are switched between input and output ports based on previously assigned VC paths. This function is normally executed in hardware in order to achieve the high performance required by ATM connections.

MPLS introduces a slight variation of the technical solutions just discussed. In MPLS, the control and forward functions are performed according to the following schema:

- Routing protocols like OSPF and BGP are used in MPLS operation to calculate paths and establish reachability.
- Path control in MPLS follows a connection-oriented approach and uses a specific protocol (label distribution protocol (LDP)) to set adequately the "MPLS labels" along the path.
- As in routers and switches, MPLS forwarding is independent from control and is based on MPLS labels.

The interesting point introduced in this schema is: Since MPLS uses a specific protocol to distribute labels (LDP), its operation can be independent of the technology used for forwarding. In other words, the control plane became independent from the type of forwarding being used. In brief, routers, ATM switches, and other technologies can be mixed in an MPLS network, providing a great degree of integration and flexibility. The next sections will explore some possible advantages and compromises resulting from this new technique for packet switching.

3.7.2   Goals and Basics

At first, it is important to observe that MPLS has been designed with its main target the large and complex networks typically found in ISPs and service providers. In other words, MPLS operation is supposed to scale and, as such, is intended to be an appropriate solution for backbones.

MPLS is a hybrid technique that allows very fast switching at the MPLS network core and conventional IP forwarding at the MPLS network borders. This hybrid solution has the global advantage of maintaining the basic IP operation encountered in many hosts, and also provides a generic way to achieve high-performance forwarding operation.

This high-performance forwarding operation can be achieved, for instance, by using ATM or frame relay switches at the network core and have their cross-connect tables "programmed" to switch according to IP routing requirements.

In brief, when considering IP routing, MPLS main advantages are:

- IP basic routing principles are preserved up to the MPLS network borders.
- Scaling and high-performance forwarding techniques are concentrated at the network core, which is suitable, for example, for ISP and network service providers.

MPLS supports many applications. These include traffic engineering (TE), virtual private networks (VPN), and tunneling applications.

7.7.3   MPLS Operation

MPLS basically assumes that the IP forwarding operation will be based on a "label." This will improve forwarding efficiency while allowing path setup to be defined in a more flexible way.

A simplified way to understand its basic operation is to describe MPLS as follows:

- Each MPLS node executes a routing protocol (OSPF, BGP, etc.) to discover paths (routes) and determine destination reachability.
- At the MPLS domain border, every incoming packet is associated with a *forward equivalent class* (FEC).
- Every defined FEC is associated with a route through the MPLS domain.
- At an MPLS domain border, packets also receive a *label* that assigns it to a specific FEC.
- Label information is distributed among the MPLS nodes before the forwarding process begins.
- Forwarding at the MPLS nodes is based on MPLS labels.
- Hop-by-hop forwarding using labels follows a label switched path (LSP).

- The forwarding process is repeated until the last MPLS node in the domain is encountered.
- When leaving the MPLS domain, packets are stripped of label information and are then forwarded by normal IP processing.

As this point, we observe that MPLS operation is based on definitions that must be examined in detail. These definitions are:

- FEC
- Labels
- LSPs
- LDP

We will discuss each one of these concepts in sequence, starting with the topology and terminology adopted by this packet-switching technique.

3.7.4   MPLS Domain

An MPLS domain is a set of nodes (routers and switches) running MPLS software for control and forwarding. MPLS domains are always within an administrative routing domain.

Figure 3.49 illustrates the typical nodes found in the MPLS topology and their terminology. Label edge routers (LERs) are devices operating at MPLS domain borders (Fig. 3.49). LERs can be further classified as "ingress" or "egress" devices. Ingress LERs are responsible for receiving and conditioning the packets entering the MPLS domain. Egress LERs are devices located at the MPLS domain exit points and are responsible for conditioning MPLS packets for normal IP processing. In brief, LERs are very important de-

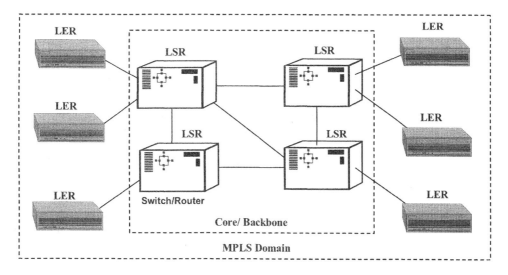

Figure 3.49   Nodes in MPLS topology.

vices that are responsible for interfacing MPLS domains with other MPLS domains or other dissimilar network.

The basic functions performed by a LER device are the following:

- To assign an FEC to packets (ingress LER).
- To assign labels to incoming packets (ingress LER).
- To participate in the establishment of "paths" (LSPs) for packets within the MPLS domain (Fig. 3.50).
- To strip labels from outgoing packets (egress LER).

Label switching routers (LSRs) are the core of the MPLS network. LSRs are typically high-performance devices (routers, ATM switches, etc.) optimized for forwarding processing.

The basic functions performed by an LSR device are the following:

- To participate in the establishment of "paths" (LSPs) for packets within the MPLS domain, in conjunction with others LSRs or LERs (Fig. 3.50).
- To "efficiently" forward labeled packets in order to achieve the best possible performance.

Figure 3.50 illustrates a path through an MPLS domain, named label switched path (LSP).

3.7.5 Forward Equivalence Class and MPLS Labels

In MPLS operation, packets are assigned to a forward equivalence class (FEC). Subsequently, the FEC is mapped to a next-hop MPLS node.

Packets assigned to the same FEC are treated indistinguishably within the MPLS do-

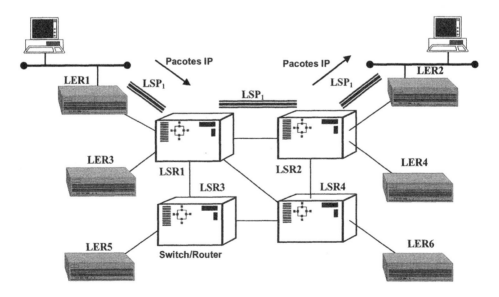

Figure 3.50 Label switched path (LSP) through a MPLS domain.

main. In other words, packets assigned to the same FEC will receive the same transport treatment at any MPLS node inside a domain independently of the packet's header contents (IP addresses, IP Precedence, etc.). This also means that, as far as their transport is concerned, packets assigned to the same FEC have, in principle, the same requirements.

Packets are assigned to an FEC only once at the MPLS domain edge by the ingress router (LER). Attaching a "label" to the packet effectively performs the packet-to-FEC mapping. Thus, by examining only the packet's label, an MPLS core node (LSR) is able to identify the FEC to which the packet is currently assigned.

Basic Principle: Packet → FEC → Label

Once packets are assigned to an FEC or, alternatively, once packets are labeled, they enter the MPLS network core and forwarding can be performed efficiently.

Each LSR device (MPLS core node) builds a table that specifies how packets are forwarded. This table is called label information base (LIB) and contains FEC-to-label bindings. Figure 3.51 illustrates LIB's contents and the next hop forwarding information used by the LSR device for a given labeled packet.

As mentioned before, the label is an identifier used to identify the packet's associated FEC. Labels have local significance. In other words, neighboring LSRs must agree on using a particular label to represent a specific FEC between them. This process is supported by the LDP, and will be discussed next. Once a label is chosen to represent an FEC between two LSRs, it has significance only to these LSR devices.

The forwarding processing is performed efficiently by using the packet's label as an index to LIB in order to identify the next hop node. No further analysis on packet's contents is executed inside the MPLS network core.

3.7.6 Label Switched Path

As illustrated in Figure 3.50, an LSP is equivalent to a path through the MPLS domain from the ingress LER to the egress LER. An LSP (route/path) has to be chosen to each FEC. In other words, associating an LSP to a particular FEC corresponds to the problem

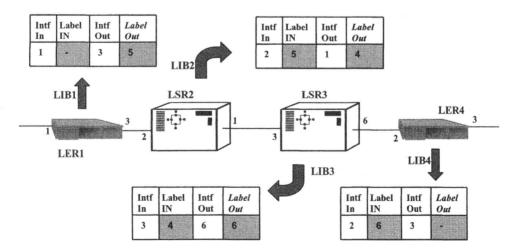

Figure 3.51 LIB and MPLS forwarding process.

of routing a set of labeled packets through the MPLS network. From an operational point of view, the LSP is set up prior to data transmission.

3.7.6.1 *LSP-to-Label Assignment: Basic Principle*   In MPLS, the decision to bind a label "L" to a particular LSP (Figure 3.51) is made by the downstream MPLS node (Figure 3.52). Label bindings are propagated from downstream nodes to upstream nodes to establish an LSP through the MPLS domain. In other words, labels are "downstream-assigned" and their distribution (LDP operation) is executed in the upstream direction.

3.7.6.2 *FEC-to-LSP Assignment Approaches*   There are two basic approaches to LSP setups (route selection) for a particular FEC in MPLS domains:

- Hop-by-hop routing and
- Explicit routing

In hop-by-hop routing, each LSR chooses the next hop (LSP) for a given FEC. This approach is equivalent to normal IP operation and each node chooses the next hop independently. Hop-by-hop routing uses conventional protocols such as OSPF and BGP for routing information decisions.

In explicit routing, an MPLS node (typically, the ingress router) specifies completely or partially the path followed by the packet in the explicit-routed LSP (ER LSP).

When the path is completely specified by the MPLS node, the LSP is "strictly" explicitly routed. Otherwise, the LSP is said to be "loosely" explicitly routed.

This approach is equivalent to the source routing operation previewed in IP options. In contrast to IP source routing operation, the packets are not flagged as source routed and do not carry the path information in the header. The explicit route is set up by FEC to LSP

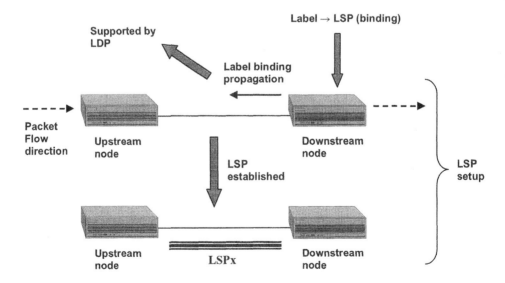

Figure 3.52   Downstream to upstream label assignment and distribution.

assignment supported by the LDP prior to packet's flow. Once established, the label assigned to the packet represents the ER LSP. This procedure allows complex computations to be realized in order to establish ER LSP. Besides this, ER LSP eliminates the actual problems found in normal IP source route operation, such as security block, header overhead, and processing overhead in high-performance routers.

Explicit routing allows the packet to follow an explicitly chosen route, which may be defined by a earlier configuration or may be defined dynamically. This approach has advantages, such as:

- The policy can be used to define routes through the network
- Traffic engineering approaches are supported

For example, nodes can make use of topological information to compute the optimal path (from ingress to egress node) through the network for quality of service or traffic engineering purposes. As another example, an explicit route can also be dynamically determined by constraint-based routing protocols such as the Constraint-based Routing LDP (CR-LDP).

3.7.7 Packet-to-FEC Assignment

A packet must be assigned to an FEC, for instance, at an MPLS network entry point (ingress LER). This assignment is realized by augmenting network layer packets with "label stacks." The packet is thereafter known as a "labeled packet."

An FEC corresponds to an aggregate of packets, all having, in principle, the same transport network requirements. In other words, once a packet is assigned to an FEC (receives a label), it will follow a specific LSP through the MPLS network.

A packet's assignment to FEC may be based on various criteria. Some of these are:

- IP addresses: complete address, prefix address, destination address, and source address
- Incoming interface
- Traffic engineering decisions
- VPN packets
- Filter based on QoS parameters (priority, ToS, IP precedence, etc.)
- Filter based on port and/or protocol, among other possible header parameters

A packet's assignment to FEC granularity may be coarse or fine grained. The level of granularity is, as far as the MPLS basic principles are concerned, an operational decision defined by operations management considering the processing resources available at routers. Packet assignment to an FEC in MPLS can be performed up to the microflow levels.

With respect to MPLS operation, a packet is initially assigned to an FEC and receives a label. In MPLS, FECs are mapped to labels, which are used at each LER/LSR to identify the packet's path (LSP) (Fig. 3.53) though the MPLS network. Thus, the packet assigned label is, in effect, that corresponding to the FEC chosen for the incoming packet.

As a final point, the FEC can also be understood as a specification indicating which packets are to be mapped to a specific LSP.

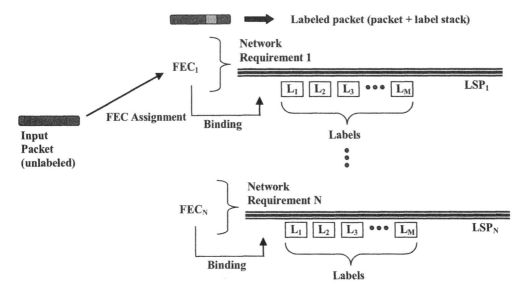

Figure 3.53   FEC and label assignments.

3.7.8   Label Distribution

MPLS architecture allows alternative methods for distributing labels among nodes and to manipulate them internally at each node. These alternative methods are used in the *hop-by-hop routing* approach, providing flexible MPLS operation and extended MPLS applicability.

First of all, there are two approaches for *FEC-to-label binding distribution.* Label bindings can be distributed for a particular FEC in two ways:

- Downstream-on-demand
- Unsolicited downstream

In downstream-on-demand, an upstream LSR explicitly requests its next hop (downstream LSR) for a particular FEC-to-label binding. In other words, the upstream LSR asks for the label, which it should use for a particular FEC (Fig. 3.54).

In unsolicited downstream (also called downstream unsolicited), a downstream LSR pushes an FEC-to-label binding to an upstream LSR (Fig. 3.54).

A second operational aspect of label distribution is when to advertise FEC-to-label binding. In MPLS architecture, two alternative methods are previewed to control label advertisement:

- *Independent* label distribution control
- *Ordered* label distribution control

In independent label distribution control, an LSR can advertise FEC-to-label mapping to its neighbors at any time (unconditional) (Fig. 3.55). In ordered label distribution control, a downstream LSR can advertise an FEC-to-label mapping only if the corresponding FEC

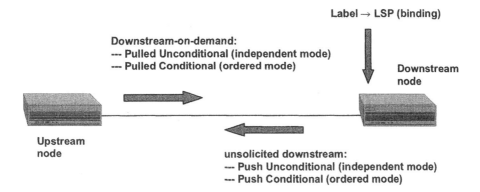

Figure 3.54   Label distribution methods: downstream-on-demand and unsolicited downstream.

already has an FEC-to-label mapping to the next hop (downstream) (Fig. 3.55). The ordered control method effectively forces the FEC-to-label biding advertisements to occur in order and sequentially, in the upstream direction, from egress node to ingress node. The independent control method, as the name suggests, allows FEC-to-label binding to be advertised in the upstream direction independently of any mapping to the same FEC in the downstream direction.

Another operational aspect concerning labels is whether each LSR should retain learned FEC-to-label binding for an LSR that is not the next hop for the FEC. In MPLS terminology, the label retention mode assumes two possibilities:

1. *Conservative* label retention mode
2. *Liberal* label retention mode

In conservative label retention, the LSR only keeps advertised label mappings, which will be used to forward packets. In this case, FEC-to-label mapping to routes, which are not used to forward packets, are discarded. The main disadvantage of conservative label-retention mode is that a new label mapping has to be obtained whenever a route change occurs. In liberal label retention mode, however, the LSR keeps all advertised la-

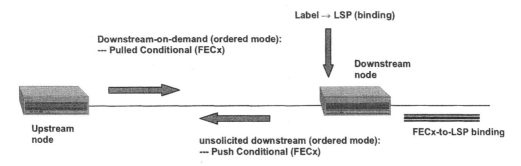

Figure 3.55   Label distribution methods: ordered control.

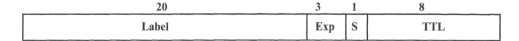

20		3	1	8
Label		Exp	S	TTL

Figure 3.56 MPLS generic label encoding entry format (shim header).

bel mappings learned from its neighbors. When the LSR uses the downstream-on-de-mand method, the requesting LSR might choose the label mappings it requires for re-tention.

3.7.8.1 MPLS Label Stack In simple terms, a label identifies the path the packet should use within an MPLS domain. Packets in MPLS networks are labeled by aug-menting them with a *label stack*. The label stack is a sequence of label entries whose general-purpose format is illustrated in Figure 3.56. In the figure, "Label" represents the label value that corresponds to the entry; "Exp" are bits left for experimental use; Bit "S" is used for stack operations, as described next; the TTL bits encode TTL values, which have the well-known "time-to-live" meaning, used in normal IP packet process-ing.

Label stacks are encoded ("shim headers") and carried with IP packets (Figure 3.57). A label stack is placed after the data link layer header and before the network layer header. The last label entry in the stack must have S bit set.

ATM, Frame Relay, LAN, and PPP Encapsulation Depending on the layer 2 tech-nology used between MPLS devices, the label can be embedded (totally or partially) in the layer 2 headers. The basic idea is that when using technologies such as ATM or frame relay, their addresses (pair VPI/VCI and DLCI) could be inferred from the MPLS label or, alternatively, their addresses can be effectively used as MPLS labels.

For LANs and point-to-point protocol (PPP) encapsulation, there is a standardized en-coding for the labeled packets (Fig. 3.58).

3.7.8.2 MPLS Label Stack Processing: Additional Considerations In the previous discussion, we have by simplification considered only single labels in MPLS la-beled packets. Generically, labeled MPLS packets carry a label stack to support, among

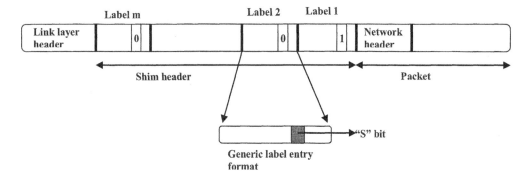

Figure 3.57 MPLS label stack carried with IP packets.

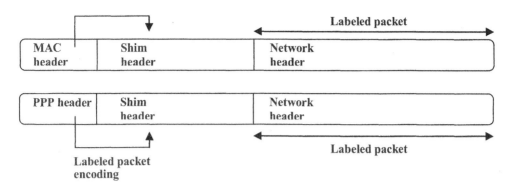

Figure 3.58   Labeled packet encapsulation.

other possibilities, LSP tunnels and MPLS hierarchy. The label stack processing follows the basic principles already defined and provides additional flexibility.

In brief, it follows the label stack processing for a labeled packet (Fig. 3.59):

- The top label is retrieved from the label stack (basic processing is always based on the top label).
- The top label is used to index the Incoming Label Map (ILM).
- The ILM points to the next hop label forwarding entry (NHLFE) entries at the LIB.
- NHLFE contains information required for label processing:
  —the stack operation to be executed (supporting hierarchy, tunnels, or conventional processing);
  —additional information, such as data-link encapsulation and label stack encoding.

Since the ILM points to multiple NHLFE entries, additional flexibility is incorporated to support, for instance, forwarding on balanced routes according to local policy management.

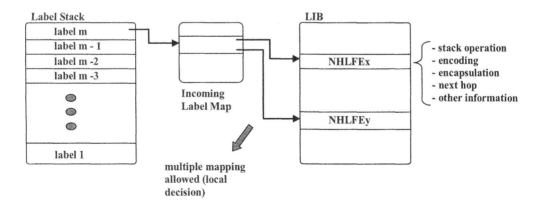

Figure 3.59   Label stack basic processing.

3.7.9 Label Distribution Protocols

Label information is distributed in MPLS domains using a protocol generically referred to as label distribution protocol (LDP). The following protocols are possible alternatives for label information distribution: LDP; RSVP; and BGP.

LDP [10] is a new standard protocol proposed by IETF for label distribution. In LDP, LSRs and LERs cooperate and exchange label information using LDP messages in a reliable LDP session. The LDP is discussed in the following section. Additionally, the constraint-based routing label distribution protocol (CR-LDP), an extension of LDP, is introduced in Section 3.7.10.

RSVP for traffic engineering (RSVP-TE) is an extension of the previously discussed resource reservation protocol, standardized by IETF for IntServ architecture, to distribute labels in MPLS domains.

With BGP, label information is exchanged, piggybacked on BGP messages.

3.7.9.1 Label Distribution Protocol As stated before, the LDP is a new protocol being defined by the IETF whose procedures and messages allow MPLS nodes to use network-layer routing information to establish LSPs. The LSPs are effectively created by *mapping* the *network-layer routing information* just mentioned to *data-link layer switched paths*.

The LDP protocol establishes reliable LDP sessions between LDP peers (MPLS nodes: LSRs and LERs) using TCP (Fig. 3.60).

In brief, LDP operation has the following phases:

* Discovery
* Session initialization
* Information exchange

In the discovery phase, "hello messages" are sent to well-known LDP port and router addresses (multicast router addresses) in order to announce neighborhood. Hello messages are periodically sent using UDP, since the basic idea is to allow the detection of potential LDP peers in the neighborhood. After the initialization phase, hello messages are also sent periodically to maintain LDP sessions as a keep-alive method.

During the session initialization phase, a TCP connection is established between LDP peers using session messages. An LDP session is then created and additional information messages could be exchanged using a reliable communication path.

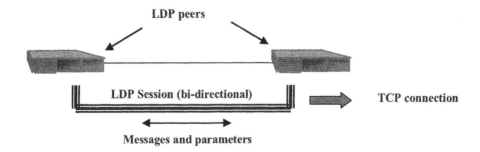

Figure 3.60 LDP basic operation.

During the information exchange phase, advertisement and notification messages are exchanged in order to create and maintain LSPs. Advertisement messages are used either to request a label or to advertise a label mapping. LDP uses these messages to create, delete, and change label mappings. As the name suggests, notification messages are used to announce additional information needed in LDP sessions or to carry error and notification information. Table 3.6 illustrates the general use of version 1 LDP protocol messages.

Table 3.6   LDP Message Types

LDP Message Type	General Use
Notification	LSR signals an event or provides information to LDP peers. Some examples are: • Fatal error (keep-alive timer expires, internal errors, etc.); and • Message formatting errors.
Hello	Supports the discovery mechanism used in LDP protocol to determine and maintain neighborhood.
Initialization	Supports session establishment between LDP peers. Examples of initialization parameters exchanged during the initialization phase are: • KeepAlive timer definition • The advertisement method used to advertise labels (unsolicited downstream or downstream on demand) • Loop detection enabling • Parameters to identify hello adjacency match • Additional parameters: ATM and frame relay session parameters (merge capability, address ranges, directionality, etc.)
KeepAlive	Supports the monitoring of LDP session integrity. KeepAlive message resets KeepAlive timer.
Address	Supports the advertisement of interface addresses. Activated interfaces should have their address advertised.
Address withdraw	Supports the deactivation of interfaces. Previously advertised address must be withdrawn whenever an LSR deactivates an interface.
Label mapping	Supports the distribution of FEC-to-label bindings to LDP peers. Label mapping messages are transmitted upon different conditions with the LSR configured as *independent distribution control* or *ordered distribution control* (Section 3.7.8).
Label request	Allows an upstream LSR to request an FEC-to-label biding (mapping). The basic parameter sent with a label request message is the FEC to which the mapping is requested. Optional parameters are a hop count (LSRs) and a path vector mainly used for loop detection.
Label abort request	This message is used to abort outstanding label request messages.
Label withdraw	Label withdraw message breaks previously defined FEC-to-label mapping. This message is used, for instance, by a downstream LSR to signal that a particular mapping should not be used.
Label release	The label release message is used by an LSR to signal to its LDP peer the release of a FEC-to-label biding. A label release message is sent, for instance, after the LSR receives a label withdraw message.

3.7.10 Constraint-Based Routing Label Distribution Protocol

Constraint-based routing (CR) is a model in which additional parameters (such as bandwidth, delay, QoS and explicit hops) are taken into consideration for packet forwarding decisions. In the CR model, the routes are typically computed at a single point, and both routing information and constraints must be distributed within the network.

The use of CR adequately supports the implementation of services and such features as:

- Load-balancing
- Traffic redirection
- VPN
- Rerouting under failure

In MPLS, the CR-LDP, an extension of the LDP protocol, supports the constraint-based routing model. CR-LDP has the same basic operation as was discussed for LDP. In addition, the CR-LDP protocol defines a mechanism, which sets up a constraint-based routing label switched path (CR-LSP) initiated at the ingress LSR and based on constraints. CR-LDP is mainly intended to support traffic engineering and, generically, to provide more flexible and robust routing decision to LDP, while the CR-LSP is an explicit routed path through the MPLS network, which is calculated at the MPLS network entry point (ingress LSR).

In a CR-LSP setup, an ER is calculated, taking not only routing information (routing tables) but also additional parameters into consideration. The idea is to consider setup characteristics and operational criteria for CR-LSP that accommodate, for instance, specific traffic and service demands.

The ER set up by CR-LDP can be strictly or loosely routed (Section 3.7.6.2). Loose ER represents flexibility for routing and rerouting. A loose ER segment allows for route definition at a higher level without specifying details. For instance, a loose ER segment could be set up automatically by LSRs based on level 3 routing information.

The LDP-CR protocol also provides information about traffic parameters that can be used for resource reservation at MPLS nodes.

3.7.10.1 CR-LDP Parameters
CR-LDP basically extends LDP operation by including additional information for LSP setup. For instance, the label request in CR-LDP includes the FEC and two fundamental sets of parameters: the ER and the traffic parameters. ER parameter corresponds to the computed LSP, and the traffic parameters, as the name suggests, represent the traffic characterization. The list of parameters for label request is as follows:

- FEC (same as LDP)
- ER
- Traffic parameters
- Preemption
- Pinning option
- Resource class
- LSPID (the CR-LSP identifier)

Following is a brief discussion of their meaning and applicability.

Explicit Route   The ER information specifies the path to be taken by the LSP being established. This information contains a list of nodes or group of nodes along the constraint-based path. This is so that after CR-LSP setup, it will traverse the entire group of nodes indicated, or a subset of it. This approach results in flexibility for fulfilling the request for constraint route decisions (Fig. 3.61).

Traffic Parameters and Resource Reservation   The traffic parameters express the required traffic characteristics for the CR-LSP. The basic parameters are: PDR, PBS, CDR, CBS, and EBS. These parameters express traffic characteristics for the LSP. Generically, they can be used for various purposes:

- To reserve resources at MPLS nodes.
- To dynamically define routes.
- To condition traffic at network entry point.
- To signal traffic characteristics to nodes supporting, for instance, DiffServ implementations.

Path Preemption   CR-LDP supports path preemption. For each hop, CR-LDP indicates the required resources. It can happen that these requirements are not fulfilled for a particular hop. CR-LDP can then reallocate paths or, in other words, to use path preemption. In path preemption, paths are reallocated. To support this facility, two priorities are defined:

- setupPriority (new CR-LSP)
- holdingPriority (existing CR-LSP)

Priorities vary from zero to seven ($0 \rightarrow 7$), and the preemption decision is based on the priority values for the existing and the new CR-LSP. This feature is very important for carriers and is a basic requirement of traffic engineering. Path preemption allows high-priority traffic LSPs to be established, even if there are not enough resources for both high- and low-priority traffic. For carriers, the preemption feature

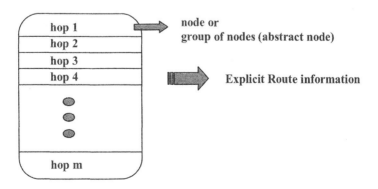

Figure 3.61   Explicit route information in CR-LDP.

is a valuable tool for network planners to assure that high-priority traffic LSPs will be set up under scarce network resource availability.

Pinning Mechanism CR-LDP also supports the route pinning feature. During CR-LSP setup the route pinning mechanism can be used to specify that the path should not be modified in case a better next hop becomes available. This prevents an LSR in the CR-LSP path from modifying its next hop, for instance, in loose routed paths. The pinning mechanism provides a method for preventing, for instance, route oscillations.

Additional Parameters CR-LDP also includes negotiation flags for each traffic parameter ("negotiable" and "not negotiable") and information concerning the service granularity ("frequency") over different time intervals. Another parameter ("weight"), weights the relative share of excess bandwidth above the committed rate. Another parameter, resource class, is a facility used to specify which links can be used by the CR-LSP. It is used to prune network topology.

3.7.10.2 CR-LDP and Traffic Engineering

Traffic engineering is one possible application of MPLS. Traffic engineering targets the efficient mapping of traffic onto a network topology. Efficient mapping means the optimization of the available network resources with respect to various criteria.

Traffic engineering has specific requirements that must be supported by the network in order to facilitate its implementation. These include:

- Adaptability to changes in network (topology, traffic load, and failure)
- Capability to support administrative policies
- Reliability
- Scalability

CR-LDP addresses these requirements, and therefore might be considered a protocol to support traffic engineering. In brief, the capabilities provided by CR-LDP are:

- Strict and loose path setup, which provides, among other possibilities, the means to support administrative policies, alternative paths, and network adaptation to changes.
- Path preemption that supports, among other possibilities, policy and network recovery procedures.
- Robust signaling by using TCP transport.
- A scalable and simple protocol with few control messages to establish, maintain, and release LSPs.

3.7.11 MPLS and ATM

MPLS can be "integrated" with ATM technology using three different approaches:

- Label-controlled ATM switching
- ATM tunneling
- Dual MPLS/ATM operation

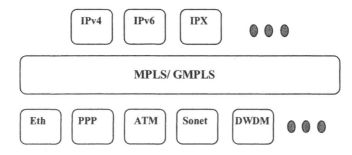

Figure 3.62 MPLS and GMPLS.

In the label-controlled ATM switching approach, ATM switches are used as LSRs. When using this approach, the ATM control software (UNI, PNNI, etc.) used by normal ATM switches to control its hardware is replaced by an IP/MPLS control software. ATM-LSRs can run network layer routing protocols and their data forwarding is based on layer 3 routes computed by these protocols. This approach therefore combines layer 3 routing with layer 2 ATM switching.

In the ATM tunneling approach, LSR devices use ATM switches as the interconnection technology between them.

In the dual MPLS/ATM operation, the ATM switch has simultaneous and independent control software for native ATM operation and IP/MPLS operation. This approach adequately supports the migration process to MPLS implementation.

3.7.12 MPLS and GMPLS: Final Considerations

As mentioned earlier, the MPLS technique can be applied to any network layer protocol (IP, IPX, and others). Besides this, MPLS can also be used with different layer 2 technologies like Ethernet, PPP, ATM, and optical network infrastructures based on SONET/SDH and DWDM (Figure 3.62).

In effect, one of the current motivations to adopt MPLS is its ability to control optical or transmission devices whose operation can be based on label swapping or label switching. The possible alternatives for applying this generalized MPLS (GMPLS) solution are numerous.

In these approaches, GMPLS and traffic engineering can be combined to control, among other devices, fiber switches, SONET and SDH switches and optical cross-connects. The IP packet forwarding processing optimization and the high throughput provided by these devices are combined to result in a robust QoS-ready multiservice network.

3.8 SUMMARY

Quality of service (QoS) approaches require both a basic background of associated principles and a general view of the alternatives available in order to adequately address the problem. In this chapter, QoS basics were initially approached by presenting the main QoS parameters and, also, by discussing the new router functionalities and how they interrelate in routers. Functions such as shaping, marking, token-bucket operation, and queuing are the basic blocks necessary for building any general QoS solution.

Based on the knowledge about basic router operation and building blocks, the standardized alternatives including IntServ, DiffServ, and MPLS, were presented. Here the main result obtained was an understanding of the architecture approach, the services previewed, as well as how router functionalities can be assembled to construct a more general solution.

The chapter then addressed an introductory approach to understanding QoS by selecting the relevant basic topics and interrelating them in order to provide a more general understanding of the subject.

REFERENCES

1. James D. McCabe, *Practical Computer Network Analysis and Design,* Morgan Kaufmann Publishers, Inc., Series in Networking, 1998

2. S. Floyd and V. Jacobson, "Random Early Detection Gateways for Congestion Avoidance," *IEEE/ACM Transactions on Networking,* vol. 1, no. 4, pp. 397–413, August 1993.

3. W. Stevens, "TCP Slow Start, Congestion Avoidance, Fast Retransmit and Fast Recovery Algorithms," *RFC 2001,* January 1997.

4. M. Christiansen *et al.,* "Tuning RED for Web Traffic," *IEEE/ACM Transactions on Networking,* vol. 9, no. 3, pp. 249–264, June 2001.

5. B. Braden *et al.,* "Recommendations on Queue Management and Congestion Avoidance in the Internet," *RFC 2309,* April 1998.

6. R. Braden, D. Clark, and S. Shenker, "Integrated Services in the Internet Architecture: An Overview," June 1994.

7. R. Braden, L. Zhang, S. Berson, S. Herzog, and S. Jamin, "Resource Reservation Protocol (RSVP)—Version 1—Functional Specification," *RFC 2205,* September 1997.

8. S. Blake, D. Black, M. Carlson, E. Davies, Z. Wang, and W. Weiss, "An Architecture for Differentiated Services," *RFC 2475,* December 1998.

9. E. Rosen, A. Viswanathan, and R. Callon, "Multiprotocol Label Switching Architecture," *RFC 3031,* January 2001.

10. L. Anderson *et al.,* "LDP Specification, *RFC 3036,* January 2001.

CHAPTER 4

A SURVEY OF CHARGING INTERNET SERVICES

BURKHARD STILLER

4.1 INTRODUCTION

Today's information society has a stringent need for advanced communication services and content, which are provided currently by a packet-switched networking technology instead of traditional circuit-switching. This is driven by the fact that provisioning of different applications on dedicated network infrastructures are inefficient [106], such as seen, for example, with the telephone network, cable TV networks, radio broadcast, and dedicated leased-line services for mission-critical data transfers. Deploying a single multiservice network infrastructure to create an integrated services network, offering services that range, e.g., from managed bandwidth services and VPNs to interactive voice, video, messaging, and eCommerce services, promises the potential for possible cost reductions, which in total is much larger than tuning networking technologies for different types of applications.

Considering the particular application support, the Internet as it exists today is designed for elastic data applications [107]. Experiences on a large scale basically are not available on reliably integrating multiple services in a single network in a commercial way. The commercial environment of tomorrow's Internet needs to revise the assumption that service customers rely on cooperation among them. Therefore, the TCP's fairness, provided by its congestion control algorithm, needs to be addressed, and, e.g., may be enforced by alternative protocol implementations in the network or may be provided by suitable economic incentives for the use of a service [61]. Because changes of transport protocols networkwide are economically difficult, an adequate distributed approach to

Managing IP Networks. Edited by Saleh Aidarous and Thomas Plevyak
ISBN 0-471-39299-5 © 2003 Institute of Electrical and Electronics Engineers

congestion control, service provisioning, and service usage is charging. In addition, due to the commercialization of the Internet, the provisioning of its services will form an open market requesting by definition an integrated charging system for services, transport, and content. For that reason, appropriate pricing schemes for communication services will provide incentives for reasonable resource usage, traditional network capacity, or bandwidth. Although solutions for methods of charging packet-switched, single-service class networks exist and are applied successful, packet-switched integrated- and differentiated-services networks have another dimension of complexity and require a completely different approach [118]. Consequently, charging for the future Internet, as the most prominent example of a packet-switched network, remains an unsolved problem even though a number of proposed approaches exist. Mainly, these problems are have three distinct causes: (1) technical reasons, (2) economic factors, and (3) operational constituents.

First, since a variety of service characterizations by QoS concepts exist [113], heterogeneous and advanced networking technology alternatives, such as ATM or Frame Relay, have been developed over time, the shape of the Internet of the future based on the IntServ [7] and the DiffServ [4] is still not fully defined. It remains unclear, if the RSVP [8] can be applied in a large backbone Internet without any loss of scalability, or if the current state of work on signaling between DiffServ domains will be able to cope with all QoS demands and traffic characterizations known from existing applications [59]. In addition, standardization work on DiffServ seems to be limited to a single provider domain [88], explicitly excluding any hint of definitions considered business-relevant, such as SLAs.

Second, an ISP today is faced with huge opportunities for growth [102] and it is challenged to increase profitability. In this highly competitive telecommunications service provider and ISP market, strategic differentiation and advanced pricing schemes for integrated multiservice networks are required in order to deal with efficient schemes, basic bandwidth allocation, or advanced QoS services to reap financial benefits of new services and to gain a competitive edge [5, 53].[1] The ability to be flexible for different and value-added services is the key factor. An efficiency gain, which is achieved in competitive markets, has a theoretical Pareto efficiency foundation, where no player can be better off without hurting any other [124]. But in a globally distributed system, such competitive markets can only be approximated. Nevertheless, a gain in efficiency in the telecommunications services market means a distributed surplus. Because the effects of multiservice provisioning onto incentive-compatible and efficient pricing schemes have not been studied in great detail, knowing how customers utilize services and therefore service demand as well as traffic profiles becomes crucial for viable multiservice pricing schemes. In addition, recent Internet service offerings and future advanced services lack another crucial component for businesses: adequate charging methods for differentiated services. For example, since the funding of transport services with revenue from separate services, such as content and entertainment offerings or advertising, is not transparent for open markets to cover network costs of transport services, different technologies for avoiding cross-subsidizing approaches are essential. In addition, high capacities provisioned in large backbone Internet networks, by separate players in the ISP market, will cross-subsidize as a viable business model.

---

[1] The number of ISPs in North America had reached about 7000 operational companies by August 1999, starting from about 1500 in February 1996.

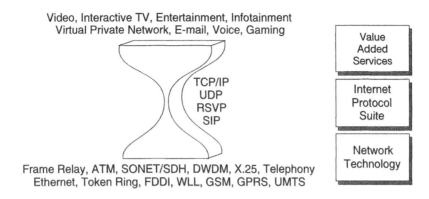

Video, Interactive TV, Entertainment, Infotainment
Virtual Private Network, E-mail, Voice, Gaming

TCP/IP
UDP
RSVP
SIP

Frame Relay, ATM, SONET/SDH, DWDM, X.25, Telephony
Ethernet, Token Ring, FDDI, WLL, GSM, GPRS, UMTS

Value
Added
Services

Internet
Protocol
Suite

Network
Technology

Figure 4.1   Internet hourglass model: value-added services, protocols, and network technology.

New telecommunication services, in particular Internet services, impose a third degree of complexity to charging support systems (CSS).[2] Different services and content, and need to be service provider overlapping. This determines the stringent need to integrate concepts for interoperable and standardized charging solutions between providers for interoperator agreements, including content delivery services and provisioning pure data transport. Finally, the performance and scalability of CSSs are major factors in their suitability for Internet services charging. While the handling of many different Internet services, millions of customers, and various technology choices in use have to be optimized on the lower levels of a CSS, the upper levels for controlling the subscriber database and for managing the money collection process perform major functions for a competitive ISP infrastructure as well. The per-customer, responsive, and on-demand functionality of a modern CSS determines its optimal characteristics, which traditional billing systems or customer care systems do not provide.

Technical, economic, and operational prerequisites are closely related. Besides its emerging popularity, even for mobile users [90], and its increasing level of interconnectivity [35], the Internet offers the central possibility of accessing different types of usage information for many services at a single network layer. This is due to the fact that most services will be transported by IP which is independent of the underlying medium-access technology. For technical and operational reasons, this eases network deployment and maintenance, since a single network protocol needs only to be supervised.[3] For commercial reasons, this allows for straightforward and interesting product offerings, where single services, each of which resides on top of the IP, are bundled and offered as a value-added service or product. Figure 4.1 shows the hourglass-model [118], which describes the relationship between network technology, Internet protocols, and value-added services. Clearly, the Internet protocol suite is the "bottleneck" for provisioning value-added services based on network technology. However, based on the Internet's years of success,

---

[2]Charging support systems are utilized to manage all economic tasks related to the commercial deployment of communication services, since operation support systems (OSS) deal with the management of technology issues and business support systems (BSS) handle customer care, customer support, and business model issues. While customer management and billing systems (CM&B) traditionally have been used for a back-office approach of handling batch-based monthly billing periods, CSS have to show a responsive, customer-oriented functionality.
[3]Different network layer protocols, such as IPx or Appletalk, become more obsolete, as estimations postulate [97].

developing appropriate means and mechanisms for this provisioning and charging task forms a challenge.

4.1.1   Outline

This overview on charging for commercial, integrated services, and packet-switched networks focuses explicitly on the case of the Internet and surveys the current state of the art and future steps for designing a flexible CSS for the Internet. Since charging for telecommunications services is not a new area as such, approaches required for charging packet-based networks show significantly different technical principles. The methodology chosen at this stage will combine known experience with solutions for the new technology.

While Section 4.2 at first discusses a scenario, and important customer and provider viewpoints, charging terms are introduced and appropriate terminology is defined to allow for an unambiguous discussion. Section 4.3 establishes an overview of related work in charging projects for the Internet as well as on traditional telecommunications systems, and summarizes metering, accounting, and mediation technology available today. To obtain a central understanding of various Internet services and technology choices, Section 4.4 elaborates on QoS methods, Internet network architecture, SLAs, and standardized data formats, which provide "hooks" for charging purposes. The relevant economic dimension is discussed in terms of pricing models for the Internet presented in Section 4.5 and ISP cost models in Section 4.6. The design of a CSS presented in Section 4.7 integrates all technical and economic issues discussed so far. Finally, major business model aspects for ISPs are outlined in Section 4.8, including provider segmentation issues as well as content charging. Section 4.9 summarizes this chapter and draws conclusions.

4.2   MOTIVATION AND TERMINOLOGY

The interest in a single multiservice network and its efficiency gains in terms of operation, utilization, and cost recovery, leads to the essential demand of appropriate technology alternatives, which will allow for the inherent differentiation of services. Let us compare this situation with a traditional business case in the toy railroad market. A store that cannot distinguish between expensive brand X model engines and cheap brand Y model engines for freight trains will have to charge all customers the same price for every engine sold. Even though these engines have extremely different values and features, they haul model trains only. Choices, if they exist at all and make sense, need to be distinguished by a set of parameters, such as degree of detail, correct coloring, or reliable technology, and each choice needs to be priced differently. With communications services, the situation is the same. Initially, communications services provide the possibility to communicate between two or multiple locations, independent of the service quality observed. However, on the one hand, customers want service choices and their explicit selection, such as services for Web surfing, fast downloads and file-transfer capabilities, or interactive gaming. On the other hand, and as a sort of causal derivation, ISPs need operational, efficient, and scalable technology, termed CSS, to charge for these service alternatives.

To provide a first overview of charging-relevant responsibilities [119], the tasks of a CSS are to be refined. In existing CSSs, sometimes called charging and accounting systems [115, 85], billing systems [22, 110], or simple charging systems [120], with different points of view and functionality included, many different tasks are subsumed. Basically, on the networking level, every provider maintains a network consisting of routers with network links between them. As illustrated in Figure 4.2, necessary functions for a CSS are metering, mediation, accounting, pricing and tariffing schemes, charge calculation, identification, and billing. While metering functions can be provided by components inside the networks on the wire and are integrated into routers, servers, or computers (active probing), they can form independent devices as well (passive probing). In either case, they generate raw accounting information (base accounting records), which show vast amounts of information. Mediation gathers, preprocesses, filters, merges, and correlates this information into accounting records, which are maintained in accounting systems. Call detail records (CDRs) [58] and Internet protocol detail records (IPDR) [21] are two examples of accounting records as agreed upon data structures (for more details, cf. Section 4.4.5). These accounting systems, in turn, forward all accumulated and perhaps abstracted accounting information through a charge calculation function toward the billing system. The charge calculation, which receives pricing and tariffing information as well as customer identification information from outside, translates the accounting information into charging records, hence, it maps the resource-oriented information into monetary, financial values. Within the charge calculation, discounting strategies, marketing-driven pricing schemes, or simply fixed prices which have been expressed in service- or customer-dependent tariff structures, can be applied on a per-customer basis. Finally, billing uses these values to prepare the invoice to be sent to the customer.

Depending on the particular system observed, setting prices and tariffs, calculating charges, or performing bill processing are integrated into a CSS. Additionally, they combine the maintenance of service classes, user profiles, customer data, identities, banking account data, and billing functions. Although these tasks can be and need to be distinguished clearly (cf. terminology as defined in Section 4.2.5), they are heavily centralized in today's CSSs. Future CSSs need to be able to integrate a variety of different charging

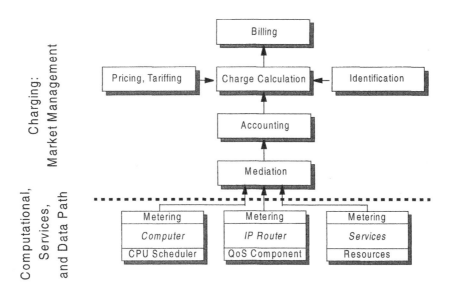

Figure 4.2   Concept of charging communications, services, transport, or even computation.

and accounting records from different communications providers or content providers, since customers' requirements are determined by the so-called "one-stop billing" approach [118]. This strongly suggests dividing existing monolithic charging systems into several components with clearly defined interfaces and interface data units. By doing so, it will become possible to exchange individual components and to integrate different components supporting different technologies without having to adapt the entire system.

Exact definitions of components and tasks of a CSS, as well as their applied nomenclature, form the basis for further comparisons and discussions. To allow for a precise specification, all charging-relevant terms are introduced below, based on an illustrating example scenario.

4.2.1 Scenario

A typical advanced communication scenario for the home[4] could include charging for communications in terms of specific transport, services, and content characteristics. Assume the presence of a single asymmetrical digital subscriber line (ADSL) at the home of a supervisory board member. To access his company, he needs a high-speed, secured, and remote VPN access. His wife organizes various activities for the local community and requires phone-conferencing facilities. The children like low-latency access to interactive gaming sites and music Web sites. These different user roles are represented contractually by a single customer, renting the ADSL line that runs from the home to an ISP. But how is charging applied?

Metering is performed on this single ADSL line. However, accounting is applied on a per-user basis to the metered and mediated data, which are correlated to the services utilized. The resulting accounting records contain, e.g., the duration of each data transfer, the obtained QoS characteristics (such as bandwidth consumed, delay encountered, and error rates experienced), and additional resource and device usage (such as the phone or a gaming device). The content may be indicated by different games played. These accounting records are fed into the charge calculation, which happens, e.g., in an administrative domain of the game provider. Pricing schemes for the ADSL service have been defined by the network provider and are adjusted to the special group of customers, which finally determines the tariff to be applied, e.g., a flat fee per month for 2 Mbit/s, proportional excess charges for bursts, and weekend reductions for VPN services. The tariff is based on the measurable QoS characteristics of a particular service and, in case of content, on the type of content distributed. All charges for services and content are calculated, possibly at different locations, and collected in multiple charging records from the billing system. A number of charging records for a certain prearranged period of time are accumulated and billed to the customer, who has been identified in advance and represents all user flows metered so far. Finally, the customer may decide at this point, or in a predefined manner, how the bill will get paid, applying traditional payment schemes or electronic systems, e.g., by credit card payments using secure electronic transactions (SET) [105] or electronic money.

4.2.2 Viewpoints

As we can see from the preceding scenario, different points of view on the CSS and its tasks exist. Concerning the customer, after service provisioning, the bill for the service

---

[4]A similar scenario for a customer premises network scenario can be defined as well.

utilized summarizes a week or month of communication activities and content. Generally speaking, there is no incentive to disconnect from the dial-up ADSL Internet connection, when there is no charge per time or volume. Therefore, only a flat fee for basic services without special requirements will be incentive-compatible. However, an always existing spending cap will limit the amount of services utilized over time. As stated in Ferrari and Delgrossi [37], the following charging properties exist from a customer's perspective: comprehensibility, controllability, predictability, stability, and fairness. With a commercial ISP, a high revenue maximization and best cost-recovery strategy should be achieved [122]. Therefore, the pricing model applied and the service bundle offered in a given market situation determines the optimization dimensions for customers and providers. The provider's charging properties need to cover settlements and should allow for a high probability of cost recovery, the competitiveness of prices, the encouragement of service usage, low implementation costs, and low usage costs. In summary and based on Stillos *et al.* [118] and Farten *et al.* [61], the customer and provider view points are clarified, which are complemented by further requests.

4.2.2.1 *Customer Point of View*

On the one hand, customers' budget constraints and spending strategies are to get as much service for as little money as possible. The underlying economic principle can be formulated as "users buy the best service bundle they can afford." With software agents and brokers, automated or optimal spending strategies for finding telecommunications service and service bundles can be used to achieve this goal. Targeted at services include the following: phone, fax, Internet access, value-added services, video-on-demand (VoD), VPN, gaming, or conferencing. These services can be chosen by software agents, working on behalf of customers in services markets, which become more and more competitive. Users only need to express their preference and budget. On the other hand, the opposite strategy may be chosen, where the quality of the service is given and the current market price returned. An implicit customer segment may be drawn here, where business customers mainly will determine their needs and will accept or reject a presented price in favor of the requested service, and where the private users will specify their budget constraints and accept or reject the service offered accordingly. This leads to explicit customer requirements:

- *Predictability of Charges*   Users want to be able to predict all of the costs of using a particular application, which include expenditures for communication services induced by this application. Therefore, an exact a priori specification of communication charges would be desirable. However, if this requirement cannot be fulfilled, a set of weaker demands can be sufficient. First, a user should be able to roughly estimate the charges. Such an estimation does not need to be exact, but should give at least a rough feeling to the user—similar to the knowledge that an international phone call of some minutes duration costs more than a dollar and not just a few cents. Second, a worst-case price should be known. Finally, a user must not be charged a higher price than previously announced, without the user's explicit approval.

- *Transparency and Accuracy of Charging*   To find out how much is spent for which application and what the reasons are for this, users need to be able to determine the costs of a particular session, e.g., if an application uses several flows, costs for each of these should be stated explicitly. Furthermore, for some users it might also be of interest to see what it is inside the network that causes major charges. This may give them information to switch to a different provider in the future. Detailed per-session information about charges can also be used to decide whether a certain service and its quality offers good value for price. Since not all users are interested in such details, each user must be able to decide how much information should be given.

- *Convenience* Charging components should not make using the communication services much more difficult. Charging mechanisms themselves, as well as the final bill based on the information gathered by the charging system, must be convenient for users. Hence, it must be possible for users to define "standard charging behavior" for their applications so they are not bothered with details during the start-up of an often-used application. On the other hand, they should be able to change such a description easily to have control over their expenditures, e.g., changing spending caps. Furthermore, most users want to have as few separate bills as possible, i.e., have contracts and thus business procedures with only one provider.

4.2.2.2 Provider Point of View From a business point of view, the costs of providing telecommunication services must be recovered in order to guarantee the stable, long-term existence of a provider. While pricing for traditional telecommunications services is well understood by companies, large as well as small ISPs still struggle to make profit [81]. Furthermore, providers want to maximize revenues, particularly in the open market of Internet services provisioning. This leads to explicit provider requirements:

- *Technical Feasibility* The charging approach and its mechanisms must be implementable and operable with little effort. Otherwise, if it becomes too complex, costs for the charging mechanisms might be higher than their gains. A set of real-life user trials needs to be performed to assure any of these statements. The added overhead for communication due to additional information transmitted between senders, network nodes, and receivers, and also for processing and storage purposes, especially in network nodes, e.g., to keep and manipulate charging information, must be as low as possible [36]. In addition, the introduction of scalable and low-effort security mechanisms is essential for any type of counterfeit-proof charging records and billing data.
- *Variety of Business Models* The business of providing network service over packet-switched networks must be sustainable and profitable to attract necessary investments into the infrastructure. It is not likely that all service providers will adopt exactly the same business model and strategies. Therefore, charging mechanisms must be flexible enough to support a large variety of business models and interoperate between multiple network domains employing different models. In addition, a charging system must be flexible enough to handle different pricing strategies, for example, during peak and off-peak times.

4.2.2.3 Further Requirements A CSS and the operation of a network with respect to charging require a set of additional requirements to be fulfilled.

- *Flexibility* When information is transmitted from a sender to one or several receivers, the flow of value associated with this information can be (1) in the same direction as that of the data flow, (2) in the opposite direction, or (3) a mixture of both, because both sides benefit from the information exchange [11]. For example, in the first case, the sender transmits a product advertisement, in the second case, the receiver retrieves a movie for playback; and in the third case, both sides hold a project meeting via a video-conferencing system. To support these different scenarios, a charging architecture must provide flexible mechanisms to allow participants in a communication session to specify their willingness to pay for charges in a variety of ways. Senders must be able to state that they will pay for some percentage of the overall communication costs or up to a specified total amount. Similarly, receivers may state what amount of costs they will cover. Additionally, charging mechanisms must allow flexibility in the distribution of communication charges among members of a multicast group [51].

- *Fraud Protection and Legal Security*   One of the most important issues demanded by participants is protection against fraud, i.e., that they do not have to pay for costs they have not incurred and that no one can misuse the system. The fear of users is that a provider may cheat or that other users may use their identity or derogate from them in any other way. Providers want to be sure users indeed pay for the used service. A prerequisite against fraud is technical security, such that users cannot damage, misuse, or intrude on the provider's communications systems. Legal security denotes the demand that in case of a failure, there is enough information to determine responsibility for it.

- *Stability of Service*   When a particular service with a certain quality has been agreed upon by the user and the provider, it must be ensured that the service indeed is delivered to the user. Hence, an exact definition of "quality assurance is met" is needed. On the other hand, users must be able to estimate the impact of such quality goals on their applications, so the definition must not be too complex. For example, multiple users want a video conference application, so they will likely request a communication service with a specified bandwidth and delay. If the provider promises delivery of this service, users expect no quality degradation and a very low probability of service disruption during the conference. Should quality degradation or service disruption occur, an appropriate refund mechanism must be applied which largely depends on the type of application, and hence, should be negotiated during setup of the communication service.

- *Reliability of Service*   In order to provide the infrastructure for an integrated packet switched network, service availability must be very reliable. Current telephone networks are designed to keep the blocking probability on the order of 10^{-4}. Similar requirements are likely to apply to integrated services networks. To assure such a low blocking probability, even during peak hours, significant effort in network and traffic engineering is necessary, which in turn must be accompanied by appropriate business calculation. A slightly different situation exists in the case of per-packet QoS guarantees without explicit flow admission control. In that case, the notion of blocking probability might be replaced by reliability of service measured in terms of probability that the promised level of QoS is violated.

4.2.3 Fairness and Utility

Assuming higher market efficiency and the views of users and providers described earlier, *fairness* defines to what extent each party profits from improved efficiency. Furthermore, fairness requires that all customers pay the same price for the same telecommunications services at the same time. In networks that do not charge for usage, i.e., the currently used Internet, fairness is defined in technical terms. Therefore, the introduction of charging needs to define a new notion of fairness, since a common sense of fairness as "an allocation where no person in the economy prefers anyone else's consumption bundle over his own" [39] does not reflect technical requirements. Historically, fairness has been considered in economics and at a later stage in resource-sharing work.

Traditionally, the notion of the fairness of network operations has two instances. One is fairness of the TCP, based on TCP congestion control algorithm and binary exponential back-off strategy in case of heavy traffic, where the protocol tries to serve all connections with the same throughput. This is a type of proportional fairness per unit bandwidth. Unfortunately, this works only for regional access without high delay variations between competing connections [25]. The other type is max-min fairness, where everyone is equal everywhere [3], i.e., max-min fairness maximizes the minimum share of sources, whose demand is not fully satisfied. For example, sources S_n demand x_i each of a single resource with capacity C. After ordering all demands x_i in $x_1 \leq \cdots \leq x_n$, S_1 is assigned a share of C/n. The reminder of $C/n - x_1$ is evenly distributed to $n - 1$ sources: $C/n + (C/n - x_1)/(n - 1)$. As long as there are leftovers, this process is iterated until the resource C is fully shared.

The concept of maximized welfare defines an additional fairness notion. In this case, a welfare function aggregates a number of utility functions, each of which increases in all of its arguments. According to [27], microfairness determines a fair distribution of network resources at a much finer granularity to applications. This affects basic data delivery, advanced data delivery, QoS, and application quality. Instead, macro-fairness is related to network mechanisms, which consider flows in a given network, such as mechanisms for fair queuing to perform a flow protection, e.g., by the WFQ scheduling strategy.

In the case of charging services, these notions have to change to so-called proportional fairness per unit charge [41, 64], which is relative to the number of charges a customer is willing to pay for. On the other hand, a market and competition mechanism is useful in providing users with the best and most inexpensive level of service, while creating incentives for network providers to supply more resources when there is sufficient demand.

However, the basic prerequisite for defining the notion of fairness requires the existence of a mechanism to express preferences of service usage. In economic terms these preferences are expressed by utility functions, where basically an outline of network services is applied to the perception of performance [26, 42]. Theoretically, utility functions are required to find an optimal resource allocation, while maximizing the utilization of the resource. This case is relevant, e.g., for ISPs to optimize their service provisioning. Therefore, service users can be modeled by their required utility or degree of satisfaction, since users value their perceived quality over price. For example, the utility function for a file-transfer application in Figure 4.3 shows that the user's satisfaction, S, is infinite, if the file can be transferred instantaneously. However, this utility decreases at a rate proportional to αt, where α defines a constant, e.g., depending reciprocally on the speed of the access link, and t depicts the transfer time. In the case where $t > S/\alpha$, a negative utility determines a file transfer that lasts too long, which changes the user's original valuation. Clearly, the larger α is, the longer the file transfer is accepted by the customer. Applying different values of α to different access speeds and assuming a 1-Mbyte file to be transferred, Table 3.1 indicates different utilities for a range of different user profiles.

In general, finding out about utility functions for all the different applications and services becomes awkward. However, two generally accepted classes of Internet applications

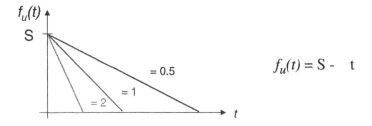

Figure 4.3 Example utility function $f_u(t)$, for a file-transfer application.

show a significantly different type of utility curve, which has been investigated by Cocchi *et al.* [26]. These characteristic curves are depicted in Figure 3.4 for elastic and real-time applications.

Assuming advance knowledge of these utility functions, they can be used as a means for distinguishing performance on the provider side; however, nonindividual or aggregated utility functions, which characterize the aggregated backbone Internet traffic or aggregated customer premises network traffic, are still an open issue for research. In addition, it remains unclear if the sound economic theory of utilities will be compliant with the user's privacy requirements. Even when an ISP knows about handling aggregated utilities, it still requires advance knowledge on a per-application basis of single input utility functions of its users and according timing information, when an application will be utilized. Even when users do not object to giving their per-application utilities to their ISP, predetermining the exact demand on an hourly or even per-minute basis is almost impossible. In addition, extensions of utility to different applications of QoS parameters, e.g., ranging from throughput to delay and jitter, are required. Finally, users evaluate charges for communication services in terms of value, which is dependent on the perceived utility of the task performed. But due to network status and congestions, the described utility may deviate from the utility perceived by the customer, therefore, investigations of the user's perception of QoS and the service started just recently, such as performed in [6], are needed.

4.2.4 Charging Tasks and Terms

Charging refers to the number of main activities to be performed for packet-switched networking and for other communications services' provisioning, if financial values are to be mapped onto resource usage or consumption. A fully operational CSS is required to accept, answer, and offer certain messages and information being exchanged over the net-

Table 4.1 Example Utilities for a File-Transfer Application

User Profile	Utility	Transfer Time (s)	α	Minimal Access Speed (Kbit/s)
Executive board member	Good	1	125.0	8000
	Acceptable	10	12.5	800
	Unacceptable	63	2.0	128
Residential user	Very well	63	2.0	128
	Good	143	1.0	56

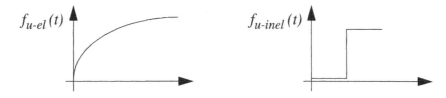

Figure 4.4   Characteristic utility functions for elastic and inelastic applications.

work. Based on the cited literature, there is a range of different, sometimes contradictory task descriptions and definitions. Therefore, the terms *metering, pricing, tariffing,* and *billing* are discussed at this stage and a unique definition is given in Section 4.2.6.

4.2.4.1 Charging and Charge Calculation

Charging is one of the most important terms in the domain considered. Based on Webster's Dictionary [128] "to charge" is defined as "to impose or record a financial obligation."

Therefore, "charging determines the process of calculating the cost of a resource by using the price for a given accounting record, which determines a particular resource consumption" [118]. Thus, charging is defined as a function that translates technical values into monetary units. The monetary charging information is included in charging records. Prices already may be available for particular resources in the accounting record or any suitable resource combination depending on the network technology or the application. Standards and research work tend to show quite a close understanding of tasks and definitions for charging.

The European Telecommunications Standardization Institute (ETSI) [33] defines charging as follows: "Charging is the determination of the charge units to be assigned to the service utilization (i.e., the usage of chargeable related elements)." In Karsten *et al.* [61] a full process point of view is defined: "Once these accounting records are collected and prices are determined in full pricing schemes on unit service, e.g., encompassing different quality levels for services or service bundles, the data for an invoice need to be calculated. The process of this calculation is termed charge calculation, performing the application of prices of unit services onto accounting records determining resource consumption. Thus, the charging function transforms mathematically unequivocal technical parameter values into monetary units. These units need to be collected, if they appear at different locations in the given networking environment, and are stored in charging records. Of course, accounting as well as charging records determine a critical set of data which need to be secured to ensure its integrity when applied to calculate monetary values or when used to compute an invoice's total." The charging process for business models offering ATM services is also called a "rating and discounting process" [112] and is "responsible for the charge calculation according to a specific pricing policy using the collected usage data." Therefore, charging mechanisms correlate service usage and calculate the charge the customer is faced with after the service utilization. Finally, according to [16]:

> Charging is the process of evaluating costs for usage of resources. Different cost metrics may be applied to the same usage of resources, and may be allocated in parallel. An example would be a detailed evaluation of resource consumption for further processing by the service

provider, and a simple evaluation of resource usage for online display of current costs. A detailed evaluation of the resource consumption can be used for generating bills to the customer, or for internal analysis by the service provider. A simple evaluation of current costs can be used for displaying an estimation of accumulated costs for the service user, or for control purposes by the customer organization or by the provider. Cost allocation assigns costs to specific endpoints, such as sender and receivers of a multicast group.

4.2.4.2 *Accounting*

Accounting is the second of the most important terms frequently used. Based on Webster's dictionary [128] "accounting" is defined as "the system of recording and summarizing business and financial transactions and analyzing, verifying, and reporting the results."

Accounting considers two different points of view. The first one is related to economic theory, where accounting relates to business processes, including profits and benefits. The second one relates to technical aspects, where technical parameters are collected. Therefore, applied to the networking environment, accounting "determines the collection of information in relation to a customer's service utilization being expressed in resource usage or consumption" [118]. Thus, accounting describes a mapping function from a particular resource usage into technical values. The information to be collected is determined by a parameter set included within an accounting record. This record depends on (1) the network infrastructure, which supports the service, e.g., IP, narrowband integrated services digital network (NISDN), ATM, or frame relay, and (2) the service provided. The content of an accounting record is of a technical nature, such as a parameter describing the duration of a phone call, the distance of a high-speed network link utilized, or the number of market transactions done. This accounting record forms the basis for further charging steps.

ETSI [33] defines accounting as "revenue sharing amongst operators." The ITU-T [54] defines terms in an economic sense: "Accounting revenue division procedure: the procedure whereby accounting revenue is shared between terminal administrations and, as appropriate, between the administrations of transit countries; Accounting rate: the rate agreed between administrations in a given relation that is used for the establishment of international accounts; Accounting rate share: the part of the accounting rate corresponding to the facilities made available in each country. This share is fixed by agreement among administrations."

The Network Working Group of the IETF has published an informal Request for Comment [14] on summarized Accounting Attributes and Record Formats. It defines an accounting server as "A network element that accepts usage events from service elements. It acts as an interface to back-end rating, billing, and operations support systems." Within this context, usage events refer to "the description of an instance of service usage," and service elements include all types of service provisioning devices, such as application bridges or gateways.

A networking technology-oriented explanation of the tasks and interfaces for accounting is presented in [61]:

> [. . .], these units need to be accounted for, traditionally performed on a percall basis over time. However, in packet-switched networks, the accounted for information may encounter a huge number of different parameters, e.g., number of packets sent, duration of a communication, number of transactions performed, distance of the communication peer, number of hops traversed, or bandwidth used. Depending on the protocol layer applied for this accounting task, only a subset of accounted for parameters are useful. In general the accounting record

determines the container for collecting this information. These records and their special appearances depend on the networking technology used, such as N-ISDN, ATM, Frame Relay, or IP. They can also be created for application services, for example, the call data record is being used for this purposes in H.323 IP telephony. Further, the Real-time Flow Measurement working group within the IETF investigates appropriate accounting mechanisms.

The accounting process applied to ATM services is defined in [112] and complies with the ITU-T process definitions just summarized from [54]. Additionally, the IETF's Authentication, Authorization, and Accounting (AAA) working group has applied the protocol Diameter (cf. Section 4.5) to specific accounting purposes. Finally, [16] states: "the process of accounting involves the following functions: collection of usage data by usage meters, creation of accounting records (data structures, or protocol data units of an accounting protocol), transport of accounting records, and collection of usage data by an accounting server."

4.2.4.3 Metering

Broad commonality and conformance can be observed for the definition of metering. ETSI [33] defines metering as ". . . the measurement of 'components' which can be used for charging such as the duration of the call . . . named also 'collection of charging information'." A full task and term definition for metering is included in [61]: ". . . there remains a single technical prerequisite for identifying and collecting accounting data. This process is called metering." Based on existing technical equipment in operation, metering tasks identify the technical value of a given parameter or resource and determine their current usage. If possible, metering can be tied to signaling events. Otherwise, it can be performed regularly, e.g., every ten seconds or every hour, it can be stimulated on other external events, such as polling requests, or it can be performed according to some statistical sampling scheme. In that case, it is closely related to network monitoring. The IETF's management information base (MIB) for switched networks and the simple network-management protocol (SNMP) [18] architectural framework can provide a means of keeping monitored data." New Zealand's approach on metering resulted in network traffic meter (NeTraMet) specifications [13] (cf. Section 4.3.2). Also for the ATM approach, network element usage metering functions are described as being responsible for the generation and reporting of accountable resource information [112].

4.2.4.4 Mediation

Mediation is concerned with the full communication service and its information level of data, such as the "begin" and "end" of communication sequences [22]. It filters, aggregates, and correlates raw data to yield different views on current network activity, and enforces business rules to package data into the form that is known to billing systems. Therefore, mediation controls a (traditionally deterministic) preprocessing of metered data according to policies and rules that have been set up by providers to minimize the amount of data collected and stored. Based on the application scenario, the final accounted-for data have to reflect the intended level of detail, e.g., guided by legal restrictions or business policies and pricing models to be applied.

4.2.4.5 Pricing and Tariffing

Pricing is the process of setting a price on a service, a product, or on content [118]. This process is an integral and critical part of business and is closely related to marketing. Prices can be calculated on a cost/profit basis or on the current market situation. For businesses selling telecommunication services, prices are set on predefined services, where the quantity used is measured, e.g., in units, time, distance, bandwidth, volume, or any combination thereof. These basic quantities to be priced are obtained from accounting devices and depend on the network type. Tariffing is a special case of pricing, normally regulated by governmental and political economic impacts [118]. Tariffs have been applied to the traditional telephone network. Karsten et al. [62] elaborate on pricing as "setting a certain price for a unit service used. Appropriate pricing of network communication provides incentives for reasonable usage of resources." In addition, a pricing scheme "describes a particular choice [. . .] and is applied to unit services offered from a communication service provider." Furthermore, a document filed with the Federal Communication Commission (FCC) or a state public utility commission by a (regulated) telephone service provider that details services, equipment, and pricing of services they provide, e.g., calling plans, is termed tariff. So-called telemanagement software uses these tariffs to determine the charge of a telephone call. For auditing purposes, telemanagement reports should match the end-of-month bill a company receives from its provider, because the same tariffs are being used to charge for calls made.

A quite similar use of pricing has been observed with respect to other related work. ETSI [33] defines pricing as "[. . .] the correlation between 'money' and 'goods' or 'service'," while it is noted that "the term is not generally used in telecommunications, the usual term being 'tariffing'." A clear distinction between price and tariff has been drawn within the M3I project (cf. [85, 119]). While "the price determines the monetary value the user owes a provider for his service provisioned and utilized, in particular it is the price per unit service. It may be based on charges and costs or it may be determined by other marketing means," price setting is defined as "the specification and the setting of prices for goods, specifically networking resources as well as services in an open market situation." Hereby the tariff "[. . .] determines [the algorithm used to] charge for a service usage. It is applied in the charge calculation for a given customer and service he utilizes to calculate the charges." The process of tariffing decides upon the algorithm used to determine a tariff for a given service and/or customer.

4.2.4.6 *Cost*

Based on [128], "cost" covers many different explanations: "The amount or equivalent paid or charged for something: Price." Obviously this usage of cost confuses mainly in technical areas. Therefore, the definition "the outlay or expenditure made to achieve an object" heads in the right direction. However, in economic accounting, various different sorts of costs are distinguished, such as general costs, capita costs, joint costs, opportunity costs, or marginal costs. Details can be obtained from, e.g., [124]. The M3I project states [119]: "Costs determine the monetary equivalent on equipment, installation, maintenance, management, operation of networks, network entities, and service provisioning. Many different types of costs can occur but it is important to note that [. . .] only costs in terms of money are of interest."

In particular, the business area of network services provisioning is considered in [61]. Since real variable costs basically do not exist or are extremely limited in nature, the term "cost per service invocation" characterizes opportunity costs (lost revenue), because resources are bound and cannot be sold otherwise. Consequently, resource usage and consumption is considered as the main cost factor. Networking is characterized by the following aspects [61]:

- High fixed costs (installation and maintenance of infrastructure)
- Low variable costs

- Fixed capacity
- Nonstorable resources and products

Business economics calls an appropriate management theory for such a business field as yield management [75]. Based on these characteristics, it is appropriate to differentiate prices according to variations in demand, instead of performing a full cost calculation for prices. The marginal return, which is given by the difference between prices for sale and variable costs, is considered to be the primary variable. The goal of a yield-management approach is to optimize the sum of marginal returns over a certain investment cycle. This sum has to exceed investments in order to allow for a profitable business.

4.2.4.7 Service Level Agreements and Interconnection

While agreements between providers are used for a long period of time in traditional telecommunications, they become important for the Internet market as well. SLAs for the Internet define formal aspects of a contract between an ISP and a customer as well as the type of traffic to be forwarded into the global Internet to allow for consistent delivery and measurement of services (cf. Section 4.4.4). SLAs are the basis for (network) interconnection between potential business partners. Traditionally, (1) it includes the collection of performance and traffic data, including availability, delay (round-trip time), and throughput measures; (2) it provides the basis for a fee calculation; (3) it offers mechanisms for data reporting and presentation; (4) it defines measurement points, such as end-to-end or switch-to-switch metrics; and (5) allows for the comparison of contracted thresholds with measured data. SLA management systems will form the key for commercial operation and management of Internet services. This covers rules applied to measurements taken inside the network, in an end-to-end fashion, or in the local loop.

According to Kilkki [69], an SLA includes, among others, definitions of the bit rate of the access link, delay information to the provider's domain, information on the network's availability including compensation and reporting activities, and timing data for repairing and installing new services. In addition, the classification rule for the stream, the specification of the traffic the customer ISP is allowed to send to the selling ISP, and the service level to be applied, e.g., best effort or premium service with bandwidth and delay, will be included. SLAs may show a (semi-)static or a dynamic behavior. While static SLAs are negotiated between the provider and a customer, dynamic SLAs change without human interactions in an automated fashion [2]. In addition, a second differentiation is made on the service quality; i.e., relative service quality and constant or variable service quality [69]. Further SLA developments address those questions of an SLA's scope, defining roles of possible interactions, the quality of privacy to be applied, e.g., encrypted/ not-encrypted, secure/insecure transmission, agreements on price, the payment method, the definition of noncompliance and reimbursement schemes, a monitoring method for service compliance, and the SLA duration [28].

Above this technical level of interest, financial interactions between providers and customers need to be considered as well [52]. While provider–provider interactions are termed "financial settlements," provider–customer interactions often are referred to as "payment." Settlements are defined as the "payment or adjustment of an account" [128], where the account in economic terms reflects the monetary equivalent for service provisioning between two business roles, such as providers and customers. These definitions lead directly to the discussion of billing and payment in the next section.

Different interconnection schemes determine various alternatives for offering, retailing, reselling, or wholesaling business schemes. However, no clear distinction is possible, since a recursive structure of the ISP market exists and relative roles in this market vary over time. In addition, the deregulated environment proposes no external entity that would be able to decide on the relationships between ISPs, customers, and their roles. Therefore, interconnection is the technical prerequisite for exchanging data. This exchange is guided and legally guarded by an SLA.

4.2.4.8 *Billing and Payment*

Billing "denotes the process of transforming the collected charging information for a customer to his/her bill" [118]. It includes the process of listing for a customer all charging information being contained in charging records that were collected over a period of time, e.g., one month. The bill summarizes all charges and indicates the amount to be paid. The bill may identify the method of payment chosen or selected, and it is transferred to customers electronically or on paper. The method of payment defines a scheme, how money is exchanged between participants, e.g., between customers and retailers or service users and providers. In general, electronic payment systems or traditional systems as utilized for traditional payment transactions are applicable.

Finally, this is similar to "the process of consolidating charging records on a per customer basis and delivering a certain aggregate of these records to a customer is termed billing" [61, 16]. The collection of these charging records requires adequate protocol support, e.g., including authentication, to allow for counterfeit-proof computation of invoices. The aggregation of monetary values (billing data) can be performed on a daily, weekly, monthly basis, or some other accepted period of time. The bill or invoice, summarizes a number of contracted details and parameters originally collected in the accounting records. Songhurst [112] distinguishes between various billing mechanisms and options based on the form of the bill (e.g., itemized or aggregated) or the time of delivery (e.g., periodic, per-call, or prepaid). The three-tiered billing architecture of Cisco systems [22] defines the process of collecting usage and accounting as billing, and refers to the sending of bills as the invoicing system.

Additionally, all bills show the amount of money to be paid by the customer to the service provider. This money may be delivered traditionally (termed payment) on paper or in an electronic-funds transfer fashion. Because new methods of payment exist, the method of how the exchange of money between buyers and sellers will be performed may include advanced electronic payments schemes.

4.2.5 Definitions of Terminology

Based on these observations, the following definitions (expanded from [121]) are utilized in the following sections:

- *Accounting* Summarized information (accounting records) in relation to a customer's service utilization. It is expressed in metered resource consumption, e.g., for the end-system, applications, middleware, calls, or any type of connections.
- *Accounting Record* An accounting record includes all relevant information acquired during the accounting process. Its internal definition can rely on Call Detail Records, Internet Protocol Detail Records, or similar standardization proposals.
- *Billing* Collecting charging records, summarizing their charging content, and delivering a bill or invoice including an optional list of detailed charges, to a user.

- *Billing Record* A billing record includes all relevant information acquired during the billing process. Its internal definition should match proposed billing-system interface standards.

- *Charge Calculation* Completing the calculation of a price for a given accounting record and its consolidation into a charging record, while mapping technical values into monetary units. Therefore, charge calculation applies a given tariff to the data accounted for.

- *Charges* Charges determine what is owed for a particular resource utilization. It is contained in a charging record.

- *Charging* The overall term "charging" is utilized as a summary word for the overall process of metering resources, enumerating their details, setting appropriate prices, calculating charges, and providing the fine-grained set of details required for billing. Note, that billing as such is not included in this definition.

- *Charging Record* A charging record includes all relevant information acquired during the charge calculation process. Its internal definition is for further definition, but may correspond to CDRs or IPDRs.

- *Charging Support System* Based on the definition of charging, the CSS implements all required tasks and interfaces that are essential and sometimes optional for managing charging-relevant data. It is concerned only with the collection of technical services data, which are mapped onto financial values, while an OSS deals with technical management tasks only.

- *Costs* Costs determine the monetary equivalent for equipment, installation, maintenance, management, operation of networks, network entities, and service provisioning. Many different types of costs can occur, but it is important to note that in the case of CSS only costs in terms of money are of interest.

- *Mediation* The task of mediation includes the filtering, aggregation, and correlation of raw, metered data. Mediation reconstructs sessions, matches measured IP addresses with users, if possible, and perform reconciliation.

- *Metering* The task of metering determines the particular usage of resources within end-systems (hosts) or intermediate systems (routers) on a technical level, including QoS, management, and networking parameters.

- *Payment* The task of payment defines the manner in which money is transferred between commercial partners to settle a rendered bill.

- *Price* The price determines the monetary value the user owes a provider for his or her service provisioned and utilized; in particular, it is the price per service unit. It may be based on charges, costs, or profits, or it may be determined by other marketing means.

- *Pricing* The specification and the setting of prices for goods, specifically networking resources and services in an open market situation. This process may combine technical considerations, e.g., resource consumption, and economical ones, e.g., applying tariffing theory or marketing, and it is part of the enterprise policy layer and requires that appropriate means of communication be in place.

- *Quality-of-Service* QoS defines the quality of a service provided. It contains technical application-level as well as network-level views and definitions. Although particular specializations exist, a commonly agreed upon definition will be used. Here, the definition from ITU-T, E. 800 [57], is applied for QoS: "The collective effect of service performance which determines the degree of satisfaction of a user of the service." Refinements are applied where necessary.

- *Service Level Agreements* An SLA defines the level of interconnection for service provisioning between providers or between a provider and a customer. The types of parameters and attributes ranges from technical values to payment schemes applied, and is still in flux.
- *Settlements* Settlements refer to the payment or adjustment of an account that needs to be enforced due to an agreed upon SLA between business roles. While important technical issues are handled by the SLA, the settlement is concerned with the financial level of interaction only.
- *Tariff* The algorithm used to determine a charge for the use of a service. It is applied in calculating the charge for a given customer and the service utilized to by that customer. Tariffs can contain, e.g., discount strategies, rebate schemes, or marketing information.
- *Tariffing* The process of deciding upon the algorithm used to determine a tariff.

4.2.6 Networking Terms

Finally, just as with the preceding charging terminology, the main networking terms and their definitions in the context of packet-switched networking are introduced, based on [61]. Resources of interest for a packet-switched communication infrastructure are given by the computing power and the buffer space of switching systems, as well as the by capacity of transmission lines (links). Computing power is a major determining factor of the number of packets that can be serviced and the amount of flow that can be handled in the case of flow-based service models. Consequently, it determines all possible computational levels of service differentiations. It should be noted that the capacity of a transmission line is useless if it cannot be fully utilized by a feeding switching system. Therefore, important resources that need to be assessed for a pricing scheme are given by the flow setup overhead (if it exists), the packet rate (and its schedulability), the traffic bandwidth (not necessarily constant), and the buffer space.

In addition, the terms packet rate and traffic bandwidth are listed separately to distinguish between two distinct units of measurement for the transmission capacity. The number of packets handled is mainly determined by the computing power of a switching system, whereas the traffic bandwidth is limited by the overall link bandwidth and throughput of a switching system. Furthermore, the input parameter for network capacity dimensioning and for pricing schemes is given by the access bandwidth of customers and adjacent providers. Eventually, this parameter defines the maximum resource QoS requests the local link.

4.3 RELATED WORK

Charging for communication services has been on the research-and-development agenda for years. However, service profiles and networking technologies changed rapidly and different communication paradigms, e.g., the shift from a circuit-switched to a packet-switched communication model, evolved. Therefore, new approaches for Internet transport, services, and content charging become necessary. This section on related work discusses major steps and projects taken for handling Internet charging. It adds a short description of accounting and mediation technologies for the Internet environment, and finishes the discussion with a brief review of traditional billing of telephony and ATM services.

4.3.1 Charging Projects

The number of projects on the Internet concerned with charging has increased quite significantly. Only a small number of recent and charging-centric work dealing with system's design and modeling is summarized below. Another overview can be found in [114]. Many projects dealing with charging and accounting functionality at the network level try to achieve a high independence from pricing models [118]. However, it has been noted that pricing in general and usage-based pricing in particular can impose a high overhead on telecommunication systems [78, 108]. Any form of usage-based pricing for various telecommunication services is interesting, because underlying resources (such as satellites, frequencies, cables, routers/switches, and most notably operating personnel) are scarce and very costly. The traditional Internet pricing model has been critiqued constantly in the past for its economic drawbacks of not being incentive-compatible [108, 24, 47]. Furthermore, it is inflexible—for example, it does not allow for combined sender/receiver payments—and does not provide economic signals, which are needed for network planning and expansion. But most importantly, the current model is based on the assumption of a single-service best effort network that provides a similar service to all customers. Therefore, the multiservice paradigm needs to be investigated with respect to heterogeneous networking infrastructures and technologies of the Internet. An early per-flow billing system for TCP flows and initial ideas on a billing service design are presented in [29] and [110], respectively. Advanced per-flow charging and accounting approaches based on reservations have been tackled in [36, 59, 62]. For the case of an integrated-services packet-switched network, the approach in [37] defines a service-dependent charging policy. Based on a list of charging properties and a cascading queuing station model, a charging formula is presented and discussed, which includes a reservation and usage portion.

4.3.1.1 Charging and Accounting Technology for the Internet   The objectives of the Swiss National Science Foundation project charging and accounting technology for the Internet (CATI) [115] included the design, implementation, and evaluation of charging and accounting mechanisms for Internet services and VPN. This covered the enabling technology support for open, Internet-based EC platforms in terms of usage-based transport service charging as well as high quality Internet transport services and its advanced and flexible configurations for VPNs. In addition, security-relevant and trust-related issues in charging, accounting, and billing processes have been investigated. Important application scenarios, such as an Internet telephony application, demonstrated the applicability and efficiency of the developed approaches [116]. This work was complemented by investigations of cost recovery for ISPs, including various investigations of suitable usage-sensitive pricing models for end-to-end communications based on reservations [36, 122], as well as SLAs between service providers [28].

4.3.1.2 Market Managed Multiservice Internet   The 5th Framework European IST project, Market-Managed Multiservice Internet (M3I) [85], aims at the design and

implementation of a next-generation system that will enable Internet resource management through market forces, specifically by enabling differential charging for multiple levels of service. This novel approach, offering a charging system, will increase the value of Internet services to customers through a greater choice in price and quality and better QoS through reduced congestion. Flexibility will be improved for the ISP, management complexity reduced, and the potential for increasing revenues is great. Price-based resource management pushes intelligence and, hence, complexity to the edges of the Internet, ensuring similar scalability and simplicity of the current network. It is intended to design a trial system, which will enable players in the Internet services market to explore sophisticated charging options and business models with their customers.

4.3.1.3 *Internet Demand Experiment*

another highly important question concerns the issue of user acceptance of pricing schemes. The Index Demand Experiment (INDEX) project was started in order to investigate user reaction when exposed to various pricing schemes for different qualities of Internet access [20, 30]. It turned out that users were not opposed to flexible pricing models. Moreover, the widespread flat-rate model, at least in its pure form, proved to tend toward waste of resources, unfairness among users, and revenue losses for ISPs. Therefore, an "alternative" ISP has been proposed, offering differentiated services with dynamic volume-based pricing and suitable feedback mechanisms to inform the users on their own patterns of consumption. These project results have become a stimulus for efforts to shift Internet pricing schemes away from the simple flat rate model.

4.3.1.4 *Lightweight Policing and Charging*

The main assumption of this work is that a multiservice packet network can be achieved by adding classification and scheduling to routers, but not policing [12]. Therefore, a lightweight, packet-granularity charging system has been investigated emulating a highly open policing function that is separated from the data path. The number of charging functions required depends on the customer's selection of services and is operated on the customer's platform. The proposed architecture includes a set of functions distributed to customers, which can include metering, accounting, and billing as well as per-packet or per-flow policing and admission control. The proposal concludes that lower cost is achieved through simplicity without sacrificing commercial flexibility or security. Different reasons for charging, such as interprovider charging, multicast charging, and open bundling of network charges with those for higher class services, are considered within the same design. A discussion of value flows in such an environment can be found in Briscoe [11].

4.3.1.5 *Edge Pricing*

The fundamental idea of edge pricing concerns pricing decisions, which are made at the edge of an ISP locally [26, 108]. Therefore, no standardized pricing models are necessary, since ISP interconnections involve bilateral agreements only, e.g., in DiffServ this will be a major part of SLAs between ISPs. This decentralized approach allows for different edges of the Internet to support differing pricing models at the same time. Furthermore, edge pricing's characteristic of transparency enables ISPs to use, adapt, and evolve pricing policies independently. In a basic approach, customers define the maximal total price they are willing to pay as a sender or a receiver of data, respectively, as well as an upper limit for the maximal number of hops. This charging information can be transmitted as part of a signaling protocol, e.g., in the RSVP header [36, 62].

4.3.1.6 Congestion Pricing

Congestion is a problem for today's packet-switched networks, particularly the current Internet. The central question is: Are there means to possibly encourage users to cooperate with the network and at the same time allow for differential QoS provisioning in the network? Emerging ways of controlling network resources use traffic-control mechanisms in terms of congestion pricing approaches to achieve differential QoS. If there is no congestion, the price for utilizing the network is zero or at a minimal value, but it increases with increasing congestion. This scheme is incentive compatible, as it gives users the choice of backing off when the network is overloaded, and allows those willing to pay more to get more. In this case, feedback signals from the network to the customer are related to shadow prices and the marginal cost of congestion. All customers are free to react as they chose, but will have to pay charges when resources are congested. Such behavior between users and the network can be considered self-management [63]. In addition, this model complies with gaming theory, since users play a game with the network [66]. Within the Internet, different algorithms can be linked to TCP or flow control schemes. In addition, the Explicit Congestion Notification (ECN) proposal [99] offers a feedback mechanism to users, which is applied as one possible example in the M3I project [85] as well as proposed in [67, 68]. Finally, the congestion pricing approach has an impact on networking infrastructure investments [46].

4.3.1.7 Cumulus Pricing Scheme

Pricing models form a scalable approach for network management. This alternative view on pricing as an economic traffic-control scheme is based on eliciting user information about expected usage patterns. Based on this information, ISPs are enabled to optimize, e.g., network configuration or admission control, with respect to objectives such as the maximization of utilization or revenue. The cumulus pricing scheme (CPS) defines a flat-rate scheme (but rates may vary over long time-scales). It provides a feedback mechanism to bring market forces into play (where this feedback is not an immediate one, but requires the accumulation of a sufficient number of discrete "flags" indicating user behavior), and it allows for a wide flexibility in terms of the technical prerequisites, especially concerning the measuring and accounting mechanisms of the required data records [121]. CPS has been developed with respect to three main dimensions—(1) customer-oriented, (2) ISP economic, and (3) ISP technical—which define the Internet pricing "feasibility problem," i.e., an optimal trade-off between the ISP's technical, the ISP's economic, and customer-oriented requirements [101]. The fundamental decision between static and dynamic schemes touches customers' desires concerning price stability, e.g., highly fluctuating auctions, whereas orienting a pricing scheme strictly according to the forces of the market induces technical infeasibility. The key to the solution proposed lies in building a contract between customer and ISP upon suitable information about the expected usage pattern of the service and influencing the actual customer behavior by a new type of feedback mechanism that is specific in terms of its relation to different time scales. Measurements take place over a short time period and allow evidence about user behavior on a medium time scale. This evidence is expressed in terms of discrete flags, so-called cumulus points, yet not triggering a reaction by themselves, but only as a result of their accumulation over a long time period. Reichl and Stiller [101] propose a framework for tariff descriptions that identifies that existing tariffs seldomly consider a time-scale mapping. It demonstrates that the design of CPS eventually even solves the feasibility problem mentioned.

4.3.1.8 Charging for Premium IP Services The ACTS project SUSIE is focused on the examination, design, implementation, and testing of solutions for charging and accounting of QoS-enhanced IP services. Driven by the need to support a wide range of possible tariff schemes and prices, the proposed charging and accounting architecture shall support a flexible set of metering solutions, the exchange of accounting information between providers and customers, and a means to provision tariffing information. Due to the fact that a wide range of application requirements and user value are in place, a tariff- dependent service selection is desirable. A charging and accounting architecture has been developed and applied to premium IP services [17]. In particular, a tariff formula language defines the description options for the charging formulas and utility curves. The Charging and Information Protocol allows for user information on current tariffs in a push and pull mode. The tariff- dependent service selection is supported by a utility-price optimizer based on user preferences, offered service classes, and applied tariffs.

4.3.2 Metering, Accounting, and Mediation Technology

A major input for CSSs is defined by the set of parameters and their values, which are measurable from the underlying networking infrastructure, including hardware and equipment, and software and communication protocols that are in place. While the lowest-layer task is defined as metering (cf. Figure 4.2 and Section 4.2.4.3), two example technology choices are mentioned at this stage.

One example is the NeTraMet [15, 13] as the first implementation of the Internet AAA architecture [80]. The NeTraMet implementation defines a meter that runs on various platforms. It collects IP packets and byte counts for traffic flows that are defined by their addresses. Addresses can be Ethernet addresses, various protocol addresses, e.g., IP or IPX, transport address information, such as IP port numbers, or combinations thereof. While the traffic flows to be observed are specified by a set of rules that are downloaded to NeTraMet by a manager, traffic flow data are collected via SNMP by a collector. Within NeTraMet's newest version, DSCPs and IPv6 implementations are supported.

A second example is given by Cisco's NetFlow product, which provides usage-based data collection to be integrated into a so-called three-tier billing architecture, where instrumentation, mediation, and billing are combined [22]. Within the instrumentation level, raw data measured at devices are collected in different data formats. The following level, "mediation," is concerned with the service and information levels of data, which begin and end the communication sequences. It filters, aggregates, and correlates raw data to yield different views on current network activity, and enforces business rules to package data into the form that is common to billing systems. The nonvolatile collection and storage platform is based technically on an accounting adjunct processor, which is necessary to relieve router memory from vast amounts of accounting data. Finally, a third-party billing system collects these mediated and packaged data. It matches these formatted data with rating systems, prices the resource usage, and outputs the record details to existing invoicing systems.

A third example covers Hewlett-Packard's Smart Internet Usage (SIU) product [111], which determines a distributed usage management system with open interfaces to a wide range of applications and data sources. Its distributed architecture was designed to scale according to growing demands with respect to numbers of services and customers. SIU collects, aggregates, and correlates data obtained from the technical infrastructure, including hardware and software components, relying on a metering tool that is in place. The configurable presentation and transformation of usage data provide the basic step to obtain information, which can be utilized for any sort of charging approach for the various services an ISP might envision.

Among various other technologies, several mediation, accounting, and billing systems exist in the market. A close similarity to various data format definitions can be observed (cf. Section 4.4.5).

4.3.3 Traditional Telecommunication Billing

Charging is not a new area, since related areas of significance for charging for data communications exist. This is due to, e.g., the length of time it took the telephone network to determine traditional telecommunications billing. Before the days of deregulation, the handling of interconnections between national telecommunication operators was based on dealing with telephone calls. As standardized in the ITU-T D Recommendations series [54], Accounting-rate systems (ARS) were devised to simplify operator-to-operator interfaces and sharing of revenues between originating and terminating operators. The accounting-revenue procedure division defines how the accounting revenue is shared between terminal administrations, and, as appropriate, between administrations of transit countries [54]. It includes the accounting-rate share as part of the accounting rate, corresponding to facilities made available in each country. This share is fixed by agreement among operators.

Thus, the ARS had to be negotiated between every separate interconnect partner. The advantage of this system is based on the fact that only bilateral agreements had to be negotiated. However, its drawback came with the liberalization of the telecommunications industry, since an ARS does not reflect the real costs of service provisioning, traffic analysis between operators is limited, and data interrogation in cases of disputes is almost impossible [74]. In addition, on the technical side, all charging capabilities (including interfaces to billing systems) were hardwired down to the switching fabric, where all data collected were tied inextricably to devices, such as line cards, crossbars, or ATM switches [22, 103]. This tight model does not offer a single degree of flexibility, particularly for different interoperable equipment, as is required for today's and tomorrow's Internet networking devices. Finally, Internet charging and SLA need to integrate multiservice agreements between providers. While telephony bearer services basically consist of a single end-to-end service class, the telephony circuit of 64-kbit/s equivalents and some predetermined delay, today's Internet services show a much larger variety of technical parameters and resource usage within the network itself. The main difference in telephony compared to the Internet is visible in the set of fixed QoS characteristics per telephone connection. The style of packet-switched networks shows major technical differences and requires different handling of charging. Thus, new concepts for Internet transport, services, and content charging are essential to develop a similar level of operation and reliability for Internet CSS.

Work on charging in the ATM environment shows commonalities, but is still significantly different from the Internet, due to at least the virtual connection principle applied. For ATM-based B-ISDN the tasks of accounting, charge calculation, and billing are required to complete a commercial services offer of integrated services. ATM charging can be expected to serve as an embracing network functionality capable of supporting the needs of service providers, retail customers, value-added service providers, and other businesses in a differentiated services market situation. VPNs offer the possibility of satisfying special enterprise needs on a closed networking environment, where an ATM-based solution is highly qualified to obtain the bandwidth and guaranteed QoS required. It guarantees maximum flexibility for a variety of different applications requiring multimedia services, it eases management overhead, and it reduces costs of operating the VPN. However, ATM-based Intranets are only affordable for medium and larger enterprises, because tariffing structures slightly favor high-volume customers.

The ATM view of accounting, charging, and billing has been preliminarily defined in [32]. The basic charging for ATM, termed "three tier charging" [72], includes the setup fee, all duration fees, and all volume fees. In contrast, two basic components of ATM tariffs are commonly identified by ETSI [31]. Charges of an access component are typically fixed per installation, and they remain constant over billing periods, which does not require any on-line measurements. However, this scheme should still allow providers to compensate and recover costs for required facilities of a service subscriber to access a service or services, e.g., facilities specifically provided to that service subscriber. In addition, these charges are independent of the utilization and are related mainly to the type of access, such as capacity provided, maintenance, or redundancy. Charges of the utilization component should be in accordance with the service requested by the service subscriber. The measurement of this utilization component usually has to be carried out. Most ATM utilization charging schemes are based on saving parameters received through the ATM signaling, e.g., including traffic contract, source and destination addresses, counting ATM cells during the ongoing call, and saving the setup time and duration of the call. Since ATM technology in the wide-area environment used to be controlled by Post, Telephone, Telegraph (PTTs), tariffing schemes defined initial approaches for public ATM networks. Legacy ATM networks still rely on conventional tariff models as applied to telephone services. Current implementations on ATM pricing models are based either on a flat rate, as for legacy leased-line tariffs, or on a two-part pricing scheme that includes a monthly access and a usage-based fee, as it has been for legacy switched-circuits tariffs. Research results on pricing ATM services have been obtained, e.g., by several ACTS projects, such as Charging and Accounting Schemes in Multi-Service ATM Networks (CA$HMAN) [112] and Contract Negotiation and Charging in ATM Networks (CANCAN) [72], as well as another Swiss project [103]. These proposals suggested different ATM pricing models to take into account various service classes offered by ATM.

4.4 INTERNET SERVICES AND TECHNOLOGY CHOICES

The different technologies for Internet services can be distinguished by their trade-off between features and complexity. While a larger set of features, such as QoS support or advanced security functionality, has the potential for a better services differentiation, the complexity of this particular technology increases. However, in order to combine these technical service differentiation methods with components for adding economic control mechanisms, these different technologies require adequate interfaces for dealing with charging-relevant information and tasks. For that reason, major QoS methods and service differentiation methods are described, Internet technology choices are discussed, and interprovider agreements, as well as suitable accounting and charging data formats, are presented.

4.4.1 Quality of Service Methods

Three major groups of QoS methods are concerned with the control of data flows in a network [113], the Internet in particular. The first group deals in the shortest amount of time with per-packet or per-flow issues, once the flow has been set up or data are transmitted. The second group handles procedures in medium time periods to signal QoS requirements to appropriate network elements. Finally, the third group provides in longest amount of time to engineer multiple traffic streams and networks as a whole.

Based on Karsten *et al.* [61], these different groups include in particular the following methods. Packet scheduling impacts the QoS experienced by a packet, since the queuing delay constitutes a portion of the total end-to-end transfer delay. Therefore, scheduling is concerned with the decision of which packet to send next on a given link. Examples include FIFO, WFQ and RED. Traffic policing and shaping deal with the task shaping traffic to either a negotiated or advertised level of service at the edges of networks or between network elements. Example mechanisms include leaky or token-bucket traffic shapers in order to ensure a controllable network load. Finally, adaptiveness determines the capability of end-systems to react to congestion in the network by evaluating signals from the network. These signals can be implicit, e.g., loss of packets, or explicit, e.g., by an ECN [99]. Dynamic and congestion-based pricing of network services are also a form of network signals proposed for managing QoS (cf. Section 4.3.1.6).

Signaling and admission control are a major representative of the second group of QoS methods. This integrated set of mechanisms builds on a session or call paradigm, where users of the network signal their requirements explicitly and the network consults local admission-control modules to accept or reject those requests. While per-flow admission control allows for statistical QoS guarantees on a per-packet basis only, admission-control procedures are either parameter- or measurement-based. An example of a proposed signaling protocol for the RSVP [8], while another one is an inter-bandwidth broker protocol [115].

Finally, long-term methods include traffic engineering, and are concerned with the distribution of traffic for a given network by mechanisms such as explicit or QoS-based routing schemes. Network design and engineering, called provisioning as well, deal with the set up and maintenance of network equipment and the design of particular instances of QoS methods based on experience, expert knowledge, heuristics, or formal optimization methods.

4.4.2 Service Differentiation Methods

Until recently, the Internet has performed on a noncommercial basis and service differentiation has not been necessary. However, with commercialization of the Internet, considered to be a commercially operated networking infrastructure and its offered services, this point of view changes. In particular, once an end-customer has to choose from, say, two different service classes, a best effort one and another one delivering some sort of bandwidth guarantees, the purely technical solution of providing these classes is not sufficient any more. The reason for this is obscured by the greedy nature of almost every, certainly the majority of, end-customers—they will always choose that service class with the best QoS. Of course, if this is the case, the service class with less QoS will become obsolete, since it is not used. In turn, users encounter similar problems as before within the better class of service due to its potential for being heavily congested. This situation will remain unchanged as long as no financial incentives for choosing a service class that is perfectly suited for the end-customer's needs are provided by the Internet.

Today's Internet does not offer service differentiation mechanisms, since the best effort type of service still dominates. In addition, the basic Internet protocol is defined by the IP, which is currently used in its Version 4 and does not provide any service class differentiation features besides the ToS field. Nevertheless, this field is only optionally used on a wide scale within IPv4. Enhancements and changes, including a flow label field [96], determine the new version IPv6 being prepared by the IETF.

An important way to make an effective service differentiation is the definition of a QoS model for services offered. According to Bradner [9], the following macroscopic facets exist. The scope defines the logical distance over which a service model is provided. The granularity identifies the smallest service unit, which is treated individually by the service model. The time period specifies the granularity in time for which services are being provided. And the control model formulates those entities, which perform the control over the network and the traffic. They can be located exclusively in the network or in end-systems, with a continuum of hybrid forms in between. However, since two distinct Internet protocol architectures are used today as approaches for a service differentiated Internet, distinct QoS models and their corresponding technology choices exist.

Another challenge is due to the fact that the application of a differentiated pricing model for differentiated Internet services gives network operators a substantial gain in efficiency. It has been shown theoretically and by simulation that this increase in efficiency depends on the traffic characteristics of applications [26, 106]. Another important factor is the degree of competition allowed by regulators. Global Internet services usually cross many different provider networks, and providers overlap each other geographically. This development not only increases competition, but also increases the choice of service offerings and the efficiency of network operation. Therefore, provisioning of differentiated services requires charging and accounting services in the Internet. The offer of multiple service classes and the precision used in appropriate pricing models depends on the way packet-based communication is handled. For example, in the medium time-scale phase of QoS methods, existing signaling protocols like RSVP [8] can provide the basis for collecting charging data [117, 59].

4.4.3 Internet Technology Choices

Starting from the presentation of the best effort model with overprovisioning, continuing to a price-based best effort, the integrated services and the differentiated services models, a combination of these approaches is discussed.

4.4.3.1 Best Effort Assuming that overprovisioning of network resources, basically bandwidth, is both possible and sufficient to sustain the single-service nature of the current Internet, an end-to-end communication is possible, where all control entities are located in end-systems [61]. Therefore, no state exists in the network and all traffic is treated at the same granularity with longer time periods, essentially equal to the length of a capacity planning cycle. The QoS method applied to this model is the network design and engineering model to provide for a superabundance of network resources. In periods of resource scarcity this model relies on the adaptiveness of end-systems. Based on another assumption that pure overprovisioning is not sufficient without an additional means of signaling besides packet loss, this additional signal is a per-packet price, depending on the internal state of the network, e.g., its congestion level. The time period of interest for this model is related to the period of price announcements and the ability to set them from the provider's side. Again, network design and engineering methods are applied, but end-systems' or users' sensitivity to pricing signals has be estimated.

Neither of these two models has been proven to be optimal or totally unsuited. In addition, the combination of technical means and an economic-driven control strategy integrates a set of not yet fully understood factors (such as packet-switched, connectionless networking technology, and the extremely high pace of network and customer growth) of a new and rapidly emerging Internet services market.

4.4.3.2 Integrated Services Internet
IntServ defines a framework in support of unidirectional end-to-end flows [7]. These flows can request certain QoS and can use a controlled-load service [129] or a guaranteed service [109]. As shown in Figure 4.5, available service classes in IntServ distinguish between best effort and guaranteed services.

However in every case, flows need to establish a context between the sender, the receiver, and intermediate nodes. Therefore, RSVP [8] has been defined as a protocol for reserving network resources for single flows, which are specified by the sender and receiver in terms of desired traffic classes, including bandwidth, delay, and loss characteristics. RSVP relies on the existence of an admission control, resource allocation, and packet-forwarding mechanism in each router to ensure that the requested QoS parameters can be guaranteed. Advantageous features of the IntServ and RSVP approach encompass a receiver-driven QoS specification, the support of multicast traffic and its merging for reservations, and the soft state approach for maintaining the context data of a flow. However, the support on a per-flow basis shows a linear scalability with respect to the number of flows and states to be kept in large backbone routers [59]. The per-flow granularity imposes overhead that may not be necessary for a certain number of situations.

4.4.3.3 Differentiated Services Internet
Due to these assumed scalability problems when handling single flows, a different framework was developed. Instead of treating a single flow as the entity of interest, the DiffServ handles Internet traffic based on the notion of aggregated, unidirectional flows and fixed numbers of service levels in terms of service profiles [4]. This approach minimizes the state to be maintained in the routers. In addition, this is supported by a domain concept, where a group of routers implements a similar number of service levels and the appropriate set of policies. This DiffServ domain is defined by a fixed boundary, consisting of ingress and egress routers. However, traffic

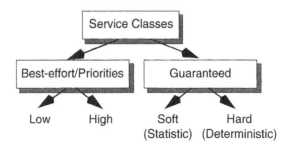

Figure 4.5 Service classes in IntServ (based on Braden et al. [7]).

traversing such a DiffServ domain is required to be marked. This marking happens on a per-IP-packet basis at the ingress routers and utilizes the DS field in an IP packet [87]. This DS field replaces the ToS field from the IPv4 protocol and accepts the definition of PHB, which in turn determine the service level such a packet will be treated by. Once the DSCP as part of the DS field has been set, the packet travels through the DS domain, and are treated equally in every interior router [89].

Therefore, since single end-to-end flows are bundled to aggregated flows with a similar behavior within a DS domain, the DS approach requires less overhead. However, the need to mark IP packets at DS borders remains. In addition, a longer termed service contract may be required between different DS domains, since a certain service level may be required. This type of flow aggregation, in conjunction with service guarantees, requires some sort of admission control, since an overutilization can lead to service degradations. SLAs are regularly set up between interconnecting ISPs in order to maintain the desired service level for the aggregated flows. An initial SLA needs to be set up between interconnected ISPs before any service is exchanged. SLAs can also be adjusted dynamically. Further details on SLAs are provided in Section 4.4.4 below.

4.4.3.4 Comparison and Combination (IntServ over DiffServ)
As presented earlier, IntServ as well as DiffServ have a number of advantages and drawbacks. Based on six classification criteria, Table 4.2 summarizes these differences for the IntServ, DiffServ, and best effort traffic architectures of the Internet.

One possible combination of IntServ and DiffServ advantages could apply to IntServ in the access and DiffServ in the core network. Local area networks (LANs) tend to show an overprovisioning of bandwidth, which does not require sophisticated resource management and signaling, if certain topology and traffic considerations are taken into account. The access network, however, utilizes RSVP to signal flow requirements from LAN-based hosts to the core's edge routers. They perform a mapping of these requirements onto particular flow aggregation types available in the DiffServ core represented by a dedicated SLA. Since core routers perform traffic forwarding based purely on PHBs, they are able to cope with many aggregated flows. Therefore, only edge routers need to keep the state of flows from their local domain.

4.4.4 Interprovider Agreements

Interprovider agreements are required between ISPs, to define terms and conditions of services for traffic exchange. Such an agreement represents a contract-like relationship,

Table 4.2 Comparison of Internet Network Architectures

Criteria	Best Effort	IntServ	DiffServ
QoS Guarantees	No	Per data stream	Aggregated
Configuration	none	Per session (dynamic)	Long-term (static)
Zone	Entire network	End-to-end	Domain-oriented
State information	None	Per data stream (in router)	(None, in BB, in edge router)
Protocols	None	Signaling (RSVP)	Bit field (DS byte)
Status	Operational	Matured	Being worked on

indicating all characteristics of the service and its implied financial settlements. Traditionally, within the Internet, ISPs engage in interconnection agreements to assure each other pervasive Internet connectivity. This allows ISPs to exchange traffic at an interconnection point, either with or without financial settlements [1]. Traditionally, these agreements do not consider QoS-related issues. More recently, SLAs are used as a means of establishing a provider/customer type of relationship between two providers. While the exact content of an SLA often depends on the specific business and technology context, the core of an SLA always includes a description of the traffic covered by the SLA and the service level that is to be applied. SLAs provide the contractual envelope for QoS-based assurances. As discussed in Kneer et al. [71] and Stiller et al. [120], the following types of SLAs can be described.

4.4.4.1 DiffServ SLAs

The DiffServ approach is based on the notion of "network domains," which can be operated by different ISPs. In a pure DiffServ world, both access and core domains would use DiffServ technology to transfer data within their domains as well as between domains. In order to indicate service commitments between domains, SLAs are employed. However, the IETF working group on DiffServ does not consider SLAs as their area of interest.

DiffServ SLAs are defined on the contract level, according to the type of underlying physical network connectivity. According to the contemplated DiffServ support for multiple service classes, an SLA also specifies a selected service class. Thus, a DiffServ SLA includes at least:

- Description of the aggregated flow to which the SLA is applicable.
- Corresponding throughput values.
- Corresponding service class, e.g., expedited/assured forwarding, determining QoS, delay or loss characteristics.

In principle, DiffServ SLAs can be defined at any granularity level, including the level of application flows. As DiffServ pursues the goal of high scalability, only a limited set of SLAs is likely to exist between any two domains, so that explicit support of individual flows through DiffServ SLAs will be an exception. Further work on SLAs and service-level specifications can be found in Salsano et al. [104].

4.4.4.2 Commercial SLAs

SLAs have emerged in the commercial domain as a result of increasing customer demand to understand what kind of service they can expect from an ISP. Such SLAs are typically tied to the provision of a network service on a long-term basis and service provision, which includes both the installation of physical equipment, e.g., routers or access lines, and the provision of a data transporting service, e.g., based on IP protocols.

In order to capture QoS aspects, SLAs include parameters similar to those considered in the DiffServ case. As an example, the SLA employed by UUNET foresees the following attributes:

- Throughput offered to customers, e.g., T1
- Round-trip latency across the provider's network
- Availability of the service

- Outage notification duration
- Duration between order and installation
- Reimbursement procedure in case of noncompliance

These SLA approaches tend to serve the same purpose: establish longer-term service relationships between adjacent ISPs, and provide assurances for traffic aggregates exchanged between them. This avoids the overhead implied by a high number of concurrent SLAs and frequent changes in terms of agreements.

4.4.4.3 Flow-based SLAs
In principle, SLAs can be applied at the service interface between ISPs, providing IP access and their end-customers. However, given that in access domains per-flow handling of traffic is a viable option, a different approach is feasible, offering superior flexibility in applying charging schemes to QoS-based traffic.

First, it is likely that QoS support within the Internet will not be pervasive. Whenever a QoS-based flow is requested by an application, the availability of such support has to be established, depending on source and destination endpoints as well as the sequence of ISPs involved. Providing SLAs dynamically on a per-flow basis allows such dependencies to be considered and automatically adapt to increasing Internet support for QoS. Second, considering QoS automatically implies a strong differentiation among Internet services. QoS can be provided at multiple levels, e.g., to support various audio qualities. Consequently, there is a need for differential and QoS-dependent pricing in order to prevent users from making use of the best QoS level only. Similarly, applying differential pricing is required in order to reflect the communication path, i.e., ISPs traversed, including source and destination locations. Both aspects lead to service costs, which can be established only if characteristics of a requested flow are known, i.e., on a per-flow basis. Third, there is an ongoing discussion on the pricing scheme that should be applied to Internet traffic. Dynamic pricing of offered services based on the current level of network usage was shown to significantly improve service characteristics a network can provide, for instance, reduce congestion and smooth traffic. Assuming such an approach, both the implied QoS level and the price provided are to be established dynamically for each new flow.

Providing flow-based SLAs captures all mentioned issues. Such SLAs are in contrast to the ones considered earlier. They directly concern application-level flows and not aggregations of traffic. Furthermore, they are likely to be set up for the required duration of communications only. Flow-based SLAs are in line with the service model proposed by IntServ, as far as the end-customer's point of view is concerned, since they want to have selectable QoS on a per-flow basis. In contrast, the arguments mentioned earlier are driven by economic considerations. ISPs want to provide incentives for end-customers to make use of more or fewer resources in the network and, in the case of dynamic pricing, ISPs want to consider the availability of free resources when setting prices. These aspects are best considered in the context of individual demand units, i.e., flows for end-customers or aggregates for enterprises.

4.4.5 Standardized Data Formats

CDRs [58], sometimes termed call detail reporting, call data records, or station message detail record (SMDR), are the most commonly known records for call-specific data, originating from telephony-based telecommunication systems and developed over many years in an environment with quite static services portfolios. Such a record defines the fundamental unit of data to be exchanged in the circuit-switched voice world. It contains data about each call made, e.g., dialed digits, the phone number dialed from, call direction, service type, associated inverse multiplexing session and port, date, time, off-hook time, on-hook time, how long the call lasted, and a circuit identifier. Virtually all telephony switches, private branch exchanges (PBXs), and ATM switches [103] produce CDRs. However, each switch product tends to produce CDRs in different formats, which means that data fields of each record may appear in a different order from one switch to another. Therefore, performance-intensive software needs to convert various CDR formats into a standard format usable by a charging system. Because the network provider can charge for bandwidth on an as-used basis, the CDR can be used to understand and manage bandwidth usage. However, they are different in that an SMDR is focused on the station (terminal) and the CDR is focused on the call itself. Therefore, the two terms should not be used interchangeably, since the formats of the records will be different. Usually, a single device, say a PBX, will produce one or the other, but not both.

To cope with networking characteristics of the Internet, mainly the packet-switched characteristic compared to the telephone network's circuit-switched system, a corresponding data specification is required. In addition, the Internet market trend to develop and deploy new services frequently raises a second dimension of complexity for an "Internet CDR." Therefore, the initiative "IPDR.org" decided to develop a basic framework for a usage specification, called IPDR, which allows different companies to develop dedicated code within the framework, support interoperability, and the usefulness of the specification [21]. It refers (1) to a functional operation, where an NDM function collects data from devices and services in a provider's network, and (2) to usage, the type of data, which shows an open, extensible, and flexible record format (the IPDR record) for exchanging usage information of essential parameters of IP-related transactions. A repository for defined IPDRs is envisioned, including the variety of services, such as email services, as well as real-time services. These definitions will form the essential elements of data exchange between network elements, OSSs, CSSs, and BSSs. The framework will provide the foundation for the development of open, carrier-grade Internet services enabling next-generation IP networks to operate efficiently and cost effectively.

The recently published informal RFC on accounting attributes and record formats [14] summarizes existing IETF and ITU-T work and discusses advantages as well as drawbacks in close detail. With respect to the Internet, the remote-access dial-in user service (RADIUS) accounting record (RAC), the DIAMETER attributes, and real-time flow measurement (RTFM) architecture are important. While RADIUS, among others, deals with start, stop, and activity data including various accounting, tunneling, and general attributes, DIAMETER being part of the AAA architecture (cf. Section 4.3.2) inherits all of them and defines a secure protocol to transfer these accounting attributes. Finally, the RTFM architecture supports flow measurements via RTFM meter readers, which read data from MIB to be stored in RTFM attributes, such as source and destination information, as well as packets and byte counts.

Additional data formats are available, but mainly with respect to a particular protocol or application. The domain name system (DNS) and the dynamic-host configuration protocol (DHCP) maintain customer profile data, which form a type of standardized data format. In addition, the lightweight directory-access protocol (LDAP) offers mechanisms with transfer capabilities for customer-profile data. However, these data formats are not generally used for the purpose of accounting.

4.4.6 Electronic Payment Systems

Aside from communication protocol relevant issues and Internet networking technology choices, a particular area of interest arises. With respect to fully integrated electronic service delivery, electronic payments for various kinds of transport and content services determine the clear necessity of pico- or micropayments. Since existing electronic payment systems are not well suited for this task, solutions have to be researched, including efficient cryptographic protocols for secure transmission of payments [98]. To implement a complete billing system successfully, legal contracts are needed that are based today mostly on verification of customers' identity by letter or telephone. This is due to the absence of efficient electronic authentication mechanisms and certification authorities. Once a contract has been established, traditional invoicing or credit card billing is the most popular way to collect money. However, electronic payment systems that provide anonymity [19] and/or small amounts [79] are still not accepted with ISPs. Today, it is not clear, whether micropayments or anonymous e-cash provide a real advantage to service providers offering usage-based pricing for their services.

4.5 PRICING MODELS

The increasing deregulation of the telecommunications market and the emerging business orientation of Internet services drive the need for appropriate pricing models for packet-based communications, which are independent of regulated aspects. Well-known and widely accepted pricing models for communication networks offering a single network service, e.g., telephony or X.25, are provider-centric, i.e., they are set to fixed values and reissued, whenever provider costs or regulations change. However, in an increasingly competitive environment, this approach of changing models is too slow. Furthermore, the deregulation opens the field of pricing in particular communication services within an open market approach [86].

Besides these changes in the overall networking environment and market situation, the selection of a set of suitable pricing models for the Internet remains an open problem. Many projects covering charging functionality on the network level, including services and sometimes content, intend to achieve complete independence from pricing models. Therefore, this section investigates pricing model constituents and then discusses existing models.

4.5.1 Pricing Model Constituents

In general, the components of pricing include three basic constituents as illustrated in Figure 4.6, each of which may be empty. First, an access fee is usually a time-periodic charge, e.g., weekly or monthly, for using an access link to the network. The price for this link depends, e.g., on the capacity of that link or its length to the provider's point of origin. This constituent does not require any on-line measurements (metering), since the data required for the price model to be defined are of a static nature, based on the installed configuration. However, metering for traditional network management purposes, such as utilization and load balancing, can be performed. Second, a per-call or connection/reservation setup fee may be included. In connection-oriented, circuit-switched networks or connectionless, packet-switched networks with reservations, different mechanisms setting up the connection and the reservation, respectively, can be charged separately. This constituent unavoidably requires on-line metering on a per-call or per-reservation basis, including corre-

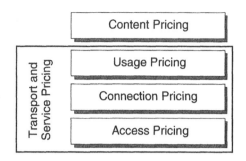

Figure 4.6 Layered components of Internet pricing.

sponding data formats for accounting for this information (cf. Section 4.4.5). Third, a usage fee may be used to charge for data transport and services on time, volume, or any particular QoS basis. This fee reflects the actual resource usage, e.g., users consume capacity. Based on economic principles of marginal cost, market mechanisms, congestion-driven schemes, or marketing policies, details of this usage fee and its corresponding pricing model have to be defined explicitly. Finally, independent of the basic transport and service fees, a content fee may be introduced. Depending on the particular application and its content, this fee may be omitted explicitly (e.g., telephony, fax, e-mail services where the "content" is provided by the user himself), billed separately (e.g., the *Wall Street Journal* on-line edition), or indistinguishably integrated into the transport and services charging (e.g., 1-900 numbers).

The traditional telecommunication services approach, as defined in [55], follows a similar approach, defining the elements "access," "invocation," and "usage," but considering a single service only and neglecting all content issues. While the access shows a subscription form and uniform periodic charge, the actual bill is based on a call or service setup attempt, which is measured in units of uniform charges or successful connections. Finally, the usage element shows the form of the call duration or the volume transmitted, which are measured in time, pulses, packets, or segments as well. Different combinations of these constituents and approaches to pricing of telecommunication services are classified in [40]. For instance, where the service is a single-voice service, traditional voice services show all three transport and services components.

The price constituents in Figure 4.6 are fully or partially reflected in Internet pricing models. An ISP usually used to charge for access and optionally for usage on a connect-time basis or on a flat rate. However, the most important pricing models for Internet services include flat fee, usage-based, reservation-based, volume-based, service class-based, and connect time-based methods, as discussed below.

Edge pricing (cf. Section 4.3.1.5) deals with another aspect of complexity reduction, only in terms of locality, concentrating the distributed nature of pricing decisions by shifting them to the edge of the ISP [108]. This concept is preferred for its simplicity, decoupling complex price negotiations between customers and various ISPs into a series of bilateral ones on different time scales, as well as for its transparence toward the customer.

4.5.2 General Characteristics of Pricing Models

Now that we know about the pricing model constituents, we can see that the targets of pricing are at least twofold. On the one hand, it acts as a means for allowing fair, financially driven resource sharing of services, and it provides an economically driven tool for traffic control functions, such as bandwidth management. On the other hand, pricing determines the approach through which providers to recover costs or increase their revenue. In general, Internet pricing needs to comply with customer demands as well as provider demands, which creates an inherent problem, since the time scales of interest to a single customer are significantly different compared to provider time scales. Therefore, to enable a comparison of particular pricing models for the Internet, time scales for Internet pricing are introduced, properties of pricing models are summarized, and relevant pricing model dimensions are derived.

4.5.2.1 *Time Scales*
Time scales define the major criteria for distributed systems to operate with feedbacks. Since, according to Section 4.2.4.1, charges are derived from prices, and since they reflect a financial feedback to utilization of a service, existing management time scales are, according to Hegering et al. [50]: short-term in minutes, medium-term in hours, and long-term in weeks or months. These scales are extended for charging purposes by an atomic scale for ultrashort times in seconds and below. As illustrated in Table 4.3, intervals and units of measurement show the relevant timing and information to be accounted for. The type of feedback is identified as well.

Applying these time scales onto pricing-controlled activities results in [120]:

1. The atomic monitoring and control level involves sending packets, round-trip times, and managing feedback between sender(s) and receiver(s).
2. The short-term intervention level is concerned with the usual duration of applications like file transfer, video conferencing, or IP phone calls. The accounting and metering tasks are closely related to these activities.
3. The medium-term service provisioning level performs billing actions and depends strongly on the usual human lifestyle habits of humans, e.g., monthly payments of rents, phone charges, or newspaper bills.
4. The long-term business/strategic level in this context determines the duration of contracts between customers and ISPs, which usually varies from several months to years. Note that contracts between ISPs may be shorter.

Therefore, as depicted in Figure 4.7, the proposed charging system operates as a management system that is capable of supporting various pricing schemes. Depending on the specific pricing model applied, different time-scales are effected. Models include usage-based and congestion pricing as a means of mediating the current network utilization, or time-of-day pricing, which is part of the strategic level, since different business models

Table 4.3 Time Scales, Measurement, and Feedback Content [121]

Time-scale Name	Measurement Intervals	Measurement Units	Feedback Content
Atomic	Milliseconds, round trip-times	Packets	Communication-relevant data
Short-term	Minutes	Flows/sessions	Application data
Medium-term	Hours/days	Billing periods	Billing data
Long-term	Weeks/months	Contract periods	Contract data

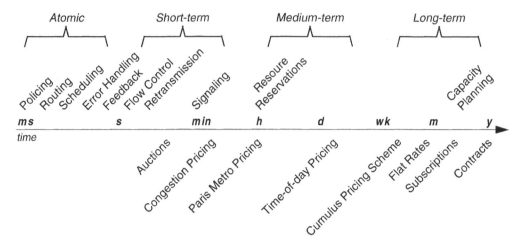

Figure 4.7   Types of feedback and relation to pricing.

are developed for different user demand and user segments.[5] An important result from this mapping of management time scales and their mechanisms in place on pricing time scales is the fact that atomic time-scale mechanisms are technically in operation, just not in an economic model. As described in the following sections, this dilemma of operating a network in smaller time scales than the customer is able to respond to single events (feedback), has been termed the "Feasibility Problem" of Internet Pricing (cf. Section 4.3.1.7 and [101]).

4.5.2.2 Pricing Model Properties

Pricing models determine the price of a communication service or application referred to. On the one hand, the price for, e.g., data transport, a service, a service invocation, a certain quality level of the service, or in general for a unit service, depends on costs, demand, and marketing considerations. They allow for service providers to recover costs or maximize their revenues. On the other hand, prices provide feedback signals to users and influence demand and usage.

Therefore, as presented in [37] and extended here, a set of pricing model properties are considered relevant, mainly based on the provider's point of view in the beginning and to the customer's point of the view afterwards (cf. Section 4.2.2). These properties encompass:

- High probability of cost recovery
- Competitiveness of prices
- Encouragement (discouragement) of customers
- Implementation and usage costs
- Comprehensibility
- Controllability, auditability, and trust
- Predictability
- Responsiveness
- Fairness

[5]For technical terms, Figure 4.7 is based on [65] extended by pricing approaches, and completed by time scales.

From the provider's point of view, to operate a network economically and efficiently, a minimal degree of cost recovery is essential and the production of revenues is intended by an applied pricing model. In addition, prices set by the pricing model shall be competitive to remain in the corresponding services market. Pricing of services needs to include incentives for customers to reward a technological, efficient use of network services and to discourage the abundant waste of network resources. Finally, the investment in the implementation of appropriate metering and accounting equipment shall be minimized.

Turning to the customer's point of view, the use of a pricing model and its necessary equipment needs to show a low usage cost limit. Comprehensibility illustrates the ease of understanding a pricing model and the simplicity of the model, particularly with respect to the tariff applied, important parameters used, and the suitability for a given communication scenario. This covers the quality of the service that has to be provided at a minimal level, and this level needs to be related to the price setting. In addition, mainly as a subjective point of view the perceived quality at the service's interface (which is not measurable today) will become equally even more important. The less a user has to think about an applied special pricing model, the better. Pricing models need a certain degree of controllability. On the one hand, this assumes that due to a user's basic amount of trust in the service provider, a price for a utilized service has to be calculable based on locally accessible information. On the other hand, the service provider has to establish means and mechanisms to ensure that the application of a published price on a utilized service remains controllable, auditable, and supervisory.

While private access to Internet services may show a predictable price of the service (flat fee) than a predictable QoS (guaranteed service with time-dependent pricing), commercial users tend to value a service that depends on the dedicated task to be performed, not the application currently used. ISPs have gained practical experience in this matter and found that residential customers prefer the option of predictable prices rather than predictable QoS (cf. [69, page 18]). However, due to the change to different and new Internet services, such as multicasting and video conferencing, it is not obvious that these assumptions will hold. In addition, the change of prices, if necessary for dynamic pricing models, should not happen too frequently, as stable prices for a reasonable period of time show a greater predictability. It always must be considered in close relation to the user group and the area of application. Responsiveness defines the feature of a pricing model to be able to inform the user on the current price for the actual service usage. Since users want feedback about charges (their calculation is based on the definitions of the price model) for their service used, it needs to be ensured that this feedback does not interfere with the task being performed currently. Therefore, the selection of an option of a push model, where feedback is given periodically, but not too often, or a pull model, where the feedback is given on request only, is left to the user. Summarizing, predictability and responsiveness for pricing models are very important and by themselves a premium service option. Finally, fairness issues in general were discussed in Section 4.2.3. Certainly, the effect of a positive willingness to pay paved the way for an economic-driven fairness notion. However, this feature is a principal disagreement with the welfare situation, where a "social fair share" of resources is intended.

Any of these properties affects one of the three dimensions of economic and social aspects (efficiency, marketing, user requirements), technical aspects (technology, services classes, parameters), and research aspects (applications, theory).

4.5.2.3 Pricing Model Dimensions

Pricing models have been proposed for almost every technical protocol architecture in an attempt to satisfy QoS demands. Thus, different and usually incompatible pricing models exist, reflecting no standardization efforts. However, from the pool of existing pricing models an important distinction must be made on whether prices are set ahead of time as a fixed (static) price or determined and potentially changed as service is provided, showing a variable (dynamic) price. As further distinctions reveal, a basic classification and differentiation has been developed [120].

The classification is based on five attributes and a number of well-defined parameters, all of which are summarized in Table 4.4. These attributes include time, space, quality (i.e., class quality characterization), technological requirements, and volume.

For the "Time" attribute, the following parameter semantics have been applied:

- *Duration* defines the elapsed time between the start and end of service usage, e.g., duration of a video conference.
- *Period* determines the committed length measured in time, which is per se independent, i.e., decoupled, of the service appliance. This commitment is usually set up in advance, e.g., a leasing period.
- *Time of day* defines the sensitivity of service usage to a given time of day. The influence of the time of day may be known in advance by the customer, e.g., weekend tariffs, or they as well may change dynamically, e.g., based on congestion in an auction system.
- *Not applicable* means that the attribute *Time, Space, Class Quality Characterization, Technological Requirement,* or *Volume* is not relevant, e.g., for the time attribute *not applicable* means, that the time has no significance at all, which can be reasonable, e.g., in a volume-based system.

For the attribute "Space" the following parameters are distinguished:

- *Distance* defines the length of the (virtual circuit) from the sender to the receiver, which is passed by messages. Its length in meters is not relevant, but rather how much infrastructure has been used to enforce the service provision.
- In contrast to distance, *route/path*, describes the relevance of where the message flow passes through, i.e., through which, how many, and what kind of routers. The route/path attribute plays in important role when particular associations are made between the chosen circuit and the service.
- The *location, distance,* and *route/path* parameters are not sufficient by themselves to describe all cases that occur for pricing models. Suppose edge-pricing has to be expressed. Saying that the distance and the route/path are not relevant implies a

Table 4.4 Pricing Model Attributes and Parameters [121]

Time	Space	Class Quality Characterization	Technological Requirements	Volume
Duration	Distance	ISP	Flow-based	Linear cumulation
period	Route/path	Customer	Class specified	Nonlinear cumulation
time of day	Location	Self-adjusting	Not applicable	Not applicable
Not applicable	Not applicable	Indifferent		
		Not applicable		

transparent network from the point of view of space. Indeed a transparent network (cloud) does not imply local importance of service provisioning. Thus *location* allows places/entities in the network that have particular importance for the pricing model, e.g., just like edge-pricing, to be considered.

The "Class Quality Characterization" attribute describes the sensitivity of pricing models to be quality classes. It mainly explores how a differentiation of quality is made and who is influencing the selection or creation of quality classes, i.e., the ISP, the customer, or both. It has to be noted that a differentiation of quality does not imply that only a fix number of classes exists.

- *ISP* sets up quality classes. Often the ISP will have a limited set of quality classes, which it may slightly adapt and distribute among customers.
- *Customer* initiates and defines quality class specification, e.g., with a signaling protocol such as RSVP.
- *Self-adjusting.* The class quality may change with network state, where the correction toward the new stable state is performed in a system-inherent manner, e.g., as with the Paris Metro Pricing approach [92].
- *Indifferent,* where no different quality classes are available.

For the attribute "Technological Requirements," the following parameters exist:

- *Flow-based:* the supporting network technology offers a clear technology for maintaining flows within the network, such as with the integrated services architecture.
- *Class-based:* the network supplies a set of discrete classes, where classes are not necessarily associated with particular technologies or QoS commitments.

Finally, the "Volume" attribute defines:

- *Linear cumulation* as the amount of data accumulated linearly, determining that every single data unit measured has the same weight.
- *Nonlinear cumulation,* which covers all other cases, where the volume of a pricing model is taken into account.

Obviously, the combination of all parameters allows for a large number of different pricing models to be identified. It is up to the designers to agree upon the most reasonable ones. As already seen with the parameter *not applicable,* pricing models are not required to be precise on all attributes. In case that a pricing model has to choose just a single parameter per attribute, this approach is inappropriate. Therefore, a supplementary notation is introduced. The two variables, x and X, describe alternatives of the importance of a given parameter on a per-attribute basis:

- x: exactly one, but an arbitrary parameter of an attribute needs to be set, e.g., for the attribute *Volume:* x = [linear cumulation | nonlinear cumulation | not applicable].
- X: at least one, but an arbitrary number of parameters of the attribute need to be set. This is required, if a combination of parameters is utilized to precisely define the scope of the pricing model, e.g., for the attribute *Space:* X = distance & route/path.

These pricing model dimensions are applied during the process of classifying existing pricing models in Section 4.5.4. However, two distinct classes of pricing models are discussed before we do that.

4.5.3   Static and Dynamic Pricing Models

Static and dynamic pricing models reflect the two general alternatives a provider needs to choose from for its service offers. Since Falkner et al. [34] discuss particular pricing models in detail, both categories of static and dynamic pricing will be evaluated and compared in the following sections. While flat-fee models show a long-term static characteristic, dynamic models may frequently change the price over time or may cover a usage-sensitive component.

4.5.3.1   Flat-Fee Models   Static models reflect the fact that no charges for calls or service usage within a specified geographical area are raised. Within the telecommunications industry, a flat fee (comparable to an "all-you-can-eat" buffet offer), or even free local telephony calls, as with some U.S.-based telephone providers, is quite common. Therefore, the adaptation of this model to a new Internet services model seemed to be straightforward. A fixed fee for the IP access is independent of the bandwidth utilized, the QoS perceived or requested, the congestion state of the network, the transmitted information, or the customer's valuation of the service. Actually, the most traditional pricing model that has been implemented for Internet services is a flat rate model, where the customer paid a flat fee for unlimited usage of the service provided.

The major advantage of static models and flat-rate schemes in particular is that charging is easy and simple to apply, since usage-based metering tasks and call timing equipment are avoided, at least for charging purposes. In consequence, accounting tasks basically do not exist, and the charge calculation is reduced to the flat fee, as defined by the pricing and tariff chosen in advance. Therefore, the resulting billing task becomes simple as well, and users know exactly what their bill will be. Billing complaints are avoided. In addition, the predictability of expected charges is deterministic, since the flat fee is known in advance and the user's budget is predictable, which reduces the risk and simplifies financial budgeting. For the provider, the revenue and cash flow estimating is simplified. Consequently, customer and provider need make only a minimal effort.

However, problems with respect to the resource utilization exist with static pricing models. Usage tends to be high, because no per-call charges are due and incentives to save resource usage are missing. Staying on-line for long periods of time from a residential location, even while not using the service at all, blocks the resource of the local phone line and switching equipment, which other users would like to use explicitly. Power users effectively penalize low usage users and could discourage demand. To solve this problem of higher provider costs, the provider could time users out after n minutes of inactivity. However, exactly determining n is difficult and will result in inefficiencies for long n's and, for short n's, in a larger overhead for new connection setups. Bandwidth assignments are made by time and by price. Even worse, bandwidth assignments are based on the customer's patience and not (social) customer valuation of the service. The major drawback of a flat-rate scheme is, however, that services differentiation is not possible at all, since the access to an ISP's point of presence will not allow for the technical differentiation of packets belonging to different services. In addition, a user differentiation, e.g., business and residential, becomes difficult, since the variations of usage are not reflected. For a profitable continuation of commercial service provisioning, a flat-rate scheme is insufficient, since they lack revenue sources. An adaptation of flat fees on a shorter time scale could be envisioned.

Strict flat-fee pricing has proven to be difficult in practice, for the U.S. as well as Europe [120]. For example, America-on-Line (AOL) and other ISPs changed from a usage-sensitive scheme (9.95 US$ monthly fee, including 5 hours and 2.95 US$ for each additional hour) to this flat-fee pricing scheme (19.95 US$ per month for unlimited access) on December 1, 1996. This led an explosion in demand that AOL initially could not cope with [84], and to blocked dial-up phone lines at the regional Bell operating companies, since they do not charge for local calls. From a customer's point of view, there is no incentive to hang up a dial-up Internet connection when there is no charge per time or volume. Hence, due to lawsuits, AOL was forced to offer extensive refunding to unsatisfied users, but finally coped with the situation and succeeded in becoming an important player in the ISP world.

European ISPs followed a more differentiated pricing model with free hours and a charge for additional hours for using the on-line service. Additionally, local phone calls have a significant price in Europe. However, Breathe Freely, a UK-based ISP, had severe problems with a flat-fee scheme. After introducing in May 2000 an unlimited access scheme for an on–off payment of 50£, the apparent lack of capacity forced the ISP to skim off the most Internet-intensive 1% of its users, because they caused real problems for the rest [82]. Finally, Breathe Freely went bankrupt at the end of 2000.

These examples clearly indicate difficulties in offering free and unmetered access to the Internet. However, without any doubt, flat-rate pricing schemes are still the most popular ones, and, hence, a reason for designing new pricing schemes. An important topic to add, in order to prevent disasters like the ones mentioned, is a defined concept of feedback to customers on their current usage patterns and their compliance to the overall network situation.

The ITU-T defines two additional variants of a flat-rate charging scheme for telephony [56]. A partial flat-rate scheme is one where a specified number of calls or call units can be made at no charge. Usage may be stimulated; however, it will be quite common that users will restrict their service usage to the exact amount of service allowed for free. A message-rate scheme is one where the metered, but untimed, call to or within a geographical region is charged at a fixed amount, independent on their duration. It is argued in [56] that users "can make long duration calls reasonably cheaply. This increases or expedites the requirement for additional equipment [. . .] resulting in additional costs," and continues, "because calls are charged at a common rate per call there may be a cost saving on equipment, there being no need for periodic pulse metering."

4.5.3.2 Overprovisioning
Flat fees are quite common, since the concept of overprovisioning is adopted. This identifies the fact that "sufficient" bandwidth is always available. This situation seems to be viable in principle, since small and further decreasing costs per bandwidth deployed in the public networking sector are observed, even though regional differences exist, e.g., between a transatlantic cable and a citywide ring. The major advantage of such an approach can be expressed by the statement: "Larger bandwidth for the same amount of money." However, since human beings are greedy in nature, no natural limit for bandwidth usage can be set. Therefore, even smaller costs are not limited by an upper bound. The major drawback is the fact that even in the case of overprovisioning and the lack of QoS and traffic control mechanisms within the network, no determin-

istically reliable service differentiation will be feasible. For example, real-time application support may not be granted, once the full bandwidth is used by all other customers, even at a very small probability.

For those reasons, flat fees and overprovisioning will not work for a services differentiated Internet, even though basic IP access and best effort services may show a strong static pricing component in their place.

4.5.3.3 Usage-Sensitive Models

Within dynamic models, all services are chargeable on a metered basis, e.g., on duration, volume, distance, or time of day. An important prerequisite for all dynamic models includes a suitable metering and accounting system, which allows for the detection of per-flow usage data, different QoS, time-of-day, and further service-specific information, which are part of the price and tariff applied. In addition, this requires resource allocation mechanisms for managing delineated resources. Usage-based pricing for telecommunication services is especially interesting, the because underlying resources used (satellites, spectrum, cables, routers/switches, and, most notably, operating personnel) are scarce and very costly. Bandwidth scarcity could be solved by installing more fibers or multiplexing on an existing fiber; however, as discussed in Section 4.5.3.2, this approach holds for certain links only, regularly for the local enterprise area, but not for the residential customer access loop or for the whole Internet. Operation of an entire and global network, and providing high quality end-to-end service, is still an expensive venture.

Therefore, major advantages of usage-based models include the fact that this system offers a wide range of service selectivity and an incentive to chose the service class really required for a current task. This allows for a service differentiation based on customer service valuation as well as reaching network efficiency (optimization of network resource utilization) and economic efficiency (Pareto efficiency), since congestion within the network can be avoided by raising prices and thus reducing customer demand. Due to potentially lower demand, the service provisioning can be maintained at a lower level and the quality can be maintained at a higher level than with flat-rate models. In this sense, potentially greedy human behavior is, at least, restricted by financial means. In addition, users are able to control to a large extent their bills for service usage, mainly based on feedback received with charging information. However, this approach requires a metered system. But insufficiencies in the performance of Internet metering, mediation, and accounting systems are fading, due to the appearance of high-performance technology solutions, including the ability to collect service-specific data at a high frequency, as is described in Section 4.3.2, and according charging systems are developed [85, 120]. Besides these dynamic technical aspects, service usage varies and, hence, the price for this usage may be influenced by the variable prices for a similar service usage at different times or locations. A good example for a dynamic pricing model is an auction with continuous price variability considered as repeated incarnations of the auctioning process [36, 124, 125].

On the problem side for usage-based schemes, it is often mentioned that pricing in general and usage-based pricing in particular, can impose a high overhead on telecommunication systems [78, 108]. However, [117] and [59] show two approaches for the Internet, which result in a manageable effort for the implementation of usage-based pricing schemes for integrated services. Besides any implementation, however, there exists a fundamental problem with usage-based pricing. This is caused by the type and precision (granularity) of the collected accounting information, which is used as the basis for pricing. For example, collecting information about connection times to an ISP rounded to 10 seconds means much less overhead than counting IP packets at each interconnection point. With current pricing models in single-service networks there is also implicit information, which can be used in the pricing process by exploiting an implicit traffic specification. However, if one aims at a more efficiently operating multiple-services network for applications with varying requirements [106], this implicit knowledge is lost and must be recovered from the information made available by the protocols employed. Billing is relatively complicated, since accounting information needs to be stored and aggregated accordingly. For the ISP, additional capital cost is required initially to provide accounting systems and user meters. Finally, revenue forecasting and budget planning will become more complicated, since demand estimations are required.

Volume-based approaches determine the form of a usage-sensitive model, since they reduce the accounting task to the traffic volume as an important parameter in terms of resource usage, but still require rather accurate monitoring of the amount of data traveling through the network. Note that delay is an equally important parameter, but even harder to be accounted for, as it is valid for further QoS parameters as well.

4.5.4 Pricing Model Classification Approaches

While flat-fee models show a fixed price and variable QoS due to unpredictable service usage, dynamic price models offer dynamic prices and variable QoS due to unpredictable service usage. But in the latter case, willingness to pay allows for the assurance of a guaranteed QoS. Usage-based service examples encompass user-defined VPNs, subscriber-activated VoD, or any value-added service, which utilizes "more" resources than regular services would require. Flat-fee examples include an email service, without multimedia attachments and chat functions, as well as a basic IP access service without any QoS requirements. These two categories outline two extreme ends of a spectrum of possible pricing schemes. Many combinations and a variety of approaches are possible.

Based on these considerations of price model components, characteristics, and types, relevant pricing models are classified and their parameter dimensions are defined (cf. Section 4.5.2.3). The following paragraphs contain an overview of important Internet pricing models that have been investigated over the last few years and have turned out to be of special importance from a practical and economic point of view.

Consider the example of a flat-rate pricing scheme. Over a fixed time, i.e., described by the attribute *time* and parameter *period,* customers can send as many packets as they like, i.e., the attribute volume is not applicable. No metering and charging entities are needed, since the volume is irrelevant in this classic flat-rate example, the *space* attribute is set to *no relevance* as well. The *quality* attribute instead may have some influence to the initial price set as the flat rate, but it is not a necessity for flat-rate pricing, so it can be set to an arbitrary parameter. In Table 4.5 the latter fact is expressed by an *x*. The volume-based (static and edge) pricing, the Paris Metro pricing (PMP) scheme [92], Vickrey Auctions [78], congestion-based pricing, and CPS [120] are also classified in the table.

Concerning the goals targeted by pricing models, a clear focus on two concurrent topics can be recognized. The first set of pricing models targets congestion in networks, i.e., congestion control and avoidance. This is a global approach covering the entire scope of an ISP's domain, representing ISP's desires in the management of limited network resources by the deployment of appropriate network technologies, e.g., ECN [99].

In contrast, the second goal to be achieved aims at individual QoS provisioning. It has to meet dedicated customer requirements, where service differentiation is available and

Table 4.5   Pricing Model Attributes and Parameters [121]

Example Pricing Model	Time	Space	Class Quality Characterization	Technological Requirements	Volume
Flat rate	Period	Not applicable	ISP	x	Not applicable
Volume-based (static and edge pricing)	Duration	Location	X	Not applicable	(Non)linear cumulation
PMP	Duration	Not applicable	Self-adjusting	Class-specified	x
Vickrey Auction	Time-of-day	X	Self-adjusting	x	x
Congestion pricing					Not applicable
CPS	Period	Location	X (ISP and customer)	Not applicable	(Non)linear cumulation

Table 4.6   Combinations of QoS Models and Pricing Schemes [61]

QoS Model	Flat Fees	Static Prices	Dynamic Prices
Overprovisioned best effort	Good fit	Likely not viable	Undecided
Price-controlled best effort	Likely not viable	Likely not viable	Good fit
Differentiated services	Likely not viable	Good fit	Good fit
Integrated services	Likely not viable	Good fit	Good fit

suitable pricing models are likewise necessary. Pricing models are strongly influenced by these goals and cannot be decoupled from the objectives of the network provider, i.e., to satisfy customer QoS requirements or to avoid and control congestion. With respect to QoS provisioning and in reflection of the networking technology discussion in Section 4.4, Table 4.6 shows an overview of pricing scheme fittings to different QoS models [61]. While flat fee denotes the current access-based pricing scheme of the Internet as described in Section 4.5.3.1, static and dynamic prices correspond to the description of Section 4.5.3.3. This includes in particular a usage-sensitive component, where a pricing scheme is based individually on the amount of resources used for a service invocation or service usage.

As discussed in Karsten et al. [61], the nature of overprovisioned best effort service is such that no service discrimination is possible, and hence, price discrimination is not appropriate.[6] Although best-effort services have been used in combination with fixed per-packet prices, this cannot be considered a useful alternative, since fixed prices do not represent the resource consumption of best-effort communication. When best-effort services are combined with resource-sensitive pricing and variable prices, it basically resembles price-controlled best-effort service. In general, it seems doubtful, whether this QoS model is capable of providing the kind of service that is needed for differentiated application demands. Even the assumption of an ever-increasing amount of transmission resources at constantly decreasing prices (overprovisioning, cf. Section 4.5.3.2), a situation of super-abundance can only exist in relation to a certain amount of aggregated demand. To attract

---

[6]The price can vary according to the customer access bandwidth, but still, this determines a flat fee for the customer on longer time scales (cf. Section 4.5.2.1).

widespread usage, such a system must be kept flexible with regard to requests from customers. Nevertheless, for reliable operation, it must be ensured that aggregated demand does not exceed an acceptable level. To combine both requirements, some kind of dynamic access control is needed (1) to ensure proper and controllable consumption of resources, and (2) to account for any premium service usage.

For a price-controlled best effort service, appropriate pricing and responsiveness of end-systems to price signals is the crucial management aspect. Because of this responsiveness of end-systems, per-packet charges provide a mechanism for dynamic access control. Under the assumption of stable price-demand patterns, it is possible to proportion capacity such that reliable operation and QoS assurances can be met statistically. However, since performance predictability can only be given under certain restrictions [94], such a service cannot provide the exclusive technology for an overall network infrastructure. Furthermore, prices are inherently variable in order to fulfill their functionality as congestion signals. It has been suggested that such a basic service be combined with higher-level entities, which act as trading or insurance brokers to remove price fluctuations or improve QoS predictability [85]. However, it may add a significant complexity to the overall system to implement such brokers and fine-grained interactions between them, if the frequency of these interactions reaches a certain limit. Future investigations need to design, simulate, and implement such systems carefully to provide evidence for their feasibility. For that reason, price-controlled best effort serves as an alternative implementation choice for certain service classes that do not specify hard QoS guarantees, e.g., similar to the controlled load service class [129].

In the differentiated service [4] and integrated services [7] models, resources are engineered or reserved according to requested service offerings. Independent of actual service implementation, some kind of admission control has to be executed on service requests in order to guarantee reliable and predictable transmission quality, as specified in the respective service classes. Since resources are allocated (more or less exclusively) to service requests and are therefore not available to others, charging has to be resource-based in order to keep the demand at a sound level and to avoid the tragedy of the commons phenomenon [48]. While these technologies gain relatively high complexity at the technical level of service provision in the network (IntServ higher than DiffServ), they also provide the most sophisticated interfaces to network management both and users (again, IntServ more than DiffServ). Consequently, the additional complexity of providing a wide range of different application services and pricing and charges for these services is lower than for price-controlled best effort approaches. Proposals for appropriate pricing models for these technology choices can be obtained from [36, 62, 77, 101, 112, 127].

4.6   ISP COST MODELS

At present, the ISP market is characterized by a set of new Internet services and interactions that differ significantly from the traditional telecommunications market. Mainly, this is due to the fact that basic IP access is extended in the case of the Internet with service offerings and content provisioning. Balancing these developments, the cost model for ISPs requires a fundamental reshaping, since traditional ways of modeling costs in a communication network do not hold any more. Therefore, the main focus of an ISP cost model is (1) to identify all relevant parameters, (2) to list their mutual relationships that contribute to the cost for providing network services to a variety of users, and (3) to include

Internet service to be considered explicitly. In a competitive market, cost modeling is helpful in two ways: first, a suitable cost model serves the ISP with respect to its internal cost management, as it helps to understand its own costs, which may have crucial influence on marketing decisions as well as operational processes. Second, a cost model provides a solid basis for calculating and determining prices, tariffs, and charges for value-added Internet services.

The earliest relevant work on ISP cost models investigates costs for Internet access using cable modems compared to the ISDNs [44]. Advances are made in Leida [75], where observations from yield management techniques are included and the set of access technologies is refined. In a first step, Leida [75] assumes that a limited set of services access classes (different bandwidths of the local loop) offered by an ISP, including dial-in analog access, dial-in ISDN access (128 kbit/s), 56 kbit/s leased-line access, and T1 leased-line access. This does not distinguish further among value-added Internet services. In a second step, a customer segmentation is performed, resulting in residential dial-in subscribers, business dial-in subscribers, business ISDN subscribers, business leased-line subscribers (56 kbit/s), and business leased-line subscribers (T1). While various assumptions about residential and business access are made, a mix of product-related (bandwidth of local loop) and customer type-related segmentation (business vs. residential customers) was achieved. The value-added service case includes investigations of two situations only: one with IP telephony in place and a second without. A different perspective was taken in the OPTIMUM project, which developed a tool for investment calculation; hence, the main goal is the investigation of investment in the telecommunication business [93]. Further features of the tool include especially network aportioning.

One characteristic of all relevant approaches of ISP cost models is their focus on concrete cases instead of developing abstract models. But concrete models lack flexibility and independence. A second characteristic of these approaches is their depth in technical and economical details, e.g., Leida [75] eventually uses more than 300 parameters for describing the model, which has major consequences with respect to the transparency of the model. In contrast to these approaches, the model ICOMO [100] is abstract, flexible, independent, and can be adapted to a set of services of interest. A trade-off has been made, e.g., between abstraction and simplicity, as it is possible to develop a purely formal model for all possible types of providers and services, but only by using an large number of parameters in contrast to the requirement of simplicity. In order to cope with them, the model starts from a purely formal and abstract view, but aims at concrete cases, which are used to feed the model and reduce its complexity. It turns out that this goal is reached by a subtle mixture of classic accounting and abstraction.

4.7 CHARGING SUPPORT SYSTEMS

Earlier work on charging and accounting in telecommunication systems has been focused on connection-oriented networks, such as the telephony network, ATM-based networks, or leased lines. However, the Internet provides a connectionless network layer, including an IP-based network service. While the set of traffic modeling parameters and service parameters for connection-oriented networks are quite well understood and agreed upon, these parameters remain heavily debated for the Internet. For example, the interpacket arrival time for an Internet service makes a significant difference for this service. However, how should a future system account for this parameter? In addition, as for connection-oriented networks, the call-blocking rate determines the level of utilization for a given topology and the potential sender is blocked in sending data into the network, while connectionless networks suffer from the problem of congestion, since in general there is no admission control available. Of course, a set of newly defined Internet services proposes the existence of such an admission control; however, a commonly agreed upon architecture has not been developed up to now. Once congestion situations can occur in a network, congestion control mechanisms are required. Traditionally, these mechanisms have operated in the purely technical domain, e.g., by dropping packets, but left out incentives to evaluate the requested service by economic measures. As discussed, sensible pricing of services in an open services market is also required [118]. However, this approach depends on the technical ability to collect and account for those data necessary to charge the customer. Therefore, a CSS provides the technology required to support price-based mechanisms for charging tasks, including the potential to perform a market-driven congestion control in the Internet along with interfacing billing systems and proving customer feedback signals on resource usage.

4.7.1 CSS Components

The CSS approach taken, provides (1) a generic and modular Internet charging system in support of various pricing schemes applicable to different communication technologies, and (2) an interface for billing systems (cf. terminology in Section 4.2.5). The goal is to identify relevant components and their relations to each other, and to create an open and complete system structure, which allows for the integration of charging support technologies available today (cf. Section 4.3.2 and Section 4.4), ranging from the data-orientated tasks (such as metering) to the money-related tasks (such as a billing interface).

Several components are needed for an Internet charging system, which have to interact to provide all offered functionalities to customers. As illustrated in Figure 4.8, a general

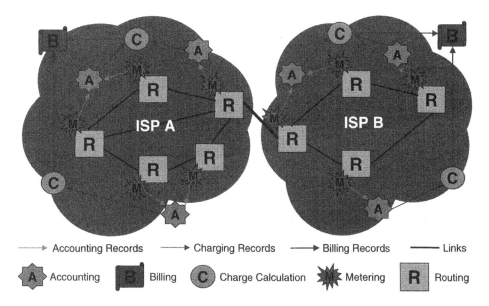

Figure 4.8 Location and replication of charging components in provider networks [120].

scenario contains interconnected communication service providers. Each provider operates a network consisting of routers and network links between them, accounting components, charge calculation components, and billing systems. Metering components are located inside the router or attached to them as separate devices. In either case, they generate accounting information, which are gathered and accumulated in an accounting component following some type of data format (cf. Section 4.4.5). In turn, it forwards the accumulated accounting information through a charge calculation function toward the billing system. The charge calculation translates the accounting information into charging records; hence, it maps resource-oriented information from accounting components into monetary values. The billing system uses these values to prepare bills that are to be sent to customers. Within the charge calculation, discounts and rebate strategies, marketing-driven pricing schemes, or simply fixed prices can be applied in terms of a selected tariff.

In the existing billing systems of today's providers, the setting of prices, the function of charge calculation, and the billing itself is integrated, even additionally combining the maintenance of service classes, user profiles, customer data, identities, and bank account data. Although these steps still can be seen clearly, they are almost completely centralized within a monolithic system. Future billing systems need to be able to integrate a variety of different charging records, even from different communication providers or content providers, since customer's demand is one-stop billing [118]. Future CSSs need to react on user requests in a short time scale, provisioning a soft real-time feedback. The move of tomorrow's CSSs from a back-end and batch-based to a front-desk and real-time-capable system are clearly visible. This strongly suggests dividing the existing monolithic systems into several components with clearly defined interfaces. By doing this, it will become possible to exchange individual components and to integrate different components supporting different technologies without having to adapt the entire system. Additionally, interfaces to metering, accounting, and other components also have to be defined, based on available technology choices (cf. Section 4.3.1.1). The goal is to define components and their relations to each other and to create an open Internet charging system architecture, which allows the charging task to be performed for various different technologies.

4.7.2   CSS DIMENSIONS

Based on these component identifications, it must be determined how these components are deployed in a particular distributed scenario with potentially several different ISPs [121]. A charging system can vary with respect to four essential dimensions, driven by the scenario (cf. Figure 4.9) and the ISP type, defining a set of different choices based on the different roles for access ISPs and core ISPs (cf. Section 4.8.3 and [71]). Depending on the ISP type, the location as well as replication of components will determine suitable and less useful components combinations. However, today there is no general set of criteria available depicting the optimal location and replication of components for a given scenario. It is expected that future work on ISP cost modeling may determine suitable design input [100].

The "Location" dimension defines where components are located. In particular, an in-house location refers to an ISP, hosting this component and providing the corresponding functionality internally. The outsourced location defines that this component and functionality are being performed outside the scope and administrative domain of the ISP. Mainly business case assumptions and the size of the ISP considered will determine the

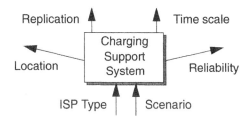

Figure 4.9 Charging support system dimensions.

final location of components in a given ISP infrastructure. In addition, security-relevant questions may arise, once the outsourcing of financial activities is intended.

The "Replication" dimension defines how many of the components considered exist in a given environment. Mainly the number of clients served by an ISP and the number of interconnection points with peering ISPs will determine the number of replicated components required. However, besides the pure replication an important issue is the interaction between these replicated components. Appropriate protocols (open, ISP-specific, or vendor-specific) need to be selected for a suitable and correct design as well as the implementation. Open interface specifications are required to provide a chance for replication.

The "Reliability" dimension defines how reliable these components have to be. The required degree of reliability depends only indirectly on the ISP type. Rather it depends on the other dimensions of location and replication previously mentioned, and heavily on the component type itself. Nevertheless, the required reliability of components is a dimension in which a specific charging system can differ from others.

Finally, "Time scales" define the last important dimension. As discussed in Section 4.5.2.1, four network management time scales are distinguished and applied to pricing-controlled mechanisms for feedback purposes.

4.7.3 Basic CSS Tasks

The CSS is supposed to support the following tasks:

- Perform accounting tasks according to service definitions. Data gathered from the physical infrastructure and mediated according to policies needs to be accounted for. This requires the knowledge of sessions, durations, or flows. Mainly, this information is derived from metered data as well, such as "begin-of-session" or "end-of-flow." If such starting and endpoints cannot be determined explicitly, heuristics need to be applied for session- or flow-detection purposes. In any case, the "length" of a communication relation will be recorded, if any usage-based charging approaches are to be supported.

- Perform multiservice accounting. The accounting task for a single service that is well known is performed by an algorithm, which utilizes a clear service specification. In the case of multiservice provisioning, these service specifications must exist and need to be maintained concurrently. Therefore, the separation of incoming data and their mapping onto the particular service in operation is essential.

- Support transport, service, and content charging. The optimal design for a CSS includes a combined approach for the three different levels of charging. Transport charging, sometimes termed network charging or network access charging, forms the basis for providing a system to deal with the transfer of data based mainly on the network infrastructure, such as the Internet.

Service charging located above this level allows for the clear distinction of different services, including different QoS requirements and resource consumptions. Services include the ones provided by a variety of service providers (cf. Kneer [71] for their different definitions and distinctions) that are offered in an open-market situation. This charging task needs to be service-independent as far as possible, to ensure future extensions and adaptations to yet unknown services. Transport charging will be integrated into this concept and may even be hidden completely.

Content charging includes the accounting tasks for information that is specifically monetary-sensitive and needs to be paid for by reading, using, or copying it. Based on the level of business interactions, it might be useful to apply content charges for certain services only, integrating invisibly by customers the underlying transport and services charging.

- Support different levels of security for charging and accounting information. All data and information related to monetary equivalents contain a certain degree of sensitivity. However, due to the dedicated level of interest, a single accounting record, a metered routing datum, or a charging record may not be a security problem, since their lifetime and validity, and therefore asset, are short. But other combinations of aggregated data, e.g., flow-related information in terms of usage information, duration, and customer identification, form critical information.

- Support auditing. Communication services offered in a market environment need mechanisms that support the proof of service delivery under well-defined circumstances. Therefore, an auditing functionality will be based on accounted for data, which may be specifically restricted, structured, or stored, depending on legal aspects, such as telecommunications acts.

4.7.4 CSS Architecture

Based on these charging system tasks, their clear separation, and design dimensions, an overall architecture for a CSS is driven by the mapping of the conceptual view onto certain components [121]. Adding their interactions and interfaces results in the CSS architecture depicted in Figure 4.10, where interactions between two neighboring providers take place on two levels. The first one is on the data path, since providers must exchange data between their networks. Interprovider information exchange happens as part of the specific protocol processing as defined in the QoS model applied, e.g., for resource reservations using the RSVP or inter-Bandwidth Broker communication, where messages are exchanged between the border routers of neighboring providers. In these cases, a type of signaling or consolidation protocol has to take care of distributed information scattered around in the network.

Since the transport of these data is not for free, ISPs will charge each other for data transported. This leads to the second level of interaction. Each provider collects information on the amount of data transported and calculates a charge for it.[7] The provider issues inter-provider invoices through a billing system to the responsible neighboring ISP's entity. Thus, information exchange between providers occurs on the level of billing systems.

---

[7]Accounting rate regimes have been applied in the traditional telephony system, however, differentiated services in the Internet require an SLA-based distinction of services exchanged and offered (cf. Section 4.4.4).

Instead of performing absolute billing between interconnected providers, they can also offset their claims against each other. A set of peering agreements and settlement schemes exist for today's ISPs; however, (1) they are defined in a quite static manner, (2) they do not allow for immediate responses to bandwidth bottlenecks or further customer and user demands, and (3) they cannot support differentiated services effectively. Besides this interprovider billing, providers bill their single customers as well.

4.7.4.1 External Components   For describing the CSS completely, an outside-first approach is taken to illustrate all components external to CSS's central component, the Internet Charge Calculation and Accounting System (ICCAS). As shown in Figure 4.10, metering is integrated in the IP router. Alternatively, it could be placed directly on the wire. Such a solution introduces supplementary expenditures, e.g., an entity needs its own IP address or requires special protocols. Furthermore, it can only monitor the actual usage of the link and has no knowledge of usage of any critical resources relevant to congestion control within the router. Therefore, the interconnection of several metering units to reconstruct the current router status is not feasible. Finally, it would be necessary, in spite of having metering units on the wire, to know the state of the router, so explicit interaction of the charging system and the router would be required. The purpose of the mediation entity is to transform metered data (of each single meter), to merge data of different meters, and to reduce the amount of data metered.

Prices are important for calculating charges of transmitted data. Since there are many different ways to set prices, a separate pricing component performs this task. It can make use of economic models or just use fixed prices set by hand (cf. Section 4.5 and Karsten [60]). For dynamic pricing models most often an input from metering is needed, since the amount of data traffic influences prices. These prices are applied in the charge-calculation component within the ICCAS. An interface to a billing system exists and is used to perform interprovider charging concerns as well as customer billing interfacing.

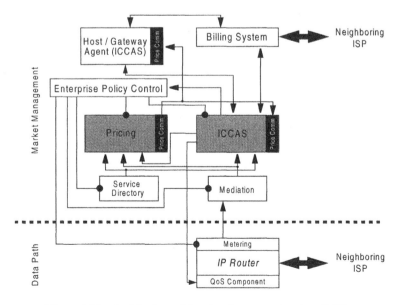

Figure 4.10   Architecture of the charging support system [120].

The policy control entity of the enterprise represents the ISP's interface for the management and supervision of all ICCAS-related entities except for the billing system. It covers and controls the ISP's business strategy with respect to its implementation and configuration of the given networking equipment and services catalog. The host/gateway agent performs two different functions. The first one is to communicate charges to hosts (users) and gateways to provide an optional feedback channel for their service usage. In this case, the host agent acts on behalf of the user. This can include the negotiation of services with the ICCAS, an automatic reaction to communicated charges, or even payment information. A host agent can also restrict the user's options, when the customer in control of these users wants to restrict the behavior of the users it pays for. In particular, this is the case for companies where the company constitutes the customer to an IPS and its employees act as users of the services offered.

Since in general a users tend to lack a complete understanding of QoS in technical terms, they will be unable to specify detailed requirements in a way that can be used as a direct input to the QoS component within the router. Instead the users have a higher, application level view of quality. This view must be translated into technical values, which can be used for setting parameters in QoS components and for charging according to technical usage data. Therefore, this translation takes place in the Service Directory.

4.7.4.2 ICCAS Architecture and Internal Components

The internal entities of the ICCAS include a charge calculation, an accounting, a customer support, and a user support component. The separation of the ICCAS into these components increases the required degree of flexibility, since these components can be physically distributed as discussed in Section 4.7.2. Embedding the ICCAS into the CSS is accomplished through eight distinct interfaces. Concerning the flow of data internally, the ICCAS has been divided into two logical paths as shown in Figure 4.11. The first, the Accounting Information Path (AIP), depicts the flow of pure charging-relevant data. On the other hand, the Control Policy Path (CPP) is used to manage and configure the ICCAS, especially all entities involved with the processing of charging data. These two paths differ mainly in the order and direction that they process data. The AIP starts from the bottom of the graph (taking raw technical data) by processing metered and mediated data as well as pricing information. It ends at the top of the graph, where complete charging records are handed over to the billing system. In contrast, the CPP starts from the top of the graph (taking business-related data) by receiving enterprise policy control information and processes down to the bottom of the graph, resulting in QoS control data to be handed over to the underlying router or optionally an agent.

The accounting component receives all metered and mediated usage data and is responsible for storing it. It must provide these stored data to other ICCAS components and interfaces for further processing, feedback, or statistic evaluation. Accounting is the central usage data storage component. The charge calculation component processes the accounted-for usage data. It calculates appropriate charges for resource usage by applying a tariff, communicated by the pricing component. To be able to determine the charges fully, it needs input from the user support component, e.g., user identifications, to apply further contract specialities.

An ISP may have many different customers. Additionally, a customer is not the same as a user, e.g., one customer might pay the bills of several users. Therefore, a customer is the one who negotiated a contract with the ISP. The content of this contract, e.g., number of users covered by the contract and their names and accounts, are managed within the customer support component. While the customer support component is responsible for

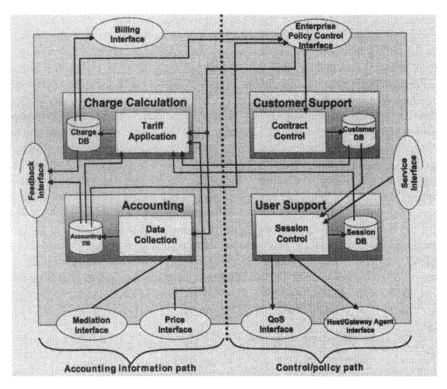

Figure 4.11 ICCAS architecture in detail [120].

keeping all contract information, the user support component is responsible for making sure that those contracts are kept safely. On the one hand, this means that it blocks any user requests that are not covered by the contract the customer, who pays for the user, has. On the other hand, is can make sure that a service requested by a user is delivered, if the contract allows it.

4.7.4.3 Open ICCAS Interfaces

All ICCAS interfaces between the components just described are designed to act (1) as protocols, allowing for open communication between two remote entities of components, or (2) as software interfaces, reflecting the clear architectural decision, that the interaction between those components happens within a common address space [120].

The QoS Interface (CPP) offers the control of routers' QoS components, where services to the customer are provided. It can be used to set QoS parameters of routers, depending on the technology in place. The Mediation Interface (AIP) is responsible for collecting data from several mediation entities, possibly even from mediation entities of different types. The usage data, which are mediated after the data gathering takes place, need to be transferred to the ICCAS. Therefore, a protocol is designed that defines rules and transmission units for transferring mediated data to the accounting component. Since the anticipated load for this interface will be high, the protocol must be highly efficient, yet extensible. The data exchanged across this interface include one of the following alternatives, which depend on the particular scenario: (1) a simple handover of data gathered by metering, or (2) a handover of data mediated based on the particular inputs from the enterprise policy control. This may result in a dedicated specification of specialized data to be required for the ICCAS, some special aggregation of these data, or even the neglect of data resulting from the gathering process. The Enterprise Policy Control Interface (CPP) is intended for changing parameters of the ICCAS after the system has been deployed. By using this interface, the enterprise policy control can install new services or request and receive charging or accounting data. The Service Interface (CPP) can be used to read service definitions out of the service directory. The Billing Interface (AIP) is responsible for sending calculated charging records to the billing system. Pricing is responsible for setting the prices used by the charge calculation component, therefore, the Pricing Interface (AIP) is used to send calculated prices to the charge calculation component. To set suitable prices, the pricing component uses price models with various input variables. Some price models need usage or charge information as input variables, hence, these variables can be communicated to the pricing component via the Feedback Interface (AIP). Finally, the Host/Gateway Agent Interface (CPP) is responsible for optional communication with the customer. Mainly, this includes the selection of services the customer can use or the transfer of a feedback signal from the service provider to a user. This interface is open for future enhancements. Further details on interfaces can be obtained from Stiller et al. [120].

4.8 BUSINESS MODEL ASPECTS

Commercially operated networks, in particular subnetworks of the Internet, follow a set of requirements that have been discussed in [37, 61, 62, 83]. They cover the fact that the business task of running a communication network must be sustainable and profitable to attract necessary investments in the infrastructure. This means that for charging systems, e.g., objectives in terms of flexibility and efficiency have to be met, which are completed by a number of criteria arising from current practice and user expectations in the areas of product liability and consumer protection in general. This is behind the need to introduce new services and charging for them.

For those reasons, a three-tiered model is introduced that interfaces with the CSS presented earlier. Based on its three layers, ISP segmentation in the lower two layers is performed and application service providers (ASP) are introduced. Because electronic content in the Internet forms an extremely important area of concern, a valuation of content versus transport is discussed and a combination of content with transport charging is proposed.

4.8.1 Market-Managed Three-Tiered Model

The infrastructure of a market managed multiservice Internet is based on an overall three-tiered model [120], as shown in Figure 4.12. This model outlines basic states and sources of information within three distinct layers as well as its interfaces to the CSS. Starting from the topmost layer, customers and providers within an Internet services market interact for any type of business based on business models as defined within the Enterprise Policy Layer (EPL). This layer defines, among others, products to be sold, i.e., services, models of business interactions between customers and providers, pricing mechanisms, and agreements on an offer. Details of relevance to the CSS can encompass, e.g., rebate systems, discounting schemes, service plans, or service pricing models. These details

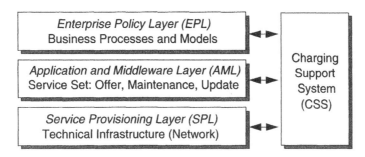

Figure 4.12 Market-managed three-tiered model.

form the business-dependent and business-central policy, which may not be completely published, but is required to provide the CSS with operational dimensions. However, to perform any type of market-driven enterprise policy, the CSS needs to offer a set of service descriptions that are applicable to all areas of enterprise policies.

Besides these business perspectives, the technical view of the market-managed approach is found in the Application and Middleware Layer (AML). It provides functions or policies that are (1) initiated due to a predetermined application or (2) acting on the application's behalf, such as a given enterprise policy. Within this layer, a set of (value-added) communication services is provided, utilized, and charged for according to customer demand. Middleware takes from the details of the technical infrastructure of the network itself. The middleware is able to provide a generic service set for offering, maintaining, and updating all types of communication services. Therefore, the CSS interface includes application-centric configuration options for particular session and service descriptions as well as more generic service descriptions according to the middleware layer functionality.

Finally, the task of service provisioning as identified in the Service Provisioning Layer (SPL) offers interfaces for the lower layer to the CSS. Therefore, data and information on the technical infrastructure (the "network") are collected and maintained depending on the service offered by the middleware layer.

4.8.2 Internet Service Provider Segmentation

In regard to the SPL of the three-tiered model, the type of service provider considered needs to offer a wider range of services from the networking domain. Hence, the focus for segmentation has to be directed to network service providers. In the current market situation, many network providers already have completed forward integration, since this allows them to reach the end-customer directly. Others remain within the backbone of the Internet. Therefore, from the position of end-customers, the distinction between two types of providers is straightforward. The first type is named telecommunications Internet service provider (TISP), and the second type pure Internet service provider (PISP) [100]. In the simplest case, the organization of these service providers consists of two levels: the lower level represents the TISP offering their services to PISPs, which are located on the upper level of Figure 4.13. Some TISPs may participate as hybrid providers in the market, i.e., they reach end-customers directly, but offer their services to other PISPs, too, as in the case for $TISP_4$.

A TISP is an enterprise owning and operating a network as well as an infrastructure of

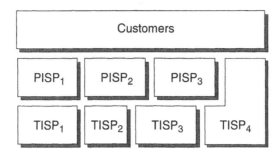

Figure 4.13 Vertical provider market structure [100].

its own, including routers, switches, and network management software, among others. This network and infrastructure includes virtually "every" necessity, i.e., the local loop, backbone links, and peerings to other backbones. Hence, the TISP segment includes former monopolists, as they become the only ones within a long-haul transmission network after the market has been deregulated. Additionally, providers exist that have taken the chance of setting up and building new networks of their own. These providers usually offer various IP services, such as voice or phone. TISPs offer services to PISPs, but they reach the end-customer directly as well, by means of forward integration. Typically, these providers possess a great deal of stamina in the market. They currently possess the largest customer base and are able to deal relatively easy with their telephone subscribers as potential IP customers.

PISPs basically do not own networking infrastructure at all, since they require TIPS or other PISP business interactions. In particular, they have to rent access from TISPs or buy services from other PISPs. Instead, their equipment is service-specific, e.g., web, multicasting, or name servers, and their portfolio offers value-added services. Moreover, these providers usually operate call centers, help desks, and hot lines in order to care for customers. The customer ought to be confident in the quality of the offered service and wants to be assisted promptly in case of failures. Current market conditions allow for the customer to choose among different offers or to change the provider, even if the transparency of the market has decreased significantly due to the deregulation and hard pricing battles among providers. Mapping these segmented provider markets into the tree-tiered model, TISPs operate on the SPL and probably on the AML. PISPs run their business in the AML, focusing on the middleware and services set. Finally, ASP operate on the AML, and are discussed in the following section.

4.8.3 Application Service Provider

ASPs deliver applications and services from distributed data centers to end-customers. The economics considered define a single business relationship between a customer and an ASP. In this case, a business model includes the series of business events and reflects all processes within an economic system [71]. In terms of electronic business systems, the ASP can be modeled by one instance and the end-customer by another, which means that these instances form the two endpoints of a communication.

ASPs offer products, content, and services on-line, e.g., via the WWW, and represent the merchant or the seller of a good. Products offered by the ASP include (1) physical and (2) nontangible goods (content). Physical goods could be purchased in stores, e.g., books, cars, or CDs. However, there are several incentives for customers to purchase products from home, such as 24-hours order service and delivery, no waiting queues at cash desks, time saving since no parking space has to be found, and electronic catalogs and navigation functions. Content offered by ASPs includes digital information in the form of bits, including the digital content of an on-line book or the digital version of a CD that can be downloaded into endcustomers' local disks. Furthermore, there exists a broad spectrum of multimedia contents and services, e.g., audio-on-demand or VoD, offered to customers on-line by the ASP.

The basic idea of an economic system established between end-customers and ASPs is well understood and feasible. Problems arise with the introduction of network performance and QoS for the delivery of Internet services. TISPs provide the physical infrastructure for the Internet and form the basic foundation of electronic commerce activities. PISPs and TISPs provide the transport of data packets over the Internet between the end-customer and the ASP. However, traffic congestion and unreliable connections on the best effort Internet are a problem for sending data, especially if wide bandwidth and reliable throughput are required, e.g., for multimedia applications or business transactions. ISPs could overcome this problem by offering services with QoS guarantees and by charging Internet users according to the service they request.

A business model for a general eCommerce scenario is shown in Figure 4.14 with an end-customer and ASP at the ends, and several intermediate ISPs. Business relationships between all parties involved are depicted, and ISPs will charge and account for Internet transportation services as well as higher-level eCommerce services. There might be a payment provider that is responsible for the financial clearing between parties. The payment provider can be a bank, a credit institution, or a trusted third party.

For the design of a business model, ISPs are differentiated into two different roles according to their scope of duties: Access ISPs (mainly PISPs and some TISPs) and Core ISPs (TISPs only). This differentiation is orthogonal to the ISP segmentation, since the definition of a particular roles of an ISP is a must for business models. Access ISPs support local access networks and provide Internet connections to the end-customer, be it directly or through a Customer Premises Network (CPN). Core ISPs increase the reach of Access ISPs to a global extent and form the backbone of the Internet. They perform data transportation by interconnecting Access ISPs. There may be more than one core ISP involved in a communicating connection between end-customer and ASP, depending on the

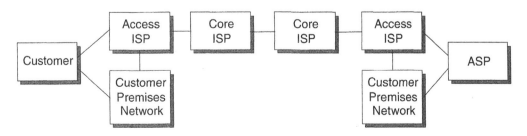

Figure 4.14 Relationships between involved parties of an eCommerce scenario.

connectivity of ISPs and their local distances. When there is only one ISP located between end-customer and ASP, it acts both as Access ISP and Core ISP, providing data transport. Thus, Access ISPs and Core ISPs can be physically identical.

An end-customer can be connected either directly to the CPN or to an Access ISP, if the end-customer is a residential user. In the first scenario, end-customers may be affiliated to a CPN, e.g., a LAN of an enterprise or a university campus, which groups end-customers and establishes the connectivity to the Access ISP. A CPN may offer additional private applications or extra conditions for data transportation to their end-customers. Therefore, a CPN represents a group of users in terms of a common policy and conceals an individual end-customer from the Access ISP.

4.8.4 Charging Content

Although, the focus of this overview has been on charging of transport services and their technological implications on the Internet networking technology, charging for content is important and becomes a substantial factor in the case of value-added services. The charge for the content of an ASP can be combined with the charge for the transportation service of the ISP, since the transport may be only a very small fraction of the overall charge. Furthermore, as mentioned earlier, the generalization of charging for services will be an important basis for the market-driven positioning of service differentiation of ISPs and ASPs. It should be noted that changes in the networking infrastructure, which are mainly due to upcoming mobile providers, will lead to new business models, since the customers in the future will dial up a connection to their mobile providers, and not a traditional ISP. This means that typical ISPs have to differentiate their services to obtain a future source of revenue due to decreasing income from stationary or mobile dial-up clients. Current investigations on including content in a wholesale approach [45] and electronic business models for content delivery and charging for them [76] lead initially to emerging areas of concern.

This section describes relevant factors that allow for the decision, whether or not it is favorable to charging content along with the transport service [71]. Figure 4.15 shows

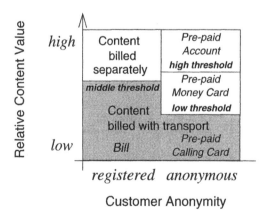

Figure 4.15 Primary influencing factors for billing content separately or including transport [71].

the primary influencing factors, namely, the relative value of content (defined as the value of content divided by the cost of transport) and required end-customer anonymity. Note that the number of bytes does not determine the value of the content as it does the current market price. For low values of content, it is more efficient to charge and bill content along with the transport service either on a single bill or through a prepaid calling card. A separate bill for the content will be provided for registered end-customers, if the relative value of content is higher than the middle threshold. If end-customers want to be anonymous and the relative value of content is between the lower and the higher threshold, prepaid calling cards can be used to pay for that content. Extremely valuable content above the high threshold requires prepaid accounts on the ASP's side with secured access rights. Content with middle as well as high values should be charged only when the transfer of content has been successful, e.g., the entire data file has been received correctly.

In addition to these primary factors, Figure 4.16 shows secondary influencing factors for deciding whether to bill separately for content or along with the transportation service. It can be assumed that there is a measure for the number of logically independent content blocks per time and the value of the full content per time.

Logically independent blocks of content are discrete and contain useful information for the customer, such as the reply on a railroad schedule request. However, financial information, e.g., stock rates, consists of a sequence of independent data packets, which are billed continuously. A backup file or a high-resolution image file can be seen as a large block of content. If only a single intermediate packet gets lost, the transmission will fail and no billing for that content should be performed. Certainly, boundaries for these loss numbers and QoS parameters are not fixed, but vary according to the application in use. For example, watching VoD can show an acceptable ratio of lost packets as long as the audio and video quality do not decrease below a certain limit. The transmission of a high number of logically independent blocks of content with a low value (lower right corner of Figure 4.16) is billed together with the transport service, if the QoS for the transport service is below a certain threshold. If QoS for the transport service increases, the QoS threshold moves to the upper left corner in Figure 4.16, the rel-

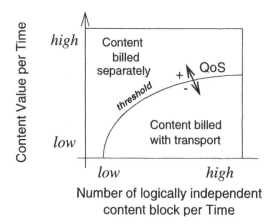

Figure 4.16 Secondary influencing factors for billing content separately or including transport [71].

ative value of content decreases, and billing of content is performed along with the transport service.

4.9 SUMMARY AND CONCLUSIONS

Today's Internet shows a clear move toward the support of differentiated services. However, purely technical mechanisms to control the access, congestion, and QoS disclose a major drawback—the lack of highly scalable mechanisms—mainly for millions of users. Therefore, economic control mechanisms, considered network management functions of the second generation, such as charging and its service-oriented derivative pricing, bridge this gap.

This chapter provided an overview of charging, the application of pricing mechanisms to Internet services, and related technology in support of these mechanisms. Determining such an approach to charging for packet-switched networks, the solution presented integrates economic mechanisms into the area of service provisioning. This extension is mainly driven by the commercialization in networking and the demand for QoS-based services, but minimized technical effort for QoS provisioning in networks.

In regard to the historic development of the Internet, two phases where economic principles have not been regarded as the major driving force can be distinguished. In the initial phase, networks were run by universities, backbones were centrally funded, and commercial use did not exist. Basically, pricing for service usage was hidden from the user and customer, and private use was almost unknown. The second phase included commercial and private users at the same time, the global deployment of the network, and its continuous extension with respect to technical mechanisms and geographical space. Simple pricing models have been implemented to support the cost recovery process of ISPs recently starting business in order to provide commercial Internet services. Limited by technical capacities of Internet protocols, driven by the run for a quick and large market share, and minor knowledge on charging packet-switched networks, flat-rate pricing schemes dominated this phase. Even though economic theory stated that an all-you-can-eat mentality is an inefficient way to price Internet services, ISPs are still offering monthly rates. Flat-fee schemes seem to offer unlimited access, but in reality they prompt an offer for a low-end QoS, at least on average.

Today the Internet is in transition between phases three and four and economic incentives play a major role. Newly developed network technology for the last mile, such as digital subscriber line technology, emerging QoS-capable Internet protocols, and an ever increasing Internet backbone capacity allows for the provisioning of new Internet services, service bundles, and applications, such as IP telephony, radio over IP, interactive TV, and other time-sensitive multimedia applications. This shift from a single-service class, best effort network to an integrated services Internet providing multiple service classes cannot be safely supported by flat-fee pricing models, since the particular resource on a per-application basis varies widely. Therefore, a completely integrated, efficient, and purely technical solution will form the immediate starting point for the fourth phase in Internet charging. All findings for an optimal balance between economic and engineering efficiency as well as user transparency and its large-scale deployment in a market managed multiservice Internet will guide commercial service suppliers and the research community. The variety of pricing schemes will be consolidated based on accounting technology, user transparency, and achievable economic efficiency. By offering flat-fee pricing for low-quality services, such as email or best effort traffic, and providing usage-based schemes for resource-consuming services, a distinction between residential user Internet access and commercial enterprise access will become a reality. High-quality end-to-end connections between the customer and service provider as well as between customers are a must. More expensive services will require a finer charging granularity than cheaper services do. Technologywise, least-cost routing functions or intelligent agents will act as price and resource brokers. Trading resources on bandwidth spot-markets has been established already for the large backbone capacity in order to provide flexibly adapted interconnectivity. Since an increasingly competitive market will exist, a trend toward dynamic pricing models can be assumed for enterprise access as well as value-added service provisioning.

Predicting the outcome of technological choices is difficult, and is specifically impossible for the Internet, but the major trend of the Internet development from a technically focused network to an economically controlled, efficient global network and distributed system is on its way. Modern accounting technology, emerging rapidly, e.g., vendors plan to ship OC-12 active measurement components and passive probes at Gigabit Ethernet [22], supports this trend. CSSs and their internal mechanisms provide the technical foundation for integrating those developments and making it happen, including front-end functionality or soft real-time feedback to customers. New economic models, implemented in terms of pricing and tariffing models, will ensure an efficient allocation of network resources. Therefore, the development of discrete, predictable, transparent, and technically feasible pricing schemes, one of them called CPS, and an ICCAS, illustrate a feasible technical solution in support of pricing tomorrow's differentiated services in the Internet. This solution will maintain parameters for customizing subscriber preferences and profiles, offer granular service control and service management features, and provide mechanisms to correlate user profiles with service profiles.

Business models for traditional ISPs will fade out as soon as providers become mobile themselves. This will be obtained by the third-generation Universal Mobile Telecommunications System (UMTS), where the typical role of an Access ISP can be performed by any mobile provider. However, due to the fact that frequencies and the currently available spectrum for sending data will be limited always, which is in clear contrast to the wired Internet backbone, efficient and user-based charging approaches have an emerging need for next-generation, packet-switched, mobile service providers. Barriers for usage-based approaches by appropriate, efficient, and technically manageable technology are being phased out. In addition, the ability to aggregate massive amounts of data, and filter, mediate, and correlate them with user and customer data eases per-customer and per-user charge calculation.

ACKNOWLEDGMENTS

The author expresses his gratitude to his senior researchers and Ph.D. students at TIK, ETH Zürich, namely P. Reichl (Sections 4.5.2.3, 4.5.4, and 4.8.2), P. Flury (Section 4.5.2.3), and J. Gerke and Hasan (Section 4.7), and his research partners T. Braun, G. Dermler, and M. Günter, (Section 4.4.4), B. Briscoe and C. Courcoubetis (Section 4.3.1.2), M. Karsten, J. Schmitt, and L. Wolf (Sections 4.2.2, 4.4.1, and 4.4.3), H. Kneer and U. Zurfluh (Sections 4.8.3 and 4.8.4), and S. Leinen. Finally, many thanks are addressed to B. Plattner for his generous support.

REFERENCES

1. J. P. Bailey, "The Economics of Internet Interconnection Agreements," in *Internet Economics*, L. McKnight and J. P. Bailey, Eds., MIT Press, Cambridge, Massachusetts, pp. 155–168, 1997.

2. Y. Bernet, J. Binder, S. Blake, M. Carlson, S. Keshav, E. Davies, B. Ohlman, D. Verma, Z. Wang, and W. Weiss, "A Framework for Differentiated Services," Internet Draft, October 1998.

3. D. Bertsekas and R. Gallager, *Data Networks*, Prentice Hall, Englewood Cliffs, New Jersey, 1987.

4. S. Blake, D. Black, M. Carlson, E. Davies, Z. Wang, and W. Weiss, "An Architecture for Differentiated Services," Internet Engineering Task Force, RFC 2475, December 1998.

5. J. Borland, "Rivalry in ISP Market Heats Up," CMP's Tech Web, *Technology News*, http://www.techweb.com/wire/story/TWB19980101S0006, January 1998.

6. A. Bouch and M. A. Sasse, "It Ain't What You Charge, It's the Way that You Do It, A User Perspective of Network QoS and Pricing," in *Proceedings of 6th IFIP/IEEE International Symposium on Integrated Network Management (IM'99)*, Boston, Massachusetts, May, pp. 639–654, 1999.

7. R. Braden, D. D. Clark, and S. Shenker, "Integrated Services in the Internet Architecture, An Overview," Internet Engineering Task Force, RFC 1633, June 1994.

8. R. Braden, S. Berson, S. Herzog, and S. Jamin, "Resource ReSerVation Protocol (RSVP)—Version 1 Functional Specification," Internet Engineering Task Force, RFC 2205, September 1997.

9. S. Bradner, "Internet Protocol Quality of Service Problem Statement," Internet Draft, September 1997.

10. B. Briscoe, Ed., "Architecture, Part I Primitives & Compositions," M3I Deliverable 2, Version 1, June 2000.

11. B. Briscoe, "The Direction of Value Flow in Connectionless Networks," 1st International Workshop on Networked Group Communication (NGC'99), Pisa, Italy, November 1999.

12. B. Briscoe, M. Rizzo, J. Tassel, and K. Damianakis, "Lightweight Policing and Charging for Packet Networks," 3rd IEEE Conference on Open Architectures and Network Programming (OpenArch 2000), Tel Aviv, Israel, March 2000.

13. N. Brownlee, "Traffic Flow Measurement, Meter MIB," RFC 2064, Internet Engineering Task Force, January 1997.

14. N. Brownlee and A. Blount, "Accounting Attributes and Record Formats," RFC 2924, Internet Engineering Task Force, September 2000.

15. N. Brownlee, C. Mills, and G. Ruth, "Traffic Flow Measurement, Architecture," RFC 2063, Internet Engineering Task Force, January 1997.

16. G. Carle, M. Smirnov, and T. Zseby, "Charging and Accounting Architectures for IP Multicast Integrated Services over ATM," 4th International Symposium on Interworking (Interworking' 98), Ottawa, Canada, July 1998.

17. G. Carle and M. Smirnov, "Charging and Accounting for Value-added IP Services," QoS Summit'99, Paris, France, November 1999.

18. J. Case, M. Fedor, M. Schoffstall, and J. Davin, "A Simple Network Management Protocol (SNMP)," RFC 1157, *Internet Engineering Task Force*, May 1990.

19. D. Chaum, "David Chaum on Electronic Commerce, How Do You Trust Big Brother?" *IEEE Internet Computing*, vol. 1, no. 6, pp. 8–16, November/December 1997,.

20. K. Chu, "User Reactions to Flat Rate Options under Time Charges with Differentiated Quality of Access, Preliminary Results from INDEX," International Workshop on Internet Service

Quality Economics, Massachusetts Institute of Technology, Cambridge, Massachusetts, December 1999.

21. S. A. Cotton, Ed., "Network Data Management—Usage (NDM-U) for IP-Based Services," *IPDR Specification Version 1.1,* June 2000.

22. Cisco Systems, *Service Providers New World News—Pricing for Profitability,* Packet, Cisco Systems, pp. 35–39, 3rd Quarter 2000.

23. Cisco Systems, "Accounting and Billing Technology," URL, http://www.cisco.com/warp/ public/cc/so/cuso/sp/sms/acct/index.shtml, January 2001.

24. D. Clark, "Combining Sender and Receiver Payments in the Internet," 24th Telecommunications Research Policy Conference, Solomon's Island, Maryland, October 1996.

25. D. Clark and W. Fang, "Explicit Allocation of Best Effort Packet Delivery Service," Tech. Rep., Massachusetts Institute of Technology, Cambridge, Massachusetts, 1997.

26. R. Cocchi, D. Estrin, S. Shenker, and L. Zhang, "Pricing in Computer Networks, Motivation, Formulation and Example," *IEEE/ACM Transactions on Networking,* vol. 1, no. 6, pp. 614–627, December 1993.

27. R. Denda, A. Banchs, and W. Effelsberg, "The Fairness Challenge in Computer Networks," LNCS, Springer-Verlag, Heidelberg, Germany, vol. 1922, 2000, pp. 208–220.

28. G. Dermler, G. Fankhauser, B. Stiller, T. Braun, M. Günter, H. Kneer, "Approaches for the Integration of Charging and Accounting into Internet Models and VPN," CATI Project Deliverable, CATI-IBM-DN-P-004-1.0, July 1999.

29. R. Edell, N. McKeown, and P. P. Varaiya, "Billing Users and Pricing for TCP," *IEEE Journal on Selected Areas in Communications,* vol. 13, no. 7, pp. 1162–1175, July 1995.

30. R. Edell and P. P. Varaiya, "Providing Internet Access, What We Learn from the INDEX Trial," Keynote Talk, Infocom'99, New York, March 1999.

31. European Telecommunications Standardization Institute (ETSI), "Parameters and Mechanisms Provided by the Network Relevant for Charging in B-ISDN," ETR 123 Rev. 1, October 1995.

32. European Telecommunications Standardization Institute (ETSI), "Considerations on Network Mechanisms for Charging and Revenue Sharing," Draft DTR/NA 010040, Version 10, October 1997.

33. European Telecommunications Standardization Institute (ETSI), "Internet Protocol (IP) based Networks," Parameters and Mechanisms for Charging," ETSI TR 101 734 V.1.1.1, Sophia Antipolis, France, September 1999.

34. M. Falkner, M. Devetsikiotis, and I. Lamdadaris, "An Overview of Pricing Concepts for Broadband IP Networks," *IEEE Communications Surveys,* pp. 2–13, 2nd Quarter 2000.

35. M. Faloutsos, P. Faloutsos, and C. Faloutsos, "On Power-Law Relationships of the Internet Topology," *ACM Computer Communication Review (SIGGCOMM'99),* vol. 29, no. 4, pp. 251–261, 1999.

36. G. Fankhauser, B. Stiller, C. Vögtli, and B. Plattner, "Reservation-based Charging in an Integrated Services Network," 4th INFORMS Telecommunications Conference, Boca Raton, Florida, March 1998.

37. D. Ferrari and L. Delgrossi, "Charging for QoS," 6th IEEE/IFIP International Workshop on Quality-of-Service (IWQoS'98), Napa, California, May 1998.

38. P. Flury, P. Reichl, J. Gerke, and B. Stiller, "Charging Considerations for Virtual Private Diff-Serv Networks," TIK Report No. 94, Computer Engineering and Networks Laboratory TIK, ETH Zürich, Switzerland, August 2000.

39. D. K. Foley, "Resource Allocation in the Public Sector," *Yale Economic Essays,* vol. 7, 1967, pp. 73–76.

40. C. Gadecki, "Usage Bills, Easier Said Than Done," *tele.com Magazine,* November 1997.

41. R. Gardner, *Games for Business and Economics,* John Wiley & Sons, New York, 1995.

42. R. Gibbens and P. Key, "Distributed Control and Resouce Pricing," ACM SIGCOM, Stockholm, Sweden, August 2000.

43. M. A. Gibney and N. R. Jennings, "Dynamic Resource Allocation by Market Based Routing in Telecommunication Networks," in *Proceedings of 2nd International Workshop on Intelligent Agents for Telecommunication Applications (IATA'98),* vol. 1437, S. Albayrak and F. S. Garijo, Eds., Springer-Verlag, Heidelberg, Germany, pp. 102–117, 1998.

44. S. E. Gillett, "Connecting Homes to the Internet, An Engineering Cost Model of Cable vs. ISDN," Massachusetts Institute of Technology, Cambridge, Massachusetts, 1995.

45. P.-L. de Guillebon, "Wholesaling for Survival and Growth," *Telecommunications, International Edition,* vol. 34, no. 2, February 2000.

46. A. Gupta, B. Jukic, D. O. Stahl, and A. B. Whinston, "Impact of Congestion Pricing on Network Infrastructure Investment," International Workshop on Internet Service Quality Economics, Massachusetts Institute of Technology, Cambridge, Massachusetts, December 1999.

47. A. Gupta, D. O. Stahl, and A. B. Whinston, "Managing the Internet as an Economic System," CISM, University of Texas at Austin, July 1994.

48. G. Hardin, "The Tragedy of the Commons," *Science,* no. 162, pp. 1243–1247, 1968.

49. A.L.G. Hayzelden and J. Bigham, "Heterogeneous Multi-Agent Architecture for ATM Virtual Path Network Resource Configuration," in *Proceedings of 2nd International Workshop on Intelligent Agents for Telecommunication Applications (IATA'98),* Vol. 1437, S. Albayrak and F. S. Garijo, Eds., Springer-Verlag, Heidelberg, Germany.

50. H.-G. Hegering, S. Abeck, and B. Neumair, *Integrated Management of Networked Systems,* Morgan Kaufmann Publishers, San Francisco, California, 1999.

51. S. Herzog, S. Shenker, and D. Estrin, "Sharing the 'Cost' of Multicast Trees, An Axiomatic Analysis," *IEEE/ACM Transactions on Networking,* vol. 5, no. 6, pp. 847–860, December 1997.

52. G. Huston, *ISP Survival Guide,* Wiley, New York, 1999.

53. G. Huston, "Interconnection, Peering, and Settlements," The Internet Summit (INET'99), San Jose, California, 1999.

54. ITU-T D-Series Recommendations, "General Tariff Principles—Definitions," D.000, Geneva, Switzerland, March 1993.

55. ITU-D.260, "General Tariff Principles, Charging and Acounting International Telecommunications Services—Charging and Accounting Capabilities to be Applied on the ISDN," Recommendation D.260, Geneva, Switzerland, March 1991.

56. ITU-D Suppl3, "General Tariff Principles, Supplement 3, Handbook on the Methodology for Determining Costs and Establishing National Tariffs," Recommendation D-Series, Supplement 3, Geneva, Switzerland, March 1993.

57. ITU-T E.800, "Quality-of-Service and Dependability Vocabulary," Recommendation E.800, Geneva, Switzerland, November 1994.

58. ITU-T Q.825, "Specification of TMN Applications at the Q3 Interface, Call Detail Recording," Recommendation Q.825, Geneva, Switzerland, 1998.

59. M. Karsten, *QoS Signaling and Charging in a Multi-service Internet Using RSVP,* Ph.D. Thesis, University of Technology, Darmstadt, Germany, July 2000.

60. M. Karsten, Ed., *Pricing Mechanisms Design (PM),* M3I Deliverable 3, Version 1.0, June 2000.

61. M. Karsten, J. Schmitt, B. Stiller, and L. Wolf, "Charging for Packet-switched Network Communications—Motivation and Overview," *Computer Communications,* vol. 23, no. 3, pp. 290–302, February 2000.

62. M. Karsten, J. Schmitt, L. Wolf, and R. Steinmetz, "An Embedded Charging Approach for

RSVP," 6th IEEE/IFIP International Workshop on Quality of Service (IWQoS'98), Napa, California, May 1998.

63. F. Kelly, "Models for a Self-managed Internet," Presented at the Department of Economics, University of Southhampton, U.K., Network Modelling in the 21st Century, The Royal Society, London, U.K., December 1999.

64. F. Kelly, A. Maulloo, and D. Tan, "Rate Control for Communication Networks—Shadow Prices, Proportional Fairness, and Stability," *Journal of the Operational Research Society,* vol. 49, pp. 237–252, 1998.

65. S. Keshav, *An Engineering Approach to Computer Networking,* Addison-Wesley, Reading Massachusetts, 1997.

66. P. Key and R. Gibbens, "The Use of Games to Assess User Strategies for Differential Quality of Service in the Internet," International Workshop on Internet Service Quality Economics (ISQE'99), Massachusetts Institute of Technology, Cambridge, Massachusetts, December 1999.

67. P. Key and L. Massoulié, "User Policies in a Network Implementing Congestion Pricing," International Workshop on Internet Service Quality Economics (ISQE'99), Massachusetts Institute of Technology, Cambridge, Massachusetts, December 1999.

68. P. Key, D. McAuley, P. Barham, K. Laevens, "Congestion Pricing for Congestion Avoidance," MSR-TR-99-15, *Microsoft Research, Cambridge, England,* February 1999.

69. K. Kilkki, *Differentiated Services for the Internet,* Macmillan Technology Series, Indianapolis, Indiana, 1999.

70. H. Kneer, U. Zurfluh, and C. Matt, "Business Model (RSVP)," Public CATI Deliverable CATIUZH-DN-P-001-2.0, March 1999.

71. H. Kneer, U. Zurfluh, G. Dermler, and B. Stiller, "A Business Model for Charging and Accounting of Internet Services," 1st International Conference on Electronic Commerce and Web Technologies, Greenwich, U.K., September 42000.

72. A. Kuiper, "Charging Methodologies for ATM, An Introduction," Cap Gemini, The Netherlands, August 1997.

73. K. Kuwabara, T. Ishida, Y. Nishibe, and T. Suda, "An Equilibratory Market-based Approach for Distributed Resource Allocation and its Application to Communication Network Control," in *Market-Based Control, A Paradigm for Distributed Resource Allocation,* E. Clearwater, Ed., pp. 53–73, 1996.

74. K. S. Lee and D. Ng, "Billing for Interconnect," *Telecommunications, International Edition,* vol. 33, no. 11, pp. 81–82, November 1999.

75. B. A. Leida, *Cost Model of Internet Service Providers, Implications for Internet Telephony and Yield Management,* Master Thesis, Massachusetts Institute of Technology, Cambridge, Massachusetts, February 1998.

76. B. Liver and G. Dermler, "The E-Business of Content Delivery," International Workshop on Internet Service Quality Economics (ISQE'99), Massachusetts Institute of Technology, Cambridge, Massachusetts, December 1999.

77. J. MacKie-Mason, "A Smart Market for Resource Reservation in a Multiple Quality of Service Information Network," Tech. Rep., University of Michigan, Ann Arbor, Michigan, September 1997.

78. J. MacKie-Mason and H. Varian, "Pricing Congestible Network Resources," *IEEE Journal on Selected Areas in Communications,* vol. 13, no. 7, pp. 1141–1149, 1995.

79. J. MacKie-Mason, and K. White, "Evaluating and Selecting Digital Payment Mechanisms," 24th Telecommunications Policy Research Conference, Solomon's Island, Maryland, October 1996.

80. D. Mitton, M. St. Johns, S. Barkley, D. Nelson, B. Patil, M. Stevens, and B. Wolff,

"Authentication, Authorization, and Accounting, Protocol Evaluation," Internet Draft, October 2000.

81. L. W. McKnight and B. A. Leida, "Internet Telephony, Costs, Pricing, and Policy," 25th Telecommunications Policy Research Conference, Alexandria, Virginia, September 1997.

82. N. McIntosh, "Heavy Surfers Pay the Price," *The Guardian,* London, August 3, 2000.

83. D. Morris and V. Pronk, "Charging for ATM Services," *IEEE Communications Magazine,* vol. 37, no. 5, pp. 133–139, May 1999.

84. A. J. Mund, "AOL's Breakdown, A Harbinger for the Internet's Future?" *Cable TV and New Media—Law and Finance,* vol. 14, no. 12, February 1997.

85. M3I, "Market Managed Multi-Service Internet," EU 5th Framework ISP Project 11429, URL, http://www.m3i.org, January 2001.

86. D. N. Newbery, *Privatization, Restructuring, and Regulation of Network Utilities,* The MIT Press, Cambridge, Massachusetts, 1999.

87. K. Nichols, S. Blake, F. Baker, and D. Black, "Definition of the Differentiated Services Field (DS Field) in the IPv4 and IPv6 Headers," RFC 2474, Internet Engineering Task Force, December 1998.

88. K. Nichols and B. Carpenter, "Definition of Differentiated Services Per-Domain-Behaviors and Rules for their Specification," Internet Draft, June 2000.

89. K. Nichols, V. Jacobson, and L. Zhang, "A Two-bit Differentiated Services Architecture for the Internet," RFC 2638, Internet Engineering Task Force, July 1999.

90. M. Nilsson, "Third-Generation Radio Access Standards," *Ericsson Review,* no. 3, pp. 110–121, 1999.

91. A. M. Noll, "Internet Pricing Versus Reality," *Communications of the ACM,* vol. 40, no. 8, pp. 118–121, August 1997.

92. A. Odlyzko, "Paris Metro Pricing, The Minimalist Differentiated Services Solution," in *Proceedings of 7th IEEE/IFIP International Workshop on QoS (IWQoS'99),* London, pp. 159–161, June 1999.

93. "Optimum, Broadband Access Networks," *Telektronikk,* vol. 95, no. 2/3, Telenor, Norway, 1999.

94. K. Park, M. Sitharam, and S. Chen, "Quality-of-Service Provision in Noncooperative Networks, Heterogeneous Preferences, Multi-Dimensional QoS Vectors, and Burstiness," in *Proceedings of 1st International Conference on Information and Computation Economies (ICE-98),* pp. 111–127, 1998.

95. C. Partridge, "A Proposed Flow Specification," RFC 1363, Internet Engineering Task Force, September 1992.

96. C. Partridge, "Using the Flow Label Field in IPv6," RFC 1809, Internet Engineering Task Force, June 1995.

97. B. Plattner, B. Stiller, and D. Bauer, "High-Performance Networks—Applications and Technology," Industry Course, Zürich, Switzerland, June 2000.

98. H. Petersen, D. Konstantas, M. Michels, D. Som, G. Fankhauser, D. Schweikert, B. Stiller, N. Weiler, R. Cantini, and F. Baessler, "MicPay, Micro-payments for Correlated Payments," SI Informatik/Informatique, No. 1, Switzerland, January 2000.

99. K. Ramakrishnan and S. Floyd, "A Proposal to add Explicit Congestion Notification (ECN) to IP," RFC 2481, Internet Engineering Task Force, January 1999.

100. P. Reichl, P. Kurtansky, J. Gerke, and B. Stiller, "The Design of a Generic Service-oriented Cost Model for Service Providers in the Internet (COSMOS)," Applied Telecommunication Symposium 2001 (ATS'01), Seattle, Washington, April 2001.

101. P. Reichl and B. Stiller, "Notes on Cumulus Pricing and Time-scale Aspects of Internet Tariff Design," TIK Report No. 97, Computer Engineering and Networks Laboratory TIK, ETH Zürich, Switzerland, November 2000.

102. L. G. Roberts, "Beyond Moore's Law, Internet Growth Trends," *IEEE Computer,* vol. 33, no. 1, pp. 117–119, January 2000.

103. F. C. Rö hmer, "Charging Information Management and its Technical Implication in a Liberalized Broadband Telecommunications Environment," *SI Informatik/Informatique, Switzerland,* no. 3, pp. 37–38, 1999.

104. S. Salsano, F. Ricciato, M. Winter, G. Eichler, A. Thomas, F. Fünfstück, T. Ziegler, and C. Brandauer, "Definition and Usage of SLSs in the AQUILA Consortium," Internet Draft, November 2000.

105. *SET, Secure Electronic Transactions,* URL, http://www.setco.org, January 2001.

106. S. Shenker, "Fundamental Design Issues for the Future Internet," *IEEE Journal on Selected Areas in Communications,* vol. 13, no. 7, pp. 1176–1188, Sept. 1995.

107. S. Shenker, "Service Models and Pricing Policies for an Integrated Services Internet," in *Public Access to the Internet,* J. Keller B. Kahin, Eds., Prentice Hall, Englewood Cliffs, New Jersey, 1995, pp. 315–337.

108. S. Shenker, D. Clark, D. Estrin, and S. Herzog, "Pricing in Computer Networks, Reshaping the Research Agenda," *ACM Computer Communication Review,* vol. 26, no. 2, pp. 19–43, April 1996.

109. S. Shenker, G. Partridge, and R. Guerin, "Specification of Guaranteed Quality-of-Service," RFC 2212, Internet Engineering Task Force, September 1997

110. A. Sirbu, "Internet Billing Service Design and Prototype Implementation," Carnegie Mellon University, Computer Science Department Tech. Rep., Pittsburgh, Pennsylvania, 1994.

111. SIU, "Smart Internet Usage," Hewlett-Packard, http://communications.hp.com/smartinternet/, January 2001.

112. D. Songhurst, Ed., *Charging Communication Networks—From Theory to Practice,* Elsevier Publisher, Amsterdam, The Netherlands, 1999.

113. B. Stiller, "QoS Methods for Managing Communicating Applications," *Journal on Integrated Computer-Aided Engineering,* vol. 6, no. 2, pp. 159–169, February 1999.

114. B. Stiller, "Pricing and Charging of Packet-based Networks," Tutorial T12, IEEE/IFIP Network Operations and Management Symposium (NOMS 2000), Honolulu, Hawaii, April 2000.

115. B. Stiller, T. Braun, M. Günter, and B. Plattner, "The CATI Project—Charging and Accounting Technology for the Internet," LNCS, Springer-Verlag, Heidelberg, Germany, vol. 1629, 1999, pp. 281–296.

116. B. Stiller, G. Fankhauser, G. Joller, P. Reichl, and N. Weiler, "Open Charging and QoS Interfaces for IP Telephony," The Internet Summit (INET'99), San Jose, California, June 1999.

117. B. Stiller, G. Fankhauser, and B. Plattner, "Charging of Multimedia Flows in an Integrated Services Network," in *Proceedings of 8th International Workshop on Network and Operating System Support for Digital Audio and Video (NOSSDAV'98),* Cambridge, England, pp. 189–192, July 1998.

118. B. Stiller, G. Fankhauser, N. Weiler, and B. Plattner, "Charging and Accounting for Integrated Internet Services - State of the Art, Problems, and Trends," The Internet Summit (INET '98), Geneva, Switzerland, July 1998.

119. B. Stiller, J. Gerke, and P. Flury, "The Design of a Charging and Accounting System," TIK Rep. No. 94, Computer Engineering and Networks Laboratory TIK, ETH Zürich, Switzerland, July 2000.

120. B. Stiller, J. Gerke, P. Reichl, and P. Flury, "The Cumulus Pricing Scheme and its Integration into a Generic and Modular Internet Charging System for Differentiated Services," TIK Rep. No. 96, Computer Engineering and Networks Laboratory TIK, ETH Zürich, Switzerland, September 2000.

121. B. Stiller, J. Gerke, P. Reichl, and P. Flury, "Management of Differentiated Service Usage by

the Cumulus Pricing Scheme and a Generic Internet Charging System," Seventh IEEE/IFIP Symposium on Integrated Network Management (IM 2001), Seattle, Washington, May 2001.

122. B. Stiller, P. Reichl, and S. Leinen, "A Practical Review of Pricing and Cost Recovery for Internet Services," *Netnomics—Economic Research and Electronic Networking,* vol. 3, no. 1, March 2001.

123. H. Tö bben, *Concept of a Market-based Routing for ATM-Networks on the Basis of Intelligent Agents,* Ph.D. Thesis (in German), TU-Berlin, DAI-Labor, Germany, April 2000.

124. H. R. Varian, *Intermediate Microeconomics—A Modern Approach,* W. W. Norton & Company, New York, 4th edition, 1996.

125. W. Vickrey, "Counterspeculation, Auctions, and Competitive Sealed Tenders," *The Journal of Finance,* vol. 16, pp. 8–37, 1961.

126. D. Walker, F. Kelly, and J. Solomon, "Tariffing in the new IP/ATM Environment," *Telecommunications Policy,* vol. 21, pp. 283–295, May 1997.

127. Q. Wang, J. Peha, and M. Sirbu, "Optimal Pricing for Integrated-Services Networks with Guaranteed Quality of Service," in *Internet Economics,* L. McKnight and J. P. Bailey Eds., MIT Press, Cambridge, Massachusetts, pp. 353–376, 1997.

128. M. Webster, *Merriam-Webster's Collegiate Dictionary,* Merriam-Webster, Inc., Springfield, Massachusetts, 10th Edition, 1996.

129. J. Wroclawski, "Specification of the Controlled-Load Network Element Service," RFC 2211, Internet Engineering Task Force, September 1997.

130. L. Zhang, S. Deering, D. Estrin, S. Shenker, and D. Zappala, "RSVP, A New Resource Reservation Protocol," *IEEE Networks Magazine,* vol. 31, no. 9, pp. 8–18, September 1993.

CHAPTER 5

IP SECURITY

MOSTAFA HASHEM SHERIF

5.1 INTRODUCTION

The goal of this chapter is to review the general principles of security in IP networks as a particular case of telecommunications networks. This chapter does not give an exhaustive treatment of the subject. It gives a description of security services in open networks and describes various security mechanisms using cryptography. Architectures for certification as well as management of encryption keys are presented. Some potential threats to security are highlighted, particularly as they relate to cracks in the protection walls of cryptography.

The chapter has four appendices. The first lists some policy considerations for securing telecommunication networks. A general overview of the symmetric and public key encryption algorithms is available in Appendices II and III, respectively. Appendix IV describes the main operations of the Digital Signature Algorithm (DSA) of ANSI X9.30:1 [1].

5.2 SECURITY OF TELECOMMUNICATIONS SERVICES

Telecommunications services build on networking technologies, operations support systems, and policies (also called methods and procedures) to allow remote access to applications as well as content management and distribution. Within this context, Recommendations X.700 [2] and X.800 [3] of the ITU-T provide a general framework to ensure the security of telecommunications services. First, security functions or services must be available. Next, these security functions must be securely managed. Finally, policies

Managing IP Networks. Edited by Saleh Aidarous and Thomas Plevyak
ISBN 0-471-39299-5 © 2003 Institute of Electrical and Electronics Engineers

should be defined and implemented to administer the security information and the information base, as well as to ensure the physical security of infrastructure (protection from fires, earthquakes, intrusions, attacks, thefts, etc.).

The complexity of securing telecommunications services today arises from several factors. Because of the worldwide phenomenon of deregulation of telecommunications, service offers are no longer vertically integrated and several operators usually collaborate to carry the traffic end-to-end. As shown in Figure 5.1, current offers of telecommunications services involve several providers end-to-end for the following components: the infrastructure for transport, the switching functions within the network, the network services; and the content management, including access, distribution, billing, and payment collection. For example, service providers can be involved in Web hosting, in disaster recovery, or in data storage networks. Content management covers the functions of customer relations management, supply management, and electronic payments. The content-level providers include broadcasters, providers of catalogues, and certification authorities. In all these instances, when a problem arises, operators at each layer need to be able to exchange authenticated information that would help in locating and resolving this problem [4, 5]. Furthermore, VPNs may span several carriers which should collaborate to ensure the continuity of service from one end to the other, even though each carrier manages its own part separately. In VPNs, customer network management (CNM) systems, such as those defined by ITU-T Recommendations X.160, X.161, and X.162 [6–8], allow end users to have controlled access to their part of the public data network for monitoring and provisioning. Clearly, the correct identification and authentication of the participants, their administrative privileges, and their traffic are essential to provide them with the services to which they have subscribed, to ensure the integrity and confidentiality of the exchanges, and to prevent users from affecting other users (inadvertently or out of malice).

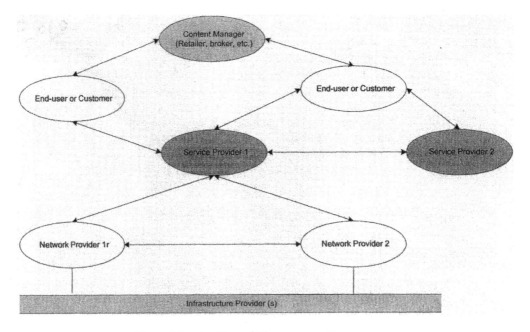

Figure 5.1 Providers of telecommunications services.

Within each network, access management to the Network Operations Center (NOC) is complicated by the fact that hundreds or technicians and applications perform specific operations. Although automation of operations is pursued to reduce cost, it requires that various OSSs communicate securely, even across administrative boundaries. It will also be necessary to preserve records of the exchanges as proof that can help resolve disputes and litigation [9]. Clearly, security in such a distributed and complex environment depends, not only on network equipment (switches, transmit trunks, and information systems), but also on the end user's terminals and the administrative policies of each operator. This is why the management systems must at least incorporate highly reliable security mechanisms to protect the telecommunication services offers.

One key assumption in this chapter is that the communications network is continuously available. Attacks on the network infrastructure, for example, the signaling, routing, or network management mechanisms, increase security exposures. Therefore, the network infrastructure must be physically protected from fires, earthquakes, floods, vandalism, etc. It also means that the network elements have been thoroughly tested to ensure the correct routing of messages and the correct functioning of various network management functions, including operations and administration, under a wide range of loads and stress conditions. ISO has issued a technical report ISO/IEC TR 13335 [10] to provide guidance on the management aspects of information security. Part 5 of this report deals with communication networks and the factors that should be taken into account to establish network security requirements. Aspects related to physical protection, software quality evaluation, risk analysis, as well as recommended security policies are outside the scope of this chapter.

5.3 SECURITY OBJECTIVES

Security exposures can affect user data and applications, the network infrastucture of the network elements themselves. Recommendations X.509 [11] and X.800 [3] of the ITU-T identify several types of information threats that can be classified as follows.

1. Passive attacks
    —Interception of the identity of one or more of the participants by a third party with a mischievous intent;
    —Data interception through clandestine monitoring of the exchanges during a communication by an outsider or an unauthorized user.
2. Active attacks
    —Replay of a previous message, in its entirety or in part, after its recording;
    —Defective or criminal manipulation of the content of an exchange by substitution, insertion, deletion, reorganization of user's data exchanged in a communication by a nonauthorized third party;
    —Users' repudiation or denial of their participation in part or in all of a communication exchange;
    —Misrouting of messages from one user to another (the objective of the security service would be to avoid the consequences of such an error);
    —Analysis of the traffic and examination of the parameters related to a communication among users (i.e., absence or presence, frequency, direction, sequence,

type, volume, etc.). This analysis would be made more difficult with the production of unintelligible additional traffic (by a fill-in traffic) and by using encrypted or random data.

—Masquerade, whereby one entity pretends to be another entity;

—Denial of service and the impossibility of accessing the resources usually available to authorized users following the prevention or interruption of a communication, or the delay imposed on time-critical operations.

Based on the preceding threats, the objectives of security measures are as follows.

- Prevent an outsider other than the participants from reading or manipulating the contents or the sequences of the exchanged messages without being detected. In particular, this third party must not be allowed to play back old messages, replace blocks of information, or insert messages from multiple distinct exchanges without detection.

- Impede the falsification of payment instructions or the generation of spurious messages by users with dubious intentions. For example, dishonest merchants or processing centers must not be capable of reutilizing information about their clients' bank accounts to generate fraudulent orders. They should not be able to initiate the processing of payment instructions without expediting the corresponding purchases. At the same time, the merchants will be protected from excessive revocation of payments or malicious denials of orders.

- Satisfy the legal requirements for valid contracts to allow conflict resolutions, particularly in the area of consumer protection and privacy protection.

- Assure access to the service according to the contractual terms.

- Give the same level of service to all customers, irrespective of their location and the variations in climate, temperature, humidity, erosion, etc.

5.4 OSI MODEL FOR CRYPTOGRAPHIC SECURITY

The well-known OSI reference model of data networks establishes a structure for exchanges in seven layers, as follows:

1. The *physical layer,* where the electrical, mechanical, and functional properties of the interfaces are defined (signal levels, rates, structures, etc.).
2. The *link layer,* which defines the methods for orderly and error-free transmission between two network nodes.
3. The *network layer,* where the functions for routing, multiplexing of packets, flow control, and network supervision are defined.
4. The *transport layer,* which is responsible for the reliable transport of the traffic between the two network endpoints as well the assembly and disassembly of the messages.
5. The *session layer,* which handles the conversation between the processes at the two endpoints.

6. The *presentation layer,* which is in charge of managing the differences in syntax among the various representations of information at both endpoints by putting the data into a standardized format.

7. The *application layer,* whose function is to ensure that two application processes cooperate to carry out the desired information processing at the two endpoints.

The ISO standard ISO 7498 Part 2 [12] (ITU-T Recommendation X.800 [3]) describes a reference model for security services in open networks. Each layer of the ISO model can offer one or more of the following security services [13]:

- *Confidentiality,* so that the exchanged messages are not divulged to an nonauthorized third party. In some applications, the confidentiality of addresses may be needed as well, to prevent the analysis of traffic patterns and the derivation of side information that could be used.

- *Integrity* of the data, i.e., proof that the message has not been altered after it was expedited and before the moment it was received. This service guarantees that the received data are exactly what have been transmitted by the sender and that they have not been corrupted, either intentionally or by error in transit in the network. Data integrity is also needed for network management data such as configuration files, and accounting and audit information.

- *Identification* of the participants by verifying a preestablished relation between a characteristic (for example, a password or cryptographic key) and an entity. This allows control of access to the network resources or to the offered services based on the privileges associated with a given identity. One entity may possess several distinct identifiers. Furthermore, some protection against denial of service attacks can be achieved using access control.

- *Authentication* of the participants (users, network elements, and network element systems), which is the corroboration of the identity that an entity claims with the guarantee of a trusted third party. Authentication is necessary to assure nonrepudiation of users as well of network elements.

- *Access control* to ensure that only the authorized participants whose identities have been duly authenticated can gain access to the protected resources.

- *Nonrepudiation,* which is the service that offers proof that the integrity of the data and of their origin in an irrefutable relation that can be verified by a third party, for example, the nonrepudiation that the sender has sent the message or that a receiver has received the message. This service can be also called authentication of the origin of the data.

Unfortunately, not all the services offered on the Internet can be easily protected. The case of mobile IP illustrates this point. According to this protocol, a mobile node outside the zone that its home agent serves must register with the foreign agent in whose region it is currently located. Yet the protocol does not provide the means to authenticate the foreign agent by initiating the exchange of the secret key that will be used to protect the resubscription data [14, pp. 134–139, 189–192].

Security services can be implemented in one or more layers of the OSI model [15–17]. The choice of the layer depends on the following criteria:

1. If the protection has to be accorded to all the traffic flow in a uniform manner, the intervention has to be at the physical or the link layers. The only cryptographic service that is available at this level is confidentiality by encrypting the data or similar means (frequency hopping, spread spectrum, etc.). The protection of the traffic at the physical layer covers all the flow, not only user data but also the information related to network administration: alarms, synchronization, update of routing table, etc. The disadvantage of the protection at this level is that a successful attack will destabilize the whole security structure, because the same key is utilized for all transmissions. At the link layer, encryption can be end-to-end, based on the source/destination, provided that the same technology is used all the way through.

2. For a selective bulk protection that covers all the communications associated with a particular subnetwork from one end-system to another end-system, network layer encipherment will be chosen. Security at the network layer is also needed to secure the communication among the network elements, particularly for link-state protocols, such as OSPF or PNNI, where updates to the routing tables are automatically generated based on received information that is then flooded to the rest of the network.

3. For a protection with recovery after a fault, or if the network is not reliable, the security services will be at the transport layer. The services of this layer apply end-to-end either singly or in combination. These services are authentication—whether *simple* by passwords or *strong* by signature mechanisms or certificates—access control, confidentiality, and integrity.

4. If a high granularity of protection is required or if the nonrepudiation service has to be assured, the encryption will be at the application layer. It is at this level that most of the security protocols for commercial systems operate, which frees them from a dependency on the lower layers. All security services are available.

It should be noted that there are no services at the session layer. In contrast, the services offered at the presentation layer are confidentiality, which can be selective such as by a given data field, authentication, integrity (in whole or in part), and nonrepudiation with a proof of origin or proof of delivery.

The secure sockets layer (SSL)/transport layer security (TLS) protocols are widely used to secure the connection between a client and a server [18, 19]. With respect to the OSI reference model, SSL/TLS lie between the transport layer and the application layer.

Nevertheless, it may be sufficient for an attacker to discover that a communication is taking place among partners, and then attempt to guess, for example:

- The characteristics of the goods or services exchanged;.
- The conditions for acquisition: delivery intervals, conditions, and means of settlement;
- The financial settlement.

The establishment of an enciphered channel or "tunnel" between two points at the network layer can constitute a shield against such types of attack. It should be noticed, however, that other clues, such as the relative time to execute the cryptographic operations, or the variations in the electric consumption or the electromagnetic radiation, can permit an analysis of the encrypted traffic and ultimately lead to breaking of the encryption algorithms [20].

5.4.1 Security Services at the Link Layer

RFC 1661 [21] defines the link-layer protocol PPP to carry traffic between two entities identified with their respective IP addresses. The Layer 2 Tunneling Protocol (L2TP), defined in RFC 2661 [22], extends the PPP operation by separating the processing of IP packets within the PPP frames from that of the traffic flowing between the two ends at the link layer. This distinction allows a remote client to connect to a network access server (NAS) in a private (corporate) network though the public Internet as follows. The client encapsulates PPP frames in an L2TP tunnel, prepends the appropriate L2TP header, and then transports the new IP packet using UDP. The IP addresses in the new IP header are assigned by the local ISP at the local access point. Figure 5.2 illustrates the arrangement where the size of the additional header ranges from 8 octets to 16 octets: 1–2 octets for PPP, 8–16 octets for L2TP. Given that the overhead for UDP is 8 octets and for the IP header it is 20 octets, the total additional overhead ranges from 37 octets to 46 octets.

Although L2TP does not provide any security services, it is possible to use IPSec to secure the layer 2 tunnel, because L2TP runs over IP. This is shown in the following section.

5.4.2 Security Services at the Network Layer

The security services at this layer are offered from one end of the network to the other. They include network access control, authentication of the users and/or hosts, and authentication and integrity of the exchanges. These services are transparent to applications and end users, and their responsibilities fall on the administrators of network elements.

The purpose of network access control is to limit actions and privileges of an entity based on network addresses of both endpoints (e.g., IP addresses). As explained earlier, this is important in link-state protocols, such as OSPF or PNNI, to protect routing tables of various network elements.

Authentication at the network layer can be simple or strong. *Simple* authentication uses a name and password pair (the password can be a one-time password), while *strong* authentication utilizes digital signatures or the exchange of certificates issued by a recognized certification authority. The use of strong authentication requires the presence of encryption keys at all network nodes, which imposes the physical protection of all these nodes.

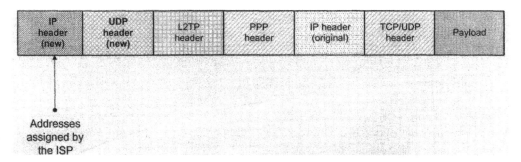

Figure 5.2 Layer 2 Tunneling with L2TP.

IPSEC is a protocol suite defined in RFCs 2401 to 2412 [23–31] to secure communications at the network layer between two peers. The overall security architecture is described in RFC 2401 [23], while a road map to the IPSec documentation is in RFC 2411 [29].

IPSec offers authentication, confidentiality, and key management. The authentication header (AH) protocol defined in RFC 2402 [23] provides the cryptographic services to authenticate and verify the integrity of the payload as well as the routing information in the original IP header. The encapsulating security payload (ESP) protocol is described in RFC 2406 [24], and gives the means to assure the confidentiality of the original payload and to authenticate the encrypted data as well as the ESP header. Both IPSec protocols provide some protection against replay attacks with the help of a monotonically increasing sequence number that is 32 bits long. Although these two mechanisms are available, in the IP version 6 (IPv6) protocol [32], IPSec makes them available with the current IP version 4. The key exchange is performed with the Internet key exchange (IKE) protocol defined in RFC 2409 [28]. (*Note:* A new ESP draft uses 64-bit sequence numbers and takes into consideration the new symmetric encryption algorithm Advance Encryption Standard (AES).)

IPSec operates in one of two modes: the transport mode and the tunnel mode. In the transport mode, protection covers the payload and transport header only, while the tunnel mode protects the whole packet, including IP addresses. The transport mode secures communication between two hosts, while the tunnel mode is useful when one or both ends of the connection is a trusted entity, such as a firewall, which provides security services to an originating device. Tunnel mode is also employed when a router provides security services to the traffic that it is forwarding [33]. Both modes are used to secure virtual private networks with IPSec, as shown in Figure 5.3. Typically, AH protocol can be used for the transport mode, while the ESP is applicable to both modes. This explains why there is a decreasing tendency to use the AH protocol.

Figure 5.4 illustrates the encapsulation in both cases. In this figure, the IPSec header represents either the ESP or both the ESP and the AH headers. Thus, routing information associated with the private or corporate network can be encrypted after establishment of a TCP tunnel between the firewall at the originating side and the one at the destination side. (*Note:* ESP with no encryption (i.e., with a NULL algorithm) is equivalent to the AH protocol, which is another reason why usage of the AH protocol is limited.)

In verifying the integrity, the contents of fields in the IP header that change in transit (e.g., the "time to live") are considered to be zero. With respect to transmission overheads, the length of the AH is at least 12 octets (a multiple of 4 octets for IPv4 and of 6 octets for IPv6). Similarly, the length of the ESP header is 8 octets. However, the overhead includes 4 octets for the initialization vector (if it is included in the payload field) as well as an ESP trailer of at least 6 octets that comprise a padding and authentication data.

Let us return back to the protection of L2TP (control data or user information) traffic with the IPSec protocol suite, as described in RFC 3193 [34]. When both IPSec and L2TP are used together, the various headers are organized as shown in Figure 5.5. (*Note:* In the 1996–1998 time frame, RSA Data Security, Inc. (RSADSI), and the Secure Wide Area Network (S/WAN) consortium were actively promoting a specific implementation of IPSec to ensure interoperability among firewalls and TCP/IP products. However, the free-software advocates cooperated under the umbrella of FreeS/WAN to distribute an open-source implementation of both IPSec and its default exchange protocol IKE written for

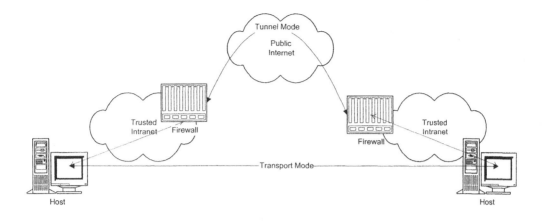

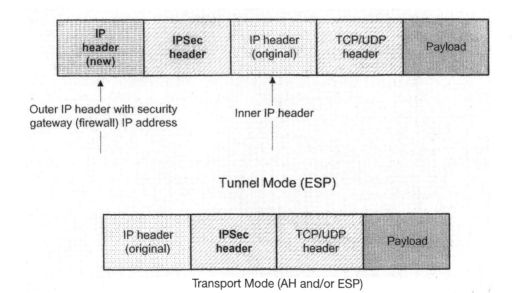

Figure 5.3 Securing virtual private networks with IPSec.

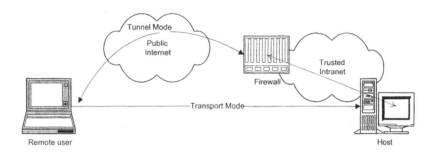

Figure 5.4 Encapsulation for IPSec modes.

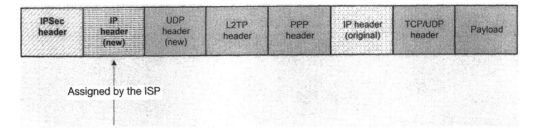

Assigned by the ISP

Figure 5.5 Encapsulation for secure network access with L2TP and IPSec.

Linux. As a consequence, S/WAN is no longer an active initiative. Details on going projects for Linux are available at http://www.freeswan.org.)

5.4.3 Application Security

Many security protocols operate at the application layer, which makes them independent of the lower layers. The whole gamut of security services is now available, namely:

1. Confidentiality, total or selective by field or by traffic flow
2. Data integrity
3. Peer entity authentication
4. Access control
5. Nonrepudiation of transmission with proof of origin
6. Nonrepudiation of reception with proof of reception

To illustrate, the Secure Shell (SSH[1]) provides security at the application layer; it allows a user to log on, execute commands, and transfer files securely. Thus, it can replace other applications, such as telnet, rlogin, rsh, rcp [35–37]. In reality, there are two distinct protocols SSH1 and SHH2. Both bind to the same TCP port. One important difference is that SSH2 has an explicit capability to secure ftp as well. Both are freely available specifications with freeware and commercial implementations. Guidelines for management of security with SSH are available [38].

In the rest of this chapter, we give an overview of the mechanisms used to implement security service. The objective is to present sufficient background for understanding the applications and not to give an exhaustive review. For a comprehensive discussion of the mathematics of cryptography and its applications, the reader can consult several excellent textbooks, such as Schneier [39] and Menezes et al. [40].

5.5 MESSAGE CONFIDENTIALITY

Confidentiality guarantees that information will be communicated solely to the parties that are authorized for its reception. Concealment is achieved with the help of encryption algorithms. There are two types of encryption: symmetric encryption, where the opera-

---

[1]Secure Shell and SSH are registered trademarks of SSH Communications Security, Ltd. of Finland.

tions of message obfuscation and revelation use the same secret key, and public key encryption, where the encryption key is secret and the revelation key is public.

5.5.1 Symmetric Cryptography

Symmetric cryptography is the tool employed in classic systems. The key that the sender of a secret message utilizes to encrypt the message is the same as the one that the legitimate receiver uses to decrypt the message. Obviously, key exchange among the partners has to occur before the communication, and this exchange takes place through other secured channels. Figure 5.6 illustrates the operation.

Let M be the message to encrypt with the encryption process E with a symmetric key K. The result will be the ciphertext C such that:

$$E[K(M)] = C$$

The decryption process D is the inverse function of E that restores the clear text:

$$D(C) = M$$

There are two main categories of symmetric encryption algorithms: block encryption algorithms and stream cipher algorithms. Block encryption acts by transforming a block of data of fixed size, generally 64 bits, in encrypted blocks of the same size. Stream ciphers convert the clear text one bit at a time by combining the stream of bits in the clear text, with the stream of bits from the encryption key using an exclusive OR (XOR).

Table 5.1 presents some algorithms for symmetric encryption commonly used in commercial applications.

The main drawback of symmetric cryptography systems is that both parties must obtain, one way or another, the unique encryption key. This is possible without too much trouble within a closed organization; on open networks, however, the exchange can be intercepted. Public key cryptography, which was proposed in 1976 by Diffie and Hellman, is one solution to the problem of key exchange [49].

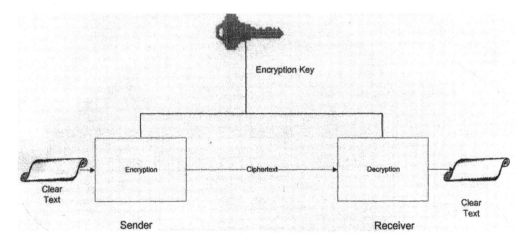

Figure 5.6 Symmetric encryption.

Table 5.1 Symmetric Encryption Algorithms in Commercial Applications

Algorithm	Name and Comments	Type of Encryption	Key Length in bits	Standard
AES	Advanced Encryption Standard	Blocks of 128, 192, or 256 bits	128, 192, or 256	FIPS 197
DES	Data Encryption Standard	Blocks of 64 bits	56	FIPS 81,1981 ANSI X3.92 [41], X3.105 [42], X3.106 [43], ISO 8372 [44], ISO/IEC 10116
IDEA (Lai and Massey [45, 46])	International Data Encryption Algorithm, apparently one of the best and most secure algorithms commercially available	Blocks of 64 bits	128	
RC2	Developed by Ronald Rivest [39, pp. 319–320]	Blocks of 64 bits	Variable, 40 bits for export from the United States	No, and proprietary
RC4	Developed by R. Rivest [39, pp. 397–398]	Stream	40 or 128	No, but posted on the Internet in 1994
RC5	Developed by R. Rivest [47]	Blocks of 32, 64, or 128 bits	Variable up to 2048 bits	No, and proprietary
SKIPJACK	An algorithm developed in the United States by the National Security Agency (NSA) for applications with the PCMCIA card Fortezza[a]	Blocks of 64 bits	80	Declassified algorithm whose Version 2.0 is available at http://csrc.nist.gov/ encryption/ skipjack-kea.htm.
Triple DES	Also called TDEA	Blocks of 64 bits	112	ANSI X9.52 [48]

[a]Fortezza is a Cryptographic Application Programming Interface (CAPI) that the NSA has defined for security applications on PCMCIA cards incorporating SKIPJACK.

5.5.2 Public Key Cryptography

Algorithms of public key cryptography introduce a pair of keys for each participant, a private key, SK, and a public key, PK. The keys are constructed in such a way that it is practically impossible to reconstitute the private key with the knowledge of the public key.

Consider two users, A and B, each having a pair of keys (PK_A, SK_A) and (PK_B, SK_B), respectively. Thus,

1. To send a secret message x to B, A encrypts it with B's public key and then transmits the encrypted message to B. This is represented by

$$e = PK_B(x)$$

2. *B* recovers the information using his or her private key SK_B. It should be noted that only *B* possesses SK_B, which can be used to identify *B*. The decryption operation can be represented by

$$x = SK_B(e) \qquad \text{or} \qquad x = SK_B[PK_B(x)]$$

3. *B* can respond to *A* by sending a new secret message x' encrypted with the public key PK_A of *A*:

$$e' = PK_A x'$$

4. *A* obtains x' by decrypting e':

$$x' = SK_B e' \qquad \text{or} \qquad x' = SK_A[PK_A x']$$

The diagram in Figure 5.7 summarizes these exchanges. Clearly, the public key is the encryption key and the private key is the recovery key.

It is worth noting that the preceding exchange can be used to verify the identify of each participant. More precisely, *A* and *B* are identified by the possession of the decryption key, SK_A or SK_B, respectively. *A* can determine if *B* possesses the private decryption key SK_B if the initial message *x* is included in the returned message x' that *B* sends. This indicates to *A* that the communication has been established with the entity that possesses SK_B. *B* can also confirm the identity of *A* in the same way.

The de facto standard for public key encryption is the algorithm RSA invented by Ronald Rivest, Adi Shamir, and Leonard Adleman in 1978 [50].

5.6 DATA INTEGRITY

The objective of the integrity service is to eliminate all possibility of nonauthorized modification of messages during their transit from the sender to the receiver. The traditional

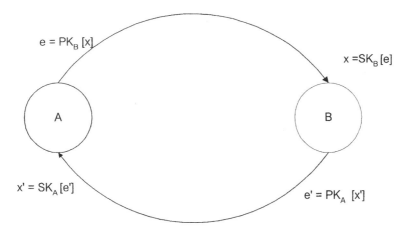

Figure 5.7 Confidentiality of messages with public key cryptography. ITU-T Recommendation X.509. (From the International Telecommunication Union, 2000. With permission.)

form to achieve this security is to stamp the letter envelope with the wax seal of the sender. Transporting this concept to electronic transactions, the seal will be a sequence of bits associated univocally with the document to be protected. This sequence of bits will constitute a unique and unfalsifiable "fingerprint" that will accompany the document sent to the destination. The receiver will then recalculate the value of the fingerprint from the received document and compare the value obtained with the value that was sent. Any difference will indicate that message integrity has been violated.

The fingerprint can be made to depend on the message content only by applying a hash function, on the message content and the sender's private key in the case of a public key encryption algorithm, or on the message content and a secret key that only the sender and the receiver know in the case of a symmetric encryption algorithm. In the first case, there are no secrets in the operation and anyone can calculate the fingerprint on the basis of the message and the hash function, provided that the hash function is known. In the second case, any person who has access to the public key of the sender and who knows the hash algorithm would be able to verify the message integrity. In the third case, only the receiver will be able to verify the integrity.

It should be noted that lack of integrity can be used to break confidentiality. For example, for some algorithms, attacks on the initialization vectors can be used to break down the confidentiality code.

5.6.1 Verification of the Integrity with a One-Way Hash Function

A *hash function* is a function that converts a sequence of characters of any length into a chain of characters of a fixed length, L, usually smaller than the original length, called a hash value. A *one-way hash function* is a function that can be calculated relatively easily in one direction, but with considerable difficulty in the inverse direction. A one-way hash function is sometimes called a compression function or a contraction function.

To verify the integrity of a message whose fingerprint has been calculated with the hash function $H( )$, this function should also be a one-way function; i.e., it should meet the following properties:

1. Absence of collisions, in other words, the probability of obtaining the same hash value with two different texts should be almost null. Thus, for a given message, x_1, the probability of finding a different message, x_2, such that $H(x_1) = H(x_2)$, is extremely small. For the collision probability to be negligible, the size of the hash value, L, should be sufficiently large.
2. Impossibility of inversion; given the fingerprint, h, of a message, x, it is practically impossible to calculate x such that $H(x) = h$.
3. A wide spread among the output values so that a small difference between two messages should yield a large difference between their fingerprints. Thus, any slight modification in the original text should, on average, affect half of the bits of the fingerprint.

Consider the message X. It will have been divided into n blocks, each consisting of B bits. If needed, padding bits would be appended to the message, according to a defined scheme, so that the length of each block reaches the necessary B bits. The operations for cryptographic hashing are described using a compression function $f(\ )$ according to the following recursive relationship:

$$h_i = f(h_{i-1}, x_i), \qquad i = 1, \ldots, n$$

In this equation, h_0 is the vector that contains an initial value of L bits and $x = \{x_1, x_2, \ldots, x_n\}$ is the message subdivided into n vectors of B bits each. Some commonly used hash algorithms are listed in Table 5.2.

For MD5 and SHA-1, the message is divided into blocks of 512 bits. The padding consists in appending to the last block a binary "1," then as many "0" bits as necessary for the size of the last block, with padding to be 448 bits. Next, a suffix of 8 octets is added to contain the length of the initial message (before padding) coded over 64 bits, which brings the total size of the last block to 512 bits of 64 octets.

In 1994, two researchers, van Oorschot and Wiener, were able to detect collisions in the output of MD5 [56], which explains its gradual replacement with SHA-1. (*Note:* Many authors use SHA-1, SHA-1, and SHA interchangeably.)

Table 5.2 Some Commonly Utilized Hash Functions

Algorithm	Name	Length of the Fingerprint (L) in bits	Block Size (B) In bits	Standardization
DSMR	Digital Signature Scheme Giving Message Recovery			ISO/IEC 9796
MCCP	Banking key management by means of public key algorithms. Algorithms using the RSA cryptosystem. Signature construction by means of a separate signature			ISO/IEC 1116-2
MD4	Message Digest Algorithm	128	512	No, but described in RFC 1320 [51]
MD5	Message Digest Algorithm	128	512	No, but described in RFC 1321 [52]
RIPEMD	Extension of MD4, developed during the European project RIPE [40, p. 380]	128	512	
RIPEMD-128	Dedicated hash function #2	128	512	ISO/IEC 10118-3 [53]
RIPEMD-160	Improved version of RIPEMD [54]	160	512	
SHA	Secure Hash Algorithm (replaced by SHA-1)	160	512	FIPS 180
SHA-1	Dedicated Hash-Function #3 (revision and correction of the Secure Hash Algorithm)	160	512	ANSI X9.30:2 [55] ISO/IEC 10118-3 [53] FIPS 180-1

5.6.2 Verification of Integrity with Public Key Cryptography

An encryption algorithm with a public key is called *permutable* if the decryption and encryption operations can be inverted, i.e., if

$$M = PK_X[SK_X(M)]$$

In the case of encryption with a permutable public key algorithm, an information element, M, that is encrypted by the private key, SK_X, of an entity, X, can be read by any user possessing the corresponding public key, PK_X. A sender can therefore sign a document by encrypting it with a private key reserved for the signature operation to produce the seal that accompanies the message. Any person who knows the corresponding public key will be able to decipher the seal and verify that it corresponds to the received message.

Another way of producing the signature with public key cryptography is to encrypt the fingerprint of the document. This is because the encryption of a long document using a public key algorithm imposes substantial computations and introduces excessive delays. It is therefore beneficial to use a digest of the initial message before applying the encryption. This digest is produced by applying a one-way hash function to calculate the fingerprint, which is then encrypted with the sender's private key. At the destination, the receiver recomputes the fingerprint. With the public key of the sender, the receiver will be able to decrypt the fingerprint to verify if the received hash value is identical to the computed hash value. If both are identical, the signature is valid. (*Note:* The signature obtained in this way is sometimes called compression, contraction, message digest, fingerprint, cryptographic checksum or message integrity check (MIC) [38].)

The block diagram in Figure 5.8 represents verification of integrity with public key encryption. In this figure "h" represents the hash function, "C" the encryption function, and "D" the decryption function. The public key algorithms that are frequently used to calculate digital signatures are listed in Table 5.8.

Even though this message allows verification of message integrity, it does not guarantee that the identity of the sender is authentic. Therefore, prior to verifying the signature in a signed message, the sender and their parameters need to be authenticated. In the case of public key encryption of the hash value, authentication requires the use of certificates, as will be explained later. (*Note:* A signature produced from a message with the signer's private key and then verified with the signer's corresponding public key is sometimes called a signature scheme with appendix [58].)

5.6.3 Blind Signature

A *blind signature* is a special procedure for a notary to sign a message using the RSA algorithm for public key cryptography without revealing the content [59, 60]. One possible utilization of this technique is to time-stamp digital payments.

Consider a debtor who would like to have a payment blindly signed by a bank. The bank has a public key, e, a private key, d, and a public modulo, N. The debtor chooses a random number, k, between 1 and N, and keeps this number secret.

The payment p is "enveloped" by applying the following formula:

$$(p\ k^e)\ \text{mod}\ N$$

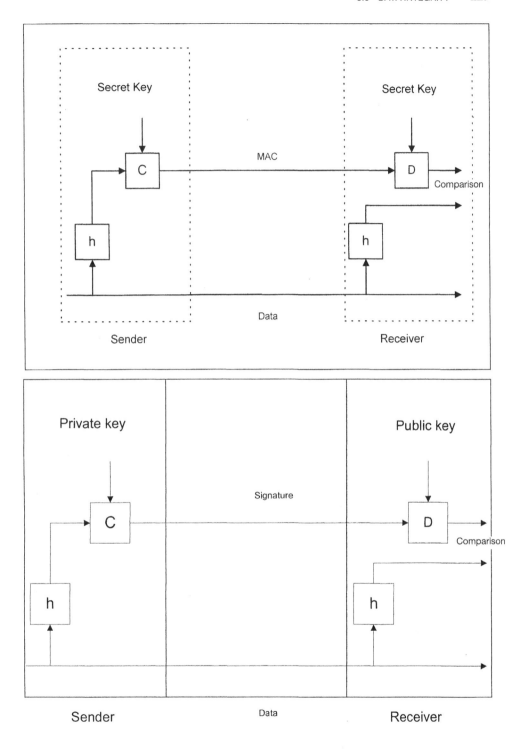

Figure 5.8 Computation of the digital signature using public key algorithms and hashing.

Table 5.3   Public Key Algorithms Used to Compute Digital Signatures

Algorithm	Comments	Length of the Fingerprint	Standard
DSA[a]	Digital Signature Algorithm, which is a variant of the ElGamal algorithm. It is a part of the Digital Signature Standard (DSS) that was proposed by the National Institute of Standards and Technology (NIST) in 1994	512 to 1024 bits	FIPS 186I ANSI X.9.30:1 [1]
ElGamal	Nondeterministic algorithm where a message corresponds to several signatures; it uses discrete logarithms [57]	Variable	—
RSA	This is the defacto standard algorithm for public key encryption; it can also be used to calculate signatures.	512 to 1024 bits	ISO/IEC 9796

[a]The United States federal government mandates the use of the DSA for signing electronic procurements.

before sending the message to the bank. The bank signs it with its private key so that

$$(p \; k^e)^d \bmod N = p^d \; k \bmod N$$

and returns the payment to the debtor. The debtor can now extract the signed note by dividing the number by k. To verify that the note received from the bank is the one that has been sent, the debtor can raise it to the e power because (as will be shown in Appendix II):

$$(p^d)^e \bmod N \equiv p \bmod N$$

The various payment protocols for digital money take advantage of blind signatures to satisfy the conditions of anonymity.

5.6.4   Verification of Integrity with Symmetric Cryptography

The message authentication code (MAC) is the result of a one-way hash function that depends on a secret key. This mechanism guarantees simultaneously the integrity of the message content and the authentication of the sender.

The most obvious way of constructing a MAC is to encrypt the hash value with a block-symmetric encryption algorithm. The MAC is then affixed to the initial message and the whole is sent to the receiver. The receiver recomputes the hash value by applying the same hash function on the received message and compares the result obtained with the decrypted MAC value. The equality of both results confirms data integrity.

The block diagram in Figure 5.9 depicts the operations where "h" represents the hash function, "C" the encryption function, and "D" the decryption function.

Another variant of this method is to append the secret key to the message that will be condensed with the hash functions.

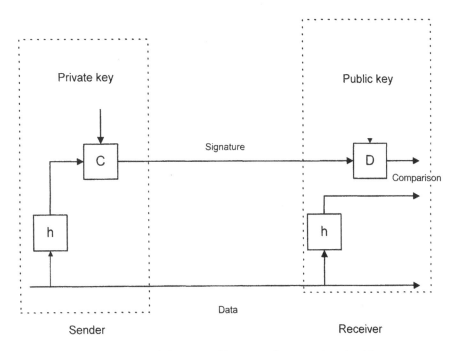

Figure 5.9   Digital signature with symmetric encryption algorithms.

It is also possible to perform the computations with the compression function $f(\ )$ and use as an initial value the vector of the secret key, k, of length L bits in the following recursion:

$$k_i = f(k_{i-1}, x_i), \qquad i = 1, \ldots, n$$

where $x = \{x_1, x_2, \ldots, x_n\}$ is the message subdivided into n vectors, each of B bits. The MAC is the value of the final output k_n. (*Note:* Some authors call the MAC the "integrity check value" or the "cryptographic checksum.")

The following keyed-hashing method augments the speed of computation in software implementation and increases the protection, even when the one-way hash algorithm experiences some rare collisions [59].

Consider the message X subdivided into n vectors of B bits each, and two keys (k_1 and k_2), each of L bits. The padding bits are added to the end of the initial message according to a determined pattern. The hashing operations can thus be described with the help of two compression functions $f_1(\ )$ and $f_2(\ )$:

$$k_i^1 = f_1(k_{i-1}^1, x_i), \qquad i = 1, \ldots, n$$

$$k_i^2 = f_2(k_{i-1}^2, k_i^1)$$

where k_0^1 and k_0^2 are the initial values of k_1 and k_2, respectively, and $x = x_1, x_2, \ldots, x_n$.

The result that this method yields is called the Nested Message Authentication Code (NMAC). It is in effect constructed by applying compression functions in sequence, the first on the padded initial message and the second on the product of the first operation after padding.

The disadvantage of this method is that it requires access to the source code of the compression functions to change the initial values. In addition, it requires usage of two secret keys. This explains the current popularity of the Hashed Message Authentication Code (HMAC) described in RFC 2104 [62]. This method uses one single key k of L bits.

Assuming that the function $H(\ )$ represents the initial hash function, the value of the HMAC is computed in the following manner:

$$HMAC_k(x) = H[\bar{k} \oplus opad \| H(\bar{k} \oplus ipad, x)]$$

In this construction, $\bar{k}$ is the vector, k, of a minimum length of L bits, which after padding with a series of "0" bits, will reach a total length of B bits. The variables *opad* and *ipad* are constants for outer padding and inner padding, respectively. The variable *opad* is formed with the octet 0x36 repeated as many times as needed to constitute a block of B bits, while the variable *ipad* is the octet 0x5C repeated as many times as need. For MD5 and SHA-1 the number of repetitions is 64. Finally, the symbols $\|$ and $\oplus$ in the previous equation denote, respectively, the concatenation and exclusive OR operations.

It should be noted that with the following representation

$$k^1 = f_1(\bar{k} \oplus ipad)$$

$$k^2 = f_2(\bar{k} \oplus opad)$$

the HMAC becomes the same as the nested MAC. (*Notes:*

1. For the SSL protocol, the HMAC is denoted as MAC.
2. In IPSec, authentication and integrity checking are done simultaneously by using one of the keyed-hashing HMACs with MD5 or SHA-1.)

5.7 IDENTIFICATION OF PARTICIPANTS

Identification is the process of ascertaining the identity of a participant (whether a person or a machine) by relying on uniquely distinguishing feature. This contrasts with authentication, which is confirmation that the distinctive identifier indeed corresponds to the declared user.

Authentication and identification of a communicating entity take place simultaneously when that party proposes to the verifier in private a secret that is only shared between them, for example, a password or a secret encryption key. Another possibility is to pose a series of challenges that only the legitimate user is supposed to be capable of answering.

Digital signature is the usual means of identification because it associates a party (a user or a machine) with a shared secret. Other methods of simultaneous identification and authentication of human users exploit biometric characteristics such as fingerprints, voice prints, the shape of the retina, the form of the hand, etc. This is elaborated in the following section.

5.7.1 Biometric Identification

Biometric identification techniques, reserved until recently for military uses and law enforcement agencies, are being considered for user identification in civilian applications. The use of biological attributes for identification and authentication bypasses some of the problems associated with cryptography (e.g., key management). This explains the interest in biometrics in large-scale civilian applications such as mobile telephony, electronic commerce, or telework.

There are two main categories of biometric features. The first category relates to behavioral patterns and acquired skills such as speech, handwriting, or keystroke patterns. In contrast, the second category comprises physiological characteristics such as facial features, iris morphology, retinal texture, hand geometry, or fingerprints. Methods based on gait, odor, or genetic composition using DNA have limited applications for on-line systems.

The usage of biometric systems includes three steps: image acquisition during the registration phase, features extraction, and identification or verification. The digital image of the person under examination originates for a sensor in the computer peripheral (a microphone, for example). This image is processed to extract a compact profile that should be unique to that person. This profile or signature is then archived in a reference database that can be centralized or distributed according to the architecture of the system. In most of these cases, registration cannot be done on-line; rather the person has to be physically present in front of a registrar to record the necessary biometric template.

Biometric identification systems ascertain the identity of the end user by matching the biometric data with an entry in a database to supplement another identifier (password, badge, etc.). Verification systems, in contrast, match biometric data with what is stored in the user credential (e.g., a smart cart) to verify access privileges.

It should be noted that biometric systems are not foolproof. The accuracy of an identification system is measured in terms of the rate of mix-up of identities and the rate of rejects of authorized identities. In contrast, the performance of biometric verification systems is assessed in terms of rate of false rejects, i.e., the rejection of authorized identities and the rate of false acceptances. These rates are interdependent, and are adjusted according to the required level of security.

The choice of a particular systems depends on several factors:

1. Accuracy and reliability of the identification or verification. The result should not be affected by the environment or by aging.
2. Cost of installation, maintenance, and operation.
3. Scale of applicability of the technique; for example, handwriting recognition is not useful for illiterate people.
4. Ease of use.
5. Reproducibility of results. In general, physiological characteristics are more reproducible than behavioral characteristics.
6. Resistance to counterfeit and attacks.

Speaker identification technology verifies the end user by comparing a digitized sample of a person's voice with a stored vocal imprint. Although the system is easy to use, its effectiveness depends on the handset characteristics, the background noise, and the link type (whether terrestrial or radio). Furthermore, under some conditions (20 hours of selected material), there are algorithms that can mimic someone's speech.

In handwriting recognition systems, the user writes on a special pad with a pressure-sensitive pen. The dynamic movement of the pen is described by tens of parameters, such as the pressure exercised on the pad, the speed and direction of the movement, the accelerations and decelerations, and the angle of the letter. One limitation of handwriting recognition is that the rate of false rejects may be too high.

Keystroke recognition techniques measure an individual's typing patterns in terms of rhythm, speed, and duration and pressure of keystrokes. The method for parameter estimation requires several repetitions of a predetermined sequence of characters (for example, the log-in and the password).

Facial scans are used for on-line or off-line identification. In the latter case, a reference image, whose size ranges from 100 to 800 octets, is stored on a smart card in the user's possession.

The retina is a special tissue of the eye that responds to light pulses by generating proportional electrical discharges to the optical nerve. In retinal recognition systems, a map of the retinal blood vessels is recorded with the help of a charge-coupled device (CCD) using reflections from a low-intensity infrared source. The descriptor is a vector of 35 octets that is not only unique to the individual but also stable over time. The main drawback of the system is that the person has to look into the infrared ray source through a special eyepiece.

A less invasive technique is the description of the iris texture with a numeric code of 256 octets (2048 bits). The person to be identified needs merely to face a desktop camera at a distance of 1 m. The accuracy is very high and the error probability is of the order of 1 for 1.2 million. It is even possible to distinguish among identical twins and to separate the two irises of the same person. Iris recognition is now being evaluated in some U.S. airports to speed up passenger processing. Another potential application is the identification of users of automatic bank teller machines for the control of access either to a physical building or equipment or to network resources. The accuracy however, may be affected by contact lenses.

The traditional method for collecting fingerprints is to swipe the finger tips (or the palm) in a special ink and then press them over paper to record a negative image. This image is processed to extract user-specific information or *minutiae*. New imaging methods allow the capture of the fingerprints with optical, optoelectronic, electric, or thermal transducers. For example, variation in the capacitance between the user's fingers and sensors on the surface of a special mouse can help draw the contour of the fingerprint. Another technique relies on a low tension alternating current injected into the fingertips to measure the changes in the electric field between a resin plate and the derma. These variations reproduce the details of the fingerprint. Thermal techniques rely on a transducer to measure the temperature gradient on the mouse's surface. Finally, optoelectronic methods employ a layer of polymers to record the image of the fingerprint that a transducer converts into a proportional electric current. In these methods, each minutia takes about 16 octets on the average; therefore, the image size varies between 500 and 5000 octets, depending on the algorithm.

Recognition of hand geometry is already in use for access control in large-scale commercial applications. Some U.S. airports (e.g., New York and Newark) are using it to accelerate the admission of frequent travelers (those with more than five entries per year). The user positions the hand on a plate between a set of guiding pins. This plate is surrounded by mirrors on three sides to capture the hand sideways and from the top with a digital camera. The hand geometry is described using 90 characteristics in the form of a 9-

octets vector. These parameters are obtained by the averaging of several (3 to 5) shots. The time for taking one picture is about 1.2 s.

5.7.2 Summary and Evaluation

Table 5.4 gives the required memory for storing selected biometric identifiers [61, 62].

At this stage and regardless of the biometric technology, there is little commonality among the various methods being proposed and/or their implementations. In addition, there are no agreed upon protocols for measuring and comparing total system performance in terms of processing speed, reliability, and security of the hardware and software package. There is also a need for standardized protocols to assess a system's vulnerability to attacks or to compare performance in an operational environment. This lack of standards is hampering the large-scale acceptance of biometric identification. Users are concerned about the long-term viability of any solution they may select and the cost of switching methods or suppliers in the future. A related concern is that of being locked into a specific implementation or supplier. Application developers, in turn, are not sure what method deserves their full attention.

Awareness of these roadblocks has spurred standardization activities to facilitate data exchanges among various implementations irrespective of the biometric method. NIST and the Federal Bureau of Investigation (FBI) have made available a large database of fingerprints gathered from crime scenes and the corresponding minutiae. This database will help developers in their effort to train and evaluate new algorithms for fingerprint recognition. In 1995, the Committee on Security Policy Board established by President Clinton chartered the Biometric Consortium (BC) to be the focal point for the U.S. government on research, development, testing, evaluation, and application of biometric-based systems for personal identification/verification. The BC cosponsors activities at NIST and at San Jose State University in California.

The U.S. Department of Defense (DOD) initiated a program to develop a standard application interface called the *Human-Authentication–Application Program Interface* (HA-API) to decouple the software of the applications from the technology used to capture the biometric data. After publishing, in April 1998, Version 2.0 of this API, activities merged with those of the BioAPI Consortium (*http://www.bioapi.org*). This consortium groups hardware and software companies as well as supplier of biometric peripherals. In March 2000, the consortium published Version 1.0 of a BioAPI and reference realizations for Windows, UNIX, Linux, and Java. All of these implementations are in the public domain.

Table 5.4 Required Storage Memory for Biometrical Identifiers

Identifier	Required Memory (in octets)
Photo image	1000–1500
Voice print	1000–2000
Handwritten scan	500–1500
Face recognition	500–1000
Fingerprint	500–5000
Iris scan	256–512
Retinal scan	35
Hand geometry	9

The BioAPI specification was the basis of the INCITS 358, a standard that the Technical Committee M1 on Biometrics for the InterNational Committee for Information Technology Standards (INCITS) has developed as an American National Standards Institute (ANSI) Standard.

In parallel, efforts within the ANSI X9.F4 working group have resulted in a common format to exchange biometric data among various systems known as Common Biometric Exchange File Format (CBEFF). This is the format to be recognized by the BioAPI. It was agreed that the International Biometric Industry Association (IBIA) (*http://www.ibia.org*) will act as the registration authority for the formats to be recognized. Finally, in X9.84 [65], ANSI has defined a data object model that is compatible with CBEFF and is suitable for securing physical and remote access within the financial industry. The standard gives guidance on proper controls and procedures for using biometrics for identification and authentication .

Other standardization initiatives are pursued by the Association for Biometrics (*http://www.afb.org.uk*) in the United Kingdom, and the *Bundesamt für Sicherheit in der Informationtechnik* (BSI—Federal Information Security Agency) (*http://www.bsi.bund.de*) in Germany. Finally, joint work by ISO and IEC aims at a standard for personal verification through biometric methods with the use of integrated circuit cards (e.g., smart cards). Potential applications include driver licenses and travel documents. The standard will be issued as ISO/IEC 7816, Part 11.

5.8 AUTHENTICATION OF PARTICIPANTS

The purpose of authentication of participants is to reduce, if not eliminate, the risk that intruders might masquerade under legitimate appearances to pursue unauthorized operations.

As has been previously stated, when participants utilize a symmetric encryption algorithm, they are the only ones who share a secret key. As a consequence, utilization of this algorithm guarantees, in theory, the confidentiality of the messages, the correct identification of correspondents, and their authentication. The key distribution servers also act as authentication servers, and the good functioning of the system depends on the capability of all participants to protect the encryption key.

In contrast, when participants utilize a public key algorithm, a user is considered authentic when that user can prove that he or she holds the private key that corresponds with the public key that is attributed to the user. A certificate issued by a certification authority indicates that it certifies the association of the public key (and therefore the corresponding private key) with the recognized identity. In this manner, identification and authentication proceed in two different ways, identity with the digital signature and authentication with a certificate. Without such a guarantee, a hostile user could create a pair of private/public keys and then distribute the public key as if it were that of the legitimate user.

Although the same public key of a participant could equally serve to encrypt the message that is addressed to that participant (confidentiality service) and to verify the electronic signature of the documents that the participant transmits (integrity and identification services), in practice a different public key is used for each set of services.

According to the authentication framework defined by ITU-T Recommendations X.500 and X.811 [66, 67], simple authentication can be achieved by one of several means:

1. Name and password in the clear.
2. Name, password, and a random number or a time stamp, with integrity verification through a hash function.
3. Name, password, a random number, and a time stamp, with integrity verification using a hash function.

Strong authentication requires a certification infrastructure that includes the following entities:

1. *Certification authorities* to back the users' public keys with "sealed" certificates (i.e., signed with the private key of the certification authority) after verification of the physical identity of the owner of each public key.
2. A database of authentication data (*directory*) that contains all the data relative to the private encryption keys, such as their value, the duration of validity, and the identity of the owners. Any user should be able to query such a database to obtain the public key of the correspondent or to verify the validity of the certificate that the correspondent would present.
3. A *naming* or *registering authority*. This authority can be distinct from the certification authority, and its principal role is to define and assign unique *distinguished names* to the different participants.

The certificate guarantees correspondence between a given public key and the entity whose unique distinguished name is contained in the certificate. This certificate is sealed with the private key of the certification authority. When the certificate owner signs documents with the private signature key, the partners can verify the validity of the signature with the help of the corresponding public key that is contained in the certificate. Similarly, to send a confidential message to a certified entity, it is sufficient to query the directory for the public key of that entity and then use that key to encrypt messages that only the holder of the associated private key would be able to decipher.

5.9 ACCESS CONTROL

Access control is the process by which only authorized entities are allowed access to the resources as defined in the access control policy. It is used to counter the threat of unauthorized operations such as unauthorized use, disclosure, modification, destruction of protected data or denial of service to legitimate users. ITU-T Recommendation X.812 [68] defines the framework for access control in open networks. Accordingly, access control can be exercised with the help of a supporting authentication mechanism at one or more the following layers: the network layer, the transport layer, or the application layer. Depending on the layer, the corresponding authentication credentials can be X.509 certificates, Kerberos tickets, simple identity, and password pairs, etc.

There are two types of access control mechanisms: identity-based and role-based. Identity-based access control uses the authenticated identity of an entity to determine and enforce its access rights. In contrast, for role-based access control, access privileges depend on the job function and its context. Thus, additional factors may be considered in the definition of the access policy, for example, the strength of the encryption algorithm, the type of operation requested, or the time of day. Thus, role-based access control provides an indirect means of bestowal of privileges through three distinct phases: the definition of roles, the assignment of privileges to roles, and the distribution of roles among users. This facilitates the maintenance of access control policies because it is sufficient to change the definition of roles to allow global updates without revising the distribution from top to bottom.

At the network layer, access control in IP networks is based on packet filtering using the protocol information in the packet header, specifically the source and destination IP addresses, and the source and destination port numbers. Access control is achieved through "line interruption" by a certified intermediary or a firewall, that intercepts and examines all exchanges before allowing them to proceed. The intermediary is thus a trusted third party that is located between the client and the server, as indicated in Figure 5.10. Furthermore, the firewall can be charged with other security services, such as encrypting the traffic for confidentiality at the network level or integrity verification using digital signatures. It can also inspect incoming and outgoing exchanges before forwarding them to enforce the security policies of a given administrative domain. However, the intervention of the trusted third party must be transparent to the client.

The success of packet filtering is vulnerable to packet spoofing if the address information is not protected and if individual packets are treated independently of other packets of the same flow. As a remedy, the firewall can include a proxy server or an application-level gateway that implements a subset of application-specific functions. The proxy is capable of inspecting all packets in light of previous exchanges of the same flow before allowing their passage in accordance to the security policy in place. Thus, by filtering incoming and outgoing electronic mail, file transfers, exchanges of Web applications, etc., application gateways can block nonauthorized operations and protect against malicious codes such as viruses. This is called a *stateful* inspection.

A third approach is to centralize management of the access control for a large number of clients and users with different privileges with a dedicated server. Several protocols have been defined to regulate the exchanges among network elements and access control servers. RFC 2865 [69] specifies Remote Authentication Dial in User Service (RADIUS) for client authentication, authorization and for collecting accounting information of the calls. In RFC 1492 [70] Cisco has described a protocol called Terminal Access Controller Access System (TACACS) which was later updated in TACACS+. Both RADIUS and TACACS+ require a secrete key between each network element and the server. Figure 5.11 depicts the operation of RADIUS in terms of a client/server architecture. The RADIUS client resides within the access control server while the server relies on an X.509 directory through the LDAP. Both X.509 and LDAP will be presented later in this chapter.

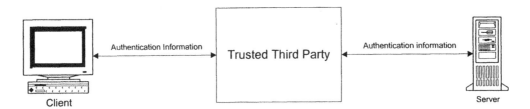

Figure 5.10   Authentication by line interruption at the network layer.

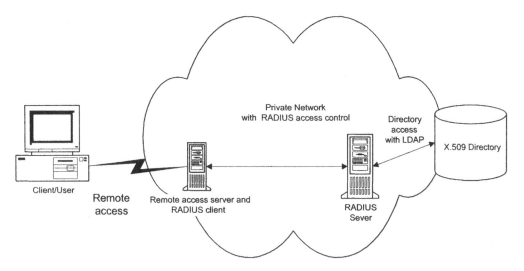

Figure 5.11   Remote access control with RADIUS.

Note that both server-to-client authentication and user-to-client authentication are outside the scope of RADIUS. Also, because, RADIUS does not include provisions for congestion control, large networks can suffer degraded performance and data loss.

Commercial systems implement two basic approaches for end user authentication: one-time password and challenge-response [16]. In a typical one-time password system, each user has a device that generates a number periodically (usually every minute) using the current time, the card serial number, and a secret key held in the device. The generated number is the user's one-time password. This procedure requires that the time reference of the access control server be synchronized with the card so that the server can regenerate an identical number.

In challenge-response systems, the user enters a personal identification number to activate hand-held authenticators (HHA), and then to initiate a connection to an access control server. The access control server, in turn, provides the user with a random number (a challenge), and the user enters this number into a hand-held device to generate a unique response. This response depends on both the challenge and some secret key shared between the user's device and the server. It is returned to the access control server to compare with the expected response and decide accordingly.

It should be noted that there are some known vulnerabilities in RADIUS or in its implementations [71].

5.9.1 Denial-of-Service

Denial-of-service attacks prevent normal network usage by blocking access of legitimate users to the network resources they are entitled to, by overwhelming the hosts with additional or superfluous tasks to prevent them from responding to legitimate requests or to slow their response time below satisfactory limits.

In a sense, denial-of-service results from failure of access control. Nevertheless, these attacks are inherently associated with IP networks for two reasons: (1) network control data and user data share the same physical and logical bandwidths, and (2) IP is a connectionless protocol where the concept of admission control does not apply. As a consequence, when the network size exceeds a few hundred nodes, network control traffic (due, for example, to the exchange of routing tables) may, under some circumstances occupy a significant portion of the available bandwidth. Further, inopportune or ill-intentioned user packets may be able to bring down a network element (e.g., a router) thereby affecting not only all end points that rely on this network element for connectivity, but also all other network elements that depend on it to update their view of network status. Finally, in distributed denial of service attacks (DDOS), a sufficient number of compromised hosts may send useless packets towards a victim around the same time, thereby affecting the victim's resources or bandwidth or both [72, 73].

As a point of comparison, the current public switched telephone network uses an architecture called common channel signaling (CCS) whereby user data and network control data use totally separate networks and facilities. It is worth noting that CCS was introduced to protect against fraud. In the old architecture, called channel-associated signaling (CAS), the network data and the user data used separate logical channels, on the same physical support. Similarly, experience has shown that ATM can be exposed to the same risks of interruption because user traffic and network control messages share the same facilities even though they are virtually distinct [74].

Let us illustrate the preceding discussion with a few examples of denial-of-service attacks using several protocols of the IP stack: TCP, Internet Control Message Protocol (ICMP), and HTTP.

- The SYN flooding attack, one of the best known mechanisms of denial-of-service, perturbs the functioning of the TCP protocol [75]. It is well known that the handshake in TCP is a three-way exchange: a connection request with the SYN packet, an acknowledgment of that request with SYN/ACK packet, and finally a confirmation from the first party with the ACK packet [76, p. 216]. Unfortunately, the handshake imposes asymmetric memory and computational loads on the two endpoints, the destination being required to allocate large amounts of memory without authenticating the initial request. Thus, an attacker can paralyze the target machine, exhausting its available resources by sending a massive number of fake SYN packets. These packets will have spoofed source addresses, so the acknowledgments are sent to hosts that the victim cannot reach or that do not exist. Otherwise, the attack may fail, because unsolicited SYN/ACK packets at accessible hosts provoke the transmission of RST packets, which upon arrival, would allow the victim to release the resources allocated for a connection attempt.

- ICMP is a protocol for any arbitrary machine to communicate control and error information back to the presumed source. Thus, an ICMP echo request, or "ping," with the victim's address falsely indicated as the source and sent to all the machines of a given network using the subnet broadcast address can flood the victim with echo replies that will overwhelm its capacities.

- The Code Red worm exploits defects in the response of some Web server to an HTTP GET request larger than the regular size (a payload of 62 octets instead of 60 octets). Under specific conditions, the buffer overflow causes an upsurge in HTTP traffic and the infection of neighboring machines, which increases network traffic, thereby causing a massive disruption [77].

Given that IP does not separate user traffic from that of the network, the best solution is to identify all with trusted certificates. However, authentication of all exchanges increases the computational load, which may be excessive in commercial applications, as the lack of success of the protocol for payments with bankcard SET has shown. Short of this, defense mechanisms will be developed on a case-by-case basis to address specific problem as they arise, for example, resource exhaustion due to the SYN attack can be alleviated by limiting the number of concurrent pending TCP connections, reducing the time out for the arrival of the ACK packet before calling off the connection establishment, blocking packets to the outside that have source addresses from outside.

Another approach is to reequilibrate the computational load among the two parties by asking the requesting client to solve a *puzzle* in the form of simple cryptographic problems before the allocated resources needed to establish a connection. To avoid replay attacks, these problems are formulated using the current time, a server secret, and additional information from the client request [78]. This approach, however, requires programs for solving puzzles specific to each application: TCP, SSL, etc, which are incorporated in the client browser.

5.10 NONREPUDIATION

Nonrepudiation is a service that prevents a person who has accomplished an act from denying it later, in part or as a whole. Nonrepudiation is a legal concept to be defined through legislation. The role of informatics is to supply the necessary technical means to support the service offer according to the law. The building blocks of nonrepudiation include the electronic signature of documents, the intervention of a third party as a witness, time-stamping, and sequence numbers. Among the mechanisms for nonrepudiation are a security token sealed with the secret key of the verifier that accompanies the transaction record, time-stamping, and sequence numbers. Depending on the system design, the security token sealed with the verifier's secret key can be stored in a tamper-resistant cryptographic module. The generation and verification of the evidence often require the intervention of one or more entities external to parties to the transaction, such as a notary, a verifier, and an adjudicator of disputes.

ITU-T Recommendation X.813 [79] defines a general framework for nonrepudiation in open systems. Accordingly, the service comprises the following measures:

- Generation of the evidence
- Recording of the evidence
- Verification of the evidence generated
- Retrieval and reverification of the evidence

There are two types of nonrepudiation services:

1. *Nonrepudiation at the Origin*   This service protects the receiver by preventing the sender from denying having sent the message.
2. *Nonrepudiation at the Destination*   This service plays the inverse role of the preceding function. It protects the sender by demonstrating that the addressee has received the message.

Threats to nonrepudiation include compromise of keys or unauthorized modification or destruction of evidence. In public key cryptography, each user is the sole and unique owner of the private key. Thus, unless the whole system has been penetrated, a given user cannot repudiate the messages that are accompanied by his or her electronic signature. In contrast, nonrepudiation is not readily achieved in systems that use symmetric cryptography. A user can deny having sent the message by alleging that the receiver has compromised the shared secret or that the key distribution server has been successfully attacked. A trusted third party would have to verify each transaction to be able to testify in cases of contention.

Nonrepudiation at the destination can be obtained using the same mechanisms, but in the reverse direction.

5.10.1 Time-Stamping and Sequence Numbers

Time-stamping of messages establishes a link between each message and the date of its transmission. This permits the tracing of exchanges and prevents attacks by replaying old messages. If clock synchronization of both parties is difficult, a trusted third party can intervene as a notary and use its own clock as reference.

Intervention of the "notary" can be either of the following:

- Off-line to fulfill functions such as certification, key distribution, and verification, if required, without intervening in the transaction.
- On-line as an intermediary in the exchanges or as an observer collecting the evidence that might be required to resolve contentions. This is a similar role to that of a trusted third party of the network layer (firewall) or at the application layer (proxy), but with a different set of responsibilities.

Let us assume that a trusted third party combines the functions of the notary, the verifier, and the adjudicator. Each entity encrypts its messages with the secret key that has been established with the trusted third party before sending the message. The trusted third party decrypts the message with the help of this shared secret with the intervening party, time-stamps it, and then reencrypts it with the key shared with the other party. This approach requires the establishment of a secret key between each entity and the trusted third party that acts as a delivery messenger. Notice, however, that the time-stamping procedures have not been normalized and each system has its own protocol.

Detection of duplication, replay, as well as the addition, suppression, or loss of messages is achieved with the use of a sequence number before encryption. Another mechanism is to add a random number to the message before encryption. All these means give the addressee the ability to verify that the exchanges genuinely took place during the time interval that the time stamp defines.

5.11 SECURE MANAGEMENT OF CRYPTOGRAPHIC KEYS

Key management is a process that continues throughout the life cycle of the keys to thwart unauthorized disclosures, modifications, substitutions, reuse of revoked or expired keys, or unauthorized use. Security at this level is a recursive problem, because the same security properties that are required in the cryptographic system must be satisfied in turn by the key management system.

The secure management of cryptographic keys relates to key production, storage, distribution, utilization, withdrawal from circulation, deletion, and archiving [80].

5.11.1 Production and Storage

Key production must be done in a random manner and at regular intervals depending on the degree of security required.

Protection of the stored keys has a physical aspect and a logical aspect. Physical protection consists of storing the keys in safes or in secured buildings with controlled access, whereas logical protection is achieved with encryption.

In the case of symmetric encryption algorithms, only the secret key is stored. For public key algorithms, storage encompasses the user's private and public keys, the user's certificate, and a copy of the public key of the certification authority. The certificates and the keys can be stored on the hard disk of the certification authority, but there is some risk of possible attacks or of loss due to hardware failure. In cases of microprocessor cards, the information related to security, such as the certificate and the keys, is inserted during card personalization. Access to this information is then controlled with a confidential code.

5.11.2 Distribution

The security policy defines the manner in which keys are distributed to entitled entities. Manual distribution by mail or special dispatch (sealed envelopes, tamper-resistant module) is a slow and costly operation that should only be used for distribution of the root key of the system. This is the key that the key distributor utilizes to send each participant their key.

An automatic key distribution system must satisfy all the criteria of security, in particular:

- Confidentiality.
- Identification of the participant.
- Data integrity by giving proof that the key has not been altered during transmission or that it was not replaced by a fake key.
- Authentication of the participants.
- Nonrepudiation.

Automatic distribution can be either point-to-point or point-to-multipoint. The Diffie–Hellman key exchange method [49] allows the two partners to construct a master key from two large numbers that have been previously exchanged in the clear. A symmetric session key is derived next, either by using this master key directly or from additional exchanges encrypted with this master key.

To distribute keys to several customers, an authentication server can also play the role of a trusted third party and distribute the secret keys to the different parties. These keys will be used to protect the confidentiality of the messages carrying the information on the key pairs.

5.11.3 Utilization, Withdrawal, and Replacement

The unauthorized duplication of a legitimate key is a threat to the security of key distribution. To prevent this type of attack, a unique parameter can be concatenated to the key, such as a time stamp or a sequence number that increases monotonically (up to a certain modulo).

The risk that a key is compromised increases proportionately with time and with usage. Therefore, keys have to be replaced regularly without causing service interruption. A common solution that does not impose a significant load is to distribute the session keys on the same communication channels used for user data. For example, in the SSL protocol, the initial exchanges provide the necessary elements to form keys that would be valid throughout the session at hand. These elements flow encrypted with a secondary key, called a key encryption key, to keep their confidentiality.

Key distribution services have the authority to revoke a key before its date of expiration after a key loss or because of the user's misbehavior.

5.11.4 Key Revocation

All user certificates must be revoked without delay for the following conditions: the user loses the right to employ a private key, if this key is accidentally revealed, or, more seriously, if the private key of a certification authority has been broken. Furthermore, these revocations have to be communicated to all the verifying entities in the shortest possible time. Similarly, the use of the revoked key by a hostile user should not be allowed. Nevertheless, the user will not be able to repudiate all the documents already signed and sent before the revocation of the key pair.

5.11.5 Deletion, Backup, and Archiving

Key deletion implies the destruction of all memory registers as well as magnetic or optical media that contain either the key or the elements needed for its reconstruction.

Backup applies only to encryption keys, and not to signature keys; otherwise, the entire structure for nonrepudiation would be put into question.

The keys utilized for nonrepudiation services must be preserved in secure archives to accommodate legal delays that may extend for up to 30 years. These keys must be easily recoverable in case of need, for example, in response to a court order. This means that the storage applications must include mechanisms to prevent unrecoverable errors from affecting the ciphertext.

5.11.6 Comparison Between Symmetric and Public Key Cryptography

Systems based on symmetric key algorithms pose the problem of ensuring the confidentiality of key distribution. This translates into the use of a separate secure distribution channel that is preestablished between the participants. Furthermore, each entity must have as many keys as the number of participants with whom it will enter into contact. Clearly, management of symmetric keys increases exponentially with the number of participants.

Public key algorithms avoid such difficulties, because each entity owns only one pair of private and public keys. Unfortunately, the computations for public key procedures are more intense than those for symmetric cryptography. The use of public key cryptography to ensure confidentiality is only possible when the messages are short, even though data compression before encryption with the public key often succeeds in speeding up the computations. Thus, public key cryptography can complement symmetric cryptography to ensure the safe distribution of the secret key, particularly when safer means such as direct encounter of the participants, or the intervention of a trusted third party, are not feasible. Thus, a new symmetric key could be distributed at the start of each new session and, in extreme cases, at the start of each new exchange.

5.12 EXCHANGE OF SECRET KEYS: KERBEROS

Kerberos is a distributed system for on-line identification and authentication as well as access control using symmetric cryptography [81]. It is widely used for remote access to resources in a university computing center (files, printers, etc.) from nonsecure machines. Kerberos is now the default authentication option in Windows 2000.

The development of Kerberos started in 1978 within the Athena project at the Massachusetts Institute of Technology (MIT), financed by Digital Equipment Corporation (DEC) and IBM. Version 5 of Kerberos, which was published in 1994, is the version currently in use .

The system is built around a Kerberos key distribution center that enjoys the total trust of all participants with whom they all have already established symmetric encryption keys. Symmetric keys are attributed to individual users for each of their accounts when they register in person.

The key distribution center consists of an authentication server (AS) and a ticket-granting server (TGS) . The AS controls access to the TGS, which in turns controls access to specific resources. Every server shares a secret key with every other server. The algorithm used for symmetric encryption is the Data Encryption Standard (DES). Finally, during the registration of the users in person, a secret key is established with the AS for each user's account. With this arrangement, a client has access to multiple resources during a session with one successful authentication, instead of repeating the authentication process for each resource. The operation is explained below.

After identifying the end user with the help of a log-in and password pair, the AS sends the client a session symmetric encryption key to encrypt data exchanges between the client and the TGS. The session key is encrypted with the symmetric encryption key shared between the user and the AS. The key is also contained in the session ticket that is encrypted with the key preestablished between the TGS and the AS.

The session ticket, also called a ticket-granting ticket, is valid for a short period, typically a few hours. During this period, it can be used to request access to a specific service; this is why it is also called an initial ticket.

The client presents the TGS with two items of identification: the session ticket and an authentication title that is encrypted with the session key. The TGS compares the data in both items to verify the client authenticity and its access privileges before granting access to the specific server requested.

Figure 5.12 depicts the interactions among the four entities: (1) the client, (2) the AS, (3) the TGS, and (4) the desired server or resource, S.

The exchanges are now explained.

Message (1): Request of a Session Ticket   A client, C, that desires to access a specific server, S, first requests an entrance ticket to the session from the Kerberos authentication server, AS. To do so, the client sends a message consisting of an identifier

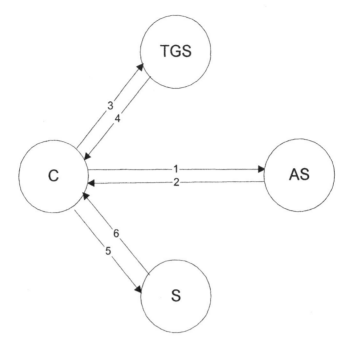

Figure 5.12   Authentication and access control in Kerberos.

(for example, a log-in and a password), the identifier of S, a time stamp, H_1, as well as a random number, Rnd, both to prevent replay attacks.

Message (2): Acquisition of a Session Ticket   The Kerberos authentication server responds by sending a message formed of two parts: (1) a session key, K_{CTGS}, and the number, Rnd, that was in the first message, both coded with the client's secret key, K_C and (2) the session ticket, T_{CTGS}, destined for the TGS and encrypted by the latter's secret key between itself and the Kerberos authentication server.

The session (ticket-granting ticket) includes several pieces of information, such as the client name, C, its network address, Ad_C, the time stamp, H_1, the period of validity of the ticket, Val, and the session key, K_{CTGS}. All these items, with the exception of the server identity, TGS, are encrypted with the long-term key, K_{TGS}, that the TGS shares with the AS. Thus,

$$T_{CTGS} = \{TGS, K_{TGS}(C, Ad_C, H_1, Val, K_{CTGS})\}$$

and the message sent to the client is

$$K_c\{K_{CTGS}, Rnd\}, \{T_{CTGS}\}$$

where $K\{x\}$ indicates encryption of the message, x, with the shared secret key, K. The client decrypts the message with its secret key, K_C, to recover the session key, K_{CTGS}, and the random number. The client verifies that the random number received is the same as that sent as a protection from replay attacks. The time stamp, H_1, is also used to protect against replay attacks. Although the client will not be able to read the session ticket because it is encrypted with K_{TGS}, it can extract it and relay it to the server.

By default the session ticket, T_{CTGS}, is valid for 8 hours. During this time, the client can obtain several service tickets for different services without the need for a new authentication.

Message (3): Request of a Service Ticket   The client constructs an authentication title, Auth, that contains its identity, C, its network address, Ad_c, the service requested, S, a new time stamp, H_2, and another random number, Rnd_2, and then encrypts it with the session key, K_{CTGS}. The encrypted authentication title can be represented in the following form:

$$\text{Auth} = K_{CTGS}(C, Ad_C, S, H_2, Rnd_2)$$

The request of the service ticket consists of the encrypted authentication title and the session ticket, T_{CTGS}:

$$\text{Service request} = \{\text{Auth}, T_{CTGS}\}$$

Message (4): Acquisition of the Service Ticket   The TGS decrypts the ticket content with its secret key, K_{TGS}, deduces the shared session key, K_{CTGS}, and extracts the data related to the client's service request. With knowledge of the session key, the server can decrypt the authentication title and compare the data in it with those that the client has supplied. This comparison gives formal proof that the client is the entity that was given the session ticket by the server. The time stamps confirm that the message was not an old message that has been replayed. Next, the TGS returns a service ticket for accessing the specific server, S.

The exchanges described by messages (3) and (4) can be repeated for all other servers available to the user, as long as the validity of the session ticket has not expired.

The message from the TGS has two parts: (1) a service key, K_{CS}, between the client and the server, S, and the number, Rnd_2, both coded with shared secret key, K_{CTGS}, and (2) the service ticket, T_{CS}, destined to the server, S, and encrypted by secret key, K_{STGS}, shared between the server, S, and the TGS.

As before, the service ticket destined for the server, S, includes several pieces of information, such as the identity of the server, S, the client's name, C, its network address, Ad_C, a time stamp, H_3, the period of validity of the ticket, Val, and, if confidentiality is desired, a service key, K_{CS}. All these items, with the exception of the server identity, S, are encrypted with the long-term key, K_{STGS}, that the ticket TGS shares with the specific server. Thus,

$$T_{CS} = \{S, K_{STGS}(C, Ad_C, H_3, Val, K_{CS})\}$$

and the message sent to the client is

$$K_{CTGS}\{K_{CS}, Rnd_2\}, \{T_{CS}\}$$

The client decrypts the message with the shared secret key, K_{CTGS}, to recover the service key, K_{CS}, and the random number. The client verifies that the random number received is the same as was sent as a protection from replay attacks.

Message (5): Service Request The client constructs a new authentication title, $Auth_2$, that contains its identity, C, its network address, Ad_c, a new time stamp, H_3, and another random number, Rnd_3, and then encrypts it with the service key, K_{CS}. The encrypted authentication title can be represented as the follows.

$$Auth_2 = K_{CS}(C, Ad_C, H_4, Rnd_3)$$

The request of the service consists of the encrypted new authentication title and the service ticket, T_{CS}:

$$\text{Service request} = \{Auth_2, T_{CS}\}$$

Message (6): Optional Response of the Server The server decrypts the content of the service ticket with the key, K_{STGS}, it shares with the TGS to derive the service key, K_{CS}, and the data related to the client. With knowledge of the service key, the server can verify the authenticity of the client. The time stamps confirm that the message is not a replay of old messages. If the client has requested the server to authenticate itself, it will return the random number, Rnd_3, encrypted by the service key, K_{CS}. Without knowledge of the secret key, K_{CS}, the server would have not have been able to extract the service key, K_{CS}.

The preceding description shows that Kerberos is mostly suitable for networks administered by a single administrative entity. In particular, the Kerberos key distribution center fulfills the following roles:

- It maintains a database of all secret keys (except of the key between the client and the server, K_{CS}). These keys have a long lifetime.
- It keeps a record of users' log-in identities, passwords, and access privileges. To fulfill this role, it may need access to an X.509 directory.
- It produces and distributes encryption keys and ticket-granting tickets to be used for a session.

5.12.1 Public Key Kerberos

The utilization of a central depot for all symmetric keys increases the potential of traffic congestion due to the simultaneous arrival of many requests. In addition, centralization threatens the whole security infrastructure, because a successful penetration of the storage could put all keys in danger [82]. Finally, management of the symmetric keys (distribution and update) becomes a formidable task when the number of users increases.

The public key version of Kerberos simplifies key management, because the server authenticates the client directly using the session ticket and the client's certificate sealed by the Kerberos certification authority. The session ticket itself is sealed with the client's private key and then encrypted with the server public key. Thus, the service request to the server can be described as follows:

$$\text{Service request} = S, PK_S \{Tauth, Kr, Auth\}$$

with

$$Auth = C, \text{certificate}, [Kr, S, PK_C, Tauth]SK_c$$

where Tauth is the initial time for authentication, Kr is a one-time random number that the server will use as a symmetric key to encrypt its answer, $\{\ldots\}$ represents encryption with the server public key, PK_S, while $[\ldots]$ represents the seal computed with the client's private key, SK_C. This architecture improves speed and security.

The operations of public key Kerberos are described in IETF RFC 1510 [83]. The official Web page for Kerberos is located at: http://web.mit.edu/kerberos/www/index.html. A frequently asked questions (FAQ) file on Kerberos can be consulted at the following address: ftp://athena-dist.mit.edu/pub/kerberos/KERBEROS.FAQ. Tung [84] contains a good compendium of information on Kerberos.

The Swedish Institute of Computer Science is distributing a free version of Kerberos, called Heidmal. This version was written by Johan Danielsson and Assar Westerlund, and includes improvements in security protocols, such as the support of Triple DES. A commercial version is TrustBroker available from CyberSafe at http://www.cybersafe.com.

5.13 EXCHANGE OF PUBLIC KEYS

5.13.1 Diffie–Hellman Exchange

The Diffie–Hellman algorithm, published in 1976, is the first algorithm for key exchange in public key algorithms. It exploits the difficulty in calculating discrete algorithms in a finite field, as compared with the calculation of exponentials in the same field.

The key exchange comprises the following steps:

1. The two parties agree on two random large integers, n and g, such that g is a prime with respect to n. These two numbers do not necessarily have to be hidden, but their choice can have a substantial impact on the strength of the security achieved.

2. A chooses a large random integer, x, and sends B the result of the computation:

$$X = g^x \bmod n$$

3. B chooses another large random integer, y, and sends to A the result of the computation:

$$Y = g^y \bmod n$$

4. A computes

$$k = Y^x \bmod n = g^{xy} \bmod n$$

5. Similarly, B computes

$$k = Y^x \bmod n = g^{xy} \bmod n$$

The value k is the secret key that both correspondents have exchanged and its size is 1024 bits (the size of the modulo n). The exponents x and y are often the same size as the prime n, but may be reduced to 160 and 256 bits. Thus a secret key has been negotiated on-line without transferring the key. Even by listening to all exchanges, it would be rather difficult to discover the key, unless there is a suitable way to calculate the discrete algorithm of X or of Y to rediscover the value of x or of y.

SSL uses the method called ephemeral Diffie–Hellman, where the exchange is short-lived, thereby achieving *perfect forward secrecy*. The Diffie–Hellman parameters are signed either with RSA or the DSA to guarantee integrity. The public keys of the various algorithms are included in the certificates that the certification authority has signed.

It should be noted that on March 29, 1997, the technique for key exchange entered the public domain.

5.13.2   Internet Security Association and Key Management Protocol

RFC 2408 [28] defines Internet Security Association and Key Management Protocol (ISAKMP), a generic framework to negotiate point-to-point security associations and to exchange key and authentication data between two parties. In ISAKMP, the term *security association* has two meanings. It is used to describe the secure channel established between two communicating entities. It can also be used to define a specific instance of the secure channel, i.e., the services, mechanisms, protocol, and protocol-specific set of parameters associated with the encryption algorithms, the authentication mechanisms, the key establishment and exchange protocols, and the network addresses. In ISAKMP, a domain of interpretation (DOI) is the context of operation in terms of the relevant syntax and semantics. RFC 2407 [26] defines the IP security DOI for security associations in IP networks within the ISAKMP framework.

ISAKMP specifies the formats of messages to be exchanged and their building blocks (payloads). A fixed header precedes a variable number of payloads chained together to form a message. This provides a uniform management layer for security at all layers of the ISO protocol stack, thereby reducing the amount of duplication within each security protocol. This centralization of the management of security associations has several advantages. It reduces connect setup time, improves reliability of software, and allows for future evolution when improved security mechanisms are developed, particularly if new attacks against current security associations are discovered.

To avoid subtle mistakes that can render a key exchange protocol vulnerable to attacks, ISAKMP includes five default exchange types. Each exchange specifies the content and the ordering of the messages during communications between the peers.

Although ISAKMP can run over TCP or UDP, many implementations use UDP on port 500. Because the transport with UDP is unreliable, reliability is built into ISAKMP.

The header includes, among other information, two 8-octet "cookies"—also called "syncookies"—which constitute an *anti-clogging* mechanism, because of their role against TCP SYN flooding. Each side generates a cookie specific to the two parties and assigns it to the remote peer entity. The cookie is constructed, for example, by hashing the IP source and destination addresses, the UDP source and destination ports and a locally generated secret random value. ISAKMP recommends including the data and the time in this secret value. The concatenation of the two cookies identifies the security association, and it gives some protection against replay of old packets or SYN flooding attacks. Protection against SYN flooding assumes that the attacker will not intercept the SYN/ACK packets sent to the spoofed addresses used in the attack. As was explained earlier, the arrival of unsolicited SYN/ACK packets at a host that is accessible to the victim will elicit transmission of an RST packet, thereby telling the victim to free the allocated resources, so that the host whose address has been spoofed will respond by resetting the connection message [78, 85].

The negotiation in ISAKMP comprises two phases: (1) the establishment of a secure channel between the two communicating entities, and (2) the negotiation of security associations on the secure channel. For example, in the case of IPSec, Phase I negotiation is to define a key exchange protocol, such as the IKE and its attributes. Phase II negotiation concerns the actual cryptographic algorithms to achieve IPSec functionality.

IKE is an authenticated exchange of keys consistent with ISAKMP. IKE is a hybrid protocol that combines aspects of the Oakley Key Determination Protocol and of SKEME. Oakley utilizes the Diffie–Hellman key exchange mechanism with signed temporary keys to establish the session keys between the host machines and the network routers. SKEME is an authenticated key exchange that uses public key encryption for anonymity and nonrepudiation and provides means for quick refreshment [84]. IKE is the default key exchange protocol for IPSec

None of the data used for key generation is stored, and a key cannot be recovered after deletion, thereby achieving perfect forward secrecy. The price is a heavy cryptographic load, which becomes more important the shorter the duration of the exchanges. Therefore, to minimize the risks from denial of service attacks, ISAKMP postpones the computationally intensive steps until authentication is established.

Unfortunately, despite the complexity of IKE, the various documents that describe it do not use the best practices for protocol engineering. For example, there are no formal language descriptions, nor are there conformance test suites available. Nevertheless, IBM has revealed some details on the architecture of its implementation [87].

Although ISAKMP has been designed in a modular fashion, implementations are often not modular for commercial or legal reasons. For example, to satisfy the restrictions against the export of cryptographic software, Version 5.0 of Microsoft Windows NT had to sacrifice the modularity of the implementation. Similarly, the version that Cisco produces, which is based on the cryptographic library of Cylink Corporation, is only available in North America (United States and Canada). It should also be noted that the MIT distributes in North America the prototype of a version approved by the DOD. (*Note:* A new version of IKE is being prepared with the aim of removing problems that were uncovered. These problems relate to the hashing function and to the protection cookies.)

5.13.3 Simple Key Management for Internet Protocols

Simple Key Management for Internet Protocols (SKIP) is an approach to key exchange that Sun Microsystems championed at one time. The principle is to exchange a master key according to the Diffie–Hellman method, then store it in a cache memory to construct the encryption key for subsequent sessions. In this manner, the protocol avoids preliminary exchanges that are needed to define the secure channel before message exchange. This may be useful in applications where efficient use of the transmission bandwidth available justifies reduced security.

SKIP operates at the network layer. The IP packets that contain the information used in SKIP have an IP AH, and their payload is encapsulated according to the ESP procedures.

Although this method allows a reduction in the number of exchanges and alleviates the cryptographic loads, its success assumes that the master key is never compromised. Interest in SKIP seems to have subsided.

5.13.4 Key Exchange Algorithm

The Key Exchange Algorithm (KEA) is an algorithm from the U.S. National Security Agency (NSA). It is based on the Diffie–Hellman algorithm. All calculations in KEA are based on a prime modulus of 1024 bits generated as per the DSA specifications of FIPS 186. Thus, the key size is 1024 bits and, as in DSA, the size of the exponent is 160 bits.

KEA is used in the cryptographic PCMCIA card Fortezza and the SKIPJACK encryption algorithm. The experimental specifications of RFC 2773 [88] describe its use for securing file transfers with ftp. Those of RFC 2951 [89] provide security to telnet sessions.

Consider its use with telnet. The aim is to replace the user-level authentication through its log-in and password being exchanged in the clear with more secure measures and to be able to authenticate the server. It is known that a telnet session is a series of exchanges on a character-by-character basis. With the combination of KEA and SKIPJACK, the encryption of the telnet bit stream can be with or without integrity protection. Without the integrity service, each character corresponds to a single octet on-line. Stream integrity uses the one-way hash function SHA-1 and requires the transmission of 4 octets for every character, i.e., it adds an overhead of 300%. (*Note:* Version 2.0 of KEA is available from NIST at *http://csrc.nist.gov/encryption/skipjack-kea.htm.*)

5.14 CERTIFICATE MANAGEMENT

When a server receives a request signed with a public key algorithm, it must first authenticate the declared identity that is associated with the key. Next, it will verify if the authenticated entity is allowed to perform the requested action. Both verifications rely on one or more certificates that a certification authority has signed. These certificates can be used for identification and authentication, for privilege verification either on an identity basis or on the basis or an assigned role. As a consequence, certification and certificate management are the cornerstone of security in open networks.

The management of the infrastructure for certification can be decentralized or centralized. Decentralized certification utilizes Pretty Good Privacy (PGP) and is very popular among Internet users [90]. This model works by reference among users and, by obviating the need for a central authenticating authority, eliminates vulnerability to attacks on the central system and prevents the potential for power abuse, which are the weak points of centralized certification. Each user therefore determines the credence accorded to a public key and assigns the confidence level in the certificate that the owner of this public key has issued. Similarly, a user can recommend a new party to members of the same circle of trust. At one time, the World Wide Web Consortium (W3C) was favoring this approach in its Digital Signature Initiative. However, absence of any collective structure forces users to manage certificates by themselves (update, revocation, etc.). The load of this management increases exponentially with the number of participants, which makes this mode of operation impractical for large-scale operations.

Centralized certification is denoted X.509 certification, using the name of the ITU-T Recommendation [11] that defines the framework for authentication in open systems. X.509 is identical to ISO/IEC 9594-8, a joint standard from the ISO and the IEC. ANSI also ratified a corresponding standard known as ANSI X9.57 [91]. The focus of the following presentation will be on X.509 certificates. For details on certification practices, the interested reader is also invited to consult specialized books on certification, for example, Ford and Baum [92, pp. 357–404] whose first author was at the time a manager in VeriSign, one of the key players in certification.

The ITU-T and the ISO/IEC have established a whole series of recommendations to describe the operation of a public key infrastructure (PKI). These are:

- X.500 (ISO/IEC 9594-1) [66] for a general view of the concepts, the models, and the services.
- X.501 (ISO/IEC 9594-2) [93] for the different models used in the Directory.
- X.509 (ISO/IEC 9594-8) [11], which defines the framework for authentication through public key cryptography using identity certificates and attribute certificates.
- X.511 (ISO/IEC 9594-3) [94], which defines the abstract services of the Directory (search, creation, deletion, error messages, etc.).
- X.520 (ISO/IEC 9594-6) [95] and X.521 (ISO/IEC 9594-7) [96], which, respectively, specify selected attribute types (key words) and selected object classes to ensure compatibility among implementations.

These recommendations specify services, protocols, messages and object classes to carry out the following functions:

- Retrieval of credentials stored in the Directory by a directory user agent (DUA) at the client side and a directory system agent (DSA) at the server's side with the Directory Access Protocol (DAP) defined in X.519 (ISO/IEC 9594-5) [97].
- Distributed searches and referrals among directory system agents with the Directory System Protocol (DSP) of X.518 (ISO/IEC 9594-4) [98].
- Information sharing among directory system agents through replication of the directory using the Directory Information Shadowing Protocol (DISP) of X.525 (ISO/IEC 9594-9) [99].

The relationship among these different protocols is shown in Figure 5.13.

X.500 [66] is the basis for security directory services in the TMN, as defined in ANSI T1.252 [100], should such security be deemed necessary. T1.252 relies on the X.500 Directory for distribution of certified public keys to authorized entities.

In IP networks, a simplified version of DAP, the LDAP, is often used for communication between user agents and system agents. LDAP is the output of the Public Key Infrastructure (X.509) (PKIX) working group of the IETF and is defined in RFC2251 [101]. The main simplifications are as follows:

1. LDAP carried directly over the TCP/IP stack, thereby avoiding some of the OSI protocols at the application layer.

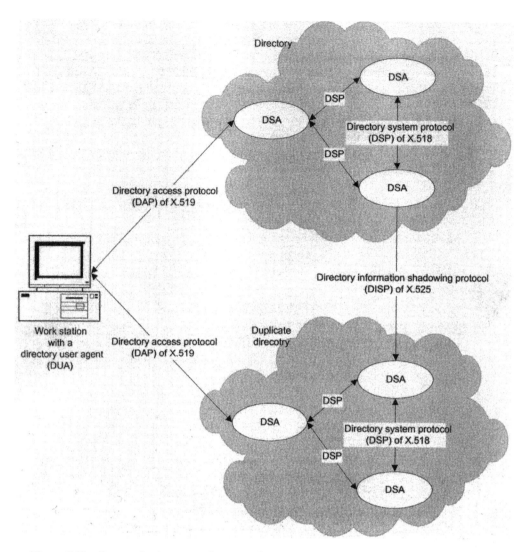

Figure 5.13 Communication protocols among the components of the directory system of X.500.

2. It uses simplified information models and object classes.

3. Being restricted to the client side, LDAP does not address what happens on the server side, for example, the duplication of the directory or the communication among servers.

4. Finally, Version 3 of LDAP, LDAPv3, does not mandate any strong authentication mechanism.

However, the latitude that LDAPv3 has allowed to developers with respect to strong authentication has resulted in some incompatibilities among different implementations of secure clients and servers. RFC 2829 [102] specifies a minimum subset of security functions common to all implementations of LSAPv3 that use the simple authentication and security layer (SASL) mechanism defined in RFC 2222 [103]. SASL adds authentication services and, optionally, integrity and confidentiality. Simple authentication is based on the name/password pair, concatenated with a random number and/or a time stamp with integrity protection using MD5. Strong authentication is achieved on a session basis using the transport layer security (TLS) protocol.

5.14.1 Basic Operation

After receiving a request encrypted using public key cryptography, a server has to accomplish the following tasks before answering:

1. Reading of the certificate presented.
2. Verification of the signature by the certification authority.
3. Extraction of the requester public key from the certificate.
4. Verification of the requester signature on the request message.
5. Verification of the certificate validity by comparison with the certificate revocation lists (CRL).
6. Establishment of a certification path between the certification authority of the requester and the authority that the server recognizes.
7. Extraction of the name of the requester.
8. Determination of the privileges that the requester enjoys.

The certificate permits the accomplishment of tasks 1 through 7 of the preceding list. In the case of payments, the last step consists of verifying the financial data relating to the requester, in particular, whether the account mentioned has sufficient funds. In the general case, the problem is much more complex, especially if the set of possible queries is large. The most direct method is to assign a key to each privilege, which increases the difficulties of key management. This topic is currently the subject of intense investigation.

5.14.2 Description of an X.509 Certificate

An X.509 certificate [11] is a record of the information needed to verify the identity of an entity. This record includes the distinguished name of the user, which is a unique name that ties the certificate owner with its public key. The certificate contains additional fields to locate its owner's identity more precisely. Each version of X.509 [11] introduces its allotment of supplementary information, although compatibility with previous versions is retained. The essential pieces of information are those that can be found in the basic certificate (Version 1), whose content is illustrated in Table 5.5.

The certificate contains the digital signature using the private key of the certification authority. It is usually recommended that a distinct key be used for each security function (signature, identification, encryption, nonrepudiation, key encryption, key agreement, etc.). Accordingly, any given entity may have several certificates.

In the initial version of X.509 [11], the hierarchical arrangement of the distinguished names followed the rules for X.500 [66]. These rules where inspired by the worldwide assignment of telephone numbers in complete accordance with Recommendation X.400 for

Table 5.5   Content of the Basic X.509 Certificate

Field Name	Description
Version	Version of the X.509 certificate
serialNumber	Certificate serial number
Signature	Identifier of the algorithm used to sign the certificate and the parameters used
Issuer	Name of the certification authority
Validity	Duration of the validity of the certificate
Subject	User's references: distinguished name, unique identifier (optional), etc.
subjectPublicKeyInfo	Information concerning the public key algorithm of the sender, its parameters, and the public key itself

electronic mail. The directory entries are described using the key words defined in Recommendation X.520 [95], a partial list of which is given in Table 5.6.

The widespread use of the Internet has spawned other models for hierarchical naming. Version 3 of X.509, which was approved in 1996, has taken this fact into account and authorized the use of a variety of distinguished names, such as the network addresses, passport or identity card numbers, Social Security numbers, Internet domain names, email addresses, and uniform resource locators (URLs) for Web applications. The certificate can include additional pointers to the certified subject (physical name; postal address; electronic address) as well as identifiers related to specific applications, such as email address, EDI identity; or even personal details, such as profession, photo ID, and bank account number. This additional flexibility requires a name registration system to ensure that any name used unambiguously identifies a certificate subject. Without this verification automatic cross-checking of directory entries will be difficult, particularly on a worldwide basis.

Starting from Version 3 of X.509 (1996), the public key certificate can contain details on the security service for which the certified public key can be used, on the duration of its validity, on any restrictions on the use of the certificates, on cross-certifications with other certification authorities, etc. For example, X.509 now provides a way for a certificate issuer to indicate how the issuer's certificate policies can be considered equivalent to a different policy used by another certification authority (Section 8.2.2.7 of X.509 (2001) on policy mapping extension).

Version 4 of X.509 (2001) introduced several certificate extensions to improve the treatment of certificate revocation and to associate privileges with the identification public key certificates or with attribute certificates.

Table 5.6   Partial List of Key Words in X.520

Key Word	Meaning
C	Country
CN	Common name
L	Locality name
O	Organization name
OU	Organizational unit name

5.14.3   Certification Path

The idea behind X.509 [11] is to allow each user to retrieve the public key of certified correspondents so they can proceed with the necessary verifications. It is sufficient therefore to request the closest certification authority to send the public key of the communicating entity in a certificate sealed with the digital signature of that authority. This authority, in turn, relays the request to its own certifying authority, and this permits an escalation through the chain of authorities, or certification path, until reaching the top of the certification pyramid, where the root authority (RA) resides. Figure 5.14 depicts this recursive verification.

Armed with the public key of the destination entity, the sender can include a secret encrypted with the public key of the correspondent and corroborate that the partner is the one whose identity is declared. This is because, without the private key associated with the key used in the encryption, the destination will not be able to extract the secret. Obviously, for the two parties to authenticate themselves mutually, both users have to construct the certification path back to a common certification authority.

Thus, a certification path is formed by a continuous series of certification authorities between two users. This series is constructed with the help of the information contained in the directory by going back to a common point of confidence. The tree structure of the certification path can be hierarchical or nonhierarchical. (*Note:* As in the system for telephone numbering, each country or region can have its own local root authority. However, to ensure worldwide communication, agreements for cross-certification among the various authorities would extend the zone of validity of their certification, by making one certification authority the subject of a certificate from another authority.)

5.14.3.1   *Hierarchical Certification Path*   According to the notational convention used in X.509 [11], a certificate is denoted by

$$authority<<user>>$$

Thus,

$$X_1<<X_2>>$$

indicates the certificate for user X_2 that authority X_1 has issued, while

$$X_1<<X_2>>\ X_2<<X_3>> \ldots X_n<<X_{n+1}>>$$

represents the certification path connecting user X_{n+1} to authority X_1. In other words, this notation is functionally equivalent to $X_1<<X_{n+1}>>$, which is the certificate that authority X_1 would have issued to user X_{n+1}. By constructing this path, another user would be able to retrieve the public key of user X_{n+1}, if that other user knows X_{1p}, the public key of authority X_1. This operation is called "unwrapping," and is represented by

$$X_{1p} \cdot X_1<<X_2>>$$

where $\cdot$ is an infix operator, whose left operand is the public key, X_{1p}, of authority X_1, and whose right operand is the certificate, $X_1<<X_2>>$, delivered to X_2 by that same certification authority. This result is the public key of user X_2.

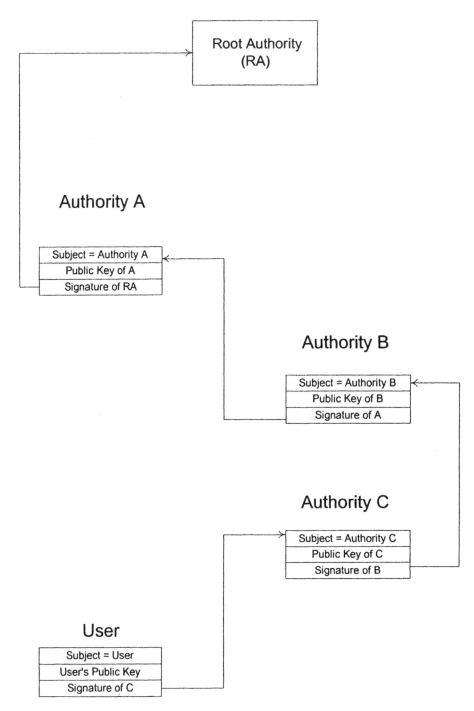

Figure 5.14 Recursive verification of certificates. (Adapted from Ford and Baum, *Secure Electronic Commerce,* Prentice Hall, 1997. With permission.)

In the example that Figure 5.15 depicts, assume that user A wants to construct the certification path toward another user, B. A can retrieve the public key of authority W with the certificate signed by X. At the same time, with the help of the certificate of V that W has issued, it is possible to extract the public key of V. In this manner, A would be able to obtain the chain of certificates:

$$X<<W>>, W<<V>>, V<<Y>>, Y<<Z>>, Z<<B>>$$

This itinerary, represented by $A \rightarrow B$, is the forward certification path that allows A to extract the public key Bp of B, by application of the operation · in the following manner:

$$Bp = Xp \cdot (A \rightarrow B) = Xp \cdot X<<W>> W<<V>> V<<Y>> Y<<Z>> Z<<B>>$$

In general, A also has to acquire the certificates for the return certification path $B \rightarrow A$, to send them to its partner:

$$Z<<Y>>, Y<<V>>, V<<W>>, W<<X>>, X<<A>>$$

When B receives these certificates from A, it can unwrap the certificates with its private key to extract the public key of A, Ap:

$$Ap = Zp \cdot (B \rightarrow A) = Zp \cdot Z<<Y>> Y<<V>> V<<W>> W<<X>> X<<A>>$$

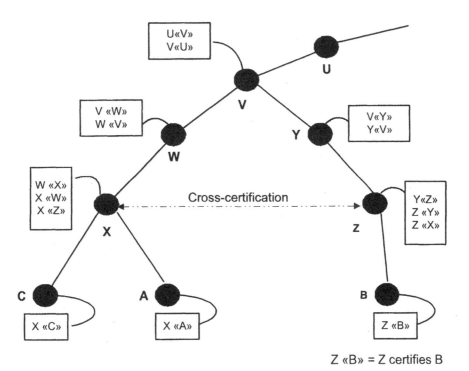

Figure 5.15   Hierarchical certification path according to X.509 [11]. (Adapted from ITU-T Recommendation X.509. Adapted from the International Telecommunication Union, 2000. With permission.)

As was previously mentioned, such a system does not necessarily impose a unique hierarchy worldwide. In the case of electronic payments, two banks or the fiscal authorities of two countries can mutually certify each other. In the preceding example, assume that authorities X and Z have cross-certified their respective certificates. If A wants to verify the authenticity of B, it is sufficient to obtain:

$$X<<Z>>, Z<<B>>$$

to form the forward certification path, and

$$Z<<X>>$$

to construct the reverse certification path. This permits the clients of the two banks to be satisfied with the certificates supplied by their respective banks.

5.14.3.2 Perspectives for Evolution   As was previously mentioned, the X.509 directory [11] was inspired by the telephone directory. However, in the absence of a central authority, the equivalence for the Internet is not exact. To resolve these difficulties, the PKIX working group of the IETF has introduced the CMP of RFC 2510 and the OCSP of RFC 2560 to support X.509-based certification on the Internet. RFC 2585 [104] describes the conventions for using the File Transfer Protocol (ftp) and the HTTP to obtain certificates and certification revocation lists from their respositories.

Some authors question the validity of transposing the design of the telephone directory to this new environment. In their view, association of a telephone number and an identity is much more stable than the link between an entity and the public key certificates. Thus, attempts have been made to come up with simple distributed authentication structures such as the simple distributed security infrastructure (SDSI) that Ronald Rivest and Butler Lampson have proposed. The design of such a system revolves around keys and not entities; i.e., it is the access to a private key rather than the identity of an entity that plays the principal role for authentication.

Work in the simple public key infrastructure (SPKI) is focused on defining an authorization model rather than an authentication model. This model avoids the need for a global naming authority, as each local authority can accord authorization in its local domain without interference of other local authorities.

If certification authorities are not organized hierarchically, the users themselves would have to construct the certification path. In practice, the number of operations to be carried out can be reduced with various strategies, for example:

1. Two users served by the same certification authority have the same certification path, and the users can exchange their certificates directly. This is the case for entities C and A in Figure 5.15.

2. If one user is constantly in touch with users that a particular authority has certified, that user could store the forward and return certification paths in memory. This would reduce the effort for obtaining the other users' certificates to a query into the directory.

3. If two users know each other's certificates, they can mutually authenticate themselves without querying the directory. This reverse certification is based on the confidence that each user has in his or her own certification authority.

The interoperability of certificates in the general case is extremely complex, given the large number of potential certification authorities. However, by limiting the field of application, the task becomes less difficult. In the United States, NIST has published the Minimum Interoperability Specifications for PKI Components (MISPC) as NIST Special Publication 800-15 [105]. MISPC includes a certificate and a certificate revocation list profile, message formats, and basic transactions for a PKI issuing signature certificates. A reference implementation is also available. An updated specification is currently being developed.

In the same spirit and to facilitate electronic exchanges with suppliers of the federal agencies by replacing handwritten signatures as a means for authentication, the Canadian government has launched the program Government of Canada Public Key Infrastructure (GOCPKI). The objective of this program is to establish uniform criteria to manage the keys and certificates among all Canadian federal agencies.

In summary, the main difficulties in establishing a public key certification infrastructure that operates on a worldwide level are (1) the lack of harmonization among the authentication practices of the various certification authorities, (2) the absence of objective criteria to measure and evaluate the performance of the certification authorities, and (3) the absence of coordination among the multiple naming authorities.

5.14.4 Procedures for Strong Authentication

Having obtained the certification path and the other side's authenticated public key, X.509 [11] defines three procedures for authentication:

1. One-way or unidirectional authentication
2. Two-way or bidirectional authentication
3. Three-way or tridirectional authentication

5.14.4.1 *One-Way Authentication*   One-way authentication takes place through the transfer of information from user A to user B according to the following steps:

- A generates a random number R^A used to detect replay attacks.
- A constructs an authentication token $M = (T^A, R^A, I_B, d)$ where T^A represents the time stamp of A (date and time) and I_B is the identity of B. T^A comprises two chronological indications, for example, the generation time of the token and its expiration date, and d is an arbitrary data. For additional security, the message can be encrypted with the public key of B.
- A sends B the message:

$$B \rightarrow A, A\{(T^A, R^A, I_B, d)\}$$

where $B \rightarrow A$ is the certification path and $A\{M\}$ represents the message M encrypted with the private key of A.

- B carries on the following operations:
  —Obtain the public key of A, A_p, from $B \rightarrow A$, after verifying that the certificate of A has not expired.

—Recover the signature by decrypting the message A{M} with Ap;. *B* then verifies that this signature is identical to the message hash, thereby ascertaining simultaneously the signature and the integrity of the signed message.

—Verifies that *B* is the intended recipient.

—Verifies that the time stamp is "current."

—Optionally, verifies that R^A has not been previously used.

These exchanges prove:

- The authenticity of A, and that the authentication token has been generated by A.
- The authenticity of B, and that the authentication token has been intended for B.
- The integrity of the identification token.
- The originality of the identification token, i.e., that it has not been previously utilized.

5.14.4.2 Two-Way Authentication
The procedure for two-way authentication adds to the previous unidirectionnal exchanges, similar exchanges but in the reverse direction. Thus:

- B generates another random number R^B.
- B constructs the message $M' = (T^B, R^B, I_A, R^A, d)$, where T^B represents the time-stamp of *B* (date and time), I_A is identity of A, and R^A is the random number received from A. T^B consists of one or two chronological indications, as previously described. For security, the message can be encrypted with the public key of A.
- B sends A the message:

$$B\{(T^B, R^B, I_A, R^A, d)\}$$

where B{M'} represents the message M' encrypted with the private key of B.

- A carries out the following operations:

—Extracts the public key of *B* from the certification path and uses it to decrypt B{M'} and recovers the signature of the message that *B* has produced. A verifies next that the signature is the same as the hashed message, thereby ascertaining the integrity of the signed information.

—Verifies that A is the intended recipient.

—Checks the time stamp to verify that the message is current.

—As an option, verifies that RB has not been previously used.

5.14.4.3 Three-Way Authentication
Protocols for three-way authentication introduce a third exchange from A to B. The advantage is the avoidance of time-stamping and, as a consequence, a trusted third party. The steps are the same as for two-way identification, but with $T^A = T^B = 0$. Then:

- A verifies that the value of the received R^A is the same as that sent to B.
- A sends *B* the message:

$$A\{R^B, I_B\}$$

encrypted with the private key of A.

- B performs the following operations:
  - —Verifies the signature and the integrity of the received information.
  - —Verifies that the received value of R^B is the same as that sent.

5.14.5 Certificate Revocation

Authentication establishes the correspondence between a public key and an identity only for a period of time. Therefore, certification authorities must refer to revocation lists, which contain certificates that have expired or have been revoked. These lists are continuously updated. Table 5.7 shows the format of the revocation list that Version 1 of X.509 has defined. The third revision of X.509 has added other optional entries such as the date of the certificate revocation and the reason for revocation.

In principle, each certification authority has to maintain at least two revocation lists: (1) a dated list of the certificates that it has issued and revoked, and (2) a dated list of all the certificates that the authorities know of and recognize as having been revoked. The root certification authority and each of its delegate authorities must be able to access these lists to verify the instantaneous state of all the certificates to be treated within the authentication system.

Revocation can be periodic or exceptional. When a certificate expires, the certification authority withdraws it from the directory (but retains a copy in a special directory, to be able to arbitrate any conflict that might arise in the future). Replacement certificates have to be ready and supplied to the owner to ensure the continuity of the service.

The root authority (or one of its delegated authorities) can cancel a certificate before its expiration date, for example, if the certificate owner's private key has been compromised or if there has been any abuse in usage. In the case of secure payments, the notion of solvency, i.e., that the user has available the necessary funds, is obviously one of the essential considerations.

The processing of the revocation lists must be speedy to alert users and, in certain countries, the authorities, particularly if the revocation is before the expiration date. Perfect synchronization among the various authorities must be attained to avoid questioning the validity of documents signed or encrypted before the withdrawal of the corresponding certificates.

Table 5.7 Basic Format of the X.509 Revocation List

Field	Comment
Signature	Identifier of the algorithm used to sign the certificates and the parameters used
Issuer	Name of the certification authority
thisUpdate	Date of the current update of the revocation list
nextUpdate	Date of the next update of the revocation list
revokedCertificates	References of the revoked certificates including the revocation date

Users must also be able to access the various revocation lists; this is not always possible because current client programs do not query these lists.

In summary, when an entity has a certificate signed by a certification authority, this means that the entry for that entity in the directory maintained by the certification authority has the following properties:

1. It establishes a relationship between the entity and a pair of public and private cryptographic keys.
2. It associates a unique distinguised name in the directory with the entity.
3. It establishes that, for a certain time, the authority is able to guarantee the correspondence between that unique distinguished name and the pair of keys.

5.14.6   Attribute Certificates

X.509 (Version 4) introduces a new type of public key certificates called *attribute certificates,* to link a subject to certain privileges separately from its authenticated identity. Attribute certificates allow the verification of the rights or prerogatives of their subject, such as access privileges [105]. Thus, once an identity has been authenticated with a public key certificate, the subject may use multiple attribute-certificates associated with that public key certificate.

Although it is quite possible to use public key identity certificates to define what the holder of the certificate may be entitled to, a separate attribute certificate may be useful in some cases, for example:

1. If the authority for privilege assignment is distinct from the certification authority.
2. A variety of authorities will be defining access privileges to the same subject.
3. The same subject may have different access permissions, depending on its role.
4. There is the possibility of delegation of privileges, in full or in part.
5. The duration of validity of the privilege is shorter than that of the public key certificate.

Conversely, the public key identity certificate may suffice for assigning privileges whenever:

1. The same physical entity combines the roles of certification authority and of attribute authority.
2. The expiration of the privileges coincides with that of the public key certificate.
3. Delegation of privileges is not permitted, or if permitted, all privileges are delegated at once.

The use of attribute certificates creates the need of a new infrastructure for their management. This is called privilege management infrastructure (PMI). When a single entity acts as both a certification authority and an attribute authority, it is strongly recommended that different keys be used for each kind of certificates.

The source of authority (SOA) is the trusted entity responsible for assigning access privileges. It plays a role similar to the root certification authority; however, the root certification authority may control the entities that can act as SOAs. An SOA can authorize the holder of a set of privileges to further delegate these privileges, in part or in full, along a *delegation path*. There may be restrictions on the power of delegation capability, for example, the length of the delegation path can be bonded and the scope of privileges allowed can be restricted downstream. To validate the delegation path, each attribute authority along the path must be checked to verify that it was duly authorized to delegate its privileges.

Attribute certification allows modification of the privileges of a role without impacts on the public key identity certificates However, privilege verification requires an independent verification of the privileges attributed to a role. This be done by prior agreement or through role-specification certificates. It is worth noting that hierarchical role-based access control allows role specifications to be more compact, because higher levels inherit the permissions accorded to subordinates.

X.509 [11] supports role-based access control (RBAC), provided that role specification certificates can be linked with the role assignments indicated in identity certificates or in attribute certificates. In addition, X.509 supports hierarchical RBAC through a "domination rule" that puts limits on the scope of delegated privileges. (*Note:* An X.509 RBAC policy for privilege management using XML is available at http://www.xml.org, and is based on work done at the University of Salford, U.K. [107].

5.15 APPLICATIONS FOR NETWORK MANAGEMENT

The first version of SNMP did not offer any security services. All management information can be accessed from the management system with read and write permissions. There are no mechanisms for authentication; messages are passed in plaintext form, and there are no sequence numbers. While the so-called "community string" could be used to identify the origin of the message, this string was not encrypted. SNMP packets are transmitted in the clear, which allows traffic analysis. Furthermore, there is no control for the integrity of the information; because there are no sequence numbers, replay attacks could not be fended off. Thus, the only way to protect Version 1 SNMP packets is through the use of IPSec.

Version 2 of SNMP allows confidentiality with DES as well as integrity verification through MD5. There is a mechanism for clock synchronization at both sides to prevent replay attacks. SNMPv2, however, does not provide a means for key distribution and management [108, pp. 285–286].

Version 3 of SNMP provides means for authentication, confidentiality, integrity verification, key management, access control, and clock synchronization. Authentication and integrity verification use the HMAC keyed-hashing algorithm, while confidentiality uses DES in the cipher block chaining (CBC) mode (see Appendix II).

A secret is constructed for communication between an SNMP manager and each of the SNMP agents that it manages . This secret is based on a nonshared secret stored in the SNMP manager and each agent's unique identifier using a hashing function (MD5 or SHA-1). The shared secret is then manually loaded in the SNMP agent. From this secret, the authentication key, the encryption key, and the initialization vector of the encryption can be derived [109, 110, pp. 202–203]. The specifications include a way for updating the various keys. SNMPv3 also offers a method for access control [111].

One major limitation in the security offered by SNMPv3 is that key update is based on the current key. Thus, if one key is compromised, an intruder can derive the next key by observing and decrypting the update exchanges. For small payloads, SNMPv3 requires about 24% more bandwidth than when SNMPv2c is secured with IPSec [112].

Finally, it has been observed in the past that many software implementations of SNMP managers do not decode the SNMP messages correctly or do not make the necessary syntax checks before interpreting and executing the commands. Thus, it is important to verify through adequate testing that the SNMP implementations behave correctly.

5.16 ENCRYPTION CRACKS

While the role of encryption is to mask the messages, the objective of cryptanalysis is to recover the message without knowledge of the encryption key. The basic approach consists of uncovering flaws in the cryptographic algorithms or in the system design that allows eavesdropping on the encrypted messages or at least spreading confusion.

The best-known cryptological attacks are of the following types:

1. Brute-force attacks where the assailant systematically tries all possible encryption keys until getting the one that will reveal the plain text.
2. Attacks on the encrypted text assuming that the clear text has a known given structure, for example, the systematic presence of a header with a known format (this is the case of email messages) or the repetition of known key words.
3. Attacks starting with the clear text, in total or in part, so as to uncover the encryption key.
4. Attacks starting with chosen plaintexts that are encrypted with the unknown key, so as to deduce the key itself.
5. Attacks by replaying old legitimate messages to evade the defense mechanisms and to short-circuit the encryption.
6. Attacks by interception of the messages (man-in-the-middle) where the interceptor inserts its eavesdrop at an intermediate point between the two parties. After interception, an exchange of a secret key, for example, the interceptor will be able to decipher the exchanged messages while the participants think they are communicating in complete security. The attacker may also be able to inject fake messages that would be treated as legitimate by the two parties.
7. Attacks by measuring the length of encryption times, of electromagnetic emissions, etc., to deduce the complexity of the operations, and hence their form.

Other techniques depend on the communication system itself. For example, corruption of the DNS can reorient packets to an attacker's address. Among the recommended measures to fend off attacks are the following [113]:

1. The explicit indication of the identity of the participants, if this identity is essential for the semantic interpretation of the message.
2. The choice of a sufficiently large key to discourage brute-force attacks, provided

that the encryption algorithm is well designed. The required key size grows with the computational power available to the adversaries.

3. The addition of random elements, a time stamp, and other nonce values that make replay attacks more difficult. However, deficient random-number generators open the possibility of attacks on secure algorithms.

In some cases, the physical protection of the whole cryptographic system (fibers, computers, smart cards, etc.) may be needed. For example, fiber bending results in a dispersion of 1–10% of the signal power; therefore, well-placed acoustic-optic devices can capture the diffraction pattern for later analysis.

In the real world, there are easier ways than cryptanalysis to break the cryptographic defenses. It is erroneous to evaluate the resistance of a cryptographic system by measuring the theoretical properties of the cryptographic algorithms used, without taking their practical implementation into account. Errors in design, gaps in implementations, or operational deficiencies, particularly if the encryption is done in software, augment the vulnerability of the system. It is well known, for example, that GSM, IEEE 802.11b, IS-41, etc., have faulty or deliberately weakened protection schemes. A catalog of the causes of vulnerability includes [113–115].

1. Nonverification of partial computations.
2. The use of defective random-number generators, because the keys and the session variables depend on a good supply source for nonpredictable bits.
3. The improper reutilization of random parameters.
4. The misuse of a hash function, which increases the chance of collisions.
5. The structural weakness of the telecommunications network.
6. The nonsystematic destruction of the clear text after encryption as well as the keys used in encryption.
7. The retention of the password or the keys in the virtual memory.
8. No checking of correct range of operation. This is particularly the case when buffer overflows can cause security flaws. Recently, a problem with Kerberos was discovered through buffer overflow within a process that administers the database.
9. The misuse of a protocol can lead to an authenticator traveling in plain text. For example, RFC 2109 [117] specifies that when the authenticator is stored in a cookie, the server has to set the Secure flag in the cookie header so that the client waits until a secure connection has been established with SSL or TLS before returning the cookie. Unfortunately, some Web servers neglect to set this flag, thereby negating that protection. The authenticator can also leak if the client software continues to use it even after the authentification is successful.

For example, when a program deletes a file, most commercial operating systems merely eliminate the corresponding entry in the index file. This allows recovery of the file, at least partially, with off-the-shelf software. The only means of guaranteeing total elimination of the data is to rewrite systematically each of the bits that the deleted file was using. Similarly, the use of the virtual memory in commercial systems exposes another vulnerability, because the secret document may be momentarily in the clear on the disk.

Systems for general commercial use must be easily accessible and affordably priced.

As a consequence, all the protective measures used in "top-secret" computers will not be used, and many compromises will be made to improve response time and the ease of use. However, if one starts from the principle that, sooner or later, any system is susceptible to unexpected attacks with unanticipated consequences, it would be useful to design the system such that any possible attack will be detected. For example, by accumulating proofs that are accepted by courts, the consequences would be alleviated and the possible damages reduced.

The starting point should be a correct definition of the type of expected threats and the eventual attack plans. The model has to take into account users' practices and the way they will be using the system, as well as the motivations for possible attacks. Such a realistic evaluation of threats and risks permits a precise understanding of what should be protected, against whom, and for how long.

5.17 SUMMARY

The task of securing telecommunications services has always been part of the role of network operators. There are two types of attacks: passive and active. Protection can be achieved with suitable mechanisms and appropriate policies. Recently, security has leaped to the forefront in priority because of changes in the regulatory environment and in technology. The fragmentation of operations that were once vertically integrated have increased the number of participants in end-to-end information transfer. In virtual private networks, customers are allowed some control of their part of the public infrastructure. Finally, security must be retrofitted in IP networks to protect from the inherent difficulties of having user traffic and network control traffic within the same pipe.

Security mechanisms can be implemented in one or more layers of the OSI mode. The choice of the layer depends on the security services to be offered and the coverage of protection.

Confidentiality guarantees that only the authorized parties can read the information transmitted. This is achieved by cryptography, whether symmetric or asymmetric. Symmetric cryptography is faster than asymmetric cryptography, but has a limitation in terms of the secure distribution of the shared secret. Asymmetric (or public key cryptography) overcomes this problem; this is why both can be combined. In on-line systems, public key cryptography is used for sending the shared secret that can be used later for symmetric encryption. Two of the public key schemes used for sharing the secrets are Diffie–Hellman and RSA. ISAKMP is a generic framework to negotiate point-to-point security and to exchange key and authentication data among two parties.

Data integrity is the service for preventing nonauthorized changes to the message content during transmission. A one-way hash function is used to produce a signature of the message that can be verified to ascertain integrity. Blind signature is a special procedure for signing a message without revealing its content.

Identification of participants depends on whether cryptography is symmetric or asymmetric. In asymmetric schemes, there is a need for authentication using certificates. In the case of human users, biometric features can be used for identification in specific situations. Kerberos is an example of a distributed system for on-line identification and authentication using symmetric cryptography.

Access control is used to counter the threats of unauthorized operations. There are two types of access control mechanisms: identity-based and role-based. Both can be managed through certificates defined by ITU-T Recommendation X.509 [11]. Denial of service is the consequence of failure of access control. These attacks are inherently associated with IP networks where network control data and user data share the same physical and logical bandwidths. The best solution is to authenticate all communications by means of trusted certificates. Short of this, defense mechanisms will be specific to the problem at hand.

Nonrepudiation is a service that prevents a person who has accomplished an act from denying it later. This is a legal concept that is defined through legislation. The service comprises the generation of evidence, their recording, and subsequent verification. The technical means to ensure nonrepudiation include electronic signature of documents, the intervention of third parties as witnesses, time-stamping, and sequence numbering of the transactions.

APPENDIX I: AREAS RELATED TO SECURITY POLICIES

Security policies cover several areas such as [16, 38]:

- Policies regarding physical security of sites and network components, including the threats from fires, earthquakes, floodings, etc, and responses to emergencies.
- Policies for *prevention,* including physical access security, personnel risk analysis, security screening, access to management information.
- Policies for *administering* cryptographic keys for network elements or certificates, etc.
- Policies for *intrusion detection:* through usage pattern analysis to detect theft of service or denial of service attacks, network security alarm software intrusion audit.
- Policies for *audits*: what should be in an event record (nature of event, time, etc.), who can specify them, how to analyzed audit trails, etc.
- Policies for *reports,* i.e., the capability of reporting events to the network management system in real time as selected by a network administrator.
- Policies for *containment.*
- Policies for *recovery,* for example, backup policies.

APPENDIX II: PRINCIPLES OF SYMMETRIC ENCRYPTION

AII.1   Modes of Algorithm Utilization for Block Encryption

The four modes for using symmetric algorithms of the block cipher type are (1) ECB mode; (2) CBC mode, (3) cipher feedback (CFB) mode, and (4) output feedback (OFB) mode.

The ECB mode is the most obvious, because each clear block is encrypted independently of the other blocks. However, this mode is susceptible to attacks by replay of blocks, which results in the perturbation of the messages even without breaking the code. This is the reason this mode is only used to encrypt random data, such as the encryption of keys during authentication.

The other three modes have in common that they protect against such types of attacks with a feedback loop. They also have the additional property that they need an initialization vector to start the computations. These values can be revealed. The difference between the three feedback modes resides in the way the clear text is mixed, partially or in its entirety, with the preceding encrypted block.

In the CBC mode, the input to the encryption module is the clear text mixed with the preceding encrypted block with an exclusive OR. This encryption operation is represented in Figure AII.1, and Figure AII.2 represents the decryption. In these figures, M_i represents the ith block of the clear message, while E_i is the corresponding encrypted block. Thus, the encrypted block, E_i, is given by

$$E_i = E_k(M_i \oplus E_{i-1}), \qquad i = 0, 1, \ldots$$

where $E_K(\ )$ represents the encryption with the secret key, K, and $\oplus$ is the exclusive OR operation. The starting value E_o is the initialization vector The decryption operation, shown in Figure AII.2 is described by

$$M_i = E_{i-1} \oplus D_K(E_i)$$

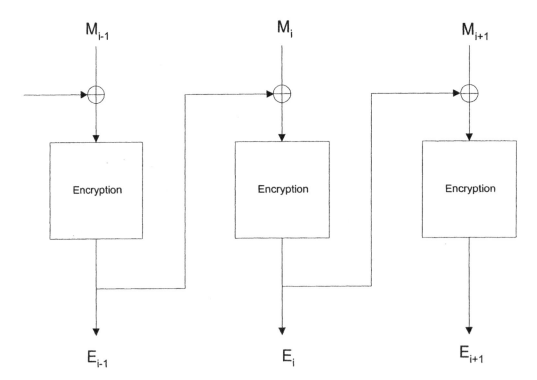

Figure AII.1   Encryption in the CBC mode.

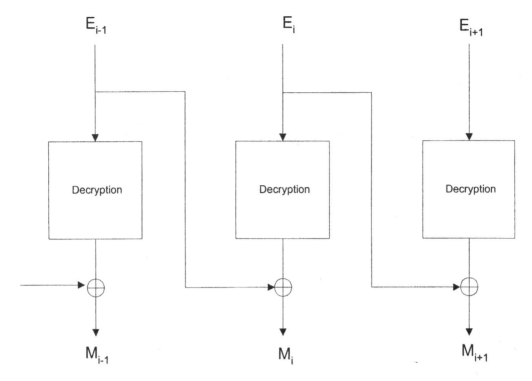

Figure AII.2   Decryption in the CBC mode.

The CBC mode is generally useful for non-real-time encryption of files, for example, to calculate the signature of a message (or its MAC). In fact, this is the method indicated in the various standards for securing financial and banking transactions: ANSI X9.9 [118], ANSI X9.19 [119], ISO 8731-1 [120], and ISO/IEC 9797 [121], as well as in the ESP protocol of IPSec

The CFB and OFB modes are more appropriate for the real-time encryption of a character stream, such as in the case of a client connected to a server.

In CFB encryption, the encryption of a block of clear text of m bits is done in units of n bits ($n = 1, 8, 32,$ or 64 bits), with $n \leq m$, in n/m cycles. At each cycle, n bits of the clear message, M_i, are combined, with the help of an exclusive OR, with the leftmost n bits of the previously encrypted block, E_{i-1}, to yield the new n bits of the new encrypted block E_i. These same n bits are then concatenated to the feedback bits in a shift register, and then all the bits of this register are shifted n positions of the left. The n leftmost bits of the register are ignored, while the remainder of the register content is encrypted, and the n leftmost bits are used in the encryption of the next n bits of the clear text. The decryption operation is identical with the roles of M_i and E_i transposed. Figure AII.3 depicts the encryption, and Figure AII.4 illustrates the decryption.

It can be seen that the block encryption algorithm is acting on both sides. The decryption operation is sensitive to bit errors, because one bit error in the encrypted text affects the decryption of ($m/n + 1$) blocks, the present one and the next (m/n). In this mode of operation, the initialization vector needs to be changed after each message to prevent cryptanalysis.

Shift register (m bits)

Clear
text
(m bits)

n bits
eliminated

$M_i = \{m_{i1},...,m_{il},...,m_{in}\}$

m_{il}

K_{il}

Encryption

e_{il} the leftmost
n bits

Figure AII.3   Encryption in the CFB mode of a block of m bits and n bits of feedback.

In the case $n = m$, the shift register can be eliminated and the encryption is done as illustrated in Figure AII.5. Thus, the encrypted block, E_i, is given by

$$E_i = M_i \oplus E_K(E_{i-1})$$

where $E_K(\;)$ represents the encryption with the secret key K.

The decryption is obtained with another exclusive OR operation as follows:

$$M_i = E_i \oplus E_K(E_{i-1})$$

which is shown in Figure AII.6.

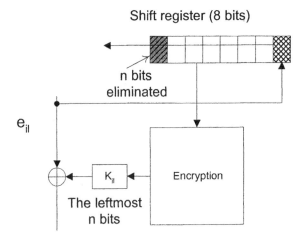

Shift register (8 bits)

n bits
eliminated

e_{il}

K_{il}

Encryption

The leftmost
n bits

Figure AII.4   Decryption in the CFB mode of a block of m bits with n bits in the feedback loop.

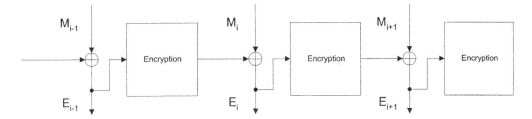

Figure AII.5   Encryption in the CFB mode for a block of n bits with a feedback of n bits.

The CFB mode can be used to calculate the MAC of a message as the last block encrypted two consecutive times. This method is also indicated in ANSI X9.9 [116] for the authentication of banking messages, as well as ANSI X9.19 [117],, ISO 8731-1 [118], and ISO/IEC 9797 [119]. In the encryption of a telnet stream with SKIPJACK $m = 64$ bits and $n = 32$ or 8 bits, depending on whether integrity is provided. These modes are denoted as CFB-8 without integrity and CFB-32 with integrity.

Finally, the OFB mode is similar to the CFB mode, except that the n bits in the feedback loop result from the encryption and are not in the ciphertext transmitted to the destination. This is illustrated in Figures AII.7 and AII.8 for the encryption and decryption, respectively.

OFB is adapted to situations where the transmission systems insert significant errors, because the effects of such errors are confined: a single bit error in the ciphertext affects only one bit in the recovered text. However, to avoid the loss of synchronization, the values in the shift registers should be identical. Thus, any system that incorporates the OFB mode must be able detect the loss of synchronization and have a mechanism to reinitialize the shift registers on both sides with the same value.

The encryption operation is represented in Figure AII.9, for the case where $n = m$, and is described by

$$E_i = M_i \oplus E_i$$

$$S_i = E_K(S_{i-1})$$

The algorithm approaches a permutation of m bits that, on average, repeats itself every $2^m - 1$ cycles. Therefore, it is recommended to utilize mode OFB only with $n = m$, i.e., the feedback size equal to the block size, to increase the security of the operation.

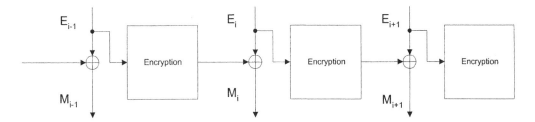

Figure AII.6   Decryption in the CFB mode for a block of n bits with a feedback of n bits.

The decryption is described by

$$M_i = E_i \oplus S_i$$

$$S_i = E_K(S_{i-1})$$

and it takes place as indicated in Figure AII.10.

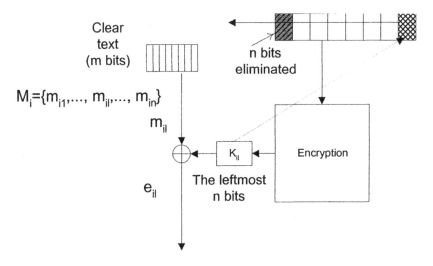

Figure AII.7   Encryption in OFB mode of a block of m bits with a feedback of n bits.

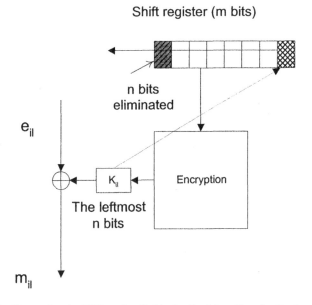

Figure AII.8   Decryption in OFB mode of a block of m bits with a feedback of n bits.

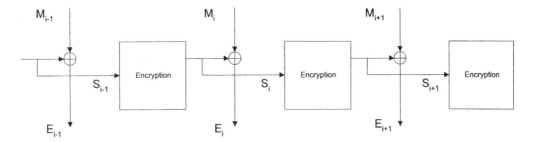

Figure AII.9   Encryption in OFB mode with a block of n bits and a feedback of n bits.

AII.2   Examples of Symmetric Block Encryption Algorithms

AII.2.1   *Advanced Encryption Standard*

The AES is the new symmetric encryption algorithm that will replace DES. It is published by NIST as FIPS 197 and is based on the algorithm Rijndael that was developed by two Belgian cryptographers. It is a block code with blocks of 128, 192, or 256 bits. The corresponding key lengths are128, 192, and 256 bits, respectively.

The selection in October 2000 came after two rounds of testing following NIST's invitation to cryptographers from around the world to submit algorithms. In the first round, 15 algorithms were retained for evaluation. The submissions came from a variety of companies, such as Deutsche Telekom, IBM, NTT, RSADSI, from Canada and South Korea, as well as from independent researchers. All the algorithms in competition operated with key lengths of 128, 192, and 256 bits. In the second round of evaluation, five finalists were retained : RC6, MARS, Rijnadel, Serpent, and Twofish. Results from the evaluation and the rational for the selection have been documented in a public report by NIST [120].

AII.2.2   *Data Encryption Standard*

DES is one of the most widely used algorithms in the commercial world for applications such as the encryption of financial documents, the management of cryptographic keys, and the authentication of electronic transactions. This algorithm was developed by IBM and then adopted as a U.S. standard in 1977. It was published in FIPS 81, then adopted by ANSI in ANSI X3.92 [40] under the name of *Data Encryption Algorithm*. This algorithm has reached the end of its useful life and is expected to be replaced by the AES.

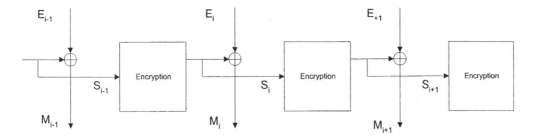

Figure AII.10   Decryption in OFB mode for a block of n bits with a feedback of n bits.

DES operates by encrypting blocs of 64 bits of clear text to produce blocks of 64 bits of ciphertext. The encryption and decryption are based on the same algorithm with some minor differences in the generation of subkeys.

The key length is 64 bits, with 8 bits for parity control, which gives an effective length of 56 bits. The operation of DES consists of 16 rounds of identical operations, each round including a text substitution followed by a bit-by-bit permutation of the text, based on the key. If the number of rounds is fewer than 16, DES can be broken by a clear text attack, which is easier to conduct than an exhaustive search.

AII.2.3 Triple DES   The vulnerability of DES to an exhaustive attack has encouraged the search of other, surer algorithms until a new standard is available. Given the considerable investment in the software and hardware implementations of DES, triple DES uses DES three successive times with two different keys. Figure AII.11 represents the schema used in triple DES.

The use of three stages doubles the effective length of the key to 112 bits. The operations "encryption–decryption–encryption" aim at preserving compatibility with DES, because if the same key is used in all operations, the first two cancel each other. As there are several ways to attack the algorithm, it is recommended that three independent keys be used [39, pp. 359–360].

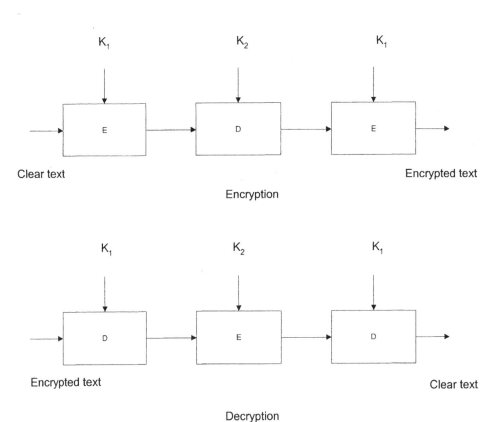

Figure AII.11   Operation of triple DES.

AII.2.4   International Data Encryption Algorithm   IDEA was invented by Xuejia Lai and James Massey circa 1991 [45]. The algorithm takes blocks of 64 bits of the clear text, divides them into subblocks of 16 bits each, and encrypts them with a key 128 bits long. The same algorithm is used for encryption and decryption. IDEA is clearly superior to DES, but has not been a commercial success. The patent is held by a Swiss company, Ascom-Tech AG, and is not subject to U.S. export control.

AII.2.5   SKIPJACK   SKIPJACK is an algorithm developed by NSA for several single-chip processors, such as Clipper, Capstone, and Fortezza. Clipper is a tamper-resistant very large-scale integrated (VLSI) chip used to encrypt voice conversation. Capstone provides the cryptographic functions needed for secure electronic commerce, and is used in Fortezza applications. SKIPJACK is an iterative block cipher with a block size of 64 bits and a key of 80 bits. It can be used in any of the four modes ECB, CBC, CFB (with a feedback of 8, 16, 32, or 64 bits), and OFB with a feedback of 64 bits.

APPENDIX III: PRINCIPLES OF PUBLIC KEY ENCRYPTION

The most popular algorithms for public cryptography are those of Rivest, Shamir, and Adleman (RSA) [50], Rabin (1979), and ElGamal [57]. Nevertheless, the overwhelming majority of proposed systems in commercial systems are based on the RSA algorithm.

It should be noted that RSADSI was founded in 1982 to commercialize the RSA algorithm for public key cryptography. However, its exclusive rights ended with the expiration of the patent on September 20, 2000.

AIII.1   RSA

Consider two odd prime numbers $\mathbf{p}$ and $\mathbf{q}$ whose product $\mathbf{N} = \mathbf{p} \times \mathbf{q}$. The values $\mathbf{p}$ and $\mathbf{q}$ are kept secret, while $\mathbf{N}$ is the modulus used in the computation which is public. When referring to the key size for RSA, what is meant is the length of the modulus $\mathbf{N}$ in bits.

Let $\varphi(\mathbf{n})$ be the Euler totient function of $\mathbf{N}$. By definition, $\varphi(\mathbf{n})$ is the number of elements formed by the complete set of residues that are relatively prime to $\mathbf{N}$. This set is called the reduced set of residues modulo $\mathbf{N}$.

If $\mathbf{N}$ is a prime, $\varphi(\mathbf{N}) = \mathbf{N} - 1$. However, because $\mathbf{N} = \mathbf{p} \times \mathbf{q}$ by construction, while $\mathbf{p}$ and $\mathbf{q}$ are primes, then

$$\varphi(\mathbf{N}) = (\mathbf{p} - 1)\,(\mathbf{q} - 1)$$

According to Fermat's little theorem, if m is a prime, and $\mathbf{a}$ is not a multiple of $\mathbf{m}$ (for example, $\mathbf{a} < \mathbf{m}$), the

$$\mathbf{a}^{\mathbf{m}-1} \equiv 1 \,(\mathrm{mod}\ m)$$

Euler generalized this theorem in the form:

$$\mathbf{a}^{\varphi(\mathbf{N})} \equiv 1 \,(\mathrm{mod}\ \mathbf{N})$$

Choose the integers $\mathbf{e}$, $\mathbf{d}$ both less that $\varphi(\mathbf{N})$ such that the greatest common divisor of $(\mathbf{e}, \varphi(\mathbf{N})) = 1$ and $\mathbf{e} \times \mathbf{d} \equiv 1 \,\mathrm{mod}\,(\varphi(\mathbf{N})) = 1 \,\mathrm{mod}\,((\mathbf{p} - 1)(\mathbf{q} - 1))$.

Let **X**, **Y** be two numbers less than **N**,

$$\mathbf{Y} = \mathbf{X^e} \bmod \mathbf{N} \quad \text{with} \quad 0 \equiv \mathbf{X} < \mathbf{N}$$

$$\mathbf{X} = \mathbf{Y^d} \bmod \mathbf{N} \quad \text{with} \quad 0 \equiv \mathbf{Y} < \mathbf{N}$$

because, by applying Fermat's little theorem,

$$\mathbf{Y^d} \bmod \mathbf{N} = (\mathbf{X^e})^\mathbf{d} \bmod \mathbf{N} = \mathbf{X^{ed}} \bmod \mathbf{N} = \mathbf{X}\varphi^{(\mathbf{N})} \equiv 1 \ (\bmod \ \mathbf{N}) = 1 \bmod \mathbf{N}$$

To start the process, a block of data is interpreted as an integer. To do so, the total block is considered as an ordered sequence of bits (of length, say, λ). The integer is considered to be the sum of the bits by giving the first bit the weight of $2^{\lambda-1}$, the second bit the weight of $2^{\lambda-2}$, and so on until the last bit, which will have the weight of $2^0 = 1$.

The block size must be such that the largest number does not exceed the modulo **N**. Incomplete blocks must be completed by padding bits with either 1 or 0 bits. Further padding blocks may be also added.

The public key of the algorithm **Pk** is the number **e**, along with **N**, while the secret key **Sk** is the number **d**. RSA achieves its security from the difficulty of factoring **N**. The number of bits of **N** are considered to be the key size of the RSA algorithm. The selection of the primes **p** and **q** must make this factorization as difficult as possible.

Once the keys have been generated, it is recommended, for reasons of security, that the values of **p** and **q** as well as all intermediate values, such as the product $(\mathbf{p} - 1)(\mathbf{q} - 1)$, be deleted. Nevertheless, the preservation of the values of **p** and **q** locally can double or even quadruple the speed of decryption.

AIII.1.1 *Practical Considerations*

To increase the speed of signature verification, suggested values for the exponent **e** of the public key are 3 or $2^{16} + 1$ (65,537) [40, p. 437]. Other variants designed to speed up decryption and signing are discussed in Boneh and Shacham [122].

For short-term confidentiality, the modulus **N** should be at least 768 bits. For long-term confidentiality (5 to 10 years), at least 1024 bits should be used. Currently, it is believed that confidentiality with a key of 2048 bits would last about 15 years.

AIII.2 Public Key Cryptography Standards

Public Key Cryptography Standards (PKCS) are business standards developed by RSA Laboratories in collaboration with many other companies working in the area of cryptography. They have been used in many aspects of public key cryptography that are based on the RSA algorithm. At the time of writing this section, their number has reached 15.

PKCS #1 (RFC 2437 [58]) defines the mechanisms for data encryption and signature using the RSA algorithm. These procedures are then utilized for constructing the signatures and electronic envelopes described in PKSC #7. In particular, PKCS #1 defines an encryption scheme based on the optimal asymmetric encryption padding (OAEP) of Bellare and Rogaway [124]. PKCS #2 and #4 have been incorporated in PKCS #1.

PKCS #3 defines the key exchange protocol using the Diffie–Hellman algorithm.

PKCS #5 describes a method for encrypting an information using a secret key derived from a password. For hashing, the method utilizes either MD2 or MD5 to compute the key starting with the password, and then encrypts the key with DES in the CBC mode.

PKCS #6 is a syntax for X.509 certificates.

PKCS #7 (RFC 2315 [125]) defines the syntax of a message encrypted using the Basic Encoding Rules (BER) of ASN.1 [126] of ITU-T Recommendation X.209 [127]. These messages are formed with the help of six content types:

1. *Data,* for clear data
2. *SignedData,* for signed data
3. *EnvelopedData,* for clear data with numeric envelopes
4. *SignedAndEnvelopedData,* for data that are signed and enveloped
5. *DigestedData,* for digests
6. *EncryptedData,* for encrypted data

The secure messaging protocol, Secure Multipurpose Internet Mail Extensions (S/MIME), as well as the messages of the SET protocol, designed to secure bankcard payments over the Internet utilize the PKSC #7 specifications.

PKCS #8 describes a format for sending information related to private keys.

PKCS #9 defines the optional attributes that could be added to other protocols of the series. The following items are considered: the certificates of PKCS #6, the electronically signed messages of PKCS #7, and the information on private keys as defined in PKCS #8.

PKCS #10 (RFC 2896 [128]) describes the syntax for certification requests to a certification authority. The certification request must contain details on the identity of the candidate for certification, the distinguished name of the candidate, his or her public key, and optionally, a list of supplementary attributes, a signature of the preceding information to verify the public key, and an identifier of the algorithm used for the signature so that the authority could proceed with the necessary verifications. The version adopted by the IETF is called Cryptographic Message Syntax (CMS).

PKCS #11 defines a cryptographic interface, called *Cryptoki* (Cryptographic Token Interface Standard), between portable devices such as smart cards or PCMCIA cards and the security layers.

PKCS #12 describes a syntax for the storage and transport of public keys, certificates, and other user's secrets. Microsoft utilizes this syntax in the new version of NT Server 5.0.

PKCS #13 describes a cryptographic system using elliptic curves.

PKCS #15 describes a format to allow the portability of cryptographic credentials such as keys, certificates, passwords, PINs, among application and among portable devices such as smart cards. (*Notes:* (1) Even though the specifications of PKCS #1, #7, and 10 have been described in IETF documents, this organization has not accepted them as standards because they mandate the utilization of algorithms that RSADSI does not offer free of charge. (2) In PKCS #11 and #15, the word *token* is used to indicate a *portable device capable of storing persistent data.*)

AllI.3   Pretty Good Privacy

PGP is considered to be the commercial system whose security is closest to military grade. It is described in one of the IETF documents, namely, RFC 1991 [129]. PGP consists of six functions:

1. A public key exchange using RSA with MD5 hashing.

2. A data compression with ZIP, which reduces the file size and redundancies before encryption. Reduction of the size augments the speed for both processing and transmission, while reduction of the redundancies makes cryptanalysis more difficult.

3. Message encryption with IDEA.

4. Encryption of the user's secret key using the digest of a sentence instead of a password.

5. An ASCII "armor" is used to protect the binary message for any mutilations that might be caused by Internet messaging systems. This armor is constructed by dividing the bits of three consecutive octets into four groups of 6 bits each and then by coding each group using a 7-bit character according to a given table. A checksum is then added to detect potential errors;

6. Message segmentation.

Although the IETF has worked on PGP, it has not adopted PGP as a standard yet because it incorporates protocols that have patent protections, such as IDEA and RSA. Current activities in the IETF attempt to use the framework of PGP, but with protocols that circumvent these restrictions.

AIII.4 Elliptic Curve Cryptography

Elliptic curves have been studied in algebraic geometry and number theory. They have been applied in factoring integers, in primality proving, in coding theory, and in cryptography [130]. Elliptic curve cryptography (ECC) is a public key cryptosystem where the computations take place on an elliptic curve. These cryptosystems are variants of the Diffie–Hellman and DSA algorithms, thereby giving rise to the Elliptic Curve Diffie–Hellman algorithm (ECDH) and the Elliptic Curve Digital Signal Algorithm (ECDSA), respectively. They can be used to create digital signatures and to establish keys for symmetric cryptography. The ECDSA algorithm is now an ANSI standard (X9.62) [131].

The elliptic curves are defined over the finite field of the integers modulo a primary number p (the Gallois field GF(p)) or that of binary polynomials (GF(2^m)). The key size is the size of the prime number or the binary polynomial in bits. Cryptosystems over GF(2^m) appear to be slower than over GF(p), but there is no consensus on that point. Their main advantage, however, is that additions over GF(2^m) do not require integer multiplications, which reduces the cost of the integrated circuits implementing the computations.

ECDSA is used for digital signing, while ECDH can be used to secure on-line key exchange. Perfect forward secrecy is achieved with the ephemeral mode of ECDH, i.e., the key is short-term. Diffie–Hellman and ECDH are comparable in speed, but RSA is much slower because of the generation of the key pair.

Typical key sizes are in the range 160 to 200 bits. The advantage of elliptic curve cryptography is that key lengths are shorter than for existing public key schemes that provide equivalent security. For example, the level of security of 1024-bit RSA can be achieved will elliptic curves with a key size in the range of 171–180 bits [132]. This is an important factor in wireless communications and whenever bandwidth is a scarce resource.

Table AIII.1 gives various computations times for digital signatures with RSA, DSA, and ECDSA on a 200-MHz Pentium Pro [133]. The results show that RSA is slower for signing and much faster for signature verification than DSA and ECDSA. Thus, from a

Table AIII.1   Computation Times for Digital Signatures with the RSA, DSA, and ECDSA Algorithms [133]

Operation	Timings in ms (on a 200-MHz Pentium Pro)		
	RSA with $N = 1024$ and $e = 3$	DSA with 1024 bits	ECDSA over GF(p) with 168 bits
Sign	43	7	5
Verify	0.6	27	19
Key generation	1100	7	17
Parameter generation	0	6500	High

Table AIII.2   Comparison of Public Key Systems in Terms of Key Length in Bits for the Same Security Level [130]

RSA	Elliptic Curve	Reduction Factor RSA/ECC
512	106	5:1
1024	160	7: 1
2048	211	10:1
5120	320	16:1
21000	600	35:1

computational speed viewpoint, RSA is more suitable for certificate verification, while Diffie–Hellman, ECDH, and ECDSA are more suitable for on-line communication.

Finally, Table AIII.2 compares the key lengths of RSA and elliptic cryptography for the same amount of security measured in terms of effort to break the system [130].

APPENDIX IV: PRINCIPLES OF THE DIGITAL SIGNATURE ALGORITHM

According to the DSA defined in ANSI X9.30:1 [1], the signature of a message M is the pair of numbers r and s computed as follows:

$$r = (g^k \bmod p) \bmod q$$

and

$$s = \{k^{-1}[H(\mathrm{M}) + xr]\} \bmod q,$$

where

- p and q are primes such that $2^{511} < \mathrm{p} < 2^{1024}$, $2^{159} < q < 2^{160}$, and q is a prime divisor of $(p-1)$, i.e., $(p-1) = mq$ for some integer m.
- $g = h^{(p-1)/q} \bmod p$ is a generator polynomial modulo p of order q, with h any integer $1 < h < (p-1)$ such that $h^{(p-1)/q} \bmod p > 1$. By Fermat's little theorem, $g^q = h^{(p-1)/q} \bmod p = 1$, since $g < p$. Thus, each time the exponent is a multiple of q, the result will be equal to 1 (mod p).

- x and k are randomly generated integers between 0 and q (i.e., $0 < x, k < q$).
- x is the private key of the sender, while the public key y is given by $y = g^x \bmod p$.
- k^{-1} is the multiplicative inverse of $k \bmod q$, i.e., $(k^{-1} \times k) \bmod q = 1$, where $0 < k, k^{-1} < q$.
- $H(\ )$ is the SHA-1 hash function.

To verify the signature the verifier computes

$$w = s^{-1} \bmod q$$

$$u_1 = H(M)\, w \bmod q$$

$$u_2 = rw \bmod q$$

$$v = (g^{u_1}\, y^{u_2} \bmod p) \bmod q$$

If $v = r$, the signature is valid.
To show this we have:

$$
\begin{aligned}
v &= \{(g^{[H(M)w \bmod q]}\, y^{rw \bmod q}) \bmod p\} \bmod q \\
&= (g^{[H(M)w \bmod q]}\, g^{xrw \bmod q}) \bmod p\} \bmod q \\
&= \{g^{[H(M)+xr]w \bmod q]} \bmod p\} \bmod q \\
&= (g^{ksw \bmod q} \bmod p) \bmod q \\
&= (g^{k \bmod q} \bmod p) \bmod q \\
&= (g^{k} \bmod p) \bmod q, \text{ since the generator is of order } q \text{ by construction,} \\
&= r
\end{aligned}
$$

Note that the random variable k is also transmitted with the signature. This means that if the verifier knows the signer's private key, they will be able to pass additional information through the channel established through the value of k.

REFERENCES

1. ANSI X9.30:1, "American National Standard—Public Key Cryptography for the Financial Services Industry: Part 1: The Digital Signature Algorithm (DSA)" (Revision of X9.30:1-1995), American Bankers Association, 1997.

2. ITU, *Management Framework for Open Systems Interconnection for CCITT Applications,* Recommendation X.700, 1992.

3. ITU, *Security Architecture for Open Systems Interconnection for CCITT Applications,* Recommendation X.800, 1991.

4. S. Covaci, L. Marchisio, and D. J. Milham, "Trouble Ticketing X Interfaces for International Private Leased Data Circuits and International Freephone Service," in *Proceedings of the IEEE Network Operations and Management Symposium (NOMS'98),* vol. 2, pp. 342–353, February 1998.

5. D. J. Milham, C. Hatch, A. Hensen, S.-T. Johnsen, and R. Moons, "European ATM Service Introduction—OSS Interconnection Between Operators," in *Proceedings of IEEE Network Operations and Management Symposium (NOMS 2000),* pp. 247–260, 2000.

6. ITU, *Architecture for Customer Network Management Service for Public Data Networks,* Recommendation X.160, 1996.

7. ITU, *Definition of Customer Network Management Service for Public Data Networks,* Recommendation X.161, 1997.

8. ITU, *Definition of Management Information for Customer Network Management Service for Public Data Networks to be Used with the CNMc Interface,* Recommendation X.162, 1996.

9. M. H. Sherif and S. Ho, "Evolution of Operation Support Systems in Public Data Networks," in *Proceedings of the 5th IEEE Symposium on Computers and Communications ISCC2000,* Antibes-Juan Les Pins, France, pp. 72–77, July 2000.

10. ISO/IEC TR 13335-5, *Information Technology—Guidelines for the Management of IT Security—Part 5: Management Guidance on Network Security,* 2001.

11. ITU, *Information Technology—Open Systems Interconnection—The Directory: Public-key and Attribute Certificate Frameworks,* Recommendation X.509 (ISO/IEC 9594-8), 2000.

12. ISO 7498-2, *Information Technology*—Open Systems Interconnection—Basic Reference Model—Part 2: Security Architecture, 1989.

13. R. W. Baldwin and, C. V. Chang, "Locking the e-Safe," *IEEE Spectrum,* vol. 34, no. 2, pp. 40–46, 1997.

14. C. E. Perkins, *Mobile IP: Design Principles and Practices,* Addison-Wesley, Reading, Massachusetts, 1998.

15. W. Ford and B. O'Higgins, "Public-key Cryptography and Open Systems Interconnection," *IEEE Communications Magazine,* vol. 39, no. 7, pp. 30–35, 1992.

16. S. E. Forrester, M. J. Palmer, D. C. McGlaughlin, and M. J. Robinson, "Security in Data Networks," *BT Technol. J.,* vol. 16, no. 1, pp. 52–75, 1998.

17. P. Rolin, "La sécurité dans les réseaux," in *Réseaux de Communication et Conception de Protocoles,* G. Juanole, A. Sehrouchni, and D. Seret, Eds., Hermès, Paris, pp. 80–103, 1995.

18. A. O. Freier, P. Karlton, and P. C. Kocher, "The SSL Protocol Version 3.0," available at http://www.netscape.com/PROD/eng/ssl3/ssl-toc.html, 1996.

19. T. Dierks and C. Allen, "The TLS Protocol Version 1.0," IETF RFC 2246, January 1999.

20. T. S. Messerges, E. A. Dabbish, and R. H. Sloan, "Investigations of Power Analysis Attacks on Smartcard," in *Proceedings of USENIX Workshop on Smartcard Technology,* Chicago, pp. 151–161, May 1999.

21. W. Simpson, "The Point-to-Point Protocol (PPP)," IETF RFC 1661, July 1994.

22. W. Townsley, A. Valencia, A Rubens, G. Pall, G. Zorn, and B. Palter, "Layer Two Tunneling Protocol L2TP," IETF RFC 2661, August 1999.

23. S. Kent and R. Atkinson, "Security Architecture for the Internet Protocol," IETF RFC 2401, November 1998.

24. S. Kent and R. Atkinson, "IP Authentication Header," IETF RFC 2402, November 1998.

25. S. Kent and R. Atkinson, "IP Encapsulating Security Payload (ESP)," IETF RFC 2406, November 1998.

26. D. Piper, "The Internet IP Security Domain of Interpretation for ISAKMP," IETF RFC 2407, November 1998.

27. D. Maughan, M. Schertler, M. Schneider, and J. Turner, "Internet Security Association and Key Management Protocol (ISAKMP)," IETF RFC 2408, November 1998.

28. D. Harkins and D. Carrel, "The Internet Key Exchange (IKE)," IETF RFC 2409, November 1998.

29. P. Glenn and S. Kent, "The NULL Encryption Algorithm and Its Use with IPSEC," IETF RFC 2410, November 1998.

30. R. Thayer, N. Doraswamy, R. Glenn, "IP Security Document Roadmap," IETF RFC 2411, November 1998.

31. H. Orman, "The OAKLEY Key Determination Protocol," IETF RFC 2412, November 1998.

32. C. Huitema, *IPv6: The New Internet Protocol,* Prentice Hall, Englewood Cliffs, New Jersey, 1996.

33. N. Doraswamy and D. Harkins, *IPSec: The New Security Standard for the Internet, Intranets, and Virtual Private Networks,* Prentice Hall, Upper Saddle River, New Jersey, 1999.

34. B. Patel, B. Adoba, W. Dixon, G. Zorn, and S. Booth, "Securing L2TP using IPsec," IETF RFC 3193, November 2001.

35. A. Carasik, "Secure Shell FAQ," Revision 1.4, http://www.tigerlair.com/ssh/faq, February 2001.

36. T. Ylönen, "The SSH (Secure Shell) Remote login Protocol," http://www.tigerlair.com/ssh/faq/ssh1-draft.txt, November 1995.

37. T. Ylönen, "SSH- Secure login Connections over the Internet," in *Proceedings of the Sixth USENIX Security Symposium,* pp. 37–42, 1996.

38. ATM Forum Technical Committee, "Methods for Securely Managing ATM Network Elements—Implementation Agreement," AF-SEC-0179.000, Version 1.0, April 2002.

39. B. Schneier, *Applied Cryptography,* John Wiley & Sons, New York, second edition, 1996.

40. A. J. Menezes, P. C. van Oorschot, and S. A. Vanstone *Handbook of Applied Cryptography,* CRC Press, Boca Raton, Florida, 1997.

41. ANSI X3.92, "American National Standard—Data Encryption Algorithm (DEA)," 1981.

42. ANSI X3.105, "American National Standard—Data link encryption," 1983.

43. ANSI X3.106, "American National Standard—Data Encryption Algorithm, Modes of Operations," 1983.

44. ISO 8372, *Information processing—Modes of Operation for a 64-bit Block Cipher Algorithm,* 1987.

45. X. Lai, J. Massey, and S. Murphy, "Markov Ciphers and Differential Cryptanalysis," in *Proceedings of Eurocrypt'91,* LNCS 547, Springer-Verlag, Berlin, pp. 17–38, 1991.

46. X. Lai and J. Massey, "A Proposal for a New Block Encryption Standard," in *Proceedings of Eurocrypt'90,* LNCS 473, Springer-Verlag, Berlin, pp. 389–404, 1991.

47. R. L. Rivest, "The RCE Encryption Algorithm," *Crypto Bytes,* vol. 1, no. 1, pp. 9–11. 1995.

48. ANSI X9.52, "American National Standard—Triple Data Encryption Algorithm Modes of Operation," 1998.

49. W. Diffie and M. E. Hellman, "New Directions in Cryptography," *IEEE Transactions on Information Theory,* vol. 22, no. 6, pp. 644–654, 1976.

50. R. L. Rivest, A. Shamir, and L. M. Adleman, "A Method for Obtaining Digital Signatures and Public Key Cryptosystems," *Communications of the ACM,* vol. 21, no. 2, pp. 120–126, 1978.

51. R. Rivest, "The MD4 Message Digest Algorithm," IETF RFC 1320, April 1992.

52. R. Rivest, "The MD5 Message Digest Algorithm," IETF RFC 1321, April 1992.

53. ISO/IEC 10118-3, *Information Technology—Security Techniques—Hash-Functions—Part 3: Dedicated Hash-Functions,* 1998.

54. H. Dobbertin, A. Bosselaers, and B. Preneel, "RIPEMD-160: A Strengthened Vervion of RIPMD," in *Proceedings of Fast Software Encryption Workshops,* LNCS 1039, Springer-Verlag, Berlin, pp. 71–82, 1996.

55. ANSI X9.30:2, "American National Standard—Public Key Cryptography for the Financial Services Industry: Part 2: The Secure Hash Algorithm 1 (SHA-1)," (Revised), American Bankers Association, 1993.

56. P. van Oorschot and M. Wiener, "Parallel Collision Search with Applications to Hash Func-

tions and Discrete Logarithms," in *Proceedings of 2nd ACM Conference on Computer and Communications Security,* pp. 210–218, November 1994.

57. T. ElGamal, "A Public-Key Cryptosystem and a Signature Scheme Based on Discrete Logarithms," in *Advances in Cryptology—CRYPTO'84 Proceedings,* Springer-Verlag, Berlin, pp. 10–18, 1985.

58. B. Kaliski and J. Staddon, "PKCS #1: RSA Cryptography Specifications Version 2.0," IETF RFC 2437, October 1998.

59. P. Chaum, "Blind Signatures for Untraceable Payments," in *Crypto82,* Plenum Press, New York, pp. 199–203, 1983.

60. P. Chaum, "Privacy Protected Payments: Unconditional Payer and/or Payee Untraceability," in *SmartCard 2000,* D. Chaum and J. Schaumüler-Bichl, Eds., Elsevier Science Publishers B.V. (North Holland), Amsterdam, pp. 69–93, 1989.

61. M. Bellare, R. Canetti, and H. Krawczyk, "Keying Hash Functions for Message Authentication," in *Advances in Cryptology—CRYPTO'96 Proceedings,* Springer-Verlag, Berlin, pp. 1–15, 1996.

62. H. Krawczyk, M. Bellare, and R. Canetti, "HMAC: Keyed-Hashing for Message Authentication," IETF RFC 2104, February 1997.

63. S. A. Sherman, R. Skibom, and R. S. Murray, "Secure Network Access Using Multiple Applications of AT&T's Smart Card," *AT&T Technical Journal,* pp. 61–72, September/October 1994.

64. S. Nanavati, M. Thieme, and R. Nanavati, *Biometrics: Identity Verification in a Network World,* John Wiley & Sons, New York, 2002.

65. ANSI X9.84 "American National Standard—Biometric Information Management and Security," 2001.

66. ITU, *Information Technology—Open Systems Interconnection—The Directory: Overview of Concepts, Models and Services,* Recommendation X.500 (ISO/IEC 9594-1), 2001.

67. ITU, *Information Technology—Open Systems Interconnection—Security Architecture for Open Systems: Authentication Framework,* Recommendation X.811 (ISO/IEC 10181-3), 1995.

68. ITU, *Information Technology—Open Systems Interconnection—Security Architecture for Open Systems: Access Control Framework,* Recommendation X.812 (ISO/IEC 10181-3), 1995.

69. C. Rigney, S. Willens, A. Rubens, and W. Simpson, "Remote Authentication Dial In User Service (RADIUS)," IETF RFC 2865, June 2000.

70. C. Finseth, "An Access Control Protocol, Sometimes Called TACACS," IETF RFC 1492, July 1993.

71. J. Hill, "An Analysis of the RADIUS Authentication Protocol," http://www.untruth.org/~josh/security/radisu/radisu-auth.html, 2001.

72. R. K. C. Chang, "Defending Against Flooding-based Distributed Denial-of-Service Attack: A Tutorial," *IEEE Communications Magazine,* vol. 40, no. 10, pp. 42–51, 2002.

73. D. Moore, G. M. Voelker, and S. Savage, "Inferring Internet Denial-of-Service Activity," in *Proceedings of the 10th USENIX Security Symposium,* Washington, D.C., August 2001.

74. M. H. Sherif, G. R. Ash, and J. Han, "Transparent Processing of Resource Management (RM) Cells that Are Not Defined in ATM-TM-011–21.00, I.371, or I.361," ATM Forum Contribution 00–479, Phoenix, Arizona, January 2001.

75. C. L. Schuba, I. V. Krsul, M. G. Kuhn, E. H. Spafford, A. Sundaram, and D. Zamboni, "Analysis of a Denial of Service Attack on TCP," in *Proceedings of IEEE Symposium on Security and Privacy,* pp. 208–223, 1997.

76. D. E. Comer, *Interworking with TCP/IP Vol I: Principles, Protocols, and Architecture,* Prentice Hall, Englewood Cliffs, New Jersey, third edition, 1995.

77. *CERT® Advisory CA-2001-19 "Code Red" Worm Exploiting Buffer Overflow in IIS Indexing*

Service DLL, CERT/CC CA-2001-19, last revised January 17, 2002; available at http://www.cert.org/advisories/CA-2001-19.html.

78. A. Juels, and J. Brainard, "A Cryptographic Countermeasure Against Connection Depletion Attacks," in *Proceedings of the Internet Society Symposium on Network and Distributed System Security,* S. Kent, Ed., IEEE Computer Society Press, New York, pp. 151–165, 1999 (also available on www.rsasecurity.com).

79. ITU, *Security Architecture for Open Systems: Non-Repudiation Framework,* Recommendation X.813 (ISO/IEC 10181-3), 1995.

80. W. Fumer and P. Landrock, "Principles of Key Management," *IEEE Journal on Selected Areas in Communications,* vol. 11, no. 5, pp. 785–793, 1993.

81. B. C. Neuman and T. Ts'o, "Kerberos: An Authentication Service for Computer Networks," *IEEE Communications. Magazine,* vol. 32, no. 9, pp. 33–38, 1994.

82. M. A. Sirbu and J. C.-I. Chuang, "Distributed Authentication in Kerberos Using Public Key Cryptography," 1996; available at http://www.cs.cmu.edut/afs/andrew.cmu.edu/inst/ini.

83. M. Sirbu and J. Chuang, "Public-Key Based Ticket Granting Service in Kerberos," IETF RFC 1510, May, 1996.

84. B. Tung, *Kerberos: A Network Authentication System,* Addison Wesley Longman, Reading, Massachusetts, 1999.

85. W. A. Simpson, "IKE/ISAMP Considered Harmful," *;login:* vol. 24, no. 6, 48–58, 1999.

86. H. Krawczyk, "SKEME: A Versatile Secure key Exchange Mechanism for Internet," in *Proceedings of the Internet Society Symposium on Network and Distributed System Security,* IEEE Computer Society Press, New York, pp. 114–127, 1996.

87. P.-C. Cheng, "An Architecture for the Internet Key Exchange Protocol," *IBM Systems Journal,* vol. 40, no. 3, pp. 721–746, 2001.

88. R. Housley, P. Yee, and W. Nace, "Encryption Using KEA and SKIPJACK," IETF RFC 2773, February 2000.

89. R. Housley, T. Horting and P. Yee, "TELNET Authentication Using KEA and SKIPJAK," IETF RFC 2951, September 2000.

90. S. L. Garfinkel, *PGP: Pretty Good Privacy,* O'Reilly and Associates, Sebastopol, California, 1995.

91. ANSI X9.57, "American National Standard—Public Key Cryptography for the Financial Services Industry: Certificate Management" (Revision of X9.57-1995), 1997.

92. W. Ford and M. S. Baum, *Secure Electronic Commerce: Building the Infrastructure,* Prentice Hall, Englewood Cliffs, New Jersey, 1997.

93. ITU, *Information Technology—Open Systems Interconnection—The Directory: Models,* Recommendation X.501 (ISO/IEC 9594-2), 2001.

94. ITU, *Information Technology—Open Systems Interconnection—The Directory: Overview of Concepts, Models and Services,* Recommendation X.511 (ISO/IEC 9594-3), 2001.

95. ITU, *Information Technology—Open Systems Interconnection—The Directory: Selected Attribute Types,* Recommendation X.520 (ISO/IEC 9594-6), 2001.

96. ITU, *Information Technology—Open Systems Interconnection—The Directory: Selected Object Classes,* Recommendation X.521 (ISO/IEC 9594-7), 2001.

97. ITU, *Information Technology—Open Systems Interconnection—The Directory: Protocol Specifications,* Recommendation X.519 (ISO/IEC 9594-5), 2001.

98. ITU, *Information Technology—Open Systems Interconnection—The Directory: Procedures for Distributed Operation,* Recommendation X.518 (ISO/IEC 9594-4), 2001.

99. ITU, *Information Technology—Open Systems Interconnection—The Directory: Replication,* Recommendation X.525 (ISO/IEC 9594-9), 2001.

100. ANSI T1.252, "Operations, Administration, Maintenance and Provisioning (OAM&P)—Security for the Telecommunications Management Network Directory," 1996.

101. M. Whal, T. Howes, and S. Kille, "Lightweight Directory Access Protocol (v3)," IETF RFC 2251, December 1997.

102. M. Wahl, H. Alvestrand, J. Hodges, and R. Morgan, "Authentication Methods for LDAP," IETF RFC 2829, May 2000.

103. J. Myers, "Simple Authentication and Security Layer (SASL)," IETF RFC 2222, October 1997.

104. R. Housley and P. Hoffman, "Internet X.509 Public Key Infrastructure—Operational Protocols: FTP and HTTP)," IETF RFC 2585, May 1999.

105. W. Burr, D. Dodson, N. Nazaria, and W. T. Polk, "MISPC—Minimum Interoperability Specifications for PKI Components," Version 1, September 1997.

106. J. Feigenbaum, "Towards an Infrastructure for Authorization," in *Proceedings of Invited Talks on Public Key Infrastructure, 3rd USENIX Workshop on Electronic Commerce,* pp. 15–19, August/September 1998.

107. D. W, Chadwick and A. Ottenko, "RBAC Policies in XML for X.509 Based Privilege Management," in *Security in the Information Society: Visions and Perspectives, Proceedings of IFIP/SEC2002,* Kluwer Academic Publishers, Norwell, Massachusetts, pp. 39–53, 2002.

108. N. Simoni and S. Znaty, *Gestion de réseau et de service: Similitude des concepts, spécificité des solutions,* InterEditions (Masson), Paris, 1997.

109. U. Blumenthal and B. Wijnen, "User-Based Security Model (USM) for Version 3 of the Simple Network Management Protocol (SNMPv3)," IETF RFC 2274, January 1998.

110. M. Rozenblit, *Security for Telecommunications Network Management,* IEEE Press, New York, 2000.

111. B. Wijnen, R. Presuhn and K. McCloghrie, "View-Based Access Control Model (VACM) for the Simple Network Management Protocol (SNMPv3)," IETF RFC 2275, January 1998.

112. H. E. Hia, "Examining How Secured SNMP Network Management Consumes Network Resources," http://filebox.vt.edu/users/hhia/SNMP-IPSec-Tests.htm, 2000.

113. M. Abadi and R. Needham, "Prudent Engineering Practice for Cryptographic Protocols," *IEEE Transactions on Software Engineering,* vol. 22, no. 1, pp. 6–15, 1996.

114. K. Fu, E. Sit, K. Smith, and N. Feamster, "Dos and Don'ts of Client Authentication on the Web," available at http://cookies.lcs.mit.edu, 2001 (a shorter version was published in the *Proceedings of the 10th USENIX Security Symposium,* Washington, D.C., August 2001).

115. B. Schneier, "Why Cryptography is Harder than it Looks," available at http://www.counterpane.com/whycrypt.html, 1996.

116. B. Schneier, "Security piftalls in cryptology," available at http://www.counterpane.com/pitfalls.html, 1998.

117. D. Kristol and L. Montulli, "HTTP State Management Mechanism," IETF RFC 2109, February 1997.

118. ANSI X9.9, "American National Standard—Financial Institution Message Authentication (Wholesale)" (Revision of X9.9-1982), American Bankers Association, 1986.

119. ANSI X9.19, "American National Standard—Financial Institution Retail Message Authentication," American Bankers Association, 1986.

120. ISO 8731-1, *Banking—Approved Algorithms for Message Authentication—Part 1:DEA,* 1987.

121. ISO/IEC 9797, *Information Technology—Security Techniques—Data Integrity Mechanism 2 1ing a Cryptographic Check Function Employing a Block Cipher Algorithm,* 1993.

122. J. Nechvatal, E. Baker, L. Bassham, W. Burr, M. Dworkin, J. Foti, and E. Roback, *Report on the Development of the Advanced Encryption Standard (AES),* National Institute of Standards and Technology, October 2000.

123. D. Boneh and H. Shacham, "Fast Variants of RSA," *CryptoBytes,* vol. 5, no. 1, pp. 1–9, 2002; available at http://www.rsa.com/rsalabs/pubs/cryptobytes.html.

124. M. Bellare and P. Rogaway, "Optimal Asymmetric Encryption—How to Encrypt with RSA," in *Advances in Cryptology—Eurocrypt'94, Workshop on the Theory and Application of Cryptographic Techniques,* A. DeSantis, Ed., *Lecture Notes in Computer Science,* Springer-Verlag, Berlin, pp. 92–111, 1995.

125. B. Kaliski, "PKCS #7: Cryptographic Message Syntax Version 1.5," IETF RFC 2315, March 1998.

126. D. Steedman, *Abstract Syntax Notation One ASN.1: The Tutorial and Reference,* Technology Appraisals, Twickenham, U.K., 1993.

127. ITU, *Specifications of Basic Encoding Rules for Abstract Syntax Notation One (ASN.1),* Recommendation X.209, 1988.

128. M. Nystrom and B. Kaliski, "PKCS #10: Certification Request Syntax Specification, Version 1.7," IETF RFC 2986, November 2000.

129. D. Atkins, W. Stallings, and P. Zimmerman, "PGP Message Exchange Formats," IETF RFC 1991, August 1996.

130. A. Menezes, *Elliptic Curve Public Key Cryptosystems,* Kluwer Academic Publishing, Boston, 1993.

131. ANSI X9.62, "American National Standard for Financial Services- Public Key Cryptography for the Financial Services Industry: The Elliptic Curve Digital Signature Algorithm (ECDSA)," American Bankers Association, 1998.

132. M. J. Wiener, "Performance Comparison of Public-key Cryptosystems," *CryptoBytes,* vol. 4, no. 1, pp. 1–5, 1998; available at http://www.rsa.com/rsalabs/pubs/cryptobytes.html.

133. G. B. Agnew, "Cryptography, Data Security, and Applications to C-commerce," in *Electronic Commerce Technology Trends: Challenges and Opportunities,* W. Kou and Y. Yesha, Eds., IBM Press, pp. 69–85, 2000.

CHAPTER 6

THE FUTURE OPTICAL INTERNET

ANDREA FUMAGALLI, JAVIER ARACIL, AND LUCA VALCARENGHI

6.1 INTRODUCTION

As of today, the Internet is the most versatile and widespread form of (virtually) free public telecommunication service. Beside constituting the universal bridge between continental, national, regional, and local networks, the term Internet has become the synonym of email, World Wide Web (WWW) surfing, *multimedia applications,* and many other services.

The Internet finds its origins in two U.S. government funded research networks, namely ARPANET (late 1960s) and NSFNET (middle 1980s). By the late 1980s, a number of subnetworks worldwide (e.g., the European IP backbone EuropaNET and EBONE [1,2]) were connected to these two networks. While the Internet transport and network layer protocols are still based on the original TCP/IP suite, developed in 1974 [3,4], evolution of the transmission medium technologies has radically changed the so-called *Internet link layer* (i.e., the physical and link layer of the ISO-OSI model). Early ARPANET and NSFNET connections were running on lines leased from telephone companies at a transmission rate of 56 kb/s. With the advent of low-loss fiber-based links, transmission rates were upgraded to 45 Mb/s. It is only during the latest few years that the combined skyrocketing increase in the number of Internet users and the augmented number of services available on the Internet have created an unprecedented demand for additional bandwidth, whose exponential growth in the long run can only be coped with by the latest advances in optical technology. These advances include *wavelength division multiplexing,* or (*WDM*), which potentially provides a per-fiber aggregate bandwidth in the Tb/s range. The impact

This work was supported in part by the NSF under contract # ANI-0082085.

of such a revolution in Internet history is so widely recognized that a name has been created to indicate the outcome of such modernization of the Internet: the *next-generation Internet* (*NGI*). Since it is commonly recognized that the NGI originates from the high transmission bandwidth provided by the optical medium, in the rest of the chapter the terms NGI and *Optical Internet* (OI) will be used interchangeably.

The aim of this chapter is to describe the basic principles of the OI and to identify its potential benefits and design challenges. The chapter consists of four sections.

Section 6.2 describes the optical layer and presents some of the enabling optical components. The concepts of first-generation optical network (FGON) (e.g., SONET/SDH) and second-generation optical network (SGON) (e.g., WDM) are introduced. In the latter case optical circuits, or lightpaths, are established between network nodes to create all-optical transparent connections, and thus to circumvent the so-called electronic bottleneck of FGON. Four alternative approaches for designing SGON are described: static and semistatic lightpath-based networks, dynamic lightpath-based networks, optical packet-switching-based networks, and optical burst switching based networks.

Section 6.3 illustrates the evolution of the Internet layering from the X.25-based solution to IP over ATM, packet over SONET (POS), and Gigabit Ethernet. Network performance, complexity, and costs of these solutions are discussed and compared with one another, with the intent to identify efficient mechanisms to transport IP packets over the optical layer. The simplified two-layer architecture known as "IP over WDM" is then presented. Flow-switching solutions, such as MPLS and multiprotocol lambda switching (MPλS or generalized MPLS) are described that allow management of the WDM layer from the IP layer using standard mechanisms and protocols.

Section 6.4 discusses the impact of traffic self-similarity on the optical network engineering process. In particular, the huge bandwidth potentially available in optical fiber poses new challenges, e.g., efficient network dimensioning, which are of no concern in the conventional relatively "low speed" Internet scenario. A thorough analysis at the TCP connection level is provided in this section with the scope of determining efficient ways to manage the optical bandwidth dynamically.

Section 6.5 identifies some of the key challenges encountered in the realization of the OI. The challenges reviewed in this last section include efficient traffic engineering in the OI, adequate network resilience schemes at both the IP layer and WDM layer, and coordination between resilience schemes available at both the IP and the WDM layer.

6.2 OPTICAL NETWORK TECHNOLOGIES

Since its dawn in the 1960s [5], fiber optics technology has undergone a continuous evolution, with innovative devices becoming available on the market on a yearly basis. As illustrated in this section, the advent of these devices has fostered the development of optical networks and their evolution from first- to second-generation architectures. An overview of the key enabling optical components is first presented, followed by a description of a number of alternative network architectures based on such components. The description of the components is kept at a high level, giving the reader a global picture, rather than providing a comprehensive description of each single component. The reader who may be interested in details of specific optical components is referred to a number of comprehensive books on the subject [5–11].

6.2.1 Optical Components

Discovery, in the 1960s, that an inexpensive thin wire of glass is capable of propagating a huge quantity of data with small signal attenuation paved the way to a long—still lasting—revolution in the way telecommunications and data networks are designed.

Fiber optics is a transmission medium made of silica (SiO_2) in which the optical signal remains confined and guided by total internal reflection. Internal reflection is achieved by means of a two-region section of the fiber: the core and the cladding. The two regions are differently doped (by means of injected impurities), leading to different refractive indices. As a result, the light beam in the core that propagates with an angle of incidence higher than the critical angle—with respect to the boundary surface between the two regions—is completely reflected and confined within the core. Fiber optics can be either *multimode*—when more than one propagation mode is possible—or *single-mode*—when only one mode propagates in the fiber. The former type of fiber is characterized by modal dispersion and low installation cost. The latter does not present modal dispersion and is more expensive to install than the former, due to the accurate signal coupling required between fibers, transmitters and receivers. Typically, three spectral regions, referred to as *windows*, are defined that have low signal attenuation in the fiber. The *first window* is in the 800–900-nm interval range—optical frequencies are conventionally characterized in terms of wavelengths—and it is generally used to transmit multimode signals. The *second* and *third windows* are, respectively, in the 1240–1340-nm and 1500–1650-nm regions, and are typically used to transmit single-mode signals. The bandwidth potentially available in each window is about 20 THz, but the actual bandwidth available for data transmission is considerably less and limited by a number of factors. Among these factors, one can enumerate the limited bandwidth of other optical components, such as transmitters, receivers, and optical amplifiers, and the limited electronic processing speed at the network nodes, the so-called "electronic bottleneck" of the first-generation optical networks.

An optical signal is generated by either a *light-emitting diode* (LED) or a *laser diode* (*laser*). The main difference between LEDs and lasers is the spectral density of the emitted light beam. The LED signal has a large spectrum and is used in conjunction with multimode fiber. LEDs are relatively inexpensive and used in networks with low data rates (e.g., FDDI), short distances, and limited power budget (e.g., LANs, fiber to the home, fiber to the curb, coarse WDM (CWDM), access networks). Instead, the laser emits a light beam with power concentrated in a narrow bandwidth. Its cost grows with its selectivity in bandwidth. Lasers are currently expensive and used in conjunction with single-mode fiber to deploy DWDM systems, in which the wavelength or channel density is high. Lasers can be designed either to operate at one fixed wavelength or to be tunable. In the latter case there is a trade-off between the laser tuning speed and its tuning range, i.e., fast tunable lasers have a small tuning range and vice versa. At the receiver node, *photodetectors* are used to convert the optical signal back into the electronic domain. When the received optical signal is weak, *avalanche photodiodes* (APDs) can be used, in which the reception of a photon generates an avalanche of photons that are easier to detect.

Optical amplifiers became commercially available in the early 1990s to regenerate the optical signal without requiring the two phase O-E-O conversion plus electrical signal amplification that was previously utilized. Without any doubt optical amplifiers constitute one of the most important milestones in the history of optical communications. By avoiding O-E-O conversion, an optical signal can be regenerated directly in the optical domain, thus circumventing the limited bandwidth of electronic circuitry. For example, a single optical amplifier can amplify a number of WDM channels simultaneously, with an aggregate throughput that by far exceeds the electronic maximum bandwidth.

Optical amplifiers can be divided into four categories: semiconductor optical amplifiers (SOAs), x-doped fiber amplifiers (xDFAs), linear optical amplifiers (LOAs), and nonlinear amplifiers (e.g., Raman amplifiers (RAs)). SOAs exploit the same principle used by lasers. An SOA is maintained under the lasing threshold in order to utilize its amplification capabilities without inducing lasing. SOAs can work in both the second and the third spectral window, offering a broadband gain characteristic and a total bandwidth of about 100 nm. Gain fluctuation, polarization dependency, high coupling loss with the fiber, and their inherent nonlinearity represent their main drawbacks. These amplifiers are suitable for single channel amplification. Doped fiber amplifiers consist of a segment of fiber optics that is doped with rare-earth chemical elements. Their behavior is based on the principle of *stimulated emission,* by which the electrons of the doped fiber, stimulated by the arriving signal photons, emit light. As a result, the incoming optical signal is amplified as it propagates through the doped fiber and absorbs the power of a *pump* signal launched into the fiber. Widely used, the *erbium-doped fiber amplifier (EDFA)* [12] is employed in the *short wavelength band (S* = 1450–1530 nm), in the *conventional wavelength band (C* = 1530–1570 nm), and in the *long wavelength band (L* = 1570–1620 nm) of the third spectral window [13]. For example, with a total available bandwidth of about 70 nm, this amplifier can amplify 80 bidirectional channels with 100-GHz spacing (0.8 nm), each transmitting at 10 Gb/s. Interesting properties of EDFA are high gain (e.g., 18 dB fiber-to-fiber), no crosstalk among the amplified channels, small noise figure, and low coupling loss. Its drawbacks are gain fluctuations, which are a function of the channel (wavelength) position in the spectrum, and large physical dimensions. Another doped fiber amplifier is the Praseodymium-Doped Fiber Amplifier (PDFA) that is employed in the second spectral window at 1300 nm. LOAs consist of the integration of an amplifier and a vertical cavity surface emitting laser (VCSEL) [14]. The circulating optical power of the VCSEL overlaps with the amplifier waveguide and permits the optical amplifier maintaining a constant gain to be linearized. They operate across the C wavelength band. LOAs have been shown to have a small gain transient (i.e., low dependence on the number of wavelengths amplified), almost constant BER in the presence of a varying number of amplified wavelengths, and small interchannel crosstalk. These properties make them suitable for metropolitan and access optical networks, where optical amplifiers may need to operate in the presence of dynamic lightpaths that operate at different data rates and are frequently set up and torn down. Nonlinear amplifiers resort to nonlinear effects of the fiber and require high power pump signal(s). In the most common nonlinear amplifier, the RA, the power of the lower wavelength (higher energy) pump is partially transferred to the higher wavelength (lower energy) data signal via excitation of fiber vibrational modes [15]. The pump's wavelength and power determine, respectively, the data wavelengths that are amplified and the amplification gain. The 3-dB gain bandwidth for a single pump RA is about 5 THz (at 1545 nm). To obtain broader gain spectra, multiple pump signals can be used in the same fiber. RAs yield high gain, are polarization independent, have a low noise figure, allow tight channel spacing at high transmission rate (e.g., 40 Gb/s with 100-GHz spacing), and can operate inside and outside the C- and L-bands of the fiber third window.

Another important optical component is the *wavelength* (or frequency) *converter.* A wavelength converter translates the wavelength of an optical signal to a desired value. In its simplest implementation, a wavelength converter consists of an SOA [6]. In this realization the wavelength converter exploits the SOAs gain saturation effect. Two signals at two different wavelengths are launched into the SOA input. One is the data signal whose wavelength is to be converted. The other is a constant signal at high power that is transmitted on the wavelength that the other information-bearing signal must be converted to. The combined power of both signals is chosen to saturate the amplifier. Consequently, the gain experienced by the incoming constant signal is a function of the power on the data signal: intervals with high power in the incoming data signal generate low power intervals in the outgoing (originally constant) signal, and vice versa. As a result, the bit pattern of the information-bearing signal (filtered out at the SOA output) is converted to the other wavelength with a reverse bit coding. With current technology, wavelength converters are expensive components.

The components described so far constitute the building blocks of a point-to-point transmission system. In order to provide networking functionalities, optical nodes must be designed that are able to switch and route the optical signal. Both *optical add/drop multiplexers* (OADMs) and *optical cross connects* (OXCs) belong to this category. An OADM node is capable of extracting one arriving optical signal from the network and replacing it with a newly injected one. While doing so, the other optical signals in the fiber are let through the OADM node unaltered. For example, in a WDM OADM, one wavelength is dropped and added, while the other wavelengths in the fiber are optically routed through the node. An OXC is an optical node that can perform routing functions on optical signals. OXCs can be built in different ways (see [5,7,8]) but their functioning principles remain the same. Depending on their routing capabilities, OXCs are usually subdivided in *fiber optical cross connects* (F-OXC), *wavelength translating optical cross connects* (WT-OXC), and *wavelength routing optical cross connects* (WR-OXC) (see Figures 6.1, 6.2, 6.3, respectively). The F-OXC is able to switch the signals of one entire fiber from the input port to the desired output port. Individual wavelengths can be added and dropped at the F-OXC. A particular implementation of this OXC is based on *microelectromechanical switch* (MEMS) [13,16–18]. The WT-OXCs and the WR-OXCs are able to switch both single fibers and single wavelengths from the input to the desired output. In the WT-OXC (WR-OXC) the wavelength of the incoming optical signal can (cannot) be converted. Recently *waveband cross connect* (WBXC) have been proposed [19]. WBXCs permit transparent switching an aggregated set of wavelengths (*wavebands*) that share the same links along part of their paths. Switching wavebands reduces the complexity of OXCs [20] but increases the complexity of routing and wavelength assignment algorithms. The configu-

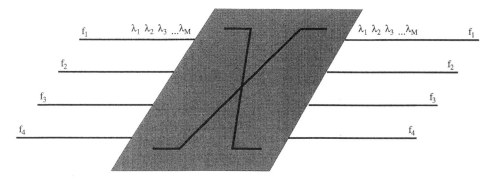

Figure 6.1 F-OXC.

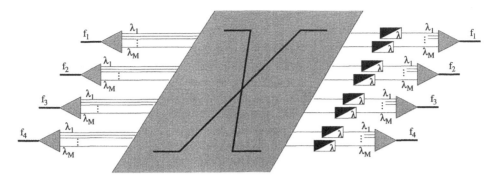

Figure 6.2 WT-OXC.

ration of an OXC can be either fixed or dynamically changed by means of an (electronic) controller (in the latter case, the component is more commonly referred to as an "optical switch").

As already mentioned, the system obtained by interconnecting the aforementioned optical components is not a mere point-to-point transport medium anymore. It presents characteristics and functions that are typical of the network layer of the ISO/OSI model. Thus, the all-optical networks (or second-generation optical networks) offer networking, multiplexing, and transport capabilities altogether. These functions have been standardized by the ITU-T to form a layered model, referred to as the Optical Layer (OL).

6.2.2 The Optical Layer

In its Recommendation G.872 [21], the ITU-T describes the functional architecture of the *optical transport network* (OTN) commonly referred to as the OL. By means of WDM, the OL provides simple routing functions that create optical circuits, or *lightpaths*, across the network. A lightpath is a point-to-point all-optical connection between physical nodes that need not be adjacent [22]. Conceptually, a lightpath is a service that belongs to the network layer of the ISO/OSI model.

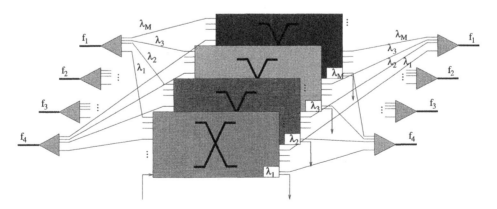

Figure 6.3 WR-OXC.

As part of the OL, three sublayers have been standardized by ITU-T:

1. Lightpath or Optical Channel (OCh)
2. Optical Multiplex Section (OMS)
3. Optical Transmission Section (OTS).

In [21] the OL is described from a network level viewpoint, taking into account an optical network layered structure, client characteristic information, client/server layer associations, networking topology, and layered functionalities that provide optical signal transmission, multiplexing, routing, supervision, performance assessment, and network survivability.

The layered structure of the optical transport network, depicted in Figure 6.4, shows the OCh section, OMS, and OTS sublayers.

6.2.2.1 *Optical Channel Section*   This sublayer provides end-to-end networking in the form of optical channels (lightpaths) for the transparent transmission of a client's data in varying desired formats, e.g., SDH STM-N, PDH 565 Mb/s, cell-based ATM, digital wrapper, IP/MPLS. To provide end-to-end networking, the following capabilities are included in the OCh sublayer:

1. OCh connection rearrangement for flexible network routing.
2. OCh overhead processing that ensures integrity of the OCh-adapted information.
3. OCh supervisory functions that enable network level operations and management functions, such as connection provisioning, exchange of QoS parameters, and network survivability (end-to-end protection and restoration).

Network components related to this sublayer include optical line terminals (OLTs) (the interface between the electronic layer and the optical layer), optical transmitters (laser, diodes), and optical receivers (photodiodes).

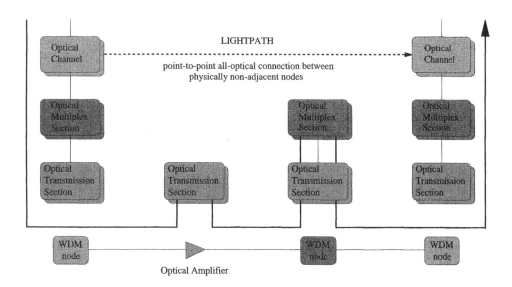

Figure 6.4   The ITU-T G.872 optical layer [7].

6.2.2.2 Optical Multiplex Section   This sublayer provides the functionalities required to manage a multiwavelength optical signal. (Notice that a "multiwavelength" signal includes as a special case the single-wavelength fiber.) The capabilities of this layer include:

• OMS overhead processing that ensures integrity of the multiwavelength OMS-adapted information.

• OMS supervisory functions that enable section level operations and management functions, such as multiplex section survivability (line protection and restoration).

Network components related to this sublayer include OADMs, OXCs (F-OXC, WT-OXC, WR-OXC), wavelength converters, optical switches, passive optical couplers/splitters (e.g., passive hub).

6.2.2.3 Optical Transmission Section   This sublayer provides the functionalities required to handle the transmission of the optical signal on various types of optical medium. The capabilities of this sublayer include:

• OTS overhead processing that ensures integrity of the OTS-adapted information.

• OTS supervisory functions that enable section level operations and management functions, such as survivability of the transmission section.

The network components related to this sublayer are primarily optical amplifiers and regenerators. The regeneration process can be of three types: 1R, when signal amplification and equalization (frequency, dispersion) are performed; 2R, when 1R, digital reshaping of the signal, and noise suppression take place; and 3R, when 2R regeneration and pulse retiming take place. Regeneration can be achieved using either optical amplifier (OA) (1R) or O-E-O conversion and electronic processing of the signal (1R, 2R, 3R).

6.2.3 All-Optical Network Architectures

Optical networks are often divided into two classes: first-generation optical networks and second-generation optical networks. In first-generation optical networks the optical signal undergoes O-E-O conversion at each node that it encounters on the route from source to destination. First-generation solutions include conventional telephone standards, e.g., SDH, SONET, and more recently proposed standards, e.g., Gigabit Ethernet. In second-generation optical networks (commonly referred to as "all-optical networks") the optical signal is optically routed at the network node, and does not require O-E-O conversion until it is received at the destination. A few promising commercial products are becoming available with all-optical features, e.g., WDM rings with OADM.

It is important to understand the potential advantages of all-optical networks when compared to first-generation optical networks [13]. All-optical networks provide transparency of the optical signal, hence, they are capable of supporting multiple protocols on the same optical transport infrastructure. Optical transparency eases the migration from one protocol to another because no major changes in the physical transport network are necessary. In all-optical networks, services such as protection and restoration switching can be provided directly at the optical layer, and made available to all higher protocols running in the network, including those protocols that do not have built-in survivability features. In all-optical networks, a significant cost reduction can be potentially achieved by reducing the amount of electronic circuitry and line terminals required in the network (the so-called electronic bottleneck of first-generation optical networks).

The significant potential advantages of all-optical networks make them one of the most promising networking solution for the next-generation Internet. This section will therefore focus on various all-optical network architectures that can be implemented using the optical components presented in Section 6.2.1. Readers interested in a survey of (the more conventional) first-generation optical networks are referred to [5,7,23].

All-optical networks can be classified in fours categories: static and semistatic lightpath networks, dynamic lightpath networks, optical packet-switching networks, and optical burst switching networks.

6.2.3.1 Static and Semistatic Lightpath Networks

Static and semistatic lightpath networks are the simplest SGON architecture. These networks, sometime referred to as "wavelength routed networks," provide point-to-point wavelength paths (lightpaths) between network nodes—e.g., IP routers—that need not be physically adjacent—e.g., directly connected by a cable. In a way that is similar to ATM or frame relay permanent virtual circuits, such static lightpaths can be used to transport data between gigabit routers that perform packet or cell forwarding in the electronic domain.

Wavelength routed networks circumvent the electronic bottleneck due to O-E-O conversion at every network node of FGON. By means of a lightpath, the connection from source to destination remains in the optical domain along its entire path. The only places where the transmitted signal is converted from and to electronics are, respectively, the source and the destination. For this reason, this approach is sometimes referred to as "single-hop" networking. The creation of lightpaths permits to build a desired logical topology (where the lightpaths constitute the links) on top of the physical topology (where the cables constitute the links). By creating a logical topology, network connectivity can be increased arbitrarily. In addition, the virtual topology can be redesigned or updated without requiring the huge investments that are necessary to modify the existing cabling of the physical topology.

The key components utilized in static and semistatic lightpath networks are OADMs and OXCs. Depending on their characteristics, OADMs and OXCs can be either configured during their production (static network) or reconfigured multiple times during the lifetime of the network (semistatic network). Manual reconfiguration is typically required in the semistatic network, to provision new lightpaths on a per-month or per-year basis.

The fundamental problem to be addressed in wavelength routed networks is the *routing and wavelength assignment* (RWA) problem. The RWA problem consists of determining for each required lightpath, a path across the physical topology and a wavelength to be used to establish the lightpath. Clearly, the cost of providing a desired logical topology in a given physical topology is affected by the algorithm used to solve the RWA problem. For example, a cost-effective solution will minimize the number of wavelengths required in the fiber to provide the desired logical topology.

In general, two scenarios are defined for the RWA problem. In the first scenario *wavelength continuity* is required along the lightpath. This is the scenario in which wavelength converters are not available in the network. In this case, once chosen, the wavelength of the lightpath cannot be changed from fiber to fiber. The RWA problem with wavelength continuity constraint is NP-complete [22]. In the second scenario, the wavelength continuity constraint is removed, and the RWA problem is greatly simplified. This is the scenario in which wavelength converters are available at the network nodes, and can be used to change the wavelength of a lightpath along its path. However, it must be remembered that wavelength converters are, at the moment, expensive components that significantly increase the overall network cost.

Besides the single-hop approach, *multihop* optical networks have been proposed. Multihop optical networks permit routing of a connection using a concatenation of multiple lightpaths, allowing O-E-O conversion of the optical signal at some "selected" intermediate nodes. Two advantages of multihop networking are: (1) reducing the span of the individual lightpath to better cope with transmission impairments, e.g., fiber chromatic dispersion [24]; and (2) performing electronic traffic multiplexing at the nodes where O-E-O conversion takes place [25]. By multiplexing multiple connections together at selected network nodes, the multihop network yields more bandwidth-efficient solutions than does the single-hop approach.

Figure 6.5 plots the network cost of a WDM ring network obtained using three approaches: First-generation optical network, single-hop network, and multihop network. The network cost is a function of γ, which represents the cost ratio between a wavelength mile and optical terminal (OT) cost. When $\gamma = 0$ the terminal cost is predominant. When $\gamma = 1$ the per mile wavelength cost is predominant. Network cost is normalized to the cost of the multihop network. The trade-off between first-generation optical networks and the single-hop network is clearly visible. The advantage of the multihop network over the single-hop network is documented in the figure. More details on this subject can be found in [25].

Another important aspect of static and semistatic lightpath networks is *survivability*. This problem is considered of paramount importance, because a sudden network fault can disrupt revenues of both network providers and network users at the same time. In general, a network is referred to as "survivable" if it provides some ability to restore ongoing connections in the event of a catastrophic failure of a network component, such as a fiber cut. Several approaches can be used to guarantee optical layer survivability [26]. Relevant parameters of a survivable network are fast recovery time, contained network resource redundancy, and simplicity of the recovery scheme.

A simple and fast protection scheme is represented by the self-healing WDM ring [26]. This scheme provides optical protection against any single-cable failure in the ring

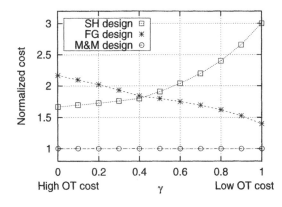

Figure 6.5 Trade-off between first-generation (FG), single-hop (SH), and multihop (MH) WDM ring design.

topology. By deflecting optical signals into a second counterpropagating fiber, the WDM ring can circumvent any single cable interruption or node fault. A recent study [27] illustrates the use of multiple WDM rings in an arbitrary topology. In this approach, a given arbitrary topology is covered with WDM rings. Lightpaths are then routed across the WDM rings to create the desired virtual topology. In this manner, if a cable fails, all lightpaths originally routed across that cable are rerouted using the WDM ring, which covers the interrupted cable. A lightpath may require a cascade of rings to reach the destination. The effect of the ring size (number of nodes) on the network cost is indicated in Figures 6.6 and 6.7. Two cost factors are considered: the total wavelength mileage required to create the virtual topology and the necessary spare resources in the WDM rings as well as the number of crossconnect ports that are required to switch a lightpath from one ring to another. As shown in Figure 6.6, the number of crossconnect ports decreases as the maximum ring size increases. Ring size is defined as the number of nodes connected to the same ring. The required wavelength mileage may be adversely affected by increasing ring size, as shown in Figure 6.7. With appropriate optimization techniques, however, it is possible to mitigate resulting wavelength mileage increase.

6.2.3.2 Dynamic Lightpath Networks
With data traffic becoming predominant over voice traffic, bandwidth flexibility is becoming a key feature in high-speed networks. A way to obtain such bandwidth flexibility in the optical layer is to resort to dynamic lightpath provisioning in which lightpaths are set up and torn down on demand. We refer to this type of network as *dynamic lightpath* networks. In such networks, lightpath re-

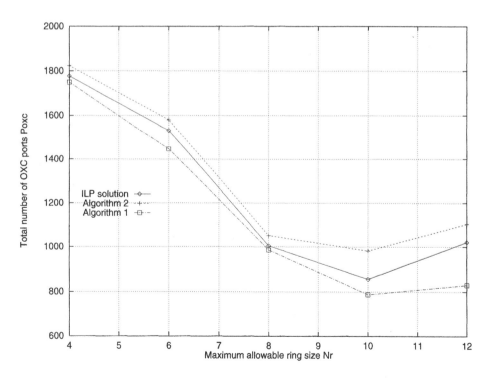

Figure 6.6 Number of OXC ports required.

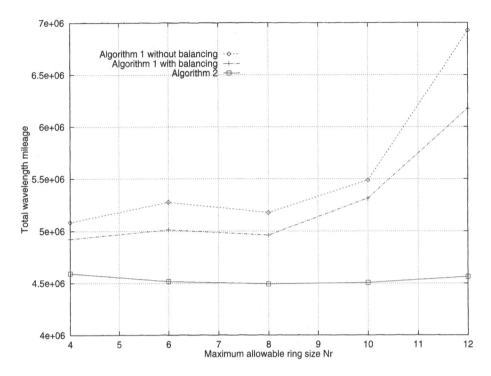

Figure 6.7 Total wavelength mileage required.

quests are expected to be generated frequently and to last for intervals of hours, minutes, and even seconds.

Similar to wavelength routed networks, dynamic lightpath networks offer the advantage of circumventing the electronic bottleneck of O-E-O at the transit nodes once the lightpath is set up. In addition, it is now possible to continuously adjust the logical network topology to best serve varying traffic patterns. The latter feature seems to be particularly suitable for today's Internet traffic. Dynamic lightpath networks are also expected to increase network utilization. When a lightpath is underutilized, it will be taken down, thus releasing some network resources that may be used more efficiently by other newly generated lightpaths.

Enabling technologies for dynamic lightpath networks include tunable transmitters, tunable receivers, and switching capabilities of both OADMs and OXCs. In order to yield satisfactory performance, the tuning and switching latencies required by these devices must be a fraction of the lightpath lifetime.

As in the case of wavelength routed networks, various algorithms for solving the RWA problem in the presence of dynamic lightpaths have been proposed. These can either require wavelength continuity or allow a lightpath to occupy distinct wavelengths on distinct network links [28]. Typical parameters that are optimized when creating lightpaths dynamically are *blocking probability*—the probability that the lightpath request is blocked due to unavailable resources—*throughput, setup delay,* and *fairness.*

Besides devising the appropriate RWA algorithm, a control protocol must be implemented to set up and tear down lightpaths. Two approaches are possible: centralized and distributed. In the centralized approach lightpath requests are sent to a controller node that has knowledge of the actual network configuration and decides whether resources are available for setting up the requested lightpath. In the distributed approach network nodes dynamically set up lightpaths utilizing a network state update protocol that discovers the actual network configuration [28,29].

Several solutions have been proposed for the implementation of dynamic lightpath networks. The optical network for regional access using multiwavelength protocols (ONRAMP) project [30–32] consists of a WDM physical ring architecture that reconfigures the network logical topology by dynamically provisioning lightpaths between network nodes. The objective of the ONRAMP project is to explore possible architectures for the access network of the NGI. In the *LightRing* [33] a WDM ring multi-token protocol is proposed that controls the distributed set up and tear down of lightpaths. In the LightRing, access to each wavelength is regulated by a token dedicated to that channel. In a distributed way, nodes can grab a token and gain access to the token-corresponding wavelength. A performance comparison between the centralized and the distributed approach can be found in [34]. Proposals by the IETF are based on adapting the MPLS control plane to control the optical layer, e.g., OADMs and OXCs. This approach is commonly referred to as MPλS, and more recently as GMPLS [35,36]. GMPLS permits to dynamically set up and tear down lightpaths in arbitrary, mesh, and network topologies.

Survivability is another important factor in dynamic lightpath networks. Due to the dynamic behavior of the network, schemes that are flexible and able to adapt themselves to network changes are preferred over fixed protection schemes previously described. Recently, solutions for dynamic provisioning of reliable connections have been proposed [37–43]. In these schemes, upon arrival of a request for setting up (tearing down) a connection, both a primary and a backup path are established (torn down) and resources along the network are reserved (released). Path calculation is based on network status information available at the source node upon arrival of the connection request. When resources for either the working or the protection path are not available, the request is blocked. Efficiency of the scheme (e.g., maximization of resource sharing, low connection request blocking) critically depends on signaling protocol convergence time. In particular, convergence time of the network status information at the nodes must be faster than connection interarrival time. It must be noticed that providing (freeing) both primary and backup resources, when the circuit is created (torn down), may require considerable signaling that may overload the control and management channel.

Restoration schemes have the potential to yield a more dynamic and less signaling demanding solution than protection schemes. Restoration schemes search for a secondary (or restoration) path to reach the destination only upon failure of the working path *without* reserving, in advance, any network spare resource. As depicted in Figure 6.8, depending on the node that computes the secondary path, restoration schemes can be divided into two classes: centralized restoration and distributed restoration. Depending on whether or not the restoration paths are computed before the occurrence of the fault, restoration schemes can be further divided in preplanned and real time [44].

Among the restoration schemes proposed so far for the WDM layer, *alternate routing[1]* (AR) [45] and *distributed restoration algorithms* (DRA) [46] are worth mentioning. Real-time DRAs [46] best utilize network resources, as they search for the secondary path only when the primary lightpath is disrupted. This approach may require heavy sig-

---

[1]Sometime referred to as diverse routing.

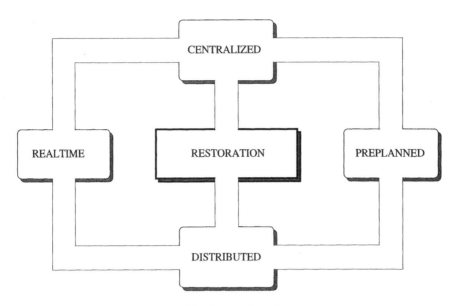

Figure 6.8 Restoration schemes.

naling when the network fault disrupts numerous connections (e.g., fiber cut), since each disrupted connection will search for a secondary path independently of others. AR schemes [45,47] are simple and provide fast recovery time by precomputing (yet not reserving) the secondary path for each active connection. Unless blocked due to lack of resources, AR schemes yield a recovery time that is merely the time necessary to set up the secondary path, which can be comparable to SONET-protection times, i.e., <50 ms [45,47].

An intermediate solution that yields relatively fast restoration time and low blocking probability is the class of *stochastic preplanned restoration* (SPR) schemes [48]. In the SPR schemes, multiple restoration paths are precomputed for each active connection. Resources along the precomputed restoration paths are not reserved. Upon failure of the working path, one of the precomputed restoration paths is randomly chosen and activated. The random selection is driven by the network status information available at the source node at the moment of failure occurrence. The selection is made with the aim of reducing the probability that the restoration path will be blocked due to lack of sufficient network resources. Figure 6.9 reports three curves that represent expected restoration blocking probability versus network load of three restoration schemes: AR, the SPR scheme with proportional weighted path choice (SPR-PW) [48] and exact solution of the integer multicommodity maximum flow (MCMF) problem with centralized control. Solution of the MCMF problem represents the theoretical optimum (minimum restoration blocking probability) for any restoration scheme.

6.2.3.3 Optical Packet-Switching Networks

Optical packet switching represents the ultimate frontier of all-optical networking. In this approach, packets are individually switched and routed in the optical domain. Statistical multiplexing of multiple data streams can be achieved in this way, while circumventing the O-E-O conversion required in conventional electronic packet-switching solutions.

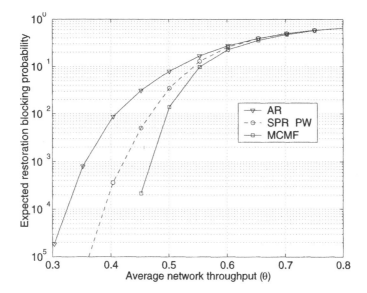

Figure 6.9 Restoration blocking probability versus network load of AR, SPR, and centralized MCMF exact solution.

Depending on how the packet header is processed at the optical node, two approaches are possible. In the *quasi-optical* approach, the packet header is converted to and processed in the electronic domain for control purposes, i.e., determining the output port intended for the arriving packet [49]. Packet payload remains in the optical domain. In the *all-optical* scenario the entire packet, header included, remains in the optical domain. Header processing can be performed by optical gates [50, 51].

With today's available technologies, neither the quasi-optical nor all-optical approach is mature, due to a number of open challenges. Some of these challenges are discussed next.

Optical packet switching imposes very stringent requirements on the optical switching node. The optical node must be able to perform some basic functions, including packet synchronization, header detection, buffering, switching, and routing in the optical domain. Since fast optical memories are not available, both synchronization and buffering require the use of cumbersome fiber delay lines (FDLs). Buffers can be implemented using *feedforward* and *feedback* delay-line structures [7, 8]. In the former case, an optical packet can be delayed (or stored) in the same FDL only once. In the latter case, an optical packet can be circulated many times in the same FDL. Header detection requires some form of packet framing and fast clock recovery of the incoming signal. The optical switch used to route the packet to the intended output port must have a switching time that is a fraction of the packet transmission time. Optical switches capable of switching in nanoseconds or subnanosecond intervals are bulky and expensive.

Some of the open issues in optical packet switching have been extensively studied over the past decade [52]. While research on all-optical header processing is still focused on enabling devices, the quasi-optical approach has been investigated in a number of network test beds, e.g., the Defense Advanced Research Projects Agency (ARPA/DARPA) sponsored contention resolution by delay lines (CORD) [53], the

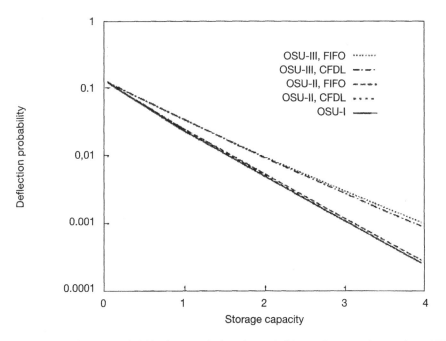

Figure 6.10 Deflection probability in an optical packet-switching node versus the number of fiber delay lines used as buffer.

European Asynchronous Transfer Mode Optical Switching (ATMOS) [54], keys to optical packet switching (KEOPS) (Advanced Communications Technologies and Services (ACTS) funded) [55], and wavelength switched-packet network (WASPNET) [56] (Engineering and Physical Sciences Research Council (EPSRC) funded). These projects have demonstrated the feasibility of optical packet switching, but not yet produced practical, off-the-shelf solutions.

An example of results obtained in these studies is found in Chlamtac and Fumagalli [57], in which a 2×2 switching node is proposed to optically store and forward packets of fixed size. A number of fiber delay lines are used in the switch to delay the arriving packets and resolve contention that may arise when two simultaneously arriving packets select the same output fiber. Three switch architectures are proposed and compared: *OSU-I*, a feedback architecture in which packets can circulate within the switch indefinitely; *OSU-II*, a feedforward architecture based on 3×3 optical switches; and *OSU-III*, a feedforward architecture based on simpler 2×2 optical switches. Figure 6.10 reports the packet deflection probability (i.e., packet is deflected to the wrong output fiber due to the lack of available delay lines) achieved by the three architectures versus the number of delay lines used in the switching node. Two control strategies are compared: FIFO and care packet first, don't care packet last (CFDL).[2]

---

[2]A packet is referred to as "don't care packet" when either of the output fibers can be used to reach its final destination using the minimum number of hops.

6.2.3.4 *Optical Burst Switching Networks*

A possible intermediate solution between dynamic lightpath networks and optical packet-switching networks is represented by *optical burst switching* (OBS) networks [58,59]. An optical burst consists of the aggregation of multiple packets and may contain several megabytes worth of data that is assembled at the edge switch or router. Once constructed, the burst is transmitted across the network optically, by utilizing a *one-way* reservation mechanism, i.e., the burst transmission is announced by a control message that is followed by the actual burst transmission. An *offset* time may be used between the control message that announces transmission of the burst and the actual burst transmission. Offset time allows the switching node to learn about the arriving burst and prepare for the appropriate switching and routing of the incoming burst.

The aim of OBS is to achieve statistical multiplexing without requiring some of the complex functions needed in optical packet switching networks. With OBS, switching time is relaxed and optical buffers can be avoided by using contention-free burst transmission scheduling [60]. Many studies have been conducted on this recently introduced concept, also indicating the possibility to integrate OBS with MPLS and generate the so-called labeled OBS (LOBS) [58].

One solution recently proposed to transmit optical bursts in WDM rings is presented in [61]. LightRing multitoken control (see Section 6.2.3.2) is adopted to transmit data bursts. Upon reception of a token, a source with an outstanding data burst ready to transmit, checks the resources available on the token-related wavelength. If no other transmission is ongoing on that wavelength, between the source and the destination, the token is released to the downstream nodes to announce transmission of the burst (which follows immediately after the token release). Since a burst transmission can occur only when a token is acquired, all transmissions are guaranteed to be contention-free, and the efficient "tell-and-go" reservation can be used, i.e., reservation of network resources and beginning of burst transmission occur simultaneously. Figure 6.11 plots the saturation throughput achieved by the LightRing reservation protocol versus the expected burst size in a 80-km ring. The total ring bandwidth (320 Gb/s) is evenly divided over W wavelengths. Figure 6.12 plots response time which includes access and transmission time versus expected burst size. Some values of W yield response times that are only marginally affected by burst size.

6.3 PROTOCOL ARCHITECTURES, SIGNALING AND FRAMING TECHNIQUES FOR THE OPTICAL INTERNET

The phenomenal advances in optical technologies are not only driving evolution of the OI, they are also fostering progressive evolution of the TCP/IP protocol stack to cope with the new gigabit speed scenario. At its origins, the Internet was built on unreliable and low-speed links, thus presenting not only congestion problems but also physical layer errors (bit error rate (BER)). Consequently, the original TCP/IP stack is oriented toward providing a reliable best-effort datagram delivery service. Soon it became clear that facilities provided by the unreliable network layer and the end-to-end TCP would not suffice to satisfy the increasing demand for multimedia services that require guaranteed QoS from the network lower layers.

ATM was adopted as a link layer that provides on-demand bandwidth to the IP flows by means of *switched virtual circuits* (SVCs). The SVCs are meant to be set up in a dy-

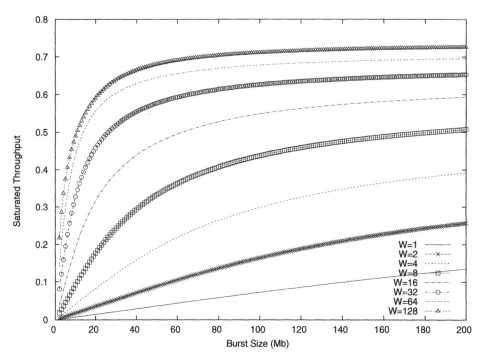

Figure 6.11 LightRing: saturation throughput versus expected burst size.

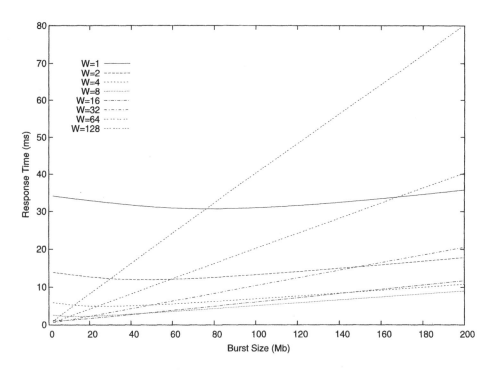

Figure 6.12 LightRing: response time versus expected burst size.

namic fashion in accordance with certain traffic flow descriptors provided by the IP. However, the complexity of provisioning dynamic bandwidth at the ATM link layer led the evolution of ATM to a mere static link layer. Nowadays, ATM *permanent virtual circuits* (PVCs) are commonly used to create links between IP routers. Such PVCs provide a constant bandwidth connection between routers. It must be pointed out that the ATM cell segmentation of the IP packet generates bandwidth inefficiency due to ATM cell headers (roughly 10%) and a significant processing burden that leads to an increase in overall network hardware cost.

In the attempt to guarantee a reliable physical layer for telephony applications, SONET and SDH standards were introduced. The SONET/SDH layer provides a reliable physical layer that the ATM layer can operate on. This includes *operations and maintenance* (OAM) features such as link protection. More recently, introduction by the ITU-T and IETF of, respectively, the OL (see 6.2.2) and the MPLS architecture [62], has led to the network layering depicted in Figure 6.13.

With the introduction of reliable protocols at the OL (e.g., second-generation optical networks) and guaranteed QoS at the IP layer (by means of MPLS), it appears that the complex multilayering architecture depicted in Figure 6.13 is no longer necessary. Some layers may be discarded to simplify the overall protocol stack and reduce network cost. In this section, we outline the evolution of OI layering by describing a number of possible realizations of IP on top of, respectively, first- and second-generation optical networks (see Figure 6.14). As part of the *first-generation optical Internet* we classify the *IP over SONET* standards and *IP over Gigabit Ethernet*. The *second-generation optical Internet* includes *IP over WDM* architectures, e.g., MPλS.

6.3.1 The First-generation Optical Internet: IP over First-Generation Optical Networks

We consider as first-generation optical internet the IP architecture based on FGONs. FGONs provide static point-to-point optical channels between physically *adjacent* IP routers. IP routers perform electronic processing of packets. The research effort in this scenario is focused on implementation of the interface between the IP and the OL that provides efficient encapsulation of IP datagrams. Both the *IP over SONET* and *IP over Gigabit Ethernet* standards are possible candidates for the interface between the IP and the optical domain.

6.3.1.1 *IP over SONET* The rationale of IP over SONET is to simplify the protocol stack, shown in Figure 6.14, by removing the ATM layer. By encapsulating IP datagrams directly on top of SONET, bandwidth efficiency is increased and the processing burden imposed by the ATM packet segmentation and reassembly avoided. However, a link layer protocol is still needed for packet delineation. Figure 6.15 illustrates how the IP packet is encapsulated in the SONET frame. Since SONET provides a byte-oriented stream service, the IP datagrams have to be delineated with a layer 2 header/trailer before being transmitted.

Current standards propose the use of HDLC-framed PPP for layer 2 framing as described in RFC 1662/2615 [63, 64]. Figure 6.16 shows the IP datagram HDLC-framed PPP encapsulation for POS, as recommended by the standard. The figure also shows the packet delineation flag that requires byte stuffing.

Two potential drawbacks may limit the application of IP over SONET architectures [65].

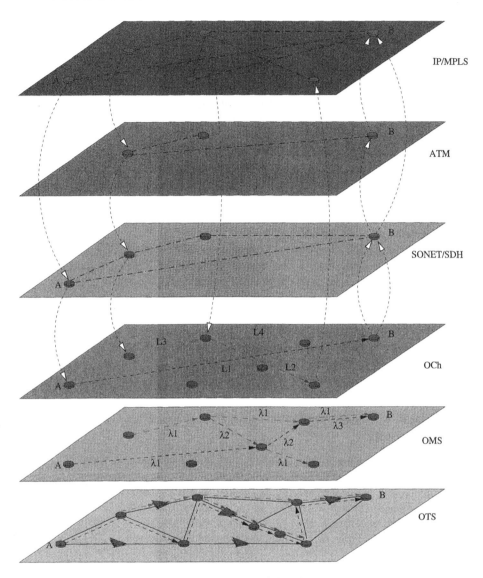

Figure 6.13   Network layering.

First of all, the use of flag 0x7E requires that the escape sequence 0x7D 0x7E is introduced in the PPP payload. Escaping a flag at gigabit rates becomes a performance bottleneck and may limit maximum transmission rate of the protocol. In addition, a malicious user may try to artificially increase the datagram length by arbitrarily inserting flag 0x7E. In doing so, the malicious user may trick the scheduling mechanisms[3] at the IP layer that sets the precedence of a certain packet over others based on the datagram size.

Second, the data scrambling provided by SONET has been shown to be insufficient. The SONET scrambler uses a simple 7-bit pseudorandom sequence,[4] which is XORed

---

[3]WFQ is an example of one well-known and widely used scheduling mechanism.
[4]$1 + x^6 + x^7$.

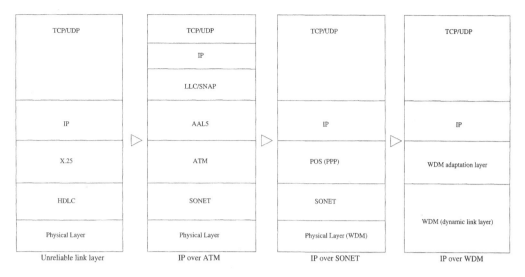

Figure 6.14 Evolution of the Internet protocol stack.

with the data in order to suppress long sequences of zeros or ones. Such long sequences of zeros and ones must be removed because they may deactivate the link due to *loss of frame* (LoF) or *loss of signal* (LoS) SONET alarms. When transmitting datagrams, the probability of still having a long sequence of zeros or ones after SONET scrambling is not negligible. An additional scrambling mechanism is thus required. At high speeds, scrambling becomes a major issue because it introduces some processing delay that can make user-perceived throughput decrease.

Due to the aforementioned drawbacks, the so-called POS standards are difficult to scale beyond OC-48 (2.5 Gb/s). To circumvent this speed limitation, other proposals for IP over SONET have been introduced, such as the *PPP over SDL* standard (RFC 2823) proposed by Lucent [66]. Figure 6.17 shows the IP frame encapsulated with PPP over

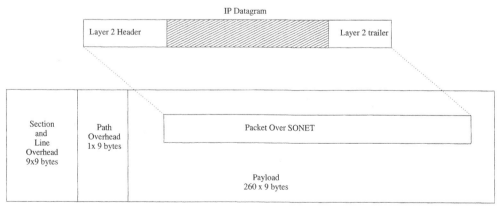

Figure 6.15 Packet encapsulation in IP over SONET.

Figure 6.16   HDLC-framed PPP encapsulation.

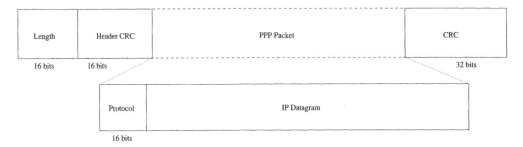

Figure 6.17   PPP SDL encapsulation.

SDL. In PPP over SDL link synchronization is achieved by means of an algorithm that is similar to I.432 ATM HEC delineation. Instead of searching for a flag (0x7E), as it is done in POS, the receiver calculates CRC over a number of bytes until it "locks" to a frame. When this happens, packet delineation is achieved and the receiver enters the SYNC state. In addition, data scrambling is performed with a self-synchronous $x^{43} + 1$ scrambler or an optional set–reset scrambler independent of user data. This makes it difficult for the malicious user to break SONET security.

Finally, it must be noted that the performance of IP over SONET, both in POS and PPP over SDL, is highly dependent upon IP packet size. Assuming that no byte stuffing (escaping 0x7E flags) is required and a 16-bit frame check sequence is adopted, the POS overhead is 7 bytes. For example, for a SONET layer offered rate of 2404 Mb/s (OC-48) the user-perceived rate on top of TCP/UDP is 2035 Mb/s for an IP packet size of 300 bytes.

6.3.1.2 IP over Gigabit Ethernet

Gigabit Ethernet is another candidate link layer for the transport of IP packets at Gb/s rates, especially in the access network [67]. There are two possible configurations for a Gigabit Ethernet: hub and point-to-point link. The latter is particularly attractive to provide access links to Gb/s users or links between gigabit routers. It must be noted that Gigabit Ethernet provides the service of an Ethernet card at Gb/s rates, i.e., asynchronous packet transport with no QoS discrimination.

In order to scale Gigabit Ethernet beyond 1 Gb/s [68] a number of solutions are being considered that are based on the principle of *inverse multiplexing*. For instance, a 10-Gb/s stream (OC-192) could be demultiplexed into four OC-48 streams (2.5 Gb/s) or eight 1.25-Gb/s streams, which could be transported by means of distinct wavelengths using 1-Gb/s Gigabit Ethernet as the link layer.

More recently, 10 Gigabit Ethernet[5] uses IEEE P802.3ae to create an new standard that

---

[5]http://www.10gea.org

still uses the IEEE 802.3 Ethernet MAC protocol with the same frame format and minimum and maximum frame size. The 802.3ae specification contains many technical innovations such as the definition of two different physical layer (PHY) types: the LAN and WAN PHY. The latter uses 64B66B encoding and SONET framing, and may be used for distances up to 40 km using single-mode fiber (1550 nm). The standard was approved at the June 2002 IEEE Standards Board meeting.

Finally, a new Internet Draft was issued recently [69] with a proposal for virtual concatenation of SONET envelopes. The aim is to provide an efficient way to carry Ethernet tributaries using SONET payloads. By allowing concatenation of envelopes at a given SONET hierarchy level, SONET bandwidth allocation granularity is improved to match the bandwidth required by Ethernet. For example, multiple VT1.5 payloads can be concatenated to produce a VT1.5-nv channel. By concatenating multiple VT1.5, it is then possible to reserve bandwidth from a 3.2-Mb/s ($n = 2$) channel to a 102.64-Mb/s ($n = 64$) channel. The latter can be used to accommodate a 10/100-Mb/s Ethernet transmission.

6.3.2 The Second Generation Optical Internet: IP over Second-Generation Optical Networks

The second-generation optical Internet, also commonly referred to as *IP over WDM*, represents a step forward in offering a high-speed efficient approach to provisioning IP services on top of OL. As described in Section 6.2.3.2, second-generation optical networks may provide dynamic resource allocation at the OL. A higher degree of flexibility is thus achieved when compared to the first-generation optical Internet, since optical bandwidth can be more efficiently handled by the client IP layer. Consequently, some of the intermediate layers between the IP and OL shown in Figure 6.13, e.g., ATM and SONET, are no longer necessary. In summary, two major benefits may derive from the use of IP over WDM: reduced network complexity and overhead and higher bandwidth flexibility.

Two possible approaches for IP over WDM are currently being debated: the overlay model and the peer model [70].

The overlay model provides two distinct control planes, one at the IP layer, the other at the OL. The overlay model is pushing the evolution of OI toward *flow switching* solutions, such as MPLS, which serve the purpose of simplifying IP routing and performing traffic engineering. Scheduling mechanisms are used to provide the transmitted IP packets with differentiated QoS on top of either static or dynamic WDM layers.

The peer model assumes that the IP layer and the OL are managed by a single control unit which has complete visibility of all network resources. The peer model is driving Internet evolution toward the so-called MPλS, which allows setup and tear down of optical circuits (lightpaths) on demand, to achieve efficient use of OL resources while circumventing the FGON electronic bottleneck.

6.3.2.1 *IP over WDM Overlay Models: Flow Switching and Gigabit Routers*

The IP over WDM overlay model assumes that the IP and WDM layers are completely decoupled. The optical network is viewed as an *autonomous system* (subnetwork) (AS) that provides connectivity to *edge IP gigabit routers,* as shown in Figure 6.18. The edge routers act as border domain gateways, and provide connectivity edge-to-edge. Such connectivity is reported to the rest of the Internet by means of BGP messages. Within the op-

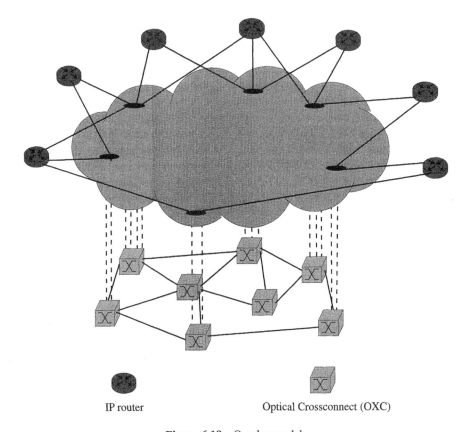

IP router   Optical Crossconnect (OXC)

Figure 6.18   Overlay model.

tical subnetwork a different routing protocol (Interior Gateway Protocol (IGP)) may be used (e.g., OSPF), which is similar to what is done in conventional ASs.

Besides end-to-end static or semistatic lightpaths, the optical network can provide flow switching mechanisms, e.g., lightpaths on-demand or burst switching. In the latter case the IP layer acts as a *client* of the OL, which is capable of providing "on the fly" resource allocation upon request. A clear advantage of the overlay model is the fact that future technology advances that will take place at the OL will not require any change of the IP layer.

The two key elements of this architecture are the concept of flow switching and gigabit routers.

Flow Switching   The idea of QoS discrimination at the link was originally introduced with the IP over ATM architecture. A network of ATM switches may provide point-to-point on-demand circuits (SVCs) in order to transport IP flows or flow bundles. As already mentioned, the use of ATM translates the problem of high-speed packet scheduling from one layer (the IP) to another (the ATM). Even though the use of fixed-size cells serves the purpose of simplifying the task, the switching and scheduling mechanism are far too elaborate for a practical implementation. As a result, current ATM implementations provide a simple static link layer to the IP.

In flow switching, the link layer is required to provide both flexible and efficient bandwidth allocation schemes and flow recognition and characterization mechanisms. The edge router must determine the flows required for a given traffic, either by automatic detection or explicit user indication. The scheduler must decide the amount of network resources that must be assigned to each flow, namely, buffer capacity and bandwidth. A number of proposals have been generated to address the flow assignment problem. In these proposals, either the IP destination address, subnetwork identifier, or HTTP file size are used to determine which flow is to be used [71, 72].

As will be shown later, most IP flows are actually short in size and duration, a fact that makes per-flow resource allocation and flow recognition a complicated matter. As a result, most flow-switching solutions existing nowadays are *tag-switching* solutions, e.g., the Cisco Tag Switching [73] and the MPLS [74]. Tag-switching solutions assign a tag to an incoming packet at the network edge so that subsequent routers perform the routing based on tag value. Tag switching is efficient and flexible. For instance, tag routing tables can be drastically simplified by addressing a set of destination subnetworks using a single tag. *Traffic engineering* of aggregated flows is possible which circumvents the problem of per-flow traffic engineering and related short time scale. For example, traffic engineering can be done at the *subnetwork granularity*. In this scenario all the connections terminating at a particular set of destination subnetworks are assigned the same tag. Suppose, for instance, that a large fraction of TCP connections from a European country are directed to U.S. servers. A tag is assigned to the corresponding IP packets in order for the edge routers to mark the packets as "directed to the US." Routers subsequently encountered by the transmitted packets will eventually route the packets to the transcontinental link by simply inspecting their tag.

On the other hand, separate resources may be assigned to the multiplexed TCP connections, resulting in segregation of flows directed to a given destination. A network operator could, for instance, assign different tags to different ISPs. Each tag is then assigned a desired capacity, as indicated by the corresponding peering agreement. Finally, a class of service (CoS) field in the MPLS tag allows one to define classes of service at the flow granularity and treat the various flows accordingly. For a detailed description of MPLS, the reader is referred to Chapter 3.

IP Gigabit Routers   The edge routers of the optical subnetwork are often referred to as gigabit routers. Design of IP gigabit routers is oriented toward providing more efficient routing table lookups so that packets and MPLS flows can be handled with minimum processing time. Gigabit Routers can be classified into three major families: centralized, decentralized, and parallel (see Figure 6.19).

The centralized router uses a single routing engine. The approach is simple, but the single routing engine may become a bottleneck. The decentralized router replicates the routing engines in the multiple line cards. If a certain route is not found in the line card routing table, the master engine is requested to handle the packet. Packets may be routed out of order due to possible delay variations that originate during update of the line card tables. The parallel router provides a parallel architecture at both the master and line card levels. The parallel architecture improves table lookup time at the cost of elaborate schemes for consistency control at high speed.

In general, the design of efficient lookup algorithms is of fundamental importance in realizing gigabit routing. Such algorithms fall into a search algorithms area that has been extensively studied over the last years. A large number of search algorithms have been

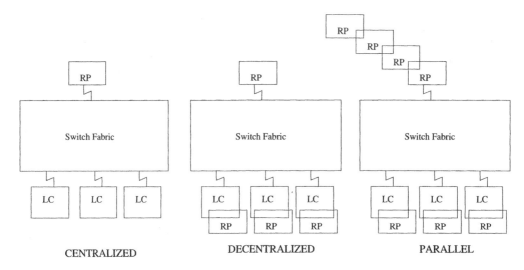

Figure 6.19   Gigabit router families.

proposed that are based on tree structures. They provide specific search optimization mechanisms at each tree level, e.g., trees with hashing tables. Tree levels can be compressed or segregated to improve the lookup time upon specific input traffic patterns. Furthermore, use of caches and *content addressable memories* (CAMs) also provide fast response times for the most frequently accessed (hot) routes. The quality of a particular algorithm is measured by the search complexity as the number of entries in the table grows. A selection of the most popular algorithms [75–80], together with the associated complexity, is shown in Table 6.1.

6.3.2.2 IP over WDM Peer Models: Multiprotocol Lambda Switching and WDM Gigabit Routers
The introduction of MPLS tag switching and its advantages has paved the way to more recent proposals that suggest the use of the MPLS control plane for controlling the OL. Use of MPLS Traffic Engineering Control to configure OADMs and OXCs has been proposed by IETF to solve the problem of finding a distributed management protocol, the so-called MPλS [81], that dynamically sets up and tears

Table 6.1   Search Complexity for Several Lookup Algorithms

Algorithm	Complexity
Binary search	$O(\log N + W)$
Patricia-trie	$O(W^2)$
Dynamic prefix tree	$O(W)$
LC-tries	$O(W/k)$
Multiresolution compressed tree	$O(\log_k N + 1)$
Hash table	$O(\log W)$
Content addressable memory	$O(W/k)$
Tree + hash table	$O(W/k)$

Note: W: bits per address, k: constant factor.

down lightpaths. A further step is represented by the proposed generalization of the MPLS control plane to manage legacy equipment, e.g., SONET crossconnects and add-drop multiplexers. This most recent proposal is referred to as GMPLS [35].

In the MPλS framework, IP and WDM layers are not independently overlayed. On the contrary, their devices are now considered as peers within the same physical network topology. As a result, IP routers are able to directly set up lightpaths in the physical network topology as they deem appropriate. For this reason, this model is known as the *peer* model (see Figure 6.20).

In simple words, the network configuration is similar to the standard MPLS network with the difference that the core MPLS routers are replaced by OXCs equipped with MPLS control plane. These OXC's are commonly referred to as Lambda Switch Routers (λSRs) (see Figure 6.21). The MPLS control plane can thus define an LSP that actually consists of a lightpath. At the MPλS network edge there are MPλS edge routers capable of aggregating IP input packets to be transmitted over the same lightpaths (the functionality is the same one provided by conventional MPLS edge routers in MPLS networks). However, the novelty is twofold: the created LSP, or lightpath, has a predetermined capacity (that is the transmission rate determined by the lightpath transmitter and receiver) and the traffic carried by the lightpath is completely orthogonal with respect to other lightpaths.

Many similarities exists between LSRs and OXCs [81]. Both LSRs and OXCs decouple the *control plane* from the *data plane*. The LSR data plane is based on label swapping to forward a packet from source to destination, whereas, the OXC data plane utilizes switching matrices. LSR performs label switching by mapping the pair (input port, input label) onto the pair (output port, output label). OXC maps (input port, input optical channel) onto (output port, output optical channel). The previous relations are determined by the control plane and are locally activated by a switch controller. The LSR control plane is used to discover, distribute, and maintain relevant state information associated with the MPLS network and instantiate and maintain LSPs. Similarly, the OXC control plane is

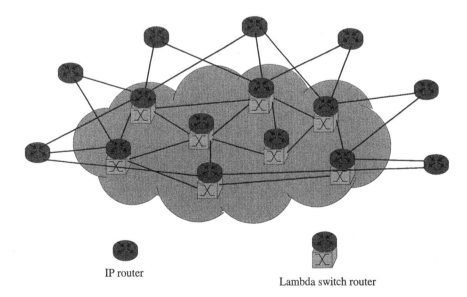

IP router

Lambda switch router

Figure 6.20   Peer model.

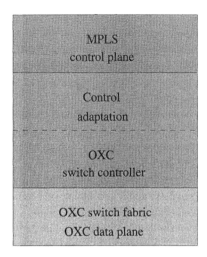

Figure 6.21 Lambda switch router.

used to discover, distribute, and maintain relevant state information associated with the OL and establish and maintain lightpaths.

The main difference between LSRs and OXCs is that OXCs are not able to perform packet level processing (e.g., aggregation and grooming), whereas, LSRs are electronic datagram devices that can perform packet level operations in the data plane. Another difference is that while in the LSR the forwarding information (tag) is carried by each individual packet. In the OXC the tag is carried, implicitly, by the lightpath's wavelength. Finally, in-band signaling is only possible in MPLS networks, whereas, in MPλS networks a separated control channel is necessary to perform out-of-band signaling.

In summary, the peer model approach is based on just one instance of routing and signaling protocols for both the electronic and optical domains. IP routing protocols (e.g., IGP such as OSPF) are used to calculate the routes and a link state advertisement (LSA) protocol distributes network state information to the network nodes. Signaling and reservation of network resources for lightpath (LSP) setup are based on MPLS signaling protocols, such as adaptations of RSVP-TE and CR-LDP [35, 82]. For network resilience, the peer model exploits the same schemes used by MPLS [26], e.g., end-to-end path restoration, path and line protection.

The MPλS peer model presents advantages and disadvantages when compared to the overlay model. It offers a framework for optical bandwidth management and provides real-time lightpath provisioning. It facilitates the coordination between IP network elements and optical network elements by resorting to the same control protocol plane used in data (MPLS) networks. It yields seamless interconnection of IP and optical networks, in accordance with the notion of second-generation optical Internet. However, it requires routing information that is specific to optical networks to be known by the IP routers. As a result, it requires a joint evolution of both the OL and the IP control plane. It is therefore expected that, from a practical point of view, the peer model is going to be less suitable than the overlay model for near-term deployment [70].

Finally, it is worth mentioning that although most of the solutions proposed so far to combine the IP layer and the OL are based on the concept of switching packets electronically and routing aggregated flows optically by means of lightpaths, some initial attempts have been made in the direction of optical packet switching. For example, WDM gigabit routers [83] combine optical switching and WDM transmission techniques to yield WDM optical packet switching. As in the case of IP gigabit routers, the main functions to be performed are packet routing (decide the packet route based on available network topology information), packet forwarding (routing table lookup and assignment of the packet to an output port), and packet switching. While efficient routing and switching mechanisms can be inherited from IP gigabit routers, the real bottleneck for WDM gigabit routers arises at the forwarding level. The high aggregate transmission rate of the wavelengths sets challenging objectives for routing table look-up. As mentioned in Section 6.2.3.3, an additional practical problem is represented by realization of inexpensive optical memories.

6.4 TRAFFIC ENGINEERING IN THE OPTICAL INTERNET

One of the open issues of OI is how to make the phenomenal amount of bandwidth supplied by the OL available to Internet applications. Available technologies in SGON provide only static lightpath configurations in which Gb/s connections are setup by management procedures. Such static lightpaths are used to transport a *high-level traffic multiplex.*

An open problem in SGON is to identify simple mechanisms that offer multiple granularities in bandwidth allotment at the optical layer (on-demand lightpaths, burst-switching, optical packet switching). In order to effectively use any of the aforementioned mechanisms, a good understanding of Internet traffic characteristics at the IP *flow* level is required.

In particular, at the coarsest level of aggregation (static lightpath), it is necessary to understand traffic characteristics obtained when a large number of flows are multiplexed. At a finer aggregation levels (burst switching, optical packet switching) a detailed characterization of IP flows is mandatory.

In this section we first describe some basic concepts of traffic *self-similarity* which is a property of high-level multiplexed Internet traffic. Then, we present a *flow level analysis* based on collected traffic traces. In conclusion, we analyze the impact of such properties on the specific scenario of the OI.

6.4.1 Self-Similarity

It is widely recognized that the multiplexing of many Internet traffic sources differs significantly from other well-known types of multiplexed traffic, such as multiplexed voice sources [84, 85]. Indeed, in contrast with voice traffic, that is Poisson modeled, Internet traffic presents self-similar characteristics.

A stationary stochastic process in discrete time $X = \{X_t, t \geq 0\} = \{X_1, X_2, \ldots\}$ is called "asymptotically second-order self-similar" with "Hurst parameter H" if for all $k \geq 1$ [86]

$$\lim_{m \to \infty} \rho^{(m)}(k) = \frac{1}{2}[(k+1)^{2H} - 2k^{2H} + (k-1)^{2H}] \tag{6.1}$$

where, $\rho^{(m)}(k)$ is the lag k autocorrelation of the aggregated process $S^{(m)} = \{X_t^{(m)}\} = \{X_1^{(m)}, X_2^{(m)}, \ldots\}$,

$$S_t^{(m)} = \frac{1}{m}(X_{tm-m+1} + \cdots + X_{tm}), \qquad t \geq 1 \tag{6.2}$$

For $1/2 < H < 1$, this means that correlation $\rho(k)$ decays to zero so slowly that [87],

$$\sum_k \rho(k) = \infty \qquad (6.3)$$

In simple words, process X has long memory or *long-range dependence*. In the specific case of the Internet traffic, such long-range dependence is observed in the packet-counting process, X_t (Figure 6.22), defined as the number of data bytes transmitted over a fixed time interval—δ ms [84,85].

As a consequence of the slow decay of the autocorrelation function, the overflow probability at intermediate router queues heavily increases when compared to a process with independent increments (Poisson). In Erramilli et al. [88], an experimental queueing analysis with long-range dependent traffic compares an original Internet traffic trace with a shuffled version of the same, i.e., with destroyed correlations. Results show a dramatic impact on server performance due to long-range dependence.

As a visual example, the packet counting process in time scales of 1, 10, and 1000 ms obtained from both a collected Internet traffic trace and a *Poisson process* is shown in Figure 6.23. We note that while the Poisson process (independent increments) tends to smooth out as the time scale of observation increases, the real traffic sample does not. Since X_t shows the long-range dependence of the Internet traffic trace, variance of the aggregate process X_t^m does not decay with the inverse of the number of samples aggregated (m).

The effect of *slowly decaying variance* can be observed by plotting the variance of the aggregated process S_t^m versus m (aggregation level) in log-log scales (Figure 6.24). For a Poisson process (independent increments) variance decays with the inverse of the number of samples (aggregation level), as predicted by the Central Limit Theorem. Instead, due to the effect of long-range dependence, decay of Internet traffic trace variance is slower than the independent case. As a result, Internet traffic trace shows significant burstiness at any time scale, not only at small time scales. We note that bursts of traffic are observed even at time scales of 1 s (see Figure 6.23). Such large bursts cause buffer overflow situations that are not captured by Poisson input traffic models.

6.4.1.1 Causes for Long-Range Dependence While there is considerable debate about long-range dependence causes [84, 85, 89–91], Willinger et al. [91] showed

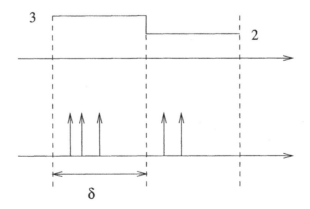

Figure 6.22 Packet-counting process (X_t).

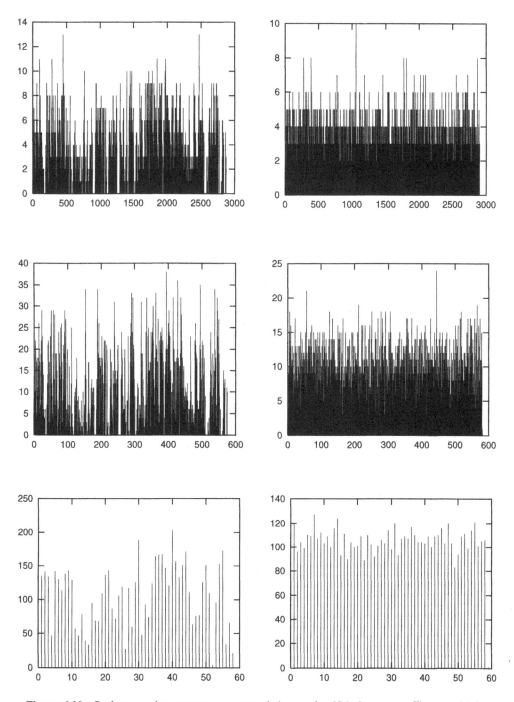

Figure 6.23 Packet-counting process over several time scales (S^m). Internet traffic trace (right-hand side) and Poisson process (left-hand side).

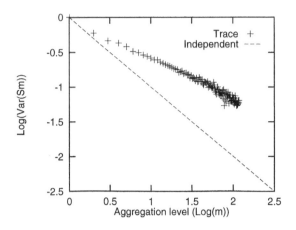

Figure 6.24   Variance-aggregation plot ($Log(Var(S^m))$) versus $Log(m)$).

that the multiplex of on–off sources with heavy-tailed on-off periods (Figure 6.25) turns out to have self-similar properties [84, 85, 89, 91]. Furthermore, Tsybakov and Georganas [86] showed that as long as the on-period of the individual connections is heavy-tailed, the resulting traffic multiplex is asymptotically second-order self-similar, even though the connection arrival process is Poisson.

A heavy-tailed random variable, R, has a distribution tail

$$P(R < r) = 1 - \left(\frac{K}{r}\right)^{-\alpha} \tag{6.4}$$

where α takes on values $1 < \alpha < 2$. The resulting random variable has finite mean but infinite variance. Parameter α in Equation (6.4) is related to the Hurst parameter H as follows [86]:

$$H = \frac{3 - \alpha}{2} \tag{6.5}$$

Values of H in the range $1/2 < H < 1$ indicate long-range dependence. Such H values correspond to α values in the range $1 < \alpha < 2$.

The Poisson-arriving heavy-tailed bursts hypothesis for long-range dependence can be verified empirically. At the Public University of Navarra the data traffic of a large

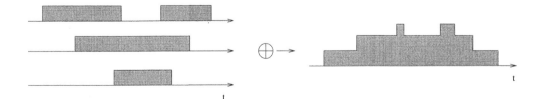

Figure 6.25   Multiplex of on–off sources.

multiplex of Internet users (1500 hosts), which share IP over ATM access links [92], has been analyzed. Traffic trace, recorded in February 2000, clearly reveals that WWW traffic is dominant. Indeed, TCP traffic percentage equals 99% in bytes transmitted, 82.8% of which (96.9% of the total number of TCP connections) are WWW connections. A detailed analysis of TCP connections recorded in the trace, focusing on *arrival process* and *connection holding time,* was performed. Hourly intervals in the morning, afternoon, and evening were observed, generating the plots reported in Figure 6.26. The plots report the *survival function* of connection interarrival time ($S(x) = P(X > x)$) in log-linear scale. The almost straight lines shown in the figure indicate that interarrival times are best modeled by an exponential random variable. Since users' traffic is independent of one another, the aggregate arrival process can be assumed to be Poisson.

Figure 6.27 and Figure 6.28 report survival functions as a function of the connection size (in bytes) and duration of the connection (in seconds) in log-log scale. The survival function of the heavy-tailed random variable defined in Equation (6.4) yields a line of slope $-\alpha$ when plotted in log-log scales. By plotting the distribution tail least-square regression line in both figures, estimated values of $\alpha = 1.2$ and $\alpha = 1.15$ were computed for size and duration, respectively. Such values are in accordance with previous studies that report values of 1.1 and 1.2 [93].

The results in Figure 6.26, 6.27, and 6.28 show that the traffic multiplex can indeed be modeled as a multiplex of Poisson arriving heavy-tailed bursts. TCP connections show a Poisson behavior in the arrival process since they originate from a multiplex of traffic originating from a large number of independent users. On the other hand, the heavy-tailed nature of connection size and duration is due to the fact that Internet file sizes can be

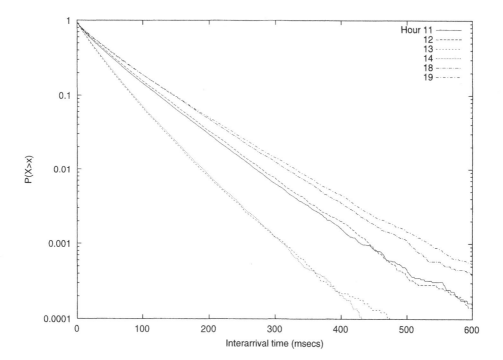

Figure 6.26 Survival function of connection interarrival time.

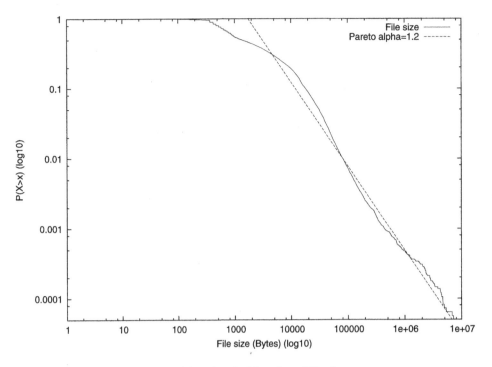

Figure 6.27   Survival function of file size.

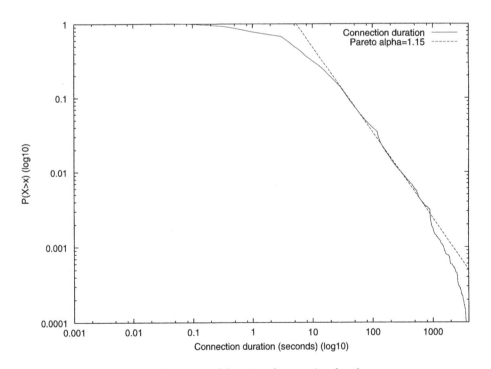

Figure 6.28   Survival function of connection duration.

modeled by a Pareto random variable (see Equation (6.4)). Pareto random variables show infinite variance whenever $1 \leq \alpha \leq 2$ and seem to be satisfactory models of the number of pages found in a book randomly chosen in a large library. The intuitive interpretation of this result is that file sizes in the Internet show a large variability, since there are a myriad of files that range from plain text to large video clips.

6.4.2 Flow Level Analysis

Considering that the most likely evolution of the OI in the near future is toward providing dynamic bandwidth allocation at the OL to support IP flows, a traffic analysis at the flow level is in order. Macroscopic analysis of traffic trace clearly indicates that the traffic sample is dominated by short TCP connections. Figure 6.29 reports the top 10 TCP ports sorted by number of connections and transmitted bytes. Note that some services generate a significant number of connections, each consisting of few bytes, such as AUTH(113), LOGIN(49), and DNS over TCP(53). However, some of the latter services are not among the top services in number of bytes transmitted. The AUTH service is normally used in conjunction with FTP, in order to allow anonymous FTP servers to authenticate the client. On the other hand, other services, such as Hotline (5501), consume a significant share of network resources (third in the amount of generated bytes) with very few connections (only 181 in a week). Hotline integrates multiple services, such as chat, file transfer, and news in the same session. As a result, the transfer of large files produces a significant amount of bytes transmitted by Hotline connections.

Traffic trace is dominated by the WWW with 80% of the total traffic in the amount of bytes, and 90% in the number of connections. We observe from Figure 6.29 that WWW uses port 80 for direct TCP connections and usually port 8080 for proxy WWW connections. The WWW is followed at a considerable distance[6] in bytes generation by the FTP (port 20 for data and port 21 for control) and Hotline, which is quite similar to FTP due to the file-transfer nature of both services. A small percentage of transmitted bytes are due to mail retrieval through POP3 (port 110), mail upload from client to server with SMTP (port 25), virtual terminal services like Telnet (port 23), and secure transactions with HTTPS} protocol (port 443). Table 6.2 presents some connection level statistics for the most popular services found in the trace. We note that WWW connections are small in size, with mean equal to 7.5 kB and 99% percentile equal to 70 kB. We also note a strong asymmetry in bytes transferred from server to client with respect to bytes from client to server, except for SMTP.

In conclusion, this analysis shows that most of traffic trace is dominated by short TCP connections due to WWW, also noted in recent studies, such as Miller et al. [94]. Such short TCP connections pose significant challenges regarding traffic engineering at the OL. As opposed to voice calls, whose call holding time justifies the use of a switched virtual circuit per call, per-flow switching in the OI is not practical except for a small percentage of connections. Thus, some flow aggregation mechanisms become necessary. While some proposals exist in the literature regarding per-port, subnetwork, or pair origin–destination address, finding an adequate flow-switching solution in the OI still remains an open issue.

---

[6]Note the logarithmic scale in the y-axis.

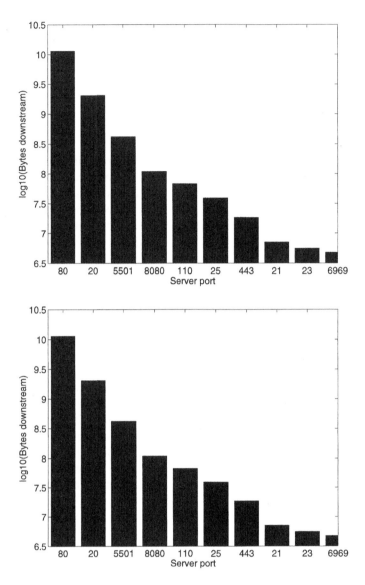

Figure 6.29 Top 10 ports (log-linear) by number of connections (top) and number of bytes transmitted (bottom).

Table 6.2 Number of Bytes and Duration of Connection

Service	Bytes per Connection Cli → Serv	Bytes per Connection Serv → Cli	Duration (s)
WWW	551	7,552	17.2
SMTP	26,394	490	40.0
POP3	69	21,494	17.1
FTPdata	0	227,603	10.6
Telnet	339	12,212	148.4

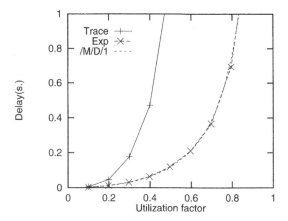

Figure 6.30 Average queue delay versus throughput for (1) Internet trace, (2) Poisson arrival of packets with exponentially distributed length, and (3) Poisson arrival of packets with deterministic length.

6.4.3 Impact on Optical Internet Traffic Engineering

From the previous section it is clear that long-range dependence of Internet traffic produces significant burstiness at any time scale. Such burstiness impacts queueing performance at intermediate routers. Figure 6.30 reports the average queue delay versus throughput curves obtained for (1) Internet trace, (2) Poisson arrival of packets with exponentially distributed length, and (3) Poisson arrival of packets with deterministic length. A dramatic performance degradation is experienced for Internet trace, which is due to the aforementioned long-range dependence effect.

An analytical expression of an infinite-queue single-server system under self-similar input[7] is presented in Norros [95]. The survival function of packet delay in the system is given by

$$P(X > x) \sim \exp\left(-\frac{(C - m)^{2H}}{2k(H)^2 c_v^2 m^2} x^{2-2H}\right) \tag{6.6}$$

where C is the link capacity, m is the input traffic mean rate, $c_v = \sigma/m$ is the standard deviation divided by input traffic mean or marginal distribution coefficient of variation [95], and $k(H) = H^H (1 - H)^{1-H}$, H being the Hurst parameter. The equation reveals that besides the utilization factor, the queueing performance depends on the input traffic long-range dependence (H parameter) and the marginal distribution variability (c_v parameter).

In optical networking, depending on the transfer mode adopted in the optical layer—dynamic lightpaths, optical bursts, etc.—the network can work at different operating points (c_v, H). For example, it has been shown that OBS serves to reduce self-similarity (H) [96]. The apparent self-similarity decrease is due to the fact that packets are aggregated to form bursts, which shifts the traffic scaling region to longer time scales. It must be observed, however, that an increase in the coefficient of variation in short time scales implies performance penalties even worse than those resulting from self-similarity [97].

---

[7]Fractional Gaussian noise.

As an example, assume that bursts of packets are used to enable the transfer of files swiftly across the network using in a single optical burst. Assuming file transmission at a line speed of 1 Gb/s using the same sequence of files as is detected in the collected Internet trace, i.e., using the time stat of the file transfer and size of the file, few curves are computed. The bits per second time series is depicted in Figure 6.31, and the marginal probability density function is plotted in Figure 6.32.

Clearly, the marginal distribution variability is increased and cannot be modeled as Gaussian. In order to model such a high-speed traffic stream, a family of random processes that have higher variability in the marginal distribution in comparison to a Gaussian process must be used [92]. Specifically, the *α-stable random processes* [98] provide non-Gaussian marginal distributions. Such processes are characterized by a higher variability (infinite variance in the marginal distribution) and do not have an analytical closed form for such a marginal distribution. The characteristic function is given by

$$E[e^{i\theta X}] = \begin{cases} e^{-\sigma|\theta|\alpha(1-i\beta(\text{sign}\theta)\tan(\pi\alpha/2))+i\mu\theta}, & \alpha \neq 1 \\ e^{-\sigma|\theta|(1+i\beta(2/\pi))(\text{sign}\theta)\ln|\theta|)+i\mu\theta}, & \alpha = 1 \end{cases} \quad (6.7)$$

with $1 < \alpha < 2$.

We note that the resulting traffic stream can be best modeled with an α-stable random variable with the following parameters: $\alpha = 1.39$, $\beta = 1$, $\sigma = 43,297$, and $\mu = 149,147$ (bytes per second), as shown in Figure 6.32.

Most interestingly, we note that input traffic now shows independent increments due to the Poissonian nature of connection arrivals and near-infinite bandwidth, which tends to

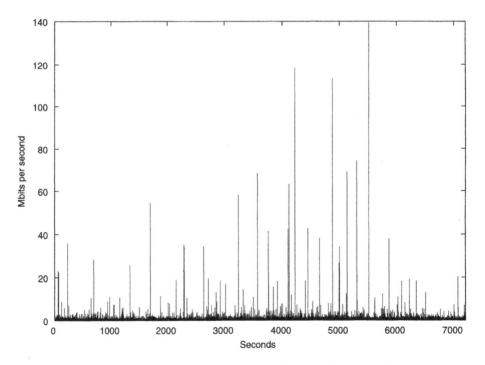

Figure 6.31 Link traffic (bytes per second) for a 1-Gb/s access link.

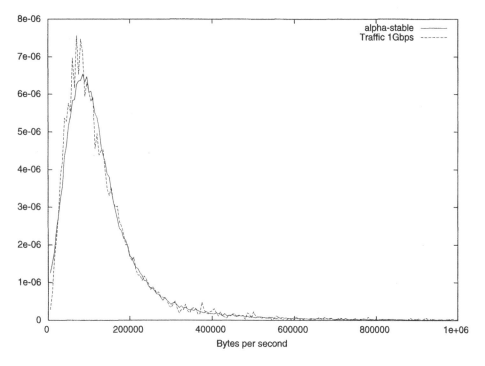

Figure 6.32 Link traffic probability density function for a 1-Gb/s access link.

make connection service times very short. The traffic marginal distribution variability is extremely large, because of the heavy-tailed nature of the size of the files transmitted over the Internet, an inherent characteristic of the current and future Internet. As a result, we note that the use of optical bursts in this scenario of "file-switching" translates dependency into marginal distribution variability. The preceding example serves to illustrate that the optical transfer mode in use, together with the traffic grooming at the edges of the optical subnetwork, may radically change the statistical characteristics of the optical network traffic load.

6.5 OPEN CHALLENGES

This final section summarizes some of the key challenges encountered in the development and deployment of the OI. These challenges include efficient traffic engineering in the OI, adequate network resilience schemes at both the IP layer and WDM layer, and coordination between resilience schemes available at both the IP and the WDM layers.

6.5.1 Traffic Engineering in the Optical Internet

Internet traffic engineering has undergone a significant evolution due to the advances in the statistical modeling of input traffic. From the oversimplified Poisson scenario to the recent discovery of the non-Poisson nature of the Internet traffic [84, 85], this field has spurred considerable research in the area of long-range dependence modeling. However, today's network operators still face the issue of how to dimension Internet links accurately. Indeed, there are no practical dimensioning rules currently available that can be used in an effective way, such as the well-known Erlang models used in designing telephone networks.

Design of the OL poses additional challenges regarding network dimensioning. The impact of recently proposed optical transfer modes, such as the dynamic lightpath provisioning and optical burst switching, will surely affect traffic characteristics at the network intermediate and destination nodes. The high variability of input traffic may even become more significant than the long-range dependence properties of current Internet traffic, thus requiring further investigation of queueing models with α-stable input [92].

In parallel, flow switching techniques, either in an overlay model (MPLS) or peer model (MPλS), require flow recognition and bandwidth reservation mechanisms that represent a challenge due to the nature of the input traffic pattern. In this regard, a number of "intelligent techniques" are being proposed that aim at performing a priori estimates of the incoming traffic, both at the multiplexed-flow and single-flow levels, in order to proactively adapt the network resources to the incoming traffic demands [99]. Whether such intelligent techniques will satisfactorily solve the problem of resource allocation at gigabit rates still remains an open issue.

6.5.2 Resilience in IP over WDM Networks

In the two-layer IP over WDM architecture, each layer can provide its own independent resilient scheme. Restoration and protection schemes can be implemented at both the IP layer (possibly using the MPLS control plane) and the WDM layer (possibly using the MPλS control plane).

In general, resilient schemes available at the network layer, such as IP (IP/MPLS), have the capability to recover multiple faults and operate at fine traffic granularity. However, these schemes are generally slow, as they require on-line processing upon failure occurrence. Dynamic routing [100] and MPLS protection switching [101] are schemes currently considered to achieve network survivability at the IP (IP/MPLS) layer.

At the OL, both the OCh section and OMS—two of the OL sublayers—feature *dynamic restoration* and *preplanned protection*. Similar to what happens at the higher layers, restoration schemes are more efficient from a capacity viewpoint, but relatively slow (typical restoration completion time is on the order of seconds or minutes). On the other hand, protection schemes may be less efficient, but they guarantee service restoration completion times of hundreds, tens, and even fractions of milliseconds.

The main difference between OCh and OMS resilient schemes is represented by the granularity at which they operate. OCh resilient schemes protect individual lightpaths, thus allowing selective recovery of OLT failures. OMS resilient schemes work at the aggregate signal level, thus recovering all lightpaths present in the failed fiber [102]. OCh resilient schemes require more spare devices, e.g., transponders, multiplexers, demultiplexers, than their OMS counterparts, because each working lightpath must be demultiplexed and multiplexed at every node in order to be individually switched [102].

Although current IP/MPLS reliability schemes offer varying levels of restoration and protection granularity (from aggregate to single flow), they cannot efficiently provide all the necessary functionalities needed by the next-generation Internet, i.e., fast restoration for real-time services. It is thus expected that both IP and WDM layers will each provide some degree of survivability against network faults.

The availability of two resilient schemes in the same network (e.g., IP dynamic routing and OL protection) poses the question of which scheme must be used to protect which traffic. The option of using both resilient schemes for all traffic may not be the most cost-effective one. A more careful design may consist of a hybrid solution in which only part of the traffic is protected by an OL resilient scheme, while the remaining part relies only on IP restoration. Some solutions exploiting this direction have been proposed. More interest on this subject has been originated since the introduction of MPλS, in which the MPLS control plane is responsible for network restoration and protection [26, 103–105].

6.5.2.1 IP over WDM Layer Resilience Coordination

The presence of different resilient schemes at different network layers requires coordination between these schemes to avoid their concurrent activation upon a single network fault [104]. In general, such coordination can be achieved in three different ways [106]: ordered response, managed response, and simultaneous response.

Ordered response is commonly achieved by resorting to *escalation strategies* that sequentially activate the different resilient schemes, starting from either the lowest or the highest network layer. Escalation strategies are governed by either explicit messaging between the different layers, or by arbitrarily setting failure detection and restoration completion times [106].

Managed response is a more sophisticated multilayer resilience strategy than the ordered response. Fault recovery procedures are managed under the supervision of a network management system that chooses the most appropriate action to take, depending on the fault nature. This scheme avoids, almost completely, multiple restoration collisions. However, due to its required large quantity of signaling, it is slow. Another potential drawback is the fact that failure of the management center may leave the entire network without any kind of resilience.

In the simultaneous response, each layer utilizes its own resilience scheme without any specific coordination with other schemes available elsewhere in the network. Consequently, multiple resilience schemes may be simultaneously activated by the same fault. This approach seems to be more economical and less complicated than the previous two. In addition, with this approach, unnecessary delays in restoring the service are avoided.

Table 6.3 summarizes some of the fault detection and restoration completion times at the IP/MPLS and WDM layers. It must be noted that MPLS resilient schemes are not yet mature and not yet experimentally tested. Similarly, OCh/OMS restoration schemes are not yet standardized. On the contrary, IP dynamic routing and OCh/OMS protection techniques are already either used in commercial networks or tested in field trials. Their characteristics are thus well known [110].

Table 6.3 Service Restoration Times of Various Resilience Techniques [107–109]

Scheme	Detection Time	Restoration Completion Time
IP dynamic routing	100 ms–180 s	1–100 s
MPLS fast (link) rerouting	0.1–100 ms	50 ms–100 ms
MPLS edge-to-edge rerouting	100 ms–80 s	1–100 s
OCh and OMS restoration	> 100 ms	≥ 50 ms
Dedicated OL protection	1–10 ms	10 μs–10 ms
Shared OL protection	1–10 ms	1–100 ms

It is also worth mentioning emerging and promising MPLS resilient schemes. Fault detection in MPLS can be achieved by exploiting different existing techniques, such as SONET/SDH-based framing alarms, OL fault-detection techniques, and IP-based KEEPALIVE, HELLO, and ICMP messages [100, 109, 111]. These detection mechanisms guarantee detection times ranging from few tenths of a millisecond to hundred of seconds. MPLS solutions may resort to control plane signaling, such as CR-LDP or modified RSVP, to perform traffic restoration, with time intervals ranging from a few dozens of milliseconds to hundreds of seconds. Due to the similarities between the MPLS and MPλS control plane, the same MPLS resilient schemes, and in particular the same signaling, can be utilized in the OL.

6.5.3 Outlook

Advent of the Internet has undoubtedly shaped the way data networks are designed and built. Opposite to the ISO-OSI layered approach, with seven well-defined, rigid, and complex protocol layers from physical to application, which even provide some redundant functionalities, the Internet protocol suite, TCP/IP, provides minimal complexity and superb reliability in the presence of faulty and noisy channels. Internet applications are built on a simple and efficient API, the BSD socket interface, which facilitates design and implementation of Internet clients and servers. As a result, a myriad of Internet applications have appeared, making the Internet evolve into a phenomenal commercial success.

In the current evolution to (gigabit speed) OI, it seems that recently proposed high-speed transfer modes, such as ATM, are being questioned in view of the latest proposed IP over WDM architectures. A parallelism to the OSI-TCP/IP evolution perhaps can be perceived at this point. While the ATM proposed a layered structure with redundant functionalities at the link, network, and transport layers, the IP over WDM architecture presents itself as a simple bandwidth-efficient alternative.

In conclusion, the IP over WDM architecture is a promising approach for realizing the OI. The IP over WDM architecture is still in its experimental phase, with a number of key issues still unresolved. Among these issues, one can find the standardization of transfer modes that support multiple granularities in bandwidth reservation, ranging up to Gb/s rates. Network resilience issues are also of fundamental importance. The challenge here is to introduce adequate resilience levels without creating unnecessary redundancies at the various protocol layers. Finally, it is expected that the OI will consist of multiple technologies and protocols, whose combination will yield network flexibility, ease of use, bandwidth efficiency, and low-cost deployment.

ACKNOWLEDGMENTS

The authors thank James Cai, Isabella Cerutti, Mikel Izal, Daniel Morato, Eduardo Magana, and Marco Tacca for providing some of the results discussed in the chapter.

REFERENCES

1. R. Sabatino and J. M. De Arce, "Implementation of the Pan-European Academic Research Network: TEN-155," *Computer Networks: the International Journal of Distributed Informatique,* vol. 31, no. 21, pp. 2253–61, November 1999.

2. F. Greisen, "EBONE and Other Parts of the European Internet," in *Proceedings of JENC7. 7th Joint European Networking Conference (JENC7). Networking in the Information Society. TERENA.* Amsterdam, The Netherlands, pp.211/1–6, 1996.

3. A. S. Tanenbaum, *Computer Networks,* Prentice Hall, Upper Saddle River, New Jersey, third edition, 1996.

4. W. R. Stevens, *TCP/IP Illustrated,* vol. 1, Addision-Wesley, Reading, Massachusetts, 1994.

5. P. E. Green, Jr., *Fiber Optic Networks,* Prentice Hall, Englewood Cliffs, New Jersey, 1993.

6. G. P. Agrawal, *Fiber-Optic Communication Systems,* John Wiley & Sons, New York, second edition, 1997.

7. R. Ramaswami and K. N. Sivarajan, *Optical Networks: A Practical Perspective,* Morgan Kaufmann Publishers, 1998.

8. R. Ramaswami and K. N. Sivarajan, *Optical Networks: A Practical Perspective,* Morgan Kaufmann Publishers, second edition, 2001.

9. L. Kazovsky, S. Benedetto, and A. Willner, *Optical Fiber Communication Systems,* Artech House, Boston, Massachusetts, 1996.

10. B. Mukherjee, *Optical Communication Networks,* McGraw-Hill, New York, 1997.

11. T. E. Stern and K. Bala, *Multiwavelength Optical Networks. A Layered Approach,* Addison-Wesley, Reading, Massachusetts, 1999.

12. E. Desurvire, *Erbium-Doped Fiber Amplifier Principles and Applications,* John Wiley & Sons, New York, 1991.

13. P. Green, "Progress in Optical Networking," *IEEE Communications Magazine,* vol. 39, no. 1, pp. 54–61, January 2001.

14. D. A. Francis, S. P. DiJaili, and J. D. Walker, "A Single-chip Linear Optical Amplifier," in *Proceedings of Optical Fiber Communication Conference and Exhibit, 2001. OFC 2001,* vol. 4, pp. PD13–P1-3, 2001.

15. T. N. Nielsen, "Raman Amplifiers in WDM Systems," in *Proceedings of LEOS '99. IEEE Lasers and Electro-Optics Society 1999 12th Annual Meeting,* LEOS, vol. 2, pp. 471–472, 1999.

16. D. J. Bishop, C. R. Giles, and G. P. Austin, "The Lucent LambdaRouter: MEMS Technology of the Future Here Today," *IEEE Communications Magazine,* vol. 40, no. 3, pp. 75–79, March 2002.

17. P. B. Chu, S.-S. Lee, and S. Park, "MEMS: The Path to Large Optical Crossconnects," *IEEE Communications Magazine,* vol. 40, no. 3, pp. 80–87, March 2002.

18. P. De Dobbelaere, K. Falta, L. Fan, S. Gloeckner, and S. Patra, "Digital MEMS for Optical Switching," *IEEE Communications Magazine,* vol. 40, no. 3, pp. 88–95, March 2002.

19. R. Izmailov, S. Ganguly, T. Wang, Y. Suemura, Y. Maeno, and S. Araki, "Hybrid Hierarchical Optical Networks," *IEEE Communications Magazine,* vol. 40, no. 11, pp. 88–94, November 2002.

20. E. Ciaramella, "Introducing Wavelength Granularity to Reduce the Complexity of Optical Cross Connects," *IEEE Photonics Technology Letters,* vol. 12, no. 6, pp. 699–701, June 2000.

21. ITU, *Draft ITU-T Recommendation for Optical Transport Networks, G.872,* July 1998.

22. I. Chlamtac, A. Ganz, and G. Karmi, "Lightpath Communications: A Novel Approach to High Bandwidth Optical WAN-s," *IEEE Transactions on Communication,* vol. 40, no. 7, pp. 1171–1182, July 1992.

23. T.-H. Wu, *Fiber Optic Survivability,* Boston, Massachusetts, Artech House, 1992.

24. I. Cerutti, A. Fumagalli, and M. J. Potasek, "Effects of Chromatic Dispersion and Self-phase Modulation in Multihop Multirate WDM Rings," *IEEE Photonics Technology Letters,* vol. 14, no. 3, March 2002.

25. I. Cerutti, A. Fumagalli, M. Tacca, A. Lardies, and R. Jagannathan, "The Multi-hop Multi-rate

Wavelength Division Multiplexing Ring," *Journal of Lightwave Technology,* vol. 18, no. 12, pp. 1649–1656, December 2000.

26. A. Fumagalli and L. Valcarenghi, "IP Restoration and WDM Protection: Is There an Optimal Choice?" *IEEE Network,* November/December 2000.

27. A. Fumagalli, M. Tacca, and I. Cerutti, "Minimizing the Number of Optical Crossconnect Ports in Mesh Networks Based on Bidirectional Line-switched WDM Self-healing Ring Protection," in *Proceedings of Eight International Conference on Computer Communications and Networks, ICCCN99,* pp. 398–403, 1999.

28. H. Zang, J. P. Jue, and B. Mukherjee, "A Review of Routing and Wavelength Assignment Approaches for Wavelength-Routed Optical WDM Networks," *Optical Networks Magazine,* vol. 1, no. 1, pp. 47–60, January 2000.

29. R. Ramaswami and A. Segall, "Distributed Network Control for Optical Networks," *IEEE/ACM Transactions on Networking,* vol. 5, no. 6, pp. 936–943, December 1997.

30. M. Kuznetsov, N. M. Froberg, S. R. Henion, H. G. Rao, J. Korn, K. A. Rauschenbach, E. H. Modiano, and V. W. S. Chan, "A Next-Generation Optical Regional Access Network," *IEEE Communications Magazine,* vol. 38, no. 1, pp. 66–72, January 2000.

31. N. M. Froberg, S. R. Henion, H. . Rao, B. K. Hazzard, S. Parikh, B. R. Romkey, and M. Kuznetsov, "The NGI ONRAMP Test Bed: Reconfigurable WDM Technology for Next Generation Regional Access Networks," *Journal of Lightwave Technology,* vol. 18, no. 12, December 2000.

32. B. Ganguly and V. Chan, "A Scheduled Approach to Optical Flow Switching in the ONRAMP Optical Access Network Testbed," in *Proceedings of Optical Fiber Communication Conference and Exhibit 2002. OFC2002,* 2002.

33. J. Cai and A. Fumagalli, "Distributed On-line Wavelength Assignment in Multi-Token Based WDM Ring Networks," Tech. Rep. EE-03-00, University of Texas at Dallas, 2000.

34. J. Cai, A. Fumagalli, and C. Guan, "Centralized vs. Distributed On-demand Bandwidth Reservation Mechanisms in WDM Ring," in *Proceedings of Optical Fiber Communication Conference and Exhibit, OFC 2001,* vol. 1, pp. MH2/1–MH2/3, 2001.

35. A. Banerjee, J. Drake, J. P. Lang, B. Turner, K. Kompella, and Y. Rekhter, "Generalized Multiprotocol Label Switching: an Overview of Routing and Management Enhancements," *IEEE Communications Magazine,* vol. 39, no. 1, pp. 144–150, January 2001.

36. A. Banerjee, L. Drake, L. Lang, B. Turner, D. Awduche, L. Berger, K. Kompella, and Y. Rekhter, "Generalized Multiprotocol Label Switching: an Overview of Signaling Enhancements and Recovery Techniques," *IEEE Communications Magazine,* vol. 39, no. 7, pp. 144–151, July 2001.

37. C. Qiao and Dahai Xu, "Distributed Partial Information Management (DPIM) Schemes for Survivable Networks—Part I," in *Proceedings of INFOCOM 2002,* vol. 1, 2002.

38. S. Sengupta and R. Ramamurthy, "From Network Design to Dynamic Provisioning and Restoration in Optical Cross-Connect Mesh Networks: An Architectural and Algorithmic Overview," *IEEE Network,* vol. 15, no. 4, July/August 2001.

39. E. Bouillet, J. F. Labourdette, G. Ellinas, R. Ramamurthy, and S. Chaudhuri, "Stochastic Approaches to Compute Shared Mesh Restored Lightpaths in Optical Network Architectures," in *Proceedings of INFOCOM 2002,* vol. 1, 2002.

40. X. Su and C.-F. Su, "An Online Distributed Protection Algorithm in WDM Networks," in *ICC 2001,* 2001, vol. 5, pp. 1571–1575.

41. D. Elie-Dit-Cosaque, M. Ali, and L. Tancevski, "Informed Dynamic Shared Path Protection," in *Proceedings of OFC 2002,* pp. 492–493, 2002.

42. B. Zhou and H. T. Mouftah, "Survivable Alternate Routing for WDM Networks," in *Proceedings of OFC 2002,* 2002.

43. C.-X. Chi, D.-W. Huang, D. Lee, and X.-R. Sun, "Lazy Flooding: A new Techniuqe for Siganling in All Optical Network," in *Proceedings of OFC 2002,* pp. 551–552, 2002.

44. Luca Valcarenghi, *Survivable IP-over-WDM Networks,* Ph.D. Thesis, University of Texas at Dallas, December 2001.

45. G. Li, J. Yates, R. Doverspike, and D. Wang, "Experiments in Fast Restoration Using GMPLS in Optical/Electronic Mesh Networks," in *Proceedings of OFC 2001,* vol. PD, pp. PD34_1–PD34_3, March 2001.

46. R. R. Iraschko and W. D. Grover, "A Highly Efficient Path-Restoration Protocol for Management of Optical Network Transport Integrity," *IEEE Journal on Selected Areas in Communications,* vol. 18, pp. 779–794, May 2000.

47. J. Yates, G. Smith, P. Sebos, C. Cannon, P. Arias, J. Rice, and A. Greenberg, "IP Control of Optical Networks: Design and Experimentation," in *Proceedings of OFC 2001,* vol. 1, pp. MH5_1–MH5_3, March 2001.

48. L. Valcarenghi and A. Fumagalli, "Implementing Stochastic Preplanned Restoration with Proportional Weighted Path Choice in IP/GMPLS/WDM Networks," *Photonic Network Communications,* vol. 4, no. 3/4, July/December 2002.

49. A. Carena, M. D. Vaughn, R. Gaudino, M. Shell, and D. J. Blumenthal, "OPERA: An Optical Packet Experimental Routing Architecture with Label Swapping Capability," *Journal of Lightwave Technology,,* vol. 16, no. 12, pp. 2135–2145, December 1998.

50. P. Toliver, I. Glesk, R. J. Runser, K.-L. Deng, B. Y. Yu, and P. R. Prucnal, "Routing of 100 Gb/s Words in a Packet-switched Optical Networking Demonstration (POND) Node," *Journal of Lightwave Technology,* vol. 16, no. 12, pp. 2169–2180, December 1998.

51. P. Toliver, K.-L. Deng, I. Glesk, and P. R. Prucnal, "Simultaneous Optical Compression and Decompression of 100-Gb/s OTDM Packets Using a Single Bidirectional Optical Delay Line Lattice," *IEEE Photonics Technology Letters,* vol. 11, no. 9, pp. 1183–1185, September 1999.

52. D. K. Hunter and I. Andronovic, "Approaches to Optical Internet Packet Switching," *IEEE Communications Magazine,* vol. 38, no. 9, pp. 116–122, September 2000.

53. I. Chlamtac, A. Fumagalli, et al., "CORD: Contention Resolution by Delay Lines," *IEEE Journal on Selected Areas in Communications,* vol. 14, no. 5, pp. 1014–1029, June 1996.

54. F. Masetti et al., "High Speed, High Capacity ATM Optical Switches for Future Telecommunication Transport Networks," *IEEE Journal on Selected Areas in Communications,* vol. 14, no. 5, pp. 979–998, June 1996.

55. C. Guillemot et al., "Transparent Optical Packet Switching: The European ACTS KEOPS Project Approach," *Journal of Lightwave Technology,* vol. 16, no. 12, pp. 2117–2134, December 1998.

56. D. K. Hunter et al., "WASPNET: A Wavelength Switched Packet Network," *IEEE Communications Magazine,* vol. 37, no. 3, March 1999.

57. I. Chlamtac and A. Fumagalli, "An Optical Switch Architecture for Manhattan Networks," *IEEE Journal on Selected Areas in Communications,* vol. 11, no. 4, May 1993.

58. C. Qiao, "Labeled Optical Burst Switching for IP-over-WDM Integration," *IEEE Communications Magazine,* vol. 38, no. 9, pp. 104–114, September 2000.

59. L. Xu, H. G. Perros, and G. Rouskas, "Techniques for Optical Packet Switching and Optical Burst Switching," *IEEE Communications Magazine,* vol. 39, no. 1, pp. 136–142, January 2001.

60. P. Mehrotra, I. Baldine, D. Stevenson, and P. Franzon, "Network Processor Design for Optical Burst Switched Networks," in *Proceedings of 14th Annual IEEE International ASIC/SOC Conference,* pp. 296–300, 2001.

61. J. Cai and A. Fumagalli, "An Analytical Framework for Performance Comparison of Bandwidth Reservation Schemes in WDM Ring," in *Proceedings of INFOCOM 2002,* 2002.

62. E. Rosen, A. Viswanathan, and R. Callon, "Multiprotocol Label Switching Architecture," RFC 3031, January 2001.

63. A. Malis and W. Simpson, "PPP over SONET/SDH," RFC 2615, June 1999.

64. A. Malis and W. Simpson, "PPP in HDLC-like Framing," RFC 1662, July 1994.

65. J. Manchester, J. Anderson, B. Doshi, and S. Davida, "IP over SONET," *IEEE Communications Magazine*, May 1998.

66. J. Carlson, P. Langner, E. Hernandez-Valencia, and J. Manchester, "PPP over Simple Data Link (SDL) Using SONET/SDH with ATM-like Framing," RFC 2823 (Experimental), May 2000.

67. R. Seifert, *Gigabit Ethernet*, Addison-Wesley, Reading, Massachusetts, 1998.

68. D. H. Su, "Standards: The IEEE P802.3ae Project for 10 Gb/s Ethernet," *Optical Networks Magazine*, vol. 1, no. 4, October 2000.

69. N. Jones and C. Murton, "Extending PPP over SONET/SDH with Virtual Concatenation, High Order and Low Order Payloads," Internet Draft <draft-ietf-pppext-posvcholo-06.txt>, December 2001.

70. B. Rajagopalan, D. Pendarakis, D. Saha, R. S. Ramamurthy, and K. Bala, "IP over Optical Networks: Architectural Aspects," *IEEE Communication Magazine*, September 2000.

71. K. Nagami, H. Esaki, Y. Katsube, and O. Nakamura, "Flow-Aggregated, Traffic Driven Label Mapping in Label-Switching Networks," *IEEE Journal on Selected Areas in Communications*, vol. 17, no. 6, pp. 1170–1177, June 1999.

72. M. Ilvesmaki, M. Luoma, and R. Kantola, "Flow Classification in Traffic Based Multilayer IP Switching—Comparison between Conventional and Neural Approach," *Computer Communications*, vol. 21, pp. 1184–1194, 1998.

73. Y. Rekhter, B. Davie, D. Katz, E. Rosen, and G. Swallow, "Tag Switching Architecture Overview," RFC 2105, February 1998.

74. *IEEE Communications Magazine, Special Issue on MPLS*, December 1999.

75. H. H. Tzeng and T. Przygienda, "On Fast Address-Lookup Algorithms," *IEEE Journal on Selected Areas in Communications*, vol. 17, no. 6, pp. 1067–1082, June 1999.

76. S. Nilsson and G. Karlsson, "IP-Address Lookup Using LC-Tries," *IEEE Journal on Selected Areas in Communications*, vol. 17, no. 6, June 1999.

77. M. Waldvogel, G. Varghese, J. Turner, and B. Plattner, "Scalable High Speed IP Routing Lookups," in *Proceedings of ACM SIGCOMM Symposium on Communications Architectures and Protocols*, Cannes, France, pp. 25–35, 1997.

78. M. Degermark, A. Brodnik, S. Carlsson, and S. Pink, "Small Forwarding Tables for Fast Routing Lookups," in *Proceedings of ACM SIGCOMM Symposium on Communications Architectures and Protocols*, Cannes, France, pp. 3–14, 1997.

79. K. Sklower, "A Tree-Based Packet Routing Table for Berkeley Unix," in *Proceedings of Winter USENIX*, Dallas, TX, pp. 93–99, 1991.

80. W. Doeringer, G. Karjoth, and M..Nassehi, "Routing on Longest-Matching Prefixes," *IEEE/ACM Transactions on Networking*, vol. 4, no. 1, pp. 86–97, February 1996.

81. D. Awduche and Y. Rekhter, "Multiprotocol Lambda Switching: Combining MPLS Traffic Engineering Control with Optical Crossconnects," *IEEE Communications Magazine*, vol. 39, no. 3, pp. 111–116, March 2001.

82. T. M. Chen and W. Wu, "Multi-protocol Lambda Switching for IP over Optical Networks," in *Proceedings of SPIE*, November 2000.

83. C. Guillemot and F. Clerot, "Optical Packet Switching for WDM IP Gigabit Routers," in *Proceedings of 24th European Conference on Optical Communication (ECOC)*, vol. 1, pp. 433–434, 1998.

84. V. Paxson and S. Floyd, "Wide Area Traffic: The Failure of Poisson Modeling," *IEEE/ACM Transactions on Networking,* vol. 4, no. 2, pp. 226–244, April 1996.

85. W. E. Leland, M. S. Taqqu, W. Willinger, and D. V. Wilson, "On the Self-similar Nature of Ethernet Traffic," *IEEE/ACM Transactions on Networking,* vol. 2, no. 1, pp. 1–15, January 1994.

86. B. Tsybakov and N. D. Georganas, "On Self-similar Traffic in ATM Queues: Definitions, Overflow Probability Bound and Cell Delay Distribution," *IEEE/ACM Transactions on Networking,* vol. 5, no. 30, pp. 397–409, June 1997.

87. J. Beran, *Statistics for Long-Memory Processes,* Chapman & Hall, London, 1994.

88. A. Erramilli, O. Narayan, and W. Willinger, "Experimental Queueing Analysis with Long-Range Dependent Packet Traffic," *IEEE/ACM Transactions on Networking,* vol. 4, no. 2, pp. 209–223, April 1996.

89. M. S. Taqqu, W. Willinger, and R. Sherman, "Proof of a Fundamental Result in Self-Similar Traffic Modeling," *ACM SIGCOMM Computer Communication Review,* 1997.

90. A. Veres and M. Boda, "The Chaotic Nature of TCP Congestion Control," in *Proceedings of IEEE INFOCOM 00,* Tel Aviv, Israel, 2000.

91. W. Willinger, M. S. Taqqu, R. Sherman, and D. V. Wilson, "Self-Similarity Through High-Variability: Statistical Analysis of Ethernet LAN Traffic at the Source Level," *IEEE/ACM Transactions on Networking,* vol. 5, no. 1, February 1997.

92. J. Aracil and D. Morato, "Characterizing Internet Load as a Multiplex of Variable Rate TCP Streams," in *Proceedings of IEEE International Conference on Computer Communications and Networks,* Las Vegas, Nevada, 2000.

93. M. E. Crovella and A. Bestavros, "Self-Similarity in World Wide Web Traffic: Evidence and Possible Causes," *IEEE/ACM Transactions on Networking,* vol. 5, no. 6, pp. 835–846, December 1997.

94. G. Miller K. Thompson and R. Wilder, "Wide-Area Internet Traffic Patterns and Characteristics," *IEEE Network,* November/December 1997.

95. I. Norros, "On the Use of Fractional Brownian Motion in the Theory of Connectionless Networks," *IEEE Journal on Selected Areas in Communications,* vol. 13, no. 6, pp. 953–962, August 1995.

96. F. Callegati et al., "On Optical Burst Switching and Self-Similar Traffic," *IEEE Communications Letters,* vol. 4, no. 3, March 2000.

97. M. Izal and M. Aracil, "On the Influence of Self-similarity on Optical Burst Switching Traffic," in *Proceedings of Globecom 2002,* Taipei, Taiwan, 2002.

98. G. Samorodnitsky and M. S. Taqqu, *Stable Non-Gaussian Random Processes,* Chapman & Hall, New York, 1994.

99. *IEEE Journal on Selected Areas in Communications, Special Issue on Intelligent Techniques In High Speed Networks,* February 2000.

100. J. Anderson, S. Manchester, J., A. Rodriguez-Moral, and M. Veeraraghavan, "Protocols and Architectures for IP Optical Networking," *Bell Labs Technical Journal,* vol. 4, no. 1, pp. 105–124, January-March 1999.

101. T. M. Chen and T. H. Oh, "Reliable Services in MPLS," *IEEE Communications Magazine,* vol. 37, no. 12, pp. 58–62, December 1999.

102. O. Gerstel and R. Ramaswami, "Optical Layer Survivability: A Services Perspective," *IEEE Communication Magazine,* vol. 38, no. 3, pp. 104–113, March 2000.

103. N. Ghani, S. Dixit, and Ti-Shiang Wang, "On ip-over-wdm Integration," *IEEE Communications Magazine,* vol. 38, no. 3, pp. 72–84, March 2000.

104. D. Colle, S. De Maesschalck, C. Develder, P. Van Heuven, A. Groebbens, J. Cheyns, I. Lievens, M. Pickavet, P. Lagasse, and P. Demeester, "Data-centric Optical Networks and Their

Survivability," *IEEE Journal on Selected Areas in Communications,* vol. 20, no. 1, pp. 6–20, Jan. 2002.

105. L. Sahasrabuddhe, S. Ramamurthy, and B. Mukherjee, "Fault Management in IP-over-WDM Networks: WDM Protection versus IP Restoration," *IEEE Journal on Selected Areas in Communications,* vol. 20, no. 1, pp. 21–33, January 2002.

106. D. Johnson, "Survivability Strategies for Broadband Networks," in *Proceedings of Global Telecommunications Conference, 1996. GLOBECOM '96,* London, vol. 1, pp. 452–456, November 1996.

107. S. Ramamurthy and B. Mukherjee, "Survivable WDM Mesh Networks, Part II—Restoration," in *Proceedings of IEEE International Conference on Communications, 1999. ICC '99,* Vancouver, Canada, vol. 3, pp. 2023 –2030, June 1999.

108. C. Metz, "IP Protection and Restoration," *IEEE Internet Computing,* vol. 4, no. 2, pp. 97–102, March-April 2000.

109. G. Hjálmtýsson, P. Sebos, G. Smith, and J. Yates, "Simple IP Restoration for IP/GbE/10GbE Optical Networks," in *Proceedings of Optical Fiber Communication Conference, OFC 2000,* Baltimore, Maryland, March 2000.

110. D. Cavendish, "Evolution of Optical Transport Technologies: From SONET/SDH to WDM," *IEEE Communications Magazine,* vol. 38, no. 6, pp. 164–172, June 2000.

111. N. Ghani, "Lambda-Labeling: A Framework for IP-over-WDM Using MPLS," *Optical Networks Magazine,* vol. 1, no. 2, pp. 45–58, April 2000.

ACRONYMS

AAA	Authentication, Authorization, and Accounting
AAP	ITU-T alternate approval process
ACTS	Advanced Communications Technologies and Services
AD	Application processing delays
ADSL	Asymmetric digital subscriber line
AES	Advanced encryption standard
AFD	Assured forwarding
AH	Authentication header
AID	Application identifier
AIP	Accounting Information Path
AML	Application and Middleware layer
ANSI	American National Standards Institute
AOL	America-Online
APD	Avalanche photodiode
API	Application programming interface
AR	Alternate routing
ARPA	Advanced Research Projects Agency
ARPANET	ARPA NETwork
ARS	Accounting-Rate Systems
AS	Autonomous system, authentication server
ASC	Accredited Standards Committee
ASC X12	Accredited Standards Committee X12—SDO for cross-industry electronic exchange of business information
ASIC	Application Specific Integrated Circuits
ASN.1	Abstract syntax notation 1

ASP	Application Service Provider
ASR	Access Service Requests
ASTM International	Formerly known as American Society for Testing and Materials
ATM	Asynchronous Transfer Mode
ATMOS	Asynchronous Transfer Mode Optical Switching
BA	TM Forum Business Agreement; behavior aggregate
BC	Biometric Consortium
BDV	Business domain view
BER	Basic encoding rules; bit error rate
BET	Business entity type
BGP	Border gateway protocol
B-ISDN	Broadband integrated services digital network
BOV	Business operation view
BPAWG	Business Process Analysis Working Group
BPDS	Business process definition specification
BPIM	Business process and information modeling
BRV	Business requirements view
BSI	*Nundesamt für Sicherheit in der Informationtechnik*
BSS	Business support system
BSV	Business service view
BT-EC	ISO-IEC JTC 1 Business Team on Electronic commerce
BTV	Business transaction view
CABS	Carrier Access Billing Systems
CAM	Content addressable memory
CANCAN	Contract Negotiation and Charging in ATM Networks
CAPI	Cryptographic application programming interface
CARE	Customer account record exchange
CAS	Channel-associated signaling
CASHMAN	Charging and Accounting Schemes in Multiservice ATM Networks
CATI	Charging and accounting technology for the Internet
CBC	Cipher block chaining
CBEFF	Common Biometric Exchange File Format
CBL	Common Business Library
CBQ	Class-based queuing
CC	Company Code
CCD	Charge-coupled device
CCP	Collaboration Protocol Profile
CCS	Common channel signaling
CDR	Call detail record
CEN	European Committee for Standardization
CE	Congestion experienced
CEN TC 251	European Standardization of Health Informatics
CFB	Cipher feedback
CFDL	Care packet first, don't care packet last
CIM	DMTF common information model
CLEC	Competitive local telephone company

CM&B	Customer management and ailing system
CMIP	Common Management Information Protocol
CMP	Certificate Management Protocol
CMS	Cryptographic message syntax
CNM	Customer network management
CORBA	Common Object Request Broker Architecture
CORD	Contention resolution by delay lines
CoS	Class of service
CPA	Collaboration Protocol Agreement
CPE	Customer-provided equipment
CPP	Control Policy Path
CPN	Customer premises network
CPS	Cumulus pricing scheme
CR	Constraint-based routing
CRL	Certification revocation list
CR-LDP	Constraint-based routing label distribution protocol
CR-LSP	Constraint-based routing LSP
CSS	Charging support system
CWDM	Coarse wavelength division multiplexing
CWR	Congestion window reduced
DAP	Directory Access Protocol
DARPA	Defense Advanced Research Projects Agency
DDOS	Distributed denial of service
DEC	Digital Equipment Corporation
DES	Data Encryption Standard
DHCP	Dynamic host configuration protocol
DiffServ	Differentiated services architecture
DIS	Draft International Standard
DISP	Directory Information Shadowing Protocol
DLCI	Data link connection identifier
DMTF	Distributed Management Task Force
DNS	Domain name system
DOD	Department of Defense
DOI	Domain of interpretation
DRA	Distributed restoration algorithms
DRR	Distributed round-robin
DS	DiffServ
DSA	Digital Signature Algorithm; directory system agent
DSCP	Differentiated-service code point
DSP	Directory System Protocol
DSS	Digital signature standard
DTD	Document-type description
DUA	Directory user agent
DWDM	Dense-wavelength division multiplexing
DWFQ	Distributed weighted-fair queuing
DWRED	Distributed weighted RED
EAN	European Article Numbering, former name of EAN International

EBONE	European BackBONE
eBusiness	Electronic business
ebXML	Electronic Business eXtensible Markup Language
EC	Electronic commerce
ECB	Electronic code book
ECC	Elliptic curve cryptography
ECDH	Elliptic Curve Diffie–Hellman
ECDSA	Elliptic Curve Digital Signature Algorithm
ECN	Explicit congestion notification
eCo	e (or eCommerce) Framework that enables businesses to dis cover each other on the WWW and determine how they can do business
eCommerce	Electronic commerce
EDE	Encryption-decryption-encryption
EDFA	Erbium-doped fiber amplifier
EDI	Electronic data interchange
EE	End-to-end (delay)
EF	Expedited forwarding
EMR	Exchange Message Record
EPL	Enterprise policy layer
EPSRC	Engineering and Physical Sciences Research Council
ER LSP	Explicit-routed LSF
eSociety	Electronic society
ESP	Encapsulating security payload
eTOM	enhanced Telecom Operations Map
ETSI	European Telecommunications Standardization Institute
EuropaNET	Europa NETwork
FAQ	Frequently asked questions
FBI	Federal Bureau of Investigation
FCC	Federal Communication Commission
FCFS	First-come first-served
FDDI	Fiber-distributed data interface
FDL	Fiber delay line
FDT	Formal description technique
FEC	Forward equivalent class
FF	Fixed filter
FGON	First-generation optical network
FIFO	First-in first-out
FoIP	Fax over IP
F-OXC	Fiber-optical cross connect
FRED	Fact RED
FSV	Functional services view
FTP	File Transfer Protocol
GMPLS	Generalized multiprotocol label switching
GOCPKI	Government of Canada Public Key Infrastructure
GPO	Government Printing Office
GPRS	General packet radio system

GPS	Generalized processor sharing
GSM	Groupe Speciale Mobile
GTDD	Global Telecommunications Data Registry
HA-API	Human-Authentication–Application Program Interface
HEDIC	Healthcare EDI Coalition
HHA	Hand-held authenticators
HL7	Health level 7—An SDO for the production and promotion of health care IT communications standards
HMAC	Hashed Message Authentication Code
HTTP	Hypertext transfer protocol
HTTPS	Hypertext transfer protocol secure
IB	Information bundle
IBIA	International Biometric Industry Association
IC	Implementation convention
ICAO	International Civil Aviation Organization
ICC	ITU Carrier Code
ICCAS	Internet Charge Calculation and Accounting System
ICMP	Internet Control Message Protocol
ICT	Information and communication technologies
IDEA	International Data Encryption Algorithm
IEC	Interexhange carrier; International Electrotechnical Commission
IETF	Internet Engineering Task Force
IGP	Interior gateway protocol
IKE	Internet key exchange
ILEC	Incumbent local telephone company
ILM	Incoming label map
IMD	Information management domain
IMO	International Maritime Organization
INCITS	InterNational Committee for Information Technology Standards
INDEX	Internet Demand Experiment
IntServe	Integrated services architecture
IP	Internet protocol
IPDR	Internet protocol detail record; Internet protocol data records
IPng	IP new generation
IPSEC	Internet Protocol Security
IPv4	IP version 4
ISAKMP	Internet Security Association and Key Management Protocol
ISDN	Integrated services digital networks
IS-IS	Intelligent scheduling and information system
ISO	Internation Organization for Standardization
ISO/IEC JTC 1/SC 7	Subcommittee for Software and System Engineering
ISO/IEC JTC 1/SC 27	Subcommittee for IT Security Techniques
ISO/IEC JTC 1/SC 31	Automatic Identification and Data Capture Techniques
ISO/IEC JTC 1/SC 32	Subcommittee for Data Management and Interchange
ISO TC 184	Technical Committee for Industrial Automation Systems and Integration

ISO TC 211	Technical Committee for Geographic Information/Geomatics
ISO TC 215	Technical Committee for Health Informatics
ISP	Internet service provider
IT	Information technology
ITU	International Telecommunication Union
ITU-T	International Organization for Standardization, Telecommunications Sector
JTC 1	Joint Technical Committee under ISO and IEC for information technology standards
KEA	Key Exchange Algorithm
KEOPS	Keys to optical packet switching
L2TP	Layer 2 Tunneling Protocol
λSR	Lambda switch router
LAN	Local-area network
LDAP	Lightweight directory access protocol (X.500)
LDP	Label distribution protocol
LED	Light-emitting diode
LER	Label edge router
LIB	Label information base
LOA	Linear optical amplifier
LOBS	Labeled OBS
LoF	Loss of frame
LoS	Loss of signal
LSA	Link state advertisement
LSP	Label switched path
LSR	Label switched router
M3I	Market-Managed Multiservice Internet
MAC	Message authentication code; medium access control
MAN	Metropolitan-area network
MCMF	Multicommodity maximum flow
MD	Message digest
MECAB	Multiple Exchange Carrier Access Billing
MEMS	Microelectromechanical switch
MF	Mulifield
MIB	Management information base
MIC	Message integrity check
MISPC	Minimum interoperability specification for PKI components
MIT	Massachusetts Institute of Technology
MOSPF	Multicast OSPF
MoU	Memorandum of Understanding
MPEG	Moving Picture Experts Group
MPLS	Multiprotocol label switching
MPλS	Multiprotocol lambda switching
MTU	Maximum transfer unit
NAS	Network access server

NECA	National Exchange Carrier Association
NeTraMet	Network traffic meter
NGI	Next-Generation Internet
NGOSS	New-generation operation support systems
NHLFE	Next hop label forwarding entry
N-ISDN	Narrowband Integrated Services Digital Network
NIST	National Institute of Standards and Technology
NL	Network latency
NMAC	Nested Message Authentication Code
NOC	Network Operation Center
NSA	National Security Agency
NSFNET	NSF Network
OA	Optical amplifier
OADM	Optical add/drop multiplexer
OAEP	Optimal asymmetric encryption padding
OAG	Open applications group
OAM	Operations and maintenance
OAM&P	Operation, administration, maintenance, and provisioning
OASIS	Organization for the Advancement of Structured Information Standards
OBS	Optical burst switching
OC	Optical channel
OCL	Object Constraint Language
OCSP	Online Certificate Status Protocol
OFB	Output feedback
OI	Optical Internet
OL	Optical layer
OLT	Optical line terminal
OMS	Optical multiplex section
ONRAMP	Optical network for regional access using multiwavelength protocol
OPWA	One path with advertising
OSI	Open Systems Interconnection
OSPF	Open shortest path first
OSS	Operation support system
OTN	Optical transport network
OTS	Optical transmission section
OXC	Optical cross-connect
PBX	Private branch exchange
PDB	Per-domain behavior
PDFA	Praseodymium-doped fiber amplifier
PDH	Plaesyochronous digital hierarchy
PGP	Pretty Good Privacy
PHB	Per-hop behavior
PHL	Physical layer
PISP	Pure ISP
PKCS	Public key cryptography standards

PKI	Public key infrastructure
PKIX	Public key infrastructure (X.509)
PMI	Privilege Management Infrastructure
PMP	Paris Metro pricing
PNNI	Private network-to-network interface
PO	Purchase order
POP	Points of presence
POP3	Post office protocol
POS	Packet over SONET
PPP	Point-to-point protocol
PPS	Packets per second
PQ	Priority queuing
PSTN	Public switched telephone network
PTT	Posts, telephone, telegraph
PVC	Permanent virtual circuit
QoS	Quality of service
RA	Raman amplifiers; root authority
RAC	RADIUS accounting record
RADIUS	Remote access dial-in user service; Remote Authentication Dial-In User Service
RBAC	Role-based access control
REA	Resource–event–agent
RED	Random early detection
RFC	Request for comments
RIP	Routing information protocol
RR	Round-robin
RSA	Rivest, Shamir, and Adleman
RSADSI	RSA Data Security, Inc.
RSVP	Resource reservation protocol
RSVP-TE	Resource reservation protocol for traffic engineering
RT	Response time
RTFM	Real-time flow measurement
RTP	Real-time protocol
RWA	Routing and wavelength assignment
S/MIME	Secure Multipurpose Internet Mail Extensions
S/WAN	Secure Wide Area Network
SASL	Simple authentication and security layer
SC	Semantic component
SDH	Synchronous digital hierarchy
SDL	Simple data link
SDO	Standards Development Organization
SDSI	Simple distributed security infrastructure
SECAB	Small Exchange Carrier Access Billing
SET	Secure electronic transactions
SF	Shared filter
SGML	Standard Generalized Markup Language

SGON	Second-generation optical network
SHA	Secure hash algorithm
SID	TM forum shared information/data model
SIM	TM forum systems integration map
SIP	Session initiation protocol
SIU	Smart Internet Usage
SKIP	Simple key management for Internet protocols
SLA	Service-level agreement
SLS	Service-level specification
SMDR	Station management detail record; station message detail record
SME	Small- and medium-size enterprise
SMTP	Simple mail-transfer protocol
SNMP	Simple network-management protocol
SOA	Semiconductor optical amplifier; source of authority
SONET	Synchronous optical network
SPKI	Simple public key infrastructure
SPL	Service provisioning layer
SPR	Stochastic preplanned restoration
SPR-PW	SPR scheme with proportional weighted
SRED	Stabilized RED
SSH	Secure Shell
SSL	Secure socket layer
STM-N	Synchronous transport module-level N
STS-N	Synchronous transport signal-N
SVC	Switched virtual circuit
SWG-EDI	Special Working Group on Electronic Data Interchange
SWIFT	Industry-owned cooperative providing secure, reliable, and standardized messaging between financial institutions
T1	Accredited Standards Committee T1-SDO for telecommunications network standards
TCA	Traffic conditioning agreement
TACACS	Terminal Access Controller Access System
TCP	Transport control protocol
TCS	Traffic conditioning specification
TDM	Time-division multiplexing
TE	Traffic engineering
TGS	Ticket-granting server
TISP	Telecommunications ISP
TLS	Transport layer security; transmission layer security
TM Forum	TeleManagement Forum
tML	telecommunications Markup Language
TMN	Telecommunications Management Network
TMN X-Interface	Interface for inter-TMN communication
TMWG	Techniques and Methodologies Working Group
ToS	Type of service
TSB	ITU-T Telecommunications Service Bureau
TSC T1M1	Technical Subcommittee for Internetwork Operations, Administration, Maintenance, and Provisioning

UCC	Uniform Code Council
UDP	User datagram protocol
UML	Unified Modeling Language
UMM	UN/CEFACT modeling methodology
UMTS	Universal mobile telecommunication system
UN/CEFACT	United Nations Centre for Trade Facilitation and Electronic Business
UN/ECE	United Nations Economic Commission for Europe
UN/EDIFACT	EDI standards developed and maintained by UN/CEFACT
UNI	User network interface
URL	Uniform resource locator
UTRAD	Unified TMN Requirements, Analysis, and Design
VC	Virtual circuits
VCI	Virtual path identifier
VCSEL	Vertical cavity surface emitting laser
VLSI	Very larger scale integration
VoATM	Voice over ATM
VoD	Video-on-demand
VoFR	Voice over frame relay
VoIP	Voice over IP
VPI	Virtual path identifier
VPN	Virtual private networks
W3C	World Wide Web Consortium
WAN	Wide-area network
WASPNET	Wavelength switched packet network
WBXC	Waveband cross-connect
WCO	World Customs Organization
WDM	Wavelength division multiplexing
WfMC	Workforce Management Coalition
WF	Wildcard filter
WFQ	Weighted fair queuing
WLL	Wireless local loop
WRED	Weighted RED
WR-OXC	Wavelength routing optical cross-connect
WRR	Weighted round-robin
WT-OXC	Wavelength translating optical cross-connect
WTO	World Trade Organization
WWW	World Wide Web
X12	EDI standards developed and maintained by ASC X12
xDFA	x-Doped fiber amplifier
XML	Extensible Markup Language: W3C recommended subset of SGML enabling the exchange of structured data over the WWW
XOR	exclusive OR

INDEX

Access charges, 176
Access control:
  centralized management, 236–237
  challenge-response systems, 237
  commercial systems, 237
  denial of service, 237–239, 267
  importance of, 11, 213, 215
  line interruption, 236
  mechanisms of, 235–236
  network layer, 236
  packet filtering, 236
  role-based (RBAC), 235, 263
Access ISPs, 199–200
Access Service Requests (ASR), 37
Accounting, 147, 155–156, 159, 165–167
Accounting rate systems (ARS), 166
Accounting record, defined, 159
Accredited Standards Committee (ASC) T1, 30
AC.1, 42
Active attacks, 213
Active probing, 147
Adaptability, eCommerce standards, 16
Administrative services, 34
Admission control, 102, 124, 163
ADSpec (advertising specification), 104–106
Advanced Communications Technologies and
    Services (ACTS), 167, 302
Advanced Encryption Standard (AES), 218, 273
Aggregate flows, 112
Agreement, REA ontology, 47, 49
All-optical network architectures:

characteristics of, generally, 294–295
dynamic lightpath networks, 297–300
optical burst switching (OBS) networks, 303,
    323
optical packet-switching networks, 300–302
overview, 294–295
static and semistatic lightpath networks, 295–297
a-stable random processes, 324, 326
Alternate routing (AR), 299
American National Standards Institute (ANSI), 234,
    251, 273, 279
America Online (AOL), 183
Application and Middleware Layer (AML), 197–198
Application, generally:
  gateways, 236
  layer, 215
  security, 220
Application service provider (ASP), 198–200
Application-specific integrated circuits (ASIC), 72
Architecture, historical perspective, 8–9. *See also*
    specific IP networks
ARPANET, 287
Arrival process, 319
ASN, Basic Encoding Rules (BER), 277
Association for Biometrics, 234
Assured forwarding (AF) per-hop behavior (PHB),
    121–122
Assured forwarding (AF) services, 110, 114–115,
    121–123
Asymmetrical digital subscriber line (ADSL),
    148–149

Managing IP Networks. Edited by Saleh Aidarous and Thomas Plevyak **345**
ISBN 0-471-39299-5 © 2003 Institute of Electrical and Electronics Engineers

Printed and bound by CPI Group (UK) Ltd, Croydon, CR0 4YY

27/10/2024

14580343-0003